# Transnational Africas Visual, Material and Sonic Cultures of Lusophone Africa

Spring/Fall 2017

**Tagus Press**
**Center for Portuguese Studies and Culture**
University of Massachusetts Dartmouth
Portuguese Literary & Cultural Studies (PLCS) 30/31

EDITORS
Mario Pereira
Christopher Larkosh
Memory Holloway

EDITORIAL BOARD
Ana Paula Ferreira (University of Minnesota)
Cristiana Bastos (Universidade de Lisboa)
Fernando Arenas (University of Michigan)

ADVISORY BOARD
Vítor Manuel de Aguiar e Silva (Universidade do Minho)
Gonzalo Aguilar (Universidade de Buenos Aires)
Luiz Felipe de Alencastro (Universidade de Paris–Sorbonne)
Maria Aparecida Ferreira de Andrade Salgueiro
    (Universidade do Estado do Rio de Janeiro)
Vincenzo Arsillo (Universidade de Veneza)
Dário Borim (University of Massachusetts Dartmouth)
Flávio Carneiro (Universidade do Estado do Rio de Janeiro)
Bruno Carvalho (Princeton University)
Alda Costa (Universidade Eduardo Mondlane)
Patricio Ferrari (Universidade de Lisboa)
Kenneth David Jackson (Yale University)
Anna M. Klobucka (University of Massachusetts Dartmouth)
Johannes Kretschmer (Universidade Federal Fluminense)
Alexander Luz (Universidade Federal Rural do Rio de Janeiro)
Nataniel Ngomane (Universidade Eduardo Mondlane)
Horst Nitschack (Universidade do Chile)
Marcus Vinicius Nogueira Soares (Universidade do Estado do Rio de Janeiro)

Carlinda Fragale Pate Nuñez (Universidade do Estado do Rio de Janeiro)
Rita Olivieri-Godet (Universidade de Rennes II)
Carmen Villarino Pardo (Universidade de Santiago de Compostela)
Rodrigo Petrônio (Poet, Essayist—FAAP— Fundação Armando Álvares Penteado)
Isabel Pires de Lima (Universidade do Porto)
Jerónimo Pizarro (Universidade de los Andes)
Andrea Portolomeos (Universidade Federal de Lavras–MG)
Valdir Prigol (Universidade Federal da Fronteira Sul)
Roberto Acizelo Quelha de Sousa (Universidade do Estado do Rio de Janeiro)
Sonia Netto Salomão (Universidade de Roma)
Nelson Schapochinik (Universidade de São Paulo)
Kathleen Sheldon (University of California Los Angeles)
Boaventura de Sousa Santos (Universidade de Coimbra)
Carlos Mendes de Sousa (Universidade do Minho)
Maria de Sousa Tavares (Universidade de Macau)
Alva Martínez Teixeiro (Universidade de Lisboa)
José Leonardo Tonus (Universidade de Paris–Sorbonne)
Sandra Guardini Teixeira Vasconcelos (Universidade de São Paulo)
Jobst Welge (Universidade de Constança)
Valquíria Wey (Universidade Nacional Autônoma do México)
Regina Zilberman (Pontifícia Universidade Católica do Rio Grande do Sul)

ASSISTANTS TO THE EDITORS
Diana G. Simões (University of Massachusetts Dartmouth)
Maggie L. N. Felisberto (University of Massachusetts Dartmouth)

**PREVIOUS ISSUES**

*Fronteiras/Borders* (PLCS 1)
  Edited by Victor J. Mendes, Paulo de Medeiros, and José N. Ornelas
*Lídia Jorge in other words / por outras palavras* (PLCS 2)
  Edited by Cláudia Pazos Alonso
*Pessoa's Alberto Caeiro* (PLCS 3)
  Edited by Victor J. Mendes
*2001 Brazil: A Revisionary History of Brazilian Literature and Culture* (PLCS 4/5)
  Edited by João Cezar de Castro Rocha
*On Saramago* (PLCS 6)
  Edited by Anna Klobucka
*A Repertoire of Contemporary Portuguese Poetry* (PLCS 7)
  Edited by Victor K. Mendes
*Cape Verde: Language, Literature & Music* (PLCS 8)
  Edited by Ana Mafalda Leite
*Post-Imperial Camões* (PLCS 9)
  Edited by João R. Figueiredo
*Reevaluating Mozambique* (PLCS 10)
  Edited by Phillip Rothwell
*Vitorino Nemésio and the Azores* (PLCS 11)
  Edited by Francisco Cota Fagundes
*The Other Nineteenth Century* (PLCS 12)
  Edited by Kathryn M. Sanchez
*The Author as Plagiarist—The Case of Machado de Assis* (PLCS 13/14)
  Edited by João Cezar de Castro Rocha
*Remembering Angola* (PLCS 15/16)
  Edited by Phillip Rothwell

*Parts of Asia* (PLCS 17/18)
  Edited by Cristiana Bastos
*Facts and Fictions of António Lobo Antunes* (PLCS 19/20)
  Edited by Victor K. Mendes
*Garrett's Travels Revisited* (PLCS 21/22)
  Edited by Victor K. Mendes and Valéria M. Souza
*Economies of Relation: Money and Personalism in the Lusophone World* (PLCS 23/24)
  Edited by Roger Sansi
*Lusofonia and Its Futures* (PLCS 25)
  Edited by João Cezar de Castro Rocha
*Literary Histories in Portuguese* (PLCS 26)
  Edited by João Cezar de Castro Rocha
*The South Atlantic, Past and Present* (PLCS 27)
  Edited by Luiz Felipe de Alencastro
*Fernando Pessoa as English Reader and Writer* (PLCS 28)
  Edited by Patricio Ferrari & Jerónimo Pizarro
*The Eighteenth Century* (PLCS 29)
  Edited by Bruno Carvalho

*Portuguese Literary & Cultural Studies* (PLCS) is an interdisciplinary, peer-reviewed hybrid online and print journal that publishes original research related to the literatures and cultures of the diverse communities of the Portuguese-speaking world from a broad range of academic, critical and theoretical approaches. PLCS is published semi-annually by Tagus Press in the Center for Portuguese Studies and Culture at the University of Massachusetts Dartmouth.

**Manuscript Policy**
*Portuguese Literary & Cultural Studies* welcomes submission of original and unpublished manuscripts in English or Portuguese appropriate to the goals of the journal. Manuscripts should be between 6,000–8,500 words in length and must be accompanied by an abstract. Manuscripts should be in accordance with the *MLA Style Manual and Guide to Scholarly Publishing* (latest version) or *The Chicago Manual of Style* (latest version) with parenthetical documentation and a list of works cited. The author is responsible for the accuracy of all quotations, titles, names, and dates. Manuscripts should be double-spaced throughout. All of the information must be in the same language (e.g., abstract, body of the article, bio-blurb). Updated guidelines are available at https://ojs.lib.umassd.edu/index.php/plcs/about/submissions#authorGuidelines. PLCS encourages submission of manuscripts in the form of a single attached MS Word document. Please send submissions to Mario Pereira, Editor, at mpereira6@umassd.edu.

Portuguese Literary & Cultural Studies 30/31

# Transnational Africas Visual, Material and Sonic Cultures of Lusophone Africa

Edited by Christopher Larkosh,
Mario Pereira and Memory Holloway

Tagus Press
UMass Dartmouth
Dartmouth, Massachusetts

Portuguese Literary & Cultural Studies 30/31
Center for Portuguese Studies and Culture/Tagus Press
University of Massachusetts Dartmouth
https://ojs.lib.umassd.edu/index.php/plcs/index
© 2018 The University of Massachusetts Dartmouth
All rights reserved
Manufactured in the United States of America
Designed by Richard Hendel
Cover design & typesetting by Inês Sena

Center for Portuguese Studies and Culture/ Tagus Press
University of Massachusetts Dartmouth
285 Old Westport Road
North Dartmouth MA 02747–2300
Tel. 508–999–8255
Fax 508–999–9272
www.portstudies.umassd.edu
*Tagus Press is the publishing arm of the*
*Center for Portuguese Studies and Culture*
*at the University of Massachusetts Dartmouth.*
Center Director: Victor K. Mendes

Cover Image: António Ole, No title, 1998, photograph on aluminium, 90x120 cm. Courtesy of the artist.

ISSN: 1521-804X (print)
ISSN: 2573-1432 (online)
ISBN: 978-1-933227-82-5 (pbk.: alk. paper)
ISBN: 978-1-933227-83-2 (Ebook)

Library of Congress Control Number: 2018933803

5 4 3 2 1

# Contents

Editor's Note xi
    MARIO PEREIRA

**Transnational Africas**

(Re)Bordering Lusophone and Transnational Africas:
    A Critical Introduction 1
    CHRISTOPHER LARKOSH

Black Women's Bodies in the Portuguese Colonial Visual Archive
    (1900-1975) 16
    FILIPA LOWNDES VICENTE

The Filmography of Guinea-Bissau's Sana Na N'Hada: From the Return
    of Amílcar Cabral to the Threat of Global Drug Trafficking 68
    FERNANDO ARENAS

Arquitetura Moderna Portuguesa na África Subsaariana 95
    JOSÉ MANUEL FERNANDES

Malangatana: *Viagem Salvadora*, Where Blood and Tears Run 114
    MEMORY HOLLOWAY

Artes Plásticas e Movimento Nacionalista em Moçambique 125
    MALANGATANA NGWENYA E PAULO SOARES
    *Introduced, transcribed and edited by Mario Pereira*

Art Topples Monuments: Artistic Practice and Colonial/Postcolonial
    Relations in the Public Space of Luanda 150
    NADINE SIEGERT

"Muamba, Banana e Cola." O Duo Ouro Negro e o Tropicalismo
    Desnacionalizador 174
    MARCOS CARDÃO

Dez perguntas para Ondjaki 192
    CHRISTOPHER LARKOSH

**Essays**

The Orders of Discourse of *Clamor Africano*: Continuity and Rupture
in the Ideology of Unitary Nationalism   199
MÁRIO PINTO DE ANDRADE
*Introduced and translated by Mario Pereira*

De Onde Menos se Espera: A Disciplina do Terror em Lygia
Fagundes Telles   225
MARIA MANUEL LISBOA

**Reviews**

Memory Holloway on António Ole: *Luanda, Los Angeles, Lisboa*   277

Dário Borim on Carlos Cortez Minchillo, *Erico Verissimo, escritor do mundo:
circulação literária, cosmopolitismo e relações interamericanas*   280

MARIO PEREIRA

## Editor's Note

It is a pleasure to publish the double issue *Transnational Africas: Visual, Material and Sonic Cultures of Lusophone Africa* (Portuguese Literary & Cultural Studies, 30/31). This is the first issue of the journal devoted specifically to visual, material and sonic cultures as well as the first issue dedicated to Lusophone Africa as a whole.

The idea for this issue emerged from conversations between Christopher Larkosh, Isabel Rodrigues, Memory Holloway and myself in March 2015. Larkosh first proposed an issue on transnational approaches to Lusophone Africa and Rodrigues suggested that we focus on visual, material and sonic cultures. Larkosh sets the terms of debate in his provocative essay "(Re)Bordering Lusophone and Transnational Africas: A Critical Introduction," which can be read simultaneously as a theoretical introduction to the issue and as an independent article on these increasingly relevant topics.

An impressive range of articles were submitted for consideration and we are grateful to the contributors for entrusting their pieces to us. We hope this special issue better integrates visual, material and sonic cultures into the interdisciplinary field of Luso-Afro-Brazilian Studies. We likewise aim to highlight the importance of transnationalism to our thinking about Africa as well as drawing attention to the continuing urgency of decolonization in countless areas. Nevertheless, the mechanics of the issue point to valuable places for improvement. We had expected to attract more submissions from scholars working in Brazil and Africa. Sonic culture deserves far more attention than it here receives, and the issue does not have a piece on cultural production in the diaspora. These are significant lacunae.

It is necessary to say a few words about the article "Black Women's Bodies in the Portuguese Colonial Visual Archive (1900-1975)" by Filipa Lowndes Vicente. The issues addressed in this article are sensitive and controversial, and the images that are analyzed and reproduced in it are disturbing and upsetting. The decision to publish the article and the images was a contested and uncomfortable one. We recognize that some readers will not agree with this decision. However, we, along with our reviewers, feel that the author took care to present the complexities and dangers of researching and writing on this topic and made a persuasive argument for having this kind of discussion in our contemporary moment.

We are also privileged to include in this special issue an essay unrelated to the organizing theme, Maria Manuel Lisboa's "De Onde Menos se Espera: A Disciplina do Terror em Lygia Fagundes Telles," which was one of the winners of the 2012 Prémio Itamaraty in Brazil.

I would like to thank Alda Costa, Delinda Collier, Drew Thompson and Heather Shirey for their always helpful advice, critical and timely input and much needed support at key moments.

Finally, on behalf of the journal, I would like to express my gratitude and warmly recognize the many contributions made by Christopher Larkosh and Memory Holloway as their three-year term as co-editors of Portuguese Literary & Cultural Studies draws to a close (February 2015–January 2018). Holloway's clarity and wisdom and Larkosh's intellectual energy and enthusiasm are unmatched. As a group, we shepherded The Eighteenth Century (PLCS 29), edited by Bruno Carvalho, to press and were responsible as co-editors for bringing Transnational Africas: Visual, Material and Sonic Cultures of Lusophone Africa (PLCS 30/31) from conception to printed volume. The success of Transnational Africas would not have been possible without their unflagging effort, intellectual dedication and undeterred commitment. Larkosh will also serve as lead editor of the forthcoming special issue, Luso-American Literatures and Cultures Today (PLCS 32), a volume he was eager to propose and has tirelessly championed for the past three years. We are very much looking forward to bringing this issue to our readers in spring 2018.

MARIO PEREIRA
Center for Portuguese Studies and Culture
University of Massachusetts Dartmouth

Transnational Africas
Visual, Material and Sonic
Cultures of Lusophone Africa

CHRISTOPHER LARKOSH

# (Re)Bordering Lusophone and Transnational Africas: A Critical Introduction

> In your text, treat Africa as if it were one country. It is hot and dusty with rolling grasslands and huge herds of animals and tall, thin people who are starving. Or it is hot and steamy with very short people who eat primates. Don't get bogged down with precise descriptions. Africa is big: fifty-four countries, 900 million people who are too busy starving and dying and warring and emigrating to read your book.
> Binyavanga Wainaina, "How to Write About Africa" (2006)

On the cover of a recently completed doctoral thesis in Luso-Afro-Brazilian Studies (Schor 2017), there is a photograph of a young woman that shows her uncovered back tattooed with a map of Africa. This map, inscribed onto the body of a woman of color, is monochrome (black ink) and without borders; its simple form may serve to evoke the importance that the idea of Africa—as One Africa—has not only for those living across the continent, but for people of African descent living in other corners of this global diaspora; it may prompt those about to read this latest issue of PLCS on "Transnational Africas" with a brief exercise in visualization of our own.

To begin: What mental map of Africa do we Lusophone literary and cultural scholars, especially those situated at the translational intersections of English and Portuguese language academia, imagine when we think about, much less begin to study and write about, 'Africa,' its art, music and other elements of visual, material and sonic culture? Is it the bare outline of the continent, one that all too often serves to stress its symbolic oneness, even if that representation may suppress important details and particularities? Or is it the colorful political map, largely of former European colonies turned independent nation-states, privileging these divisions or others on the continent (language, ethnicity, physical topography)? Or perhaps an art historical map, which superimposes characteristic objects across a backdrop of a continent now repurposed as blackboard, a surface on which to teach, one that may or may not be depicted with political borders?

Or perhaps a combination of all of these: an outline of an Africa left largely blank, except for five notable exceptions: those independent nation-states once under Portuguese rule and now known as the PALOP (Países Africanos de Língua Oficial Portuguesa)? For these countries, most scholars reading this introduction will hopefully need no geography lesson: we already know the way they stretch from one end of the African continent to the other, and if we are honest with ourselves, how, despite their distance from one another and lack of contiguity, we all-too-often continue to imagine them both together with one another, in the same measure that we think of them as somehow separate from both their immediate neighbors and the more distant political entities, ones that condition any number of ways of seeing, mapping, bordering and knowing, and yes, researching and teaching Africa.

With this understanding of geography as one more form of visual culture in mind (and one that all too often serves to oversimplify or generalize), another example of possible alternative mapping from recent scholarship might be helpful here, one that is found at the start of the 2007 collection of scholarly articles *Cultures of the Lusophone Black Atlantic*, edited by Nancy Priscilla Naro, Roger Sansi-Roca and David Treece. In this book, which draws its most unmistakable source of inspiration from the title of the British cultural theorist Paul Gilroy's seminal 1993 work *The Black Atlantic*, the map of the Atlantic that appears as a supplementary introduction of sorts, features sites that not only fall neatly within the current political boundaries of Lusophone Africa, but also numerous others that complicate the boundaries of this now presumably postcolonial cultural construct. Ironically enough, by including the often obscured sites of the Portuguese colonial encounter, ones still undeniably "black," but here examined in the context of Lusofonia, the Atlantic Ocean is marked with numerous place names as geographical points of reference that allow for a more comprehensive view of the cultures that have come into contact with the Portuguese over the last 500 years.

This view of Lusofonia, though it perhaps can never be completely inclusive in its scope and complexity, is still a distinct configuration in relation to those studies of Portuguese language in the world that continue to equate the cultural, literary and communicational concept of Lusofonia with the political organization of nation-states that use it as their official language, the CPLP (e. g., Ashby 2017). At the same time, it also does not seem fair to reduce this concept to being simply a more 'modernized,' or even explicitly 'liberal,' reincarnation of Portuguese colonialism. At least from the unofficial, diasporic perspective of, say, the

Portuguese-language communities of southeastern New England, which are not part of any former colony or present-day Portuguese-speaking country, yet are no less Portuguese-speaking than countless others on a world map, this concept of Lusofonia never assumed any overlap with the former Portuguese Empire. But even if it did—to characterize the idea of Lusofonia as a form of colonialism, liberal or otherwise, can only serve to deflect attention from the very real, and undeniably more violent and exploitative (if not always overtly genocidal) institutional structures that were at the organizational heart of the European colonialism, to which the Portuguese colonialism was certainly no exception, despite any residual presence of apologists in Portuguese academic and intellectual circles that may remain.

This is why the disarticulation of colonial borders and mental mapping is so important as researchers continue to elaborate models of Lusophone linguistic community in Africa and beyond, that do not follow earlier colonial models, nor attempt to replicate its oppressive structures. To imply that they do seems more like a denial of the worst abuses of colonialism than a valid critique of scholars and cultural workers often attempting to find ways forward from a variety of political perspectives that cannot be conflated and dismissed as "liberal," that is, if that word can even be said to mean anything specific given its varied definitions across Western languages and political cultures, to say nothing of Africa and the rest of the Global South.

But to return to Lusophone Africa and its Black Atlantic: in the aforementioned volume, one example stands out in this remapping of Portuguese colonial space along a new set of visual, territorial and cultural coordinates. I am referring to Milton Guran's article on the Agudás of Benin, a community comprising both formerly enslaved people and former traders who returned to the city of Ajudá on the coast of Benin to play "a special role in the political, economic and religious life" of the city and surrounding region, especially in Porto-Novo, often called "The Brazilian Dream" to refer to the important contributions of Brazilian returnees there as well (Guran 148).

Perhaps because of these detailed accounts of the lives and cultural identity of Brazilians in this African port city, I was surprised to find that there was no mention of Portugal's tiniest former colonial territory, a miniscule enclave on the African continent, at first governed from São Tomé, only about a square kilometer in size, and later no larger than a small military fort (2 hectares). It was set within what was to become French colonial territory, in a coastal area along the Gulf of Guinea that later became the newly independent nation of Dahomey, only to be renamed the People's Republic of Benin by the Marxist-Leninist government of President Matthieu Kérékou in 1975.[1]

Even if these historical details may have escaped some of us until now, those among us still obsessed with the Portuguese "pink bits" on any political or cultural map of Africa, if not the Global South, will know exactly what I am talking about: it is that cartographical curiosity named São João Baptista de Ajudá, a dubious candidate if there ever was one for territorial autonomy of any kind, given that it was no larger than a small compound, not to mention one whose very existence as a separate territorial entity was tied inextricably to its history as a transit point for enslaved people for the New World. It was only expunged from political map of Africa when the newly declared Republic of Dahomey (later Benin) demanded that it be returned in 1961, shortly after the country's political independence from France in 1960. As most Portuguese colonial scholars will recall, 1961 was also that *annus horribilis* considered by many to be the critical turning point in the history of Portuguese colonialism; one which saw the increasing political unrest in Angola, Mozambique and Guinea-Bissau tied to growing independence movements, a year that ended with the annexation of the remaining Portuguese territories in India in December of that year. As was to be expected, the Salazarist-controlled press in Portugal was quick to reassert its claim to the tiny parcel, in spite of the clear absurdity of preserving a territory too small to even be represented on most maps of Africa without an inset map, even if in this particular case it would have to be one that could function with the precision of a microscope.

Whatever the justifications might have been for this refusal to surrender even a single square centimeter of ground, in a colonial conflict, one that would only intensify and continue to spread in years to come, it was only after the Carnation Revolution of 1974 that all Portuguese claims on this postage-stamp-sized colony were renounced once and for all; nonetheless, this reluctance to face the facts of loss of empire is all too often how colonialism operates as a discourse, both by its administrators and colonial settlers or in the writings, not to mention the research of its latter-day apologists as witnessed in the recent spectacle at the academic journal *Third World Quarterly*: magnifying the inviolable integrity of its own territorialized discursive spaces, however minuscule, while ignoring or simply remaining in denial of the broader historical and cultural realities that lie beyond its fortified enclosure of control.

In spite of these and other factual evidence at our disposal, so it is today as well in many respects, as we once again find ourselves obliged to state the obvious to a handful of Western scholars who continue to engage in the whitewashing of the dirtier chapters of European colonialism in Africa and elsewhere, with the recent row over calls to retract an article defending colonialism at the academic journal *Third World Quarterly* perhaps only the most publicized example.[2] While earlier issues of PLCS dedicated to the literatures of African nation-states no doubt do their part to place our focus firmly in a postcolonial, if not explicitly decolonial, mindset, much as theorists like Walter Mignolo continue to insist (Mignolo 2011), the work in the double issue of PLCS, *Parts of Asia* (17/18), edited by Cristiana Bastos, made the question all the more explicit: while concerned with the vast and varied encounter between Portuguese culture and those found across the diverse landscape of South, Southeast and East Asia, the critique that exhorts scholars to transcend the cultural, linguistic and with them the ideological confines of the colonial enclave and set aside one's own culturally ingrained "colonial nostalgia" (Bastos 17, Larkosh 190) is just as timely now as it was ten years ago, and in the process, perhaps displacing a measure of what Paul Gilroy identifies as "colonial melancholia" as well (Gilroy 2006).

Many of the enslaved people who were eventually to settle on plantations in Brazil would later return to inhabit cities in the region, perhaps most notably to Lagos in Nigeria and Porto-Novo, whose Portuguese names attest to the cultural dimension that survives to this day, a cultural presence especially visible in examples of the so-called "Brazilian architecture" found in these cities' older neighborhoods. Once considered the epitome of modernity, many of these buildings are in danger of disappearing, especially in Lagos, as an unfortunate casualty of the frenetic expansion that characterizes the transformation of this and other megacities of the Global South as they develop their own urbanistic understandings of the modern and the new, for a twenty-first century in which these conurbations already dominate the list of the world's most populated metropolitan areas. With such undeniable facts in mind, these sites of cultural production are increasingly connected not just to a former colonial metropolis but above all to one another. In this way, they are already constructing their own concrete understandings of a postcolonial cultural centrality all the more undeniable with each new transformation.

On a smaller urban scale, a more immediate example can be found closer to home for us here in New England. When visitors enter the African collection at the Museum of Fine Arts in nearby Boston, one of the first things they might notice as they walk in are the Benin bronzes from what is today part of southwestern Nigeria placed near the entrance (see studies by Blackmun, Dark and Forman for further examples). These artworks, often stolen and resold to museums around the world, depict not only native warriors, but also the Portuguese, who arrived on the coasts of the Gulf of Guinea, reaching the port of Gwatto and making contact with the *oba* or king of the Edo Kingdom as early as 1485. The Portuguese soldiers are dressed in metal armor and firearms much like the ones that Edo warriors themselves would begin to use and incorporate into portraits of their own leaders and military figures.

While these artifacts of earliest contact from Edo visual culture are well-known, though perhaps not an integral part of what we learn about when we think of, say, introductory course in Lusophone cultural studies, what is given less attention is the ways that these techniques and thematics continue to influence contemporary bronze casting in the Edo culture to this day. Perhaps such examples can even be said to suggest a series of challenges to the ways in which the teaching of 'Africa' as a relatively undifferentiated and 'othered' cultural space in Portuguese (-language) literary and cultural studies related to Africa might be shifted to some extent, perhaps even towards a more historically grounded sensibility to so-often impermanent and redrawn borders: not only of countries in Africa, but of the academic institutions we ourselves may find ourselves in as we read this and consider, to give just one example, the increasing visibility of students of African descent in Portuguese programs, whether from Cape Verde, Brazil, or just as likely in many cases, from the US, Portugal and other European countries with significant and growing African diaspora populations.

It is this awareness of the realities of the majority of Portuguese speakers in the world today that underscores the urgency of imagining more inclusive futures for academic disciplines, whether in the humanities in general, or Luso-Afro-Brazilian Studies in particular, and with it, the full-scale "decolonization of the $21^{st}$-century university" itself: that is, if a recent essay by Achille Mbembe, that Cameroonian colonial historian and decolonial thinker whose work transits any number of global educational institutions in South Africa, the US, Europe and elsewhere, is any indication of possible new directions. Regardless of the possible directions that our own programs and institutions may choose, Mbembe makes a convincing argument that, while it may escape the attention of many of those who continue to implement the neoliberal model of the all-administrative university, there are other scholars, above all in Africa and elsewhere in the Global South, who know that another kind of more radically inclusive and ideologically diverse university remains possible.

So what is perhaps most interesting for the purposes of this issue of PLCS on *Transnational Africas* is the emphasis not only on visual, material, sonic and textual representations—ones conditioned, if not indelibly marked, by the Portuguese colonial/imperial gaze and the territorial boundaries it encourages—but perhaps more importantly, the shift in focus toward the representations of the native peoples they encountered and continue to interact with: both in what today are considered the recognized limits of Lusophone Africa or beyond, no matter whether in Portuguese, African languages and creoles, or other European and global languages.

## Other Africas, African Others

Such examples complicate and expand current understandings of a vast and diverse continent such as Africa on the basis of its colonial and post-independence national borders, and by extension, the commonly held view that linguistic identity is and must invariably remain at the heart of national identity or cultural perspective, when it may be the case that cultural identity in the nominally Lusophone world has always been more of a complex set of multilingual or translational engagements, and not just between Portuguese and other spoken and written languages officialized by nation-states and their empires or preserved as one vehicle for colonized peoples' cultural resistance. Other forms of native cultural production can be found in the messages conveyed in visual and sonic culture, and it is for this reason that these forms of cultural expression are at the center of this volume's focus.

What other, more fluid paradigms of identity might emerge from the study of the visual arts, not to mention other material forms of cultural production in which written, spoken and recorded language is not a necessary or essential element? And how does such creative expression allow for a divergent vision of Africa, one in which ideas, images and other visual material can cross boundaries, reshape cultural spaces, and contest subsequent interpretations of African art and culture that remain to these official linguistic and cultural paradigms?

Moreover, every model of identity implies, both within it and beyond its borders, a clear concept, or at the very least, a vague understanding, of alterity: that often uncertain zone of otherness that borders and conditions, if not permeates, any contemporary understanding and articulation of self. Take the writings of Gayatri Chakravorty Spivak, the Indian postcolonial theorist who, along with her collaborator Ranajit Guha, is to be credited for recontextualizing the Gramscian concept of the subaltern in discussions of postcoloniality in the Global South. In 2008, Spivak published a book with the ambitious title *Other Asias*, which takes on the daunting task of speaking about a vast and diverse continent beyond her native country and culture to think in "other" terms: Armenia, Afghanistan, *inter alia*. It was this book, with its discussions of postcoloniality across borders and new forms of continental thought that can be seen as providing one theoretical model for this renewed discussion on alternative, divergent forms of transnationality. In the disciplinary context of Lusophone African studies, this understanding of otherness as elaborated by Spivak (not to mention "others") can also extend to any number of other modes of creative expression, be it visual culture, popular media culture, cinema, architecture, or music.

What can this context of "Other Africas" bring to transnational Lusophone African literary and cultural studies? How might non-Lusophone and even non-linguistic forms of expression modify our way of researching and understanding what we have come to call Lusophone Africa, for lack of a better term? What of our academic engagement is explicitly committed to decolonizing these cultural spaces, and with them our own universities and the ways we interact with them as institutions?

## Futures, Utopias and Other Regenerations

Other research that is just as important to mention here as we attempt to imagine other paradigms for transnational Africas is that theoretical and critical work that assists us, not just in visually conceptualizing, but materially implementing a different set of futures for Africa, ones distinct from both its colonial past and its often stubbornly neocolonial present. What forms of futurity can we imagine for Africa through its visual, material and sonic culture, however Utopian that notion may seem in theory or impossible to achieve in practice?

In the area of Luso-Afro-Brazilian Studies, certain examples of recent scholarship come to mind: for instance, that of Yoruba-speaking Nigerian academic Niyi Afolabi's *Golden Cage: Regeneration in Lusophone African Literature and Culture*, which departs from and proposes an approach to mainly Angolan and Mozambican literary figures (Honwana, Rui, Couto, Ba Ka Khosa) by way of the recurrent and much-discussed theme of regeneration found in the works of another

Yoruba-speaking Nigerian, the internationally celebrated author Wole Soyinka. While the text may begin like so many others with a political map of Africa in which Lusophone African countries are colored in, with black ink, and thus singled out, the text itself allows for a much broader pan-African context for discussion, especially to Nigeria, not only Africa's most populous country, but also, along with its Western neighbor Benin, quite possibly the logical starting point from which new transborder discussions between Lusophone and other African literatures and cultures can be reinitiated, especially in the varied forms of transatlantic religious syncretism and other elements of diasporic transculturation that find their origins here. This kind of comparative research between nominally 'Lusophone' and other cultural sites may offer new possibilities for regeneration, if not by giving greater recognition to those African scholars who could contribute far more to this discussion.

Another set of futures can be found in the 2015 collection of essays edited by Francisco Bethencourt, published under the title *Utopia in Portugal, Brazil and Lusophone African Countries*; perhaps most notable in this context of transnational Africas is the one by the currently Macau-based São Tomean scholar of Lusophone African literature Inocência Mata, who interprets the Utopian longings that emerge both in the works by Pepetela in relation to relevant theoretical texts (Bignotto, Mannheim) and, perhaps more importantly, in the concrete context of current political realities in Angola and by extension, elsewhere in Africa. Especially when their messages are juxtaposed and understood alongside one another, these theoretical examples cannot but serve as yet another kind of programmatic warning to those who hope to imagine futurity not only through works of literature and culture, but also, at least to some extent, through the ongoing political consolidation processes of nation-states and their all-too-fragile institutions. As Mata notes:

> in the end, the bureaucratic utopia, or rather, what has been instated as a bureaucratic programme, has replaced the political-social utopia, and its purpose has a dystopic characteristic to it. It is the natural outcome of the 'victorious vanquished' because a utopia in power is a contradiction in terms. Which to use Karl Mannheim's statement in my epigraph, is the same as saying that only in Utopia and revolution is there true life. The institutional order is always-only the evil residue that remains from ebbing Utopias and revolutions. Hence, the road of history leads from one topia over a Utopia to the next topia, etc. (Mata 180).

Mata's sobering conclusion on the prospects of imagining cultural futures through the political lens of the nation-state may appear to leave little hope within current institutional and ideological confines, even as new cultural objects continue to emerge and propose new models for creative activity. How, then, might we create a future that takes these warning signals of politicized institutional and ideological overreach into account?

Limiting ourselves to literary scholarship, however, would be to miss the point of this special issue of PLCS: to continue to extend the corpus of cultural materials that form the basis of our research and teaching beyond literature in a way that recognizes the undeniable importance of other forms of visual, sonic and material culture. From the field of contemporary art, one recent collection of essays in particular sets off in a markedly different direction: the 2016 collection *African Futures: Thinking About the World in Word and Image*, which documents the multi-city African Futures festivals held simultaneously in the three African cities of Johannesburg, Lagos and Nairobi the year before. While any exact definition of the term "Afrofuturism" that emerges as the guiding principle of this exhibition may have to be deferred for a more in-depth discussion than I am permitted here, the sheer number of essays on the ways that African artists incorporate their vision of future into their own recent work in visual, material and sonic culture—i.e., both from within the current conventional confines of what we identify as 'Lusophone Africa' such as the Angolan artist Kiluanji Kia Henda, but also, and perhaps more importantly, *beyond*—does much to temper any pessimism regarding the role cultural workers can still have in making and remaking workable concepts of futurity. In the concluding essay, Achille Mbembe reappears for the purposes of our discussion to ponder the significance of an Africa at the moment of its "planetary turn": one in which China continues its economic externalization on the Continent, and environmental forces caused by human exploitation of the entire planet also expose it to an ever-greater fragility. His final thoughts, however, are not bare economic ones, but part of a broader argument that shifts the focus back to one of Africa's most important unresolved issues: that of race, racism and racialization, playing themselves out on an increasingly global scale:

> New configurations of racism are emerging worldwide. Because race-thinking increasingly entails profound questions about the nature of the human species in general, the need to rethink the politics of racialization and the

terms under which the struggle for racial justice unfolds—here and elsewhere in the world—today has become ever more urgent. Racism is still acting as a constitutive supplement to nationalism. How do we create a world beyond nationalism? [...] But simply looking to past and present, local and global rearticulations of race will not suffice. To tease out alternative possibilities for thinking life and human futures in this age of neoliberal individualism, we need to connect in entirely new ways the project of non-racialism to that of human mutuality. In the last instance, non-racialism is truly about radical sharing and universal inclusion. (Mbembe 334-335)

In a commentary clearly directed both to thinkers and to practitioners in the area of visual culture, Mbembe provides yet another reminder of how interdisciplinary and transnational work on Africa, whether by Black African scholars or by those in other cultural environments, can ignore crucial questions of racialization only at its own risk. Regardless of the additional sites of cultural activity that will no doubt be revealed as the discipline continues its work in this direction of its ever-uncertain limits and futures in an irreversibly globalized context, the articles in the collected volumes cited, both in this critical introduction and by others that comprise this issue of PLCS, are also indicative of an ever-increasing number of divergent sites of scholarly research and transmission of knowledge in our field and beyond that not only engage critically with the colonial engagement of a single European colonial power in Africa, but that also reference a number of sensory examples that go beyond the limits of Portuguese or any other written language in order to assist in visualizing this complex cultural conversation across the borders of African nation-states. At the same time, this approach serves to complicate naïve or nostalgic understandings of the colonial enclave and its claims of the epistemological or symbolic primacy of its own cultural production, much less its presumed cultural or racial superiority in relation to that of native colonized peoples.

**This Issue**
With issues of PLCS already dedicated to the literatures, cultures and other expressive traditions of Angola, Mozambique and Cape Verde, as well as one that, with contributions from both within and beyond the officially Lusophone world, does much toward meeting the objective of critically problematizing and recognizing the multiplicity of culturally specific uses that the concept of Lusofonia

finds a number of unnoticed forms of reinvention and regeneration. This double issue of PLCS takes the discussion forward, allowing us to revisit cultural production in and beyond those spaces usually considered part of Lusophone Africa, but as have seen, Africa, like any other continent or territorial entity, is always subject to remappings, and with them, new understandings of space, ways of seeing, hearing and otherwise sensing culture as it continues to change.

It is for this reason that the focus for this issue will be broadening the focus beyond literary studies to privilege visual, material and sonic culture. While the Portuguese language, as well as literature and political discourse in Portuguese, continues to shape discussions on cultural identity within all five Lusophone African nation-states, visual culture can play a critical role in questioning the primacy of language and literature, not just in providing alternative models for nascent national identities and division of space within the official linguistic frameworks predicated by officializing institutions such as the CPLP or Lusofonia, but also because in its transnational circulation, art may well encourage a more flexible and nuanced approach to (trans-)national identity.

While some scholars in the field still tend to conflate the concept of Lusofonia, in Africa and elsewhere, with any of its institutional incarnations that claim to speak for it in its entirety, others may well find themselves more concerned with its contested borders and the inherent limitations of current disciplinary models, as new interactions with and between other African and global sites enter into contact with and transform this conversation, perhaps radically: whether in connection to the three countries that have already been the subject of issues of PLCS (Angola, Mozambique, Cape Verde), or in others such as São Tomé and Principe and Guinea-Bissau still to be given the same degree of critical attention.

It might well be less-studied examples of local, native cultures, the cultural transit of cross-border regions, or the emergent transnational political systems where new perspectives might emerge; just as important for us, however, will be the ways that they are interpreted, incorporated and reflected in the "Other," still undeniably (geo-)political institutional and academic spaces that we occupy and inhabit as scholars, not only where Lusofonia once again 'meets' Africa, but also vice versa.

NOTES

1. These successive names for the country now known as Benin provide yet another example of how newly independent African states reference the cultural achievements of native kingdoms in their own projects of national consolidation according to their own narratives of power and authority (e.g., Ghana, Mali; consider also the renaming of other states in the 1970s to indicate concentrations of political power: e.g., Central African Republic/Central African Empire or Congo/Zaire). Regardless of the degree of cultural or geographical overlap that these newly independent states share with their historical precursors; in the case of Benin, it was actually because of the lack of connection with any of the ethnic groups in the country that President Kérékou considered it a more neutral, and thus more suitable choice for the country as a whole. And if these details on the consolidation of national identities seem irrelevant to a discussion of Lusophone Africa or, if you prefer, the Black Atlantic, we can go back to limiting our focus to officially Portuguese territories, regardless of their relative lack of importance in the overall cultural identity of the region (which is quite possibly one of the reasons why Guran chose to leave any mention of it out of his article).

2. Of most interest to Lusophone scholars concerned with the historiography of Portuguese colonialism in the article in question, if not the the apologetic turns on European colonialisms it has attempted to relegitimize, are perhaps those arguments which critique the political legacy of Guinea-Bissauan liberation leader Amílcar Cabral (at one point going so far as to propose that this country allow its former colonial master to return and colonize an off-shore island, and that if this were to occur, the country would somehow be transformed into another Macao or Goa, the two other former Portuguese colonial territories that the author of this article seems to consider postcolonial success stories). While it is not my place to speculate on, much less prescribe, what the correct economical or political course for post-independent Lusophone Africa might be, one might do well to defer to the recent collection of scholarly articles by English-speaking Black Studies scholars on Amílcar Cabral, one that in both its title (A Luta Continua) and its wide range of academic contributions that it brings to this discussion, make a more compelling counterargument for his continued relevance for postcolonial researchers on Lusophone Africa, not to mention other parts of the continent and beyond (Saucier ed., 2017).

WORKS CITED

Afolabi, Niyi. *The Golden Cage: Regeneration in Lusophone African Literature and Culture*. Trenton, NJ/Asmara, Eritrea: Africa World Press, 2001.

Ashby, Sarah. *The Lusophone World: The Evolution of Portuguese National Narratives*. Brighton/Portland/Toronto: Sussex Academic Press, 2017.

Bastos, Cristiana, ed. *Parts of Asia*. PLCS 17/18 (2010).

Blackmun, Barbara Winston, ed. "Contemporary Contradictions: Bronze casting in the Edo Kingdom of Benin." In Salami and Visoná, 389-407.

Dark, Philip J. C. *An Introduction to Benin Art and Technology*. Oxford: Clarendon Press, 1973.

Flaherty, Colleen. "Much of *Third World Quarterly*'s Editorial Board Resigns, Saying the Controversial Article Failed to Pass Peer Review." *Inside Higher Ed*, September 20, 2017. Online.

Forman, W. and B. and Philip Dark. *Benin Art*. London: Artia, 1960.

Gilroy, Paul. *The Black Atlantic: Modernity and Double Consciousness*. London/New York: Verso, 1993.

———. *Postcolonial Melancholia*. New York: Columbia UP, 2006.

Guran, Milton. "Agudás from Benin: 'Brazilian' Identity as a Path to Citizenship." In Maro, Sansi-Roca ad Treece, eds. *Cultures of the Lusophone Black Atlantic*. New York: Palgrave Macmillan, 2007.

Gilroy, Paul. *The Black Atlantic: Modernity and Double-Consciousness*. Cambridge, MA: Harvard UP, 1995.

———. *Postcolonial Melancholia*. New York: Columbia UP, 2006.

Heidenreich-Seleme, Lien and Sean O'Toole, eds. *African Futures: Thinking About the Future in Word and Image*. Bielefeld/Berlin: Kerber Verlag, 2016.

Larkosh, Christopher. "Passages to Our Selves: Translating Out of Portuguese in Asia." In Bastos, Cristana, ed. *PLCS* 17/18 (2010): 189-216.

Mata, Inocência. "From Utopia to Prophecy: The Meanderings of the Heterotopia of Nation in African Literatures." In Bethencourt, Francisco, ed. *Utopia in Portugal, Brazil and Lusophone African Countries*. Bern: Peter Lang, 2015.

Mbembe, Achille Joseph. "Decolonizing the University: New Directions." Online.

———. "Africa in the New Century." In Heidenreich-Seleme and O'Toole, eds. 315-335.

Mignolo. Walter. *The Darker Side of Western Modernity: Global Futures, Decolonial Options*. Durham: Duke UP, 2011.

Saucier, P. Khalil. *A Luta Continua: (Re) Introducing Amilcar Cabral to a New Generation of Thinkers*. Trenton/London/Cape Town: Africa World Press, 2017.

Schor, Patricia. *Disencounters with Africa in the Portuguese language: Postcolonial literature and theory in the Portuguese postempire*. Ph.D. thesis, University of Utrecht, 2017.

Spivak, Gayatri Chakravorty. *Other Asias*. Malden, MA/Oxford: Blackwell, 2008.

Wainaina, Binyavanga. "How to Write About Africa?" *Granta* 92: "The View from Africa." 19. January 2006.

CHRISTOPHER LARKOSH is Associate Professor of Portuguese at UMass Dartmouth. He has published and lectured around the world in a number of global languages, not only in relation to Portuguese-speaking, postcolonial and diasporic cultures, but also others including Quebec, Argentina, Italy, France, Germany, Turkey, South and East Asia, as well as on the transnational, transcultural and gendered interactions between them. He is the author of numerous articles in academic journals such as *Social Dynamics*, *TOPIA*, *TTR* and *The Translator*, as well as the Routledge/Taylor & Francis journal *Translation Studies*, for which he also contributed as Reviews Editor from 2012 to 2014. He served a two-year term as Director of Tagus Press from 2015 to 2017, and continues to serve as an Editor for its scholarly journal Portuguese Literary & Cultural Studies, as well as literary editor for its Portuguese in the Americas series. He also currently serves on the Editorial Board of the internationally recognized Montréal-based translation journal *Meta*. He is the editor of *Re-Engendering Translation: Transcultural Practice, Gender/Sexuality and the Politics of Alterity* (London/New York: St. Jerome/Routledge, 2011) and has co-edited two additional volumes in transcultural studies, one entitled *Writing Spaces*, compiled in collaboration with colleagues in Taiwan (Kaohsiung: NSYSU Press, 2013), and another entitled *KulturConfusão: German-Brazilian Interculturalities* (Berlin: De Gruyter, 2015). His forthcoming book, *The Queerness of Translation*, will be published by Routledge in 2019.

FILIPA LOWNDES VICENTE

# Black Women's Bodies in the Portuguese Colonial Visual Archive (1900-1975)

ABSTRACT: The pervasiveness of images of black women's unclothed bodies in the Portuguese colonial visual archive from the late nineteenth century to the 1970s—in photographic postcards, propaganda leaflets, colonial exhibition ephemera or as illustrations in newspapers—demonstrates that the gendered and racialized body of (unnamed) women was a powerful trope of colonial hegemony.

The Portuguese colonial context, similar to other colonial contexts, reveals the banalization of the practice of white men photographing black colonized women. Is resistance or participation in the "event of photography" possible for these photographed women? This article will discuss some of the issues and challenges of dealing with these images through specific case studies: postcards of semi-naked African women between the ethnographic and the erotic; images of women exhibited in colonial exhibitions; private photographs of Portuguese soldiers next to African women; but also the counter narratives to an hegemonic visuality.

Where are these images now? Where were they in the past? Who saw them and in what contexts? How were they kept and classified? How were they reproduced? Their endless potential for reproduction, circulation and intermediality points to the heterogeneous nature of this legacy. How can we decolonize this visual archive? The question of ethics, one which scholars, curators and archivists have been debating for the past few decades, will also be addressed. Reproducing and exhibiting images of abuse and exploitation might replicate what one seems to criticize. Are the university, the archive, the museum, or the academic journal critical enough to counteract the risks of perpetuating the violence?

KEYWORDS: Photography, visual culture, colonialism, images of black women, Portuguese colonial Africa

RESUMO: A omnipresença de imagens de mulheres negras seminuas no arquivo visual do colonialismo português desde finais do século XIX até à década de 1970—em postais fotográficos, folhetos propagandísticos, publicações relacionadas com exposições coloniais ou ilustrações em jornais—demonstra como os corpos racializados de mulheres (anónimas) foi um poderoso agente de hegemonia colonial.

O contexto colonial português, à semelhança de outros impérios, revela a banalização da prática de homens brancos, provenientes da metrópole, fotografarem mulheres africanas habitantes dos espaços colonizados. Este artigo discutirá alguns dos temas e desafios que se colocam perante estas imagens, através de estudos de caso específicos: postais de mulheres a sugerir uma fronteira ténue entre o etnográfico e o erótico; imagens de mulheres expostas em exposições coloniais; fotografias pessoais de soldados portugueses ao lado de mulheres africanas; mas também as contra-narrativas a esta hegemonia visual.

Onde estão hoje essas imagens? E onde estavam no passado? Quem é que as viu e em que contextos? Como é que foram guardadas e classificadas? Como e onde foram reproduzidas? O seu potencial infinito de reprodução, circulação e intermedialidade ajuda a explicar a heterogeneidade deste legado. Como é que podemos descolonizar este arquivo visual? As questões éticas—que têm sido debatidas por académicos, artistas, curadores e arquivistas nas últimas décadas—também serão exploradas. Reproduzir imagens de abuso e desigualdade é um gesto que corre o risco de reforçar aquilo que se quer abordar criticamente. Será que a universidade, o arquivo, o museu ou a revista académica são espaços suficientemente críticos para conter o risco de perpetuar, no presente, a violência do passado?

PLAVRAS-CHAVE: Fotografia, cultura visual, colonialismo, imagens de mulheres negras, África colonial Portuguesa

## 1. Widely Available for Visual Consumption:
## Images of Black Women in Colonial Contexts

From the late nineteenth century until the 1970s, there was a thriving global industry of "colonial" postcards where unclothed black women's bodies circulated openly. In the 1930s and 1940s, (white) women, children and men could view the naked breasts of black women in daylight at public exhibitions and gardens in Lisbon and Paris (Figs. 1-7). The unequal value placed on these bodies meant an unequal access to their viewing. Those black bodies could be subject to a close-up look because they came from distant geographies of subalternity that somehow "belonged" to the viewers. Possession (or the desire for possession) implied, among other things, the right to see. The pervasiveness of images of black women's bodies in the Portuguese as well as in other European colonial contexts—in photographic postcards, colonial propaganda leaflets, colonial exhibition ephemera or as illustrations in newspapers and magazines—demonstrates that the gendered and racialized body of (unnamed) women was a powerful trope of colonial hegemony.

This is an heterogeneous and diverse archive and it would be narrow to think of these images only in relation to their common qualities. In a pioneering article on photography in Angola, published in 1990, Beatrix Heintze explored some of this diversity.[1] Christraud M. Geary has established a wide classification of "anthropometric" and "ethnographic" photographs, the first grouped according to "types" and "geographical origins" (Figs. 8-10) and the latter according to daily activities, which included motherhood among them.[2] Within the many sub-genres of these categories, some women appear posing toward the camera. In others, there is a staged reenactment. Geary also adds a relevant category in relation to which, I would argue, little is known for the Portuguese colonial case: that of "images of pride and confidence" where black women appear in studio-like interior spaces, seated, dressed and posing centrally to the camera.[3] In these images—photographs that were often printed as postcards—which provide counter narratives to the kinds of images I will analyze in this article, women actively participate in the photographic "event," to use Ariella Azoulay's expression.[4] These were probably private, commissioned portraits that the photographer later used for commercial postcard printing not necessarily with the photographed women's knowledge.

The subject of representations of female black bodies has been framed through different scholarly approaches: there is an extensive scholarly literature on visual representations of blacks and blackness;[5] another approach focuses on the intersection of the visual with colonial contexts; and there is scholarship which concentrates specifically on the visual or photographic history of the black body, with some studies dedicated specifically to the female body[6] and some of these are dedicated to individual case-studies.[7] Another relevant critical approach to photographic history and theory is the one that reflects on an African or Black relationship to photography.[8] In 1981, the Algerian Malek Alloula published a pioneering study entitled, *Le Harem Colonial: Images d'un Sous-érotisme* (translated as *The Colonial Harem*). In his analysis of eroticized colonial photographic postcards of Algerian women, Alloula applied Edward Said's idea of Orientalism, something that had not yet been done for postcards in studies of visual culture.[9]

The colonization of the body—the female colonized body—by the male colonizer had the metaphoric resonance of the colonial experience itself: the "civilized" white European conquering the "wild" territory as well as the untamed body of the black woman. The ambivalence between the native woman and the prostitute, the racialized body as one available for male consumption, was played out in many of the photographic postcards that circulated widely and globally with more or less reference to their places of origin.[10] A white male identity was inseparable from the actual process of the construction of colonial states, and many of its practices, discourses and experiences were gendered.[11] These images were the visual translation of the widespread language imbued with difference, inequality and violence that were current within the vast printed culture produced in the colonial context.

These black women did not look like the white colonizing men's sisters, mothers or wives. Images of white women's undressed or naked bodies were also flourishing in the visual economy of the turn of the nineteenth century, but they did so within the private, male sphere of vision, placed in the circumscribed spheres of eroticism or pornography. These images of white women's bodies circulated out of sight and outside of accepted morality. They were not available in the public realm of post office circulation, family photographic albums or current paper ephemera from newspapers to leaflets, available to all, as was the case with black women's bodies.

This visual availability should be analyzed next to the actual availability of black women's bodies in European public spaces at the turn of the nineteenth century—from universal or colonial exhibitions to zoological and public gardens. In this article I explore this line of inquiry through the case of "Rosinha" or "Rosita," the black woman brought from a Portuguese colony to be exhibited in the 1934 Colonial Exhibition of Porto whose anonymity was somehow replaced by a process that turned her into an iconic figure with an invented, and more easily pronounceable, Portuguese name. In this case, the image making of her (semi-naked) body through widely accessible postcards was the visual and reproductive translation of the actual exhibition of her body in a particular space and time—that of a temporary exhibition which was designed for a Portuguese public and which aimed to make known, promote and encourage the national colonial enterprise. This case study exemplifies a much wider phenomenon, which has been studied widely in the French context, that of the "Human Zoos" which displayed human beings, mostly in public spaces in major European cities.[12]

Within this ideological context, there was space for women to have their breasts on view, in leisurely spaces such as gardens, *jardins d'acclimatation* and exhibitions. Black women's bodies were visually available to women, children and men, in broad daylight and in official, acceptable and accessible spaces in striking contrast to those spaces where images or displays of white women's exposed bodies could be observed—in circumscribed, private spaces, intended only for a "male gaze," to use Laura Mulvey's much quoted idea of women as an on-screen object of desire for a male cinema viewership.[13]

However, even if breasts were at the center of this erotic gaze, there was another body feature, which was repeatedly given as the motive for the photograph—hair. A significant quantity of postcards or printed photographs in the Portuguese colonial context, as well as in others, reinforced this with a few words in the caption: "Typos e Penteados (Huíla)" is the Angolan postcard Geary reproduces in her chapter,[14] but many others could be cited over a long period of time. For example, in the 1940s and 1950s Elmano Cunha e Costa's ethnographic photographic projects were organized around a visual survey of women's hairstyles (Fig. 6), while in 1965 the Italian military man and journalist who was in Angola with his French companion Anne Dominique Gaüzes, who was also a photographer, published a book on *Penteados de Angola*.[15]

At the time of writing, in 2017, these white/black differences persist in those spaces where these images exist today and in the ways that they are consumed, seen and collected. The material legacies of colonialism now thrive in the contemporary vintage postcard market; and so do the colonial categories. White women's exposed bodies would be classified in the sections labeled "erotic" or "pornographic." Equivalent black bodies can be filed in multiple categories: "Angola," "Africa," "colonial," "ethnic," "anthropological," "colonial exhibition," "human zoos," etc. This leads me to another question that will be explored in this article: the enduring persistence in the present of the racism and violence of the past. Therefore, I am interested in thinking about these images in the past but also in the present.[16] Where are they today? In what contexts do they circulate? Where and how are they on sale? How are they viewed, kept, talked about, classified? Who collects them and why?

Use of these materials in the contemporary moment as historical or scholarly sources leads me to a point I find more and more poignant the more I look at and hold these kinds of materials—the words, printed or manuscript, that are written next to, or behind, the images. This need to think of images next to words, the visual next to the written, is not as obvious as it may seem. The growing global tendency to digitize images may seem to make them more easily available—even in archival and academic contexts. However, this digital format moves away from the materiality that I argue is fundamental to the ways in which we must approach and analyze these documents. To look at the image printed in a photographic postcard is a gesture that should be followed by turning the object over and reading what is written on the other side, in printed letters or in manuscript ones.

Very often, the word, handwritten by an identified or non-identified person, addresses the postcard image in a way with which we are familiar from our smartphones, simultaneously image/word makers and circulation devices. It is easy to insert the picture postcard in the genealogy of our contemporary, private, individual uses of word and image, but there is a striking difference. If now this combination of word and image tends to be in the same frame, the same gaze, the same two-dimensional surface, an object such as the postcard demands a material approach where touch, movement (turning the object over) and tri-dimensionality are necessary for full apprehension. Therefore, if the printed words with which the images are identified are a relevant historical source—the banality of labels such as "Black Venus," "Black Beauty," "African Venus" or "Angolan Beauty"—so are the manuscript words someone has written on the other side or over the image itself. These words, as will be discussed below, can be more disturbing—racist, violent, humiliating—than the image itself. The image is often the trigger for the words someone has written. This "someone" is often the historical agent who is seldom heard, read or acknowledged, someone who lived a colonial experience, but who probably wrote little more than the texts found on the back of postcards sent to the metropolis. Most of the Portuguese "colonial" photographic (or picture, as seen in Figs. 14-16) postcards for sale today in commercial spaces were objects produced in colonial spaces (even if printed elsewhere), bought in Portuguese colonies by white Portuguese men or women and sent to the colonial metropolis.

Most of these postcards are now in the former colonial metropolis, a fact that is itself relevant to understanding the movements and "traveling" of these objects and the banality of their existence. Postcards are difficult to date, because one of their characteristics is that they are always undated, a strategy used to make them commercially valid for a longer period of time. In addition, an image could be printed in a postcard much later than its making. However, each object often provides clues to its chronology or at least to the time of its circulation through stamp or manuscript dates, as well as its printed legends and even technical characteristics. As with photography, the black-and-white postcard was replaced by those printed in full color. What is striking when we think diachronically is the pervasiveness of the postcard image of the black African woman who inhabited colonized territories through time, in the case of Portuguese colonialism, into the 1970s; from black and white to color.

Beyond the contemporary collecting of colonial objects, there is another way in which the present uses of past, troubled and painful materials lead us into ethical questions: that is the ways in which these images are re-printed and re-produced in the context of academia and exhibitions. Is a critical and deconstructive frame of analysis sufficient to legitimize their showing and circulation yet again? Is it possible to decolonize these images while simultaneously and consciously putting them before new eyes in seminar or conference PowerPoint presentations, in scholarly books, in thematic exhibitions or in academic journals such as this one? To think about, look at or write on these images means inevitably having to confront the violence that was implicit in many of them and with the past uses of that violence embedded in their making and consumption. Is there a difference between "showing" problematic images and "quoting" problematic words? Does the very act of seeing, which can be immediate and undemanding, as distinct from the act of reading, a slower and apparently intellectually more demanding exercise, make it more ethically challenging to reproduce difficult images than to reproduce difficult words? How can we analyze these images as historical sources, while preserving or returning to these women the dignity, individuality and subjectivity that was threatened, or even destroyed, in the past making and the past (and present) uses of these images?

These are the main questions I will address in this article. To do so I will focus on specific case studies that can be seen as a mapping for further approaches. To identify a much larger quantity of visual sources would enable other questions to be posed and more definitive conclusions to be made. One such unanswered question would involve a thorough comparison with other European colonizing nations such as Belgium, Great Britain, Italy and France. The vast bibliography that in recent decades has concentrated on "colonial visual culture," as it tends to be named in British historiography, or "colonial iconography," as it tends to be named in French historiography, does not include the Portuguese colonial visual archive as a source, a problem, or a comparative frame. More extended transcolonial and transnational comparative studies could enable researchers to detect possible nuances and differences within the more evident conclusion—that black African female bodies became a common visual trope within the context of all European nations that were formerly colonizers in Africa. The European colonial visual archive reveals the banalization of the practice of white men belonging to the military, administrative, scientific or commercial colonial European experiences, photographing black colonized women and making them available to a much wider public through reproduction techniques in a thriving global market of visual consumption.

## 2. Where are the images? Where were they reproduced? Archives, Postcards, Newspapers, Leaflets

The second half of the nineteenth century witnessed a reproductive revolution, which had a growing and overwhelming impact on the ways images could be circulated, owned and seen. From the time of photography's disputed invention in 1839 to the invention of lithography and many other kinds of reproductive techniques, the viewing of word and image, at first separately and then together, became an increasingly democratic, less expensive and widespread experience.[17] When we overlap this chronology of technological and photographic developments with that of the formation of modern European empires, the result is discernible: the colonial, and this includes colonized territories and peoples in Africa as well as in Asia, became a central subject within the visual mapping of the world.

By the final decades of the nineteenth century the conditions existed for the development of the photographic postcard (by the 1870s with printed lithographed designs and by the 1880s with photographic images): on the one side, a small rectangle/framed space for the reproduction of a drawing or photograph; on the other side, the space for the written word, the address of the recipient and the words the sender could freely choose to write.[18] A few words describing the image or identifying the publisher were almost always printed, usually on the reverse side of the postcard, sometimes over the image itself.

Already in the twentieth century printing techniques enabled newspapers to add more and more photographic images next to their written texts. Likewise, other kinds of printed matter became increasingly common. Exhibition-goers could have their experience mediated by booklets and leaflets, with rich graphic work, while catalogues and books and all kinds of printed matter made wide use of the new possibilities of reproducing images next to words. It is also worth thinking about the relationship between images and words on the same printed page. Very often there is a direct relationship between the text and the image. However, it is common to have photographic images of unnamed black women, mostly with bare breasts, to "illustrate" articles on colonial subjects with no relation at all to the image beyond suggesting a very broad idea of the "colonial." (Fig. 17)

This new banality of images (much more was seen by many more) is relevant to understanding the ways in which many more people, in many more places could receive, see, buy and send postcards. It is also relevant to think of them as being objects as well as images: to focus on their materiality leads us to focus on the spaces where they are today. They are in public and private spaces, in commercial and non-commercial ones. They can be in archives and libraries, homes and in all kinds of commercial spaces, from flea markets, to secondhand bookshops to online postcard merchants. As we shall see, the ways in which they are classified or archived can also shape our understanding of them.

Many public archives separate photography from textual, manuscript and written documents. The archival fractures that divide image from word and separate documents that were together at the moment of their making had, and will continue to have, an impact on the ways in which we think about images and the kinds of history we can write. In addition, images of women's bodies, black and nude, can be present in many archives, though they may not listed in the classification entries. Even an archive that is ostensibly synonymous with masculinity, such as the Military Historical Archive, can—if approached from a gender-conscious perspective—reveal the presence of women, in photography as well as in the interstices of many official textual documents.[19]

The political and the intimate, the public and the personal, the state and the private are intertwined, not necessarily in hierarchical or separate ways. The intimate, the sexual, the affective and the many layers of gendered violence are encountered in the colonial archive, and a major source for its study are the images of almost always unnamed and unknown black women in photographs or in photographic postcards that are simultaneously so exposed and so imperceptible. "Black Venus," "Black Beauty" and other such classifications were widely used to name unidentified women in written and visual materials published in colonial contexts. Most often, they are printed by the editors, at other times it is the manuscript text in a postcard that reproduces the clichéd trope of associating the color of skin with the aesthetic label of those who should be looked at. (Figs. 1 and 10)

## 3. Inside/Outside:
## The Photographic Studio Versus the Natural, Outdoor Setting

Since the 1850s there had been two clear traditions within photography—one inside a studio space and another outdoors, where the photographer could be a traveler and a landscaper. The latter genealogy was the one to benefit more from technological developments that enabled the camera to have more control over natural light. While we tend to associate "colonial photography" with the outside—and certainly the widespread practice of making images of humans as "types," photographed where they were and as they were, contributed to this—it is important to acknowledge that studio photography became popular in India and in Africa from very early on, and that women often commissioned their own portraits.[20] Many of these photographers were African or Indian, and many of the people who paid to be photographed were also African or Indian, often with the status of colonized subjects.[21] This is another implicit distinction relevant to our case—indigenous elites would choose to have their portrait taken in photographic studios (or in outdoor spaces where a background canvas simulated a studio) and pay for it. This created a very different power relationship than the one that existed in the widespread images of "natives" outdoors, where it is much more difficult to understand the degree of control involved in allowing themselves to be photographed.

Most of the images of black, half-naked women printed in postcards were taken in outside spaces, and this is relevant to their meaning. The outside space can become a kind of justification for the photographic act—they were "naturally" like that, that was how they usually were, and the photographer had merely captured a "reality" with which he did not interfere. After the 1880s, when cameras became lighter, easier and faster devices, "instantaneous" photography would develop and the photographer could take snapshots—just by clicking the button—outside the studio space. Therefore, a major underlying justification for circulating images of women with bare breasts was the notion that that was how they actually went out in public spaces outside the home (Figs. 9, 10, 12, and 13).

This Western distinction between the inside space as the space for intimacy, privacy, and therefore nakedness, and the outside, as the space for the public, the communal, the constrained, was implicit in the widespread uses of these images of black women. In those images revealing the open sky and natural landscape, the photographer could more easily embody the role of a mere witness of the women who were already unclothed before his arrival. He became a simple observer who only enabled others to observe what he had seen by taking the picture. This ambiguity, leaning toward a visual tradition informed by ethnography, travel inquiry and knowledge gathering, was in fact a main legitimizer for the open circulation of these images. They were already semi-naked—it was not the photographer who undressed them nor the photographic encounter that determined it, as was the case with the pornographic visual economy that had developed since the invention of photography.

How many similar images are there of naked white women before a male photographer? As soon as it was invented, photography was put to many uses, and certainly pornography was one of them. The major difference between the circulation and reception of these images was that when the women were white they were destined to a kind of private male view, shared by a selective and elitist gaze. Even though erotic photographic postcards showing naked women became so widespread in France that they became known as "French Postcards," they were nevertheless meant for a male gaze. On the contrary, black women were available to a wider spectatorship, potentially to all that could see, including other women and children. The color of their skin made for an ontological difference—belonging to the space of the colonized, the subjugated and racially inferior, a space that implied distance and differentiation, their bodies could be looked at independently of who was looking and where. The ethnographic contained (or justified) the erotic.

For a long time images of naked white women did not make the transition from private archive to public print space. However, what happens later when, around the 1970s, the development of the tourist industry has an impact on the seaside postcard industry, which begins to portray topless women on beaches accompanied by indecent sentences? Certainly there is an objectification of the female body for male visual consumption, which transcends ethnic or national distinctions. However, the persistence and widespread nature of the exposed bodies of black women is the result of the ongoing complicity of patriarchy with colonialism, different structures of inequality that were often entangled even when the resistance to and denouncing of colonialism did not always acknowledge it.

## 4. Rosinha, or the Empire as Object of Desire:
### The 1934 Colonial Exhibition in Porto

Rosa, Rosinha or Rosita was the "Portuguese" name given to the most frequently mentioned "sight" exhibited at the Portuguese Colonial Exhibition.[22] This event, which took place in 1934 in Porto, Portugal's second most important city after Lisbon, was clearly inspired by the 1931 Parisian Exposition Coloniale, where the display of human beings brought from the French colonies was also a major visual trope. Therefore, unlike the vast majority of African women who were photographed and made to circulate, she had a name, even if it was not her real Islamic name, which was considered too difficult to pronounce and to write. Use of the suffix "-inha" or "-ita" created the diminutive versions of Rosa, a strategy that was employed to make her seem more familiar and closer to the majority of the Portuguese public to whom Africa, even if "theirs," was a remote reality. A member of the Balanta community, she had been brought from the recently conquered colony of Guinea. The Portuguese colonial presence had not been there long enough for her to begin to cover her naked body. Underlying this legitimacy to display her naked breasts to the vast public of men, women and children—more than one million according to official records—in the daylight of a public garden in the center of Porto in the mid 1930s was the fact that she was black and came from a space dominated by Portugal.

Her "Portuguese" name appeared many times in the printed material related to the first (and the last) exhibition to carry the designation of "colonial" to be held in Portugal. Rosita's presence helped account for the public success of the exhibition and her printed image—accessible to anyone to take home—further multiplied the impact of her image and name. Domingos Alvão was the official photographer of the exhibition, and his images were reproduced in catalogues and leaflets but mainly through that most popular object of the early twentieth century, the photographic postcard. Like the exhibition itself, the postcard was meant to prompt imaginative travels. In the exhibition, the public was physically separated from Rosita by a pond—a small, metaphorical Atlantic, easier to cross, with Africa on the other side of the water. In Domingos Alvão's close-ups of her, distance was further annulled.

During a period when the Portuguese colonial project demanded more settlers to occupy the African territories, Rosita was to encourage exhibition-goers to make this departure by embodying the empire as an object of desire.[43] On display in Porto, she herself embodied "Africa." Rosa represented not the dangerous and threatening Africa of the earlier expeditions or the later "pacification campaigns," the name given to the Portuguese military expeditions which fought African resistance to their presence, but a luscious and desirable Africa, close enough to be attainable by the common man, precisely those whom the exhibition wanted to turn into potential settlers. The association of the masculine with territorial and sexual conquest, already implicit in the colonial as well as the slave experience, became visible both within the exhibition and the photographs that multiplied it.

In the process of having her name as much as her body colonized, Rosita's image was reproduced and put into circulation beyond the limits of the exhibition visitors' gaze. Alvão, the author of all her official images, chose to photograph her in different visual narratives. In some of the images, Alvão photographs Rosita next to other members of the community who were also brought from Guinea. (Fig. 2) However, in other photographs Rosita stands alone. Either her bare breasts were contained within an ethnographic tradition or she was made to raise her arms in the recognizable visual code also present in Picasso's *Demoiselles de Avignon,* or in thousands of other images of women's naked breasts lingering in the moving boundaries between pornography and eroticism. With "Beleza Bijagoz," an unnamed women also exhibited in 1934, leaning against a tree, there is no doubt of the outside space she occupies. (Fig. 1) Nature and nakedness was the winning combination of the "ethnographic informed realism" that had in the color of the skin its major criteria.[24] The photograph was taken in Porto, but it was important for it to seem as though it were taken in Guinea, the photographer here mimicking the geographical game played by the exhibition itself. In the encounters between the African women and Alvão, the photographer is in the position of the exhibition viewer, thus reinforcing the black female body's visual (and sexual) availability to all; she was not merely available to the photographer.

In a book published in Luanda on the representation of Angola at the 1934 exhibition, a similar duality emerges. In an article on the Bank of Angola, a "black beauty of Huíla," with her arms raised, is printed next to an erotically toned down "Black Mucancala."[25] (Fig. 17) The image of the modern architecture of the bank next to the images described as that "curious Angolan tribe," "one of the lowest species in the human scale" contributed to the trivial language of colonial justification. Gender hierarchies are likewise implicit. The bank, the building, the colonial exhibition, as well as the picture book that promoted it, were all male, Portuguese, enterprises; Africa was female. As in Alvão's double "Rositas," the eroticized and the exoticized claimed each other's presence in an ambiguous frontier where the differentiation between one and the other was to be made by the colonizer.

During a research stay in Porto in 2001, I went to a photography shop named Alvão in the city center. The owners, no longer the original photographer's family, helpfully brought me everything that was left in the shop archive. One of the albums had photographs of the colonial exhibition glued to its pages and small manuscript sentences next to some of the images. I was struck and disturbed by one of the sentences written by hand next to one of the images (I cannot remember which) where Rosita appears next to some Guinean men in the same reconstructed village. I copied it in my notebook: "Who is going to sleep with Rosita tonight?" was the comment. Visually available as much to white men as to black men, looking at her—in a photograph or in person—becomes the first act of other potential ones, the sexual or the colonial encounter.

The Colonial Exhibition of 1934—where the "ethnographic exhibitions" with more than 300 women, men and children from Cabo Verde, Guinea, Angola, Mozambique, India, Macau and Timor became the most popular—epitomized a new kind of colonial project. Focused on encouraging Portuguese immigration to Portugal's African territories and eager to rival other European empires, the Portuguese state needed to invest more in promoting the colonies within the metropolis, and the exhibition, with its recourse to all visual devices available, became the best way to achieve this.[26] Beyond Rosita's village, in another pavilion, a big diorama with life-size figures showed black women dressed in Western clothes being taught how to cook and sew by patient white nuns dressed in their habit. Domesticity and religion were rehearsed in a display that emphasized the role of Portuguese evangelization in Africa, actually one of the few official roles women could assume in the colonizing enterprise. In this case, inequality was established between women, the white nun as teacher and the black woman as pupil. Far from being contrary to what Rosita represented, these unnamed black women, dressed in modest clothes and dedicated to tasks appropriate to females symbolized, we could argue, what Rosita could become after the affirmation of the Portuguese male presence in Guinea. Portuguese male colonizers were stimulated by the overt sexualization of black women in colonial propaganda, but they also needed someone to cook for them and sew their clothes. Within the space of the exhibition these two distinct models could coexist and contribute to the same aim.

## 5. Mother and Child: The Nurturing Body Versus the Sexualized Body

This leads me to another pervasive trope within representations of black women: that of a mother holding a baby.[27] In the United States and in Brazil,[28] it was the black "mammy," or the "mãe negra," as slave or paid laborer, the black woman who breastfed and cared for the white child. In the European colonial visual archive, the black woman appears mostly as the mother of her own children.

Their bosoms become de-eroticized by breastfeeding, a nurturing act, or by carrying a child on their backs. This is the main subject of a large quantity of photographic postcards of African women which circulated over a long period of time from the late nineteenth century to the 1970s, and even later. I was especially attentive to these kinds of racialized mother and child visual representations, when, in 2014, I found this image at a street market mixed in with many other photographs. (Fig. 18)[29] Unlike photographs that are located in family albums, which are kept by their owners and embedded in strong personal narratives of memory and affect, many other photographs have been separated from their owners and have become mute, lost, and lonely. These are "found photographs" which are to be found in commercial spaces or flea markets or simply in the garbage. Even when they are associated with other photographs, they are further fragmented by the commercial space, which allows the consumer or collector to purchase a single photograph from a group or set of multiple photographs.

It struck me, the combination of mother and child, like an icon; the somehow unstaged quality of the image; the way the mother is looking at the viewer; the image of Churchill printed on the fabric. Nothing in this black and white photograph with a white irregular frame provides information about its space or time. The woman is dressed in a fabric which reproduces the image of Winston Churchill, who is dressed in a military uniform. Is the "V" of Victory linked to the victory of the Allies at the end of World War Two or the British Victory in the Second Anglo-Boer War, which took place in Southern Africa from 1899 to 1902, and in which Churchill served as a young soldier? In any case, the fabric refers to the British political and colonial context.

However, the words written on the back of the photograph point us in other directions. "Victor," the name of the man who signed the text written in blue ink and probably the one who took the photograph and dated it. His manuscript words describe the woman seen in the photograph as the wife of a soba of the Dembe region, only to add that "the women from the North of Angola do not seem so, but they are more stupid than the ones from the South." He also adds that the women from the south carried their children on their backs, whereas the ones from the north—as the one photographed here—carried them on their bosom because they considered it more "beautiful." Although "Victor" somehow begins by identifying the woman in her specificity, even though in relation to her husband's social position, he then places her within a much wider category of "women of the north," and adds an insulting generalization.

## 6. "Just to say a few words":
## Backs of Postcards as Documents of the Banality of Racism

The words written on the back of this photograph shattered the dignity and subjectivity of those portrayed, something, I would argue, the image somehow preserved. The back of colonial postcards, a democratized authorial space, even for those who seldom wrote, can be a privileged historical document for locating the blatant, spoken racism that other kinds of written conventions may limit or contain. After recognizing the banality of these texts, I have been made much more aware of the words written by unknown persons on the back of colonial postcards. The ways in which the sender uses the images to initiate a dialogue with the recipient, within the long-distance conversation enabled by postcards, exposes distinct and entangled threads of the colonial experience, especially those embedded in racially and gendered structural violence (Figs. 8, 11, 13 and 18).

Throughout the year 1975, for example, a Portuguese man sends his mother a series of photographic color postcards with images of South African black women and men. I acquired three of them in 2017, in the major street flea market in Lisbon, the twice-weekly Feira da Ladra. This was the year of the independence of Angola and Mozambique, and that important detail may or may not explain why he sent South African postcards and why he sent them from South Africa. (Fig. 11) Did he move to South Africa in the aftermath of independence? Or was he already there? Mobility between different African colonies had always been an important feature, and photography was also witness to those transcolonial movements. In his words, however, the major distinction was between "us" and "them," the European and the African, the former colonizers and the formerly colonized. It did not matter whether they were "colonies" or "nations." His words strike us in other ways. They traveled from South Africa to Portugal, a country that was going through major transformations, the end of its right-wing New State and the end of its centuries-old empire, but in their unabashed racism—openly conveyed within the postcard's rectangle—nothing seems to have changed. The empire had ended, but many of the ideas that had sustained it were still there.

## 7. White Male Soldiers Photographed Next to Black Female Locals:
## The Persistence of a Typology

The final typologies of images I will address were the last to be produced within the promiscuous one-hundred-year-long relationship between the Portuguese empire and photography, between the 1870s and 1970s.[30] They contain a violent entanglement of many of the subjects we have so far discussed. First, the maternal body is the same as the sexualized body; second, the encounter between photographer-photographed is further complicated by the appearance of a third character. The Portuguese soldier engages both with the photographer as invisible accomplice and with the women as forced accomplices. And third, the disturbing ways in which these images transform the invisible into the visible. (Figs. 19-21). The black and white photographs reproduced here are glued together in a private album, next to other images, such as color commercial postcards from Guinea (Figs. 22-24). Within this album, the personal visual passage of a Portuguese military man through Guinea is mixed with other photographs. The banality of his photographed gestures are reinforced by the fact that they were considered acceptable enough to become part of the narrative.

The common practice of abuse, coercion and sexual violence toward colonized women that tends to be invisible in the archive (and that is also part of its violence) here appears banal enough to be staged in a performance for the camera; and that reinforces its disturbing abuse. Sexual or physical violence directed toward women was, one could argue, prevalent in Portugal and in Angola, independent of context and race. But would photography be used in the same way in both places? This is not simply an "event" that is taking place and that is captured by the camera. This is an "event" (to use Azoulay's idea again) that happens because the camera is there, and there is an implicit agreement between photographer and photographed (but not all of those being photographed) that that is what should be seen when the image is revealed. Troubling and brutal, the abuse is exposed blatantly on the surface of the print—and in our faces.

Looking at the photographic lens, the young man, dressed in his military uniform, was conscious of the performative experience he was enacting. He wanted to be seen, both in the present and in the future. If all photographs are, as Azoulay has stated, "the result of an encounter of several protagonists, mainly photographer and photographed, camera and spectator," where can we place these girls/women within this encounter? Distant from home, and in a geographical space where inequality was not just implicit but at the very heart of the colonial contract, the young man was empowered. In one of the images, the girl's body becomes a mannequin—passive, stiff, inanimate—sexualized only by the crude hands of the man-boy. (Fig. 19) Lifting her dress, exhibiting her for the camera while squeezing her breasts, he shows clearly who is in command. All positions are uncomfortable, staged, artificial, in a way that has nothing to do with the discomfort of posing for a portrait with the fake smile that was invented a few decades after photography itself. In the group image, nothing seems strange at first glance. (Fig. 20) A group of African women, men, children and babies are posing for a camera. But upon a second, closer look, a sole white man appears, and the effect is striking and troubling. At first glance he seems hidden, only his smile (the only one), his boots (the only footwear) and his hand (on the girl's breast) gradually emerge, making an effort to appear in the photographic space. What choice was available to the girl in his lap?

The ambiguous presence of the baby, in one of the other photographs, contributes to the disruption. Is this a couple with their first child? No. Isn't she pregnant? Where is the (black) father? The soldier holds the baby in one arm. His other arm performs that common gesture of manly protection and affect that we can see in thousands of photographs—with one striking difference. Instead of resting on her shoulder, the hand goes down to her breast, grabbing her with a gesture that highlights our impotence. The image of the Lusotropical couple thus becomes a cruel parody. (Fig. 21)

Next to these four images about which we know little—only that they belong to the photographic album from Guinea compiled by the young soldier who appears in the images and who is now an old man living in Lisbon, the former metropolitan capital of the "overseas provinces"—we could place the photograph used by the artist Vasco Araújo in an installation at an exhibition held in Lisbon a few years ago.[31] This is another image of an interracial couple, entitled "Guiné 1962," with a white Portuguese soldier and a Guinean woman. He has one hand on her pregnant abdomen and the other on her breast. Would he be photographed like that next to a Portuguese woman, in an open space? No, he would not. The fact that he would not be photographed with such gestures with his white girlfriend or wife in his Portuguese village was what, for me, disrupted the image.

After participating in a guided visit by the artist, I along with several others scattered around the exhibition spaces. However, in reference to this image, I overheard a conversation that troubled me as much as the photograph itself had done. Two good-looking couples in their sixties commented jokingly on the image: "They really knew how to enjoy themselves!"; "There you go, what a man!" The critical context of the exhibition was not enough to prevent those responses of complicity toward the soldier's gesture as seen in the reproduction of the photograph on display in the show. Once again, I realized that one of my interests in these images resides in the ways in which they are seen, viewed, placed, and commented on today. The ways in which images of black women's bodies continue to be trivialized, colonized, subject to the same kind of viewership to which they were subjected within the colonial contexts that both produced and legitimized them.

Therefore, the ways in which black women appear in photographs and postcards in the period of the African colonial wars, from 1961 to 1975, is a particularly relevant subject and one that deserves a profound and thorough study. First, because the quantity of white Portuguese soldiers who, while in the African colonies, were photographed next to local black women, very often with exposed, nude breasts, is disturbingly banal. Such a study would demand deep research within the photographic legacies still kept in the homes of former soldiers or their children; as well as in some public archives, such as the Arquivo Histórico Militar; and in informal and unofficial associations, groups or networks of former soldiers who use photography as a bonding practice of memory, experience sharing and a defying of trauma. The images can now often be found online, on those digital platforms that unite very different men who were grouped together in the territory of the colonial wars. Previously, they used to be shown in slide shows at private gatherings or printed next to autobiographical narratives of soldier's experiences.[32] The digital revolution, however, has turned these small, restricted groups into more public events.

This is a necessarily delicate subject and one that may turn photography into a particularly contested space made of contradictory and conflicting discourses. What may be for us a problematic visual document of different kinds of inequality, injustice and violence—gender, ethnic or political—may be, for others, a mere snapshot of daily routine in the context of war, even a visual reminder of some of the few moments of joy, laughter, affection and lightness which contrasted with the hard and traumatic challenges of young men being turned into fighters without having a choice to refuse it. The places and ownership of the photographs today is a determining factor for thinking about them. They are mostly in the possession of those who were on the side of power, the power of being a white male in the military uniform of the colonizing country combating the independence aspirations of the colonized. They are not in the homes or families of the black women who were also there in the images. This means that their contemporary uses, narratives and discourses—the memories they trigger in the present—belong to those who were already in control in the past at the moment the photograph was taken. As the Brazilian poet Ana Martins Marques writes, "como as fotografias por direito pertencem/aos que não saíram na fotografia."[33]

Is it relevant for this distinction to consider the differences between those images in which the women are alone in the frame and those in which the women are seen next to Portuguese soldiers? Independently of being represented or not, it is predominantly the white male soldier who has control over the photographing process. How can we acknowledge the participation of women within the photographic event? The men were those who owned the cameras, those who had the power to coordinate the performative nature of the act of photographing and those who—now—have them in their possession (or in the possession of their families after their death). There are many questions which are difficult to answer. Where were these photographs shown and viewed? In Africa or back home in Portugal? Were there cases when more than one print was made to be distributed to all the photographed, including the women? How can we know more about these women's roles in the photographing process? Their interest in photography? Their possession of their own image? How common was the use of personal filming cameras? The role of black women in the photographing process, on the other hand, will necessarily be a fragmented history of individual stories and cases, one much more difficult to identify and narrate. As has been often repeated and demonstrated in gender approaches to history, women's history in the present is always determined by the scarcity, invisibility or negligence of sources in the past.

Independently of being present in the image itself next to a black woman or just on the invisible side of the lens, it was the Portuguese soldier who was in charge of the performative gestures. Those who had the camera in hand, made the gesture of centralizing the lens, making decisions according to the complexity of the camera itself, and pressing the button; those who were being photographed, decided the ways in which their bodies were made still (that stillness everyone knew by then to be a condition for the act of posing) and the ways in which their bodies should be placed in relation to the women's bodies. The man's arm over the woman's or women's shoulder(s) is a common example of these kinds of gestures. However, as Elizabeth Edwards has underlined, "whatever the assymetries of power relations, the act of photography was participatory and intersubjective by definition."[34] On the other hand, Ariella Azoulay has called attention in her groundbreaking publications to the fact that "every photograph of others bears the traces of the meeting between the photographed persons and the photographer, neither of whom can, on their own, determine how this meeting will be inscribed on the resulting image."[35] This approach shifts the protagonism from the photographer, the photographed, and the photograph to the *act* itself, to the "event of photography" and the ways in which we, now or in the future, continue to be part of the "event" as spectators.

## 8. An Ongoing Project: The Last Images of the Colonial Visual Archive

In this subject, as in many other historical subjects whose conflictive nature persists into the present, researchers thinking critically about images from a distant and detached present and considering them under the prism of subjection or inequality may be confronted with the profoundly different ways in which the photographers/photographed/owners of the photographs engage with them. This makes it a particularly difficult subject and one that only recently has started to be addressed in critical artistic and scholarly approaches. Júlia Garraio, for example, has written an interesting article in which she addresses the meanings and implications of the pervasiveness of black women's bodies in the late Portuguese colonial empire, a subject that dialogues with her other work on sexual violence against women in the context of war, mainly during World War Two.[36] Afonso Dias Ramos wrote a Ph.D. thesis on the relationship between political violence and photography in contemporary art, particularly within the transnational context surrounding the liberation and the civil conflict in Angola (1961-2002).[37] In addition, Maria José Lobo Antunes is pursuing a research project on the place of photography in the African colonial wars, which will certainly address one of its most persistent typologies, that of Portuguese soldiers being photographed next to black Angolan, Mozambican or Guinean women.[38] Antunes's research will make an important contribution to the wider subject of the relationship between Portuguese soldiers and African women and, more specifically, to the different kinds of gender and sexual violence against African women by Portuguese soldiers in the context of the colonial wars, a subject still imbued with the taboos associated with all historical moments marked by the triviality of violence.

When in 2014 I edited the book *O Império da Visão: Fotografia no Contexto Colonial Português*, I consciously chose the cutoff date of 1960 precisely because I considered the years from the beginning of the colonial wars in 1961 to the independence of the last Portuguese colony in Africa in 1975 to be too vast and multiple (and difficult), and felt this period deserved a specific research project in itself. When I wrote the proposal for the project in 2008, academia was not yet addressing the delicate and recent historical moment of the wars of independence, as it now is. Afonso Ramos's article was the exception among the thirty contributions to *O Império da Visão* because he analyzed the role played by photography as a conflict trigger at the onset of the war in Angola.[39] Another subject that should have deserved more space and reflection in the book was the banalization of black women's bodies in the Portuguese colonial context—only Carlos Barradas addressed the issue.[40]

A more recent book edited by Elsa Peralta, Bruno Góis and Joana Gonçalo Oliveira challenged both Maria José Lobo Antunes and myself to think about the photographs that were on display in the exhibition *Retornar* and the overall relationship between photography and this historical moment.[41] The book forms part of a larger research project that was carried out in relation to the temporary exhibition on the thousands of women, men and children who, after independence, were compelled for various reasons to leave the former Portuguese colonies in Africa where they had lived and "return" to the former colonial metropolis where many of them had never been. These people became known as the "retornados," the "returned," a problematic term which is being critically addressed by many scholars as well as artists, writers and cultural thinkers. The quantity of interesting research projects now taking place will result in the continuing enrichment of the growing field of studies on the recent Portuguese colonial legacy and its interstices with the visual.[42] The richness and disturbing quality of the Portuguese visual archive of the recent colonial wars—the latest in the European context—is finally now beginning to be addressed from many angles.

## 9. Collecting the Colonial: The Persistence of the Past in the Present

As a collector of many different nineteenth– and twentieth-century documents, a woman in a male-dominated world, I am continually confronted with the banality of both the colonial materials and the colonial ideologies themselves: when I hesitated on purchasing a 1950s calendar at Lisbon's main flea market, the seller, a woman, told me that if I did not take it, she would sell it to a client who buys "pretas nuas;" when I asked for Portuguese colonial photographs at a photographic fair in a Russell Square hotel in London, the seller showed me some of the most violent images I had ever seen of African women with German military men. I had to look away. According to a Lisbon-based postcard seller, the combination of black, colonial, woman and nakedness is one of his most profitable categories. The male-dominated collecting market in the present reproduces the uses to which these images were subjected in the past. From the Hottentot Venus being displayed around Europe in the early nineteenth century to the wide visual uses of black bodies two hundred years later, there are continuities that go beyond the chronologies of slavery and colonialism.

And this leads me, finally, to a central question, one which scholars, curators and archivists have been discussing for the past few decades: that of ethics. Images of abuse, pain and exploitation retain their strength and can perpetuate what one seems to criticize. Are institutions—the university, the archive, the museum—enough to counteract the risks of reproducing the violence? Can we show Rosinha, and all these unnamed "Black Venuses," as well as the anonymous soldiers, who can now be old men still dealing with the experience of being sent from a remote Portuguese village to the unpredictable sceneries of the African colonial wars? In the 1990s, Mieke Bal wrote an essay entitled "A Postcard from the Edge" in which she problematizes scholarly exercises such as the one in this article.[43] For her, context and critique were not enough to justify the showing of these images yet again. They still encourage the voyeuristic gaze that victimizes the women portrayed one more time.

Saidiya Hartman took a radical gesture—on the one hand, she refused the PowerPoint culture of "showing again" (as she did in a 2017 conference at Brown University)[44] and by so doing, she preserved the dignity of the black girls and women who are portrayed in the photographs she was analyzing; on the other hand, she uses informed fiction to say more about these women than the historical archive allows.[45] If history and the archives themselves reproduce forms of oppression and the eradication of many human beings—like women slaves subjected to rape by their owners and middlemen—then she goes beyond the "boundaries of the archive" to tell the stories documents do not fully tell.

When Mieke Bal published "A Postcard from the Edge" twenty-two years ago, most of the authors writing on this subject were male, and for Bal it was relevant to ask "Who does the looking?" Would Bal ask the same question in 2017? For this reason, my position as a scholar writing on this subject also needs to be addressed. I am a woman, and that is a relevant factor to the ways in which many of these images and texts strike me and affect me. I am not a black woman, however, and I question myself about what would change if that were my viewing position. Questions of "who does the looking?" (or "the writing?" or "the speaking?") have become central to many contemporary discussions on the politics of racial and gender identities, even if they are much more acute in countries such as the USA or South Africa than in other places, perhaps because their official and state-sponsored racism is so recent and because they have more active and activist people with a political consciousness regarding gender and racial inequalities. The ethics of representation go much further than the frontiers of the academy, when contemporary experience daily confronts us with the problematic legacies of the past.

Now, some of the most challenging work on the intersections of visual culture and the colonial, slavery, politics and "blackness" is written by women scholars who also include gender in their approaches: from Elizabeth Edwards to Patricia Hayes or Christraud M. Geary, from Tamar Garb to Ariella Azoulay. Some are black women, such as Saidiya Hartman, Tina Campt and Krista Thompson.[46] Ethics has been a central issue for all of them. Certainly, the new scholarship on gender, race and visuality is also the result of this new generation of "women speakers," black and white, who are more aware of questions of gender, going back to the archive—written, material and visual—and finding what was there but had not previously been found.

## 10. Counter-narratives:
## African Women's Images in African Studio Portraits

By the early twentieth century, photographic studios were widely available in African urban ports to Africans both as photographers and as sitters.[47] Over the past few decades, scholarship has increasingly emphasized this point. Patricia Hayes, for example, in a 1998 review of *The Face of the Country: A South African Family Album, 1860-1910*, a book project based on a compilation of two-hundred photographs in the collection of the South African Library in Cape Town, argued that "blacks were not entirely on the fringes of this visual economy."[48] She does so in order to question the book's argument that photographic representations of blacks tended to fit into two categories, the ethnographic one and the domestic one, where black subjects appear in the role of domestic workers in white households. Hayes, however, is also careful to explain that these categories depend on the nature of the archive itself, an official space which as such tended to receive and keep those materials of families from specific, privileged, white, social groups.

Beyond the "defeated and the domesticated," there is a substantial corpus of images of Africans taken in photographic studios from the late nineteenth century onwards.[49] More recent studies have focused on these visual archives that work as a counter narrative to the "colonial visual archives" which had dominated research approaches and topics. In an essay published in 2013, Christopher Pinney, a scholar with a long and creative history of thinking about photography in spaces that have been colonized by Europeans, such as India, questioned the idea of "colonial photography."[50] By doing this he was calling attention to the limits and problems of looking at photography produced in a geographical space with the "lens" of the "colonial," the theoretical frame that had determined most of the work on African or Indian photography for many decades. Scholars such as Christopher Pinney, Elizabeth Edwards and Patricia Hayes, among others, have contributed to making the relations between photography and colonial spaces more complex, fragmenting its meanings beyond the homogenizing and hegemonic place where it tended to be placed. The "colonial" should not prevent us from seeing other things that might also be there. And these other things can be dignity, resistance, subjectivity and self-consciousness, even when the "photographic event," to use Azoulay's expression once again, took place in a colonial and unequal context.

African women were a major object of the "desiring gaze" that was an integral part of the male dominated colonial ethos and the photographic experience certainly became a major way of materializing it. Furthermore, the possibilities of multiplying one image and making it travel further disseminated what became a colonial trope—the image of the unnamed African woman with her body partially exposed. However, even within and beyond this trope there were many other images of black women and to search for them can also be a way of questioning the banality of the images they 'counter narrate.' Not by chance, the questioning of the colonial as the central framework of analysis coincided with increasing scholarly attention to Black, African or Indian photographic practices.

This scholarly literature is diverse, as we have seen: from photography as an empowering tool, in the uses made by former North American slaves, such as Sojourner Truth and Frederick Douglass; to family and private uses of images by blacks at home and abroad; and to African photographers and photographic studios, those which were often the spaces where African women chose to go alone or with other family members to have their portraits taken and thus to possess an image of themselves for themselves or for others. It must be recalled, however, that even this kind of private image sometimes traversed a commercial frontier into a public sphere, most probably without the knowledge of the portrayed sitter. This happened when a studio photographer saw in these images of black women a potential consumer market and turned them into photographic postcards, most probably without their knowledge or consent.

There were, therefore, many black women being photographed because they wanted to be photographed, and they had the access and the means to do so. However, these images tended to remain in the private sphere of those who were represented and had paid for them. They were not reproduced in postcards and colonial newspapers. Therefore, visual counter narratives to the dominant trope of the black typified or eroticized woman existed at this time, but their presence was not strong enough to create a contemporary alternative to the hegemonic banality of the exposed African female body, widely reproduced in postcards and print culture.

Recent studies have provided new insights into these counter-narrative photographic practices and uses, but the scholars working on them had to look beyond the culture of reproduction and circulation that characterized those images featuring the dominant tropes of the "defeated," the "domesticated" and, we could add, the "sexualized and racialized female body," devoid of self-identity and subjectivity. While reproducibility through a panoply of materials—postcards, newspapers, colonial propaganda leaflets and books or colonial exhibition printed matter—multiplied the impact of semi-naked or eroticized African female bodies in wide geographical spaces, the photographic portraits of black women that depended on their own choice tend to remain hidden in private homes, as part of well-kept or forgotten family albums, or within the archives of photographic studios.[51] Therefore, the uses, movements and reproductive uses of images need to be taken into account as much as the images themselves. The legacies of the visual archive from the past, found in public archives, libraries, markets or online postcard commercial sites, are much more visible and accessible than those other images of black women that also existed but that did not fit a popular or dominant visual culture of what was consumed and collected. (Fig. 25)

Even though I am concentrating in this article solely on photography, it is important to acknowledge other media, such as that of painting. Laura Knight, for example, a female student at the Slade School of Arts in London in the early twentieth century, was by 1926 painting a portrait of a black identified woman, Pearl Johnson, an African-American nurse at the racially segregated maternity ward of Baltimore Hospital, and a civil rights activist who had involved the British painter in the movement. A woman such as Pearl Johnson exemplifies a wider phenomenon of intellectually and politically aware African-American women who also incorporated photography into their lives, thus contributing to the formation of black family albums, which can be placed in contrast to the public, popular and massive circulation of racist or subordinated images of African-Americans in a country where racial segregation was part of everyday life.[52]

Contemporary art practices have also offered a means of critically engaging with the visual legacies of colonialism, especially those authored by women who come from places where colonialism and racial discrimination linger as more or less distant legacies. These artistic practices, as well as many of the exhibitions that theoretically frame them, go beyond written scholarly work, but they often share the same critical idiom. Some artists have specifically addressed the vast colonial visual archive of eroticized black women, mainly through postcards and illustrated newspapers, but the majority of them deal with broader issues of the politics of race and gender in past and present settings.[53] Many female black artists have thus greatly contributed to the decolonization of the black female body, problematizing its sexualization and subjugation, most often by a Western male colonizing paradigm that lingers into the present in different ways, and inscribing it within the unbound meanings and possibilities of subjectivity and agency.

I would like to conclude with the work of the black British artist Lynette Yiadom-Boakye, *Ever The Women Watchful* (2017). It is not a photograph but a painting that represents two black women looking through a pair of binoculars toward something, which we, the observers of the painting, do not see. It reminds me of the painting that was done by the North American artist Mary Cassatt while she was in Paris: *In the Loge*, from 1878. This painting has been used by feminist art historians, namely Griselda Pollock, to reclaim the female's right to gaze, to observe, to see (as well as to paint): the "female gaze." A woman in her theater box uses her binoculars to gaze down at what is going on in the theatrical space that we do not see.

These two paintings, separated by more than one hundred years, serve as counter-narratives to the strong visual paradigms that tend to place women, different kinds of women, socially, ethnically, nationally, in the place of that which is observed, gazed upon and appropriated. Even if there were multiple differences in the ways female bodies were made into images, reproduced and circulated, these were indissociable from the color of their skin, the political and social spaces they inhabited and the weaker or stronger voices they possessed. Some women had more of a voice than others. Women also looked back. Most, however, did not have the tools to materialize it through the instruments of writing, painting or photography. To find and analyze past and present female counter-narratives can also be a way of contesting the lasting silences of the past, the silences of the images of those women who never saw themselves portrayed in the photographs.

NOTES

1. Beatrix Heintze, "In pursuit of a chamaleon: Early ethnographic photography from Angola in context," *History in Africa*, vol. 17 (1990), pp. 131-156. I thank António Araújo, Afonso Dias Ramos, Djaimilia Pereira de Almeida and Inês Galvão for reading and commenting on this text.

2. Christraud M. Geary, "The Black Female Body, the Postcard, and the Archives," in Barbara Thompson, ed., *Black Womanhood: Images, Icons, and Ideologies of the African Body* (Hanover, NH: Hood Museum of Art, Dartmouth College; University of Washington Press, 2008), pp. 147-152.

3. Christraud M. Geary, "The Image of the Black in Early African Photography," in David Bindman, Suzanne Preston Blier and Henry Louis Gates Jr., eds., *The Image of the Black in African and Asian Art* (Cambridge, Mass.; London: The Belknap Press of Harvard University Press, 2017), pp. 141-166, p. 159-165; Geary, "The Black Female Body...," pp. 152-156.

4. Ariella Azoulay, *Civil Imagination. A Political Ontology of Photography* (Brooklyn, NY: Verso, 2012)

5. David Bindman, Suzanne Preston Blier and Henry Louis Gates Jr., eds., *The Image of the Black in African and Asian Art* (Cambridge, Mass.; London: The Belknap Press of Harvard University Press, 2017). This is the Companion volume to the series published between 2010 and 2017 in 5 volumes; Adrienne L. Childs and Susan H. Libby, *Blacks and Blackness in European Art of the Long Nineteenth Century* (Farnham, Survey: Ashgate, 2014); Henry Louis Gates, Jr., "The Black Person in Art: How should S/He be portrayed," in *Black American Literature Forum*, Vol. 21, No. 1/2 (Spring-Summer 1987), pp. 3-24.

6. Geary, "The Image of the Black in Early African Photography," pp. 141-166; Barbara Thompson, ed., *Black Womanhood: Images, Icons, and Ideologies of the African Body* (Hanover, NH: Hood Museum of Art, Dartmouth College; University of Washington Press, 2008). Exhibition Catalogue; Geary, "The Black Female Body...," pp. 143-160; Deborah Willis and Carla Williams, *The Black Female Body: A Photographic History* (Philadelphia: Temple University Press, 2002); Gen Doy, "More than Meets the Eye...Representations of Black Women in Mid-19$^{th}$-century French Photography," in *Women's Studies International Forum*, Vol. 21, No 3, 1998, pp. 305-319.

7. See the many studies on Sara Bartman or Hottentot Venus as she was also known; as well as, for example, Ciraj Rassool and Patricia Hayes, "Science and Spectacle: /Khanako's South Africa, 1936-1937," in Wendy Woodward, Patricia Hayes and Gary Minkley, eds., *Deep hiStories: Gender and Colonialism in Southern Africa* (Amsterdam; New York: Rodopi, 2002), pp. 117-161.

8. Some examples: Tina M. Campt, *Listening to Images* (Durham: Duke University Press, 2017); Tina M. Campt, *Image Matters: Archive, Photography and the African Diaspora* (Durham: Duke University Press), 2012; Tina M. Campt, *Other Germans: Black Germans and the Politics of*

*Race, Gender and Memory in the Third Reich* (Ann Harbor: University of Michigan Press, 2004); Leigh Raiford, "Photography and the Practices of Critical Black Memory," *History and Theory*, vol. 48, No.4, Theme issue: Photography and Historical Interpretation (December 2009), pp. 112-129; *In/Sight: African Photographers from 1940 to the Present*, Exhibition Catalogue (New York: Guggenheim Museum, 1996).

9. Malek Alloula. *The Colonial Harem* (Minneapolis: University of Minnesota, 1986).

10. Ayo Abiétou Coly, "Housing and Homing the Black Female Body in France: Calixthe Beyala and the Legacy of Sarah Baartman and Josephine Baker", in Barbara Thompson, ed., *Black Womanhood: Images, Icons, and Ideologies of the African Body* (Hanover, NH: Hood Museum of Art, Dartmouth College; University of Washington Press, 2008), pp. 259-277, p. 272.

11. Patricia Hayes, "'Cocky' Hahn and the 'Black Venus': the Making of a Native Commisioner in South West Africa, 1915-46," in *Cultures of Empire: A Reader. Colonizers in Britain and the Empire in the Nineteenth and Twentieth Centuries* (London: Taylor and Francis, 2000), pp. 329-355, p. 350. The article was first published in *Gender and History* 8, 3 (November 1996): pp. 364-92.

12. *Human Zoos: the Invention of the Savage*, edited by Pascal Blanchard, Gilles Boetsch and Nanette Jacomijn Snoep (Arles; Paris: Actes Sud, Musée du Quai Branly, 2011). Exhibition Catalogue; *Zoos Humains: de la Vénus Hottentote aux Reality Shows*, edited by Nicolas Bancel, Pascal Blanchard, Gilles Boetsch, Éric Deroo, Sandrine Lemaire, (Paris: Éditions La Découverte, 2002); Filipa Lowndes Vicente, Review of *Zoos Humains: de la Vénus Hottentote aux Reality Shows*, edited by Nicolas Bancel, Pascal Blanchard, Gilles Boetsch, Éric Deroo, Sandrine Lemaire, (Paris: Éditions La Découverte, 2002), in *Estudos do Século xx*, n.º 3, 2003, pp. 389-395.

13. Laura Mulvey, "Visual pleasure and narrative cinema," Screen, Autumn 1975, 16 (3), pp. 6–18.

14. Geary, "The Black Female Body...", pp. 143-160, p. 148

15. Elmano Cunha e Costa, *Catálogo da exposição de penteados e adornos femininos das indígenas de Angola*. Agência Geral das Colónias (S.l.: s.n., 1951); Dante Vacchi, *Penteados de Angola*, Lisbon: Author's Edition printed at Litografia de Portugal, Text in Portuguese, French and English, 1965.

16. There are now many closed and ongoing research projects and a vast bibliography on subjects related to colonial memories and post-memories in the Portuguese context. For example: 2015-2020—"MEMOIRS-Children of Empires and European Postmemories", coordinated by Margarida Calafate Ribeiro, European Research Council Grant; 2017-2022, "CROME—Crossed Memories, Politics of Silence: The Colonial-Liberation Wars in Postcolonial Times," coordinated by Miguel Cardina, European Research Council Grant. Examples of publications: Ângela Campos, *An Oral History of the Portuguese Colonial War: Palgrave Studies in Oral History* (Basingstoke: Palgrave Macmillan, 2017); Boaventura de Sousa Santos,

*Epistemologies of the South: Justice Against Epistemicide* (New York: Routledge, 2016); Margarida Calafate Ribeiro; António Sousa, Ribeiro, eds., *Geometrias da Memória: configurações pós-coloniais* (Porto: Afrontamento 2016); Manuela Ribeiro Sanches, ed., *Malhas que os impérios tecem: Textos anti-coloniais, contextos pós-coloniais* (Lisbon: Edições 70, 2011); Rosa Cabecinhas and João Feijó, "Collective Memories of Portuguese Colonial Action in Africa: Representations of the Colonial Past among Mozambicans and Portuguese Youths," in *International Journal of Conflict and Violence*, Vol. 4 (1) 2010, pp. 28—44; Manuela Ribeiro Sanches, ed., *"Portugal não é um país pequeno": Contar a Império na pós-colonialidade* (Lisbon: Cotovia, 2006); Manuela Ribeiro Sanches, ed., *Deslocalizar a "Europa": Antropologia, arte, literatura e história na pós-colonialidade* (Lisbon: Cotovia. 2005);

17. Here I will not include those printed illustrations, very often based on photographs, which became so popular within illustrated journals worldwide. On this subject see: Leonor Pires Martins, *Um Império de Papel: Imagens do Colonialismo Português na Imprensa Periódica Ilustrada (1875-1940)* (Lisbon: Edições 70, 2012).

18. Christraud M. Geary and Virginia-Lee Webb, eds., *Delivering Views: Distant Cultures in Early Postcards* (Washington: Smithosian Institution Press, 1998); Aline Ripert and Claude Frère, *La Carte postale: son histoire, sa fonction sociale* (Lyon: Presses Universitaires de Lyon; Paris: Editions du CNRS, 1983).

19. Filipa Lowndes Vicente and Inês Vieira Gomes, "Inequalities on Trial: Conflict, Violence and Dissent in the Making of Colonial Angola (1907-1920)" in Francisco Bethencourt, ed., *Inequality in the Portuguese-Speaking World* (Eastbourne: Sussex Academic Press, 2018), pp. 217-242.

20. Geary, "The Black Female Body...," pp. 152-156.

21. Geary, "The Image of the Black in Early African Photography," pp. 141-166, pp. 143-159; Christraud M. Geary, "Through the Lenses of African Photographers: Depicting Foreigners and New Ways of Life, 1870-1950," in David Bindman and Henry Louis Gates Jr., eds., *The Image of the Black in Western Art: The Twentieth Century: The Impact of Africa*, vol. V (Cambridge, Mass.: The Belknap Press, 2014), pp. 87-99.

22. I first wrote on the case of Rosinha for a newspaper article: Filipa Lowndes Vicente, "Rosita ou o Império como um objecto de desejo," *Público*, 25 de Agosto de 2013 which was then translated into French: "Rosita. La Vénus noire de Porto," *Books.fr: livres & idées du monde entier*, n.º 52, Março 2014, pp. 50-53. See also the exhibition catalogue of Domingo's Alvão photographs of the 1934 Porto Colonial Exhibition: Maria do carmo Serén, ed., *A Porta do Meio: a Exposição Colonial de 1934: Fotografias da casa Alvão* (Oporto: Centro Português de Fotografia, 2001).

23. See the excelent article by Isabel Morais, "'Little Black Rose' at the 1934 Exposição Colonial Portuguesa," in *Gendering the Fair: Histories of Women and Gender at World's Fairs*, edited by T.J. Boisseau and Abigail M. Markwyn, foreword by Robert W. Rydell (Urbana:

University of Illinois Press, 2010), pp. 19-36. For a recent overview on colonial exhibitions see Nadia Vargavtig, *Des Empires en carton: Les expositions coloniales au Portugal et en Italie* (Madrid: Casa de Velazquez, 2016).

24. Elizabeth Edwards, "Anthropology and Photography (1910-1940)," in *The Image of the Black in Western Art*, vol. V, 2014 pp. 47-62, p. 48.

25. "O Banco de Angola na Exposição Colonial," in *A Província de Angola: Número extraordinário dedicado à Exposição Colonial Portuguesa e em honra da Restauração de Angola*, 15 Aug. 1934 (Luanda : Empresa Gráfica de Angola, 1934), p. 18.

26. On the encouragement of colonial emigration, see the work of Cláudia Castelo, *Passagens para África. O Povoamento de Angola e Moçambique com naturais da Metrópole (1920-1974)* (Porto: Afrontamento, 2007).

27. Geary, "The Black Female Body…" and Kimberly Wallace-Sanders, "The Body of a Myth: Embodying the Black Mammy Figure in Visual Culture," in Barbara Thompson, ed., *Black Womanhood: Images, Icons, and Ideologies of the African Body* (Hanover, NH: Hood Museum of Art, Dartmouth College; University of Washington Press, 2008), pp. 143-160, p. 149; pp. 163-179.

28. Lilia Moritz Schwarcz has been exploring this subject both in her written work and through the curating of exhibitions: Lilia Moritz Schwarcz, "Black Nannies: Hidden and Open Images in the Paintings of Nicolas-Antoine Taunay," *Women's History Review*, 2017, pp. 1-18; Boris Kossoy and Lilia Moritz Schwarcz, *Um Olhar Sobre o Brasil: a Fotografia na Construção da Imagem da Nação: 1833-2003* (Rio de Janeiro: Objetiva; Fundación Mapfre, 2012).

29. I previsouly wrote on this image in Filipa Lowndes Vicente, "Introduction", in Filipa Lowndes Vicente (ed.), *O Império da Visão: Fotografia no Contexto Colonial português (1860-1960)*, (Lisbon: Edições 70, 2014), pp. 11-29.

30. I have already written about these photographs in the book chapter: Vicente, Filipa Lowndes Vicente, "Retornar não é possível. Fotografia nas partidas, nos regressos e na distância," in Elsa Peralta, Bruno Góis, Joana Gonçalo Oliveira, eds., *Retornar: Traços de memória do fim do Império* (Lisboa: Edições 70, 2017), pp. 197-212. Júlia Garraio has also written on them in the article "Perdidas na exposição? Desafiar o imaginário colonial português através de fotografias de mulheres negras," in Ribeiro and Ribeiro, eds., *Geometrias da memória*: 279-303.

31. Vasco Araújo, *Botânica*, Exhibition at MNAC (Museu Nacional de Arte Contemporânea) from March 13, 2014 to May 18, 2014, curated by Emília Tavares. I have already written on this exhibition in Vicente "Introduction," pp. 11-29.

32. Maria José Lobo Antunes, *Regressos Quase Perfeitos. Memórias da Guerra em Angola* (Lisboa: Tinta da China, 2016).

33. Ana Martins Marques, "As casas pertencem aos vizinhos…," in *O LIvro das Semelhanças. Poemas* (São Paulo: Companhia das Letras, 2015), p. 60

34. Edwards, "Anthropology and Photography (1910-1940)," pp. 47-62, p. 53

35. Azoulay, *Civil Imagination* (New York: Verso, 2012); Azoulay, *The Civil Contract of Photography* (London: Zone Books, 2008).

36. Garraio, Júlia, "Perdidas na exposição? Desafiar o imaginário colonial português através de fotografias de mulheres negras," in Ribeiro and Ribeiro, eds., *Geometrias da memória*: 279-303.

37. Afonso Dias Ramos's PhD (2017) at University College London is titled "Imageless in Angola: Living through the aftermath of war. Reinventing the photographic medium in a transnational age."

38. Since April 2017 Maria José Lobo Antunes has been a postdoctoral researcher at the Institute of Social Sciences-University of Lisbon where she is developing the project "Image, war and memory: colonial war photography in private collections and in institutional archives," funded by the Fundação para a Ciência e a Tecnologia.

39. Afonso Ramos, "Angola 1961, o horror das imagens,", Filipa Lowndes Vicente, ed., *O Império da Visão: Fotografia no Contexto Colonial português (1860-1960)*, (Lisbon: Edições 70, 2014), pp. 397-432.

40. Barradas, Carlos, "Descolonizando enunciados: a quem serve objectivamente a fotografia?" in *O Império da Visão: Fotografia no Contexto Colonial português (1860-1960)*, (Lisbon: Edições 70, 2014), pp. 447-460. See also by the same author: "Poder ver, poder saber. A fotografia nos meandros do colonialismo e pós-colonialismo," *Arquivos da Memória-Número Temático "Antropologia, Arte e Imagem,"* 2009, 5-6, 59-79.

41. Filipa Lowndes Vicente, "Retornar não é possível: Fotografia nas partidas, nos regressos e na distância" and Maria José Lobo Antunes, "O que se vê e o que não pode ser visto: Fotografia, violência e Guerra," in Elsa Peralta, Bruno Góis, Joana Gonçalo Oliveira, eds., *Retornar: Traços de memória do fim do Império* (Lisbon: Edições 70, 2017), pp. 197-212; pp. 213-224.

42. In this article I am not addressing the moving image—documentary, cinema or home movies: on this see all the work of Maria do Carmo Piçarra, for example, Maria do Carmo Piçarra and Teresa Castro, *(Re)imagining African Independence. Film, Visual Arts and the Fall of the Portuguese Empire* (Oxford: Peter Lang, 2017); Jorge Seabra, *África Nossa: o Império Colonial na Ficção Cinematográfica Portuguesa, 1945-1974* (Coimbra: Imprensa da Universidade de Coimbra, 2011); Joana Pimentel, "La Collection Coloniale de la Cinemateca Portuguesa", *Journal of Film Preservation* 64 (2002), pp. 22-30. On the artistic uses of the Colonial Film Archive see the work of Teresa Castro: Teresa Castro, "In-Between Memory and History: Artists' Films and the Portuguese Colonial Archive", in Piçarra and Castro, eds, *(Re)imagining African Independence*, pp. 205-223; on television documentaries see Afonso Dias Ramos, "Rarely penetrated by camera or film: NBC's *Angola: Journey to a War* (1961)", pp. 111-130.

43. Mieke Bal, "A Postcard from the Edge", *Double Exposures: The Subject of Cultural Analysis* (New York: Routledge, 1996), pp. 195-224.

44. Saidiya Hartman, "The Beauty of the Ungovernable" within the Seminar *Imperial Origins of Racialized Lives: From Enslavement to Black Lives Matter*, Mellon Sawyer Seminar on Displacement, Brown University, 7th April 2017.

45. Saidiya Hartman, "Venus in two Acts," in *Small Axe*, Number 26 (vol. 12, Number 2), June 2008, pp. 1-14.

46. Krista Thompson, "The Evidence of things Not Photographed: Slavery and Historical Memory in the British West Indies," *Representations*, vol. 113, No.1 (Winter 2011), pp. 39-71.

47. Erin Haney, *Photography and Africa* (London: Reaktion Books, 2010), pp. 49-55, 71-76.

48. Patricia Hayes, "Visual History in Photographs," review of Karel Schoeman, *The Face of the Country: A South African Family Album, 1860-1910* (Cape Town, Pretoria, Johannesburg: Human and Rousseau, 1996), in *The Journal of African History*, vol. 39, No. 1 (1998), pp. 168-170.

49. Hayes refers here to the important project taken by Santu Mofokeag, *The Black Photo Album/Look At Me: 1890-1950*, "a series of digitally reworked 19th century, colonial portraits of Black South African families" which was exhibited at Tate Gallery.

50. Christopher Pinney, "What's photography got to do with it?" in *Photography's Orientalism: New Essays on Colonial Representation*, edited by Ali Behdad and Luke Gartlan (Los Angeles: Getty Research Institute, 2013), pp. 33-52.

51. For example the *Foto Melo* Photographic Studio in Mindelo, Cabo Verde (Cape Vert). This was the main photographic studio on the Cape Verdean Island of São Vicente for around a century, 1890 to 1990. It was founded by Djindjon (João Henriques) de Melo, and continued by his son Papim (Eduardo Ernesto) de Melo and finally, by another younger member of the family, therefore three generations of men. The archive of the Foto Melo has more than 150 thousand photographs, a major part being from individual studio portraits, commissioned by the local population across many generations. In 2011 the Centro Cultural Português do Mindelo, with the financial support of the Portuguese Instituto Camões started a conservation, digitalization and cataloguing process, which involved different people but which was never concluded due to the discontinuation of financial aid. I thank my colleague at the ICS-University of Lisbon, João Vasconcelos for this information on the photographic studio, as well as Inês Vieira Gomes, PhD candidate at the same Institute, for first telling me about this studio.

52. Deborah Willis, "Picturing the New Negro Woman," in *Black Womanhood: Images, Icons, and Ideologies of the African Body* (Hanover, NH: Hood Museum of Art, Dartmouth College; University of Washington Press, 2008), pp. 227-245.

53. Ifi Amadiume, "African Women's Body Images in Postcolonial Discourse and Resistance to Neo-Crusaders" and Barbara Thompson, "Decolonizing Black Bodies: Personal Journeys in the Contemporary Voice," in Barbara Thompson, ed., *Black Womanhood: Images,*

*Icons, and Ideologies of the African Body* (Hanover, NH: Hood Museum of Art, Dartmouth College; University of Washington Press, 2008), pp. 49-69, pp. 279-311.

BIBLIOGRAPHY

Alloula, Malek. *The Colonial Harem*. Minneapolis: University of Minnesota, 1986.

Amadiume, Ifi. "African women's body images in postcolonial discourse and resistance to neo-crusaders." In *Black Womanhood: Images, Icons, and Ideologies of the African Body*, edited by Barbara Thompson, 49-69. Hanover, NH: Hood Museum of Art, Dartmouth College in association with University of Washington Press, 2008.

Antunes, Maria José Lobo. "O que se vê e o que não pode ser visto: fotografia, violência e Guerra." In *Retornar: Traços de memória do fim do Império*, edited by Elsa Peralta, Bruno Góis, and Joana Gonçalo Oliveira, 213-224. Lisbon: Edições 70, 2017.

Antunes, Maria José Lobo. *Regressos quase perfeitos: memórias da guerra em Angola*. Lisbon: Tinta da China, 2016.

Azoulay, Ariella. *Civil Imagination. A Political Ontology of Photography*. Brooklyn, NY: Verso, 2012.

Azoulay, Ariella. *The Civil Contract of Photography*. London: Zone Books, 2008.

Bal, Mieke. "A Postcard from the Edge." In *Double Exposures: The Subject of Cultural Analysis* (New York: Routledge, 1996) pp. 195-224.

Bancel, Nicolas, Pascal Blanchard, Gilles Boetsch, Éric Deroo, and Sandrine Lemaire, ed. *Zoos Humains: de la Vénus Hottentote aux Reality Shows*. Paris: Éditions La Découverte, 2002

"Banco (O) de Angola na Exposição Colonial." In *A Província de Angola*. Número extraordinário dedicado à Exposição Colonial Portuguesa e em honra da Restauração de Angola, 18. Luanda : Empresa Gráfica de Angola, 1934.

Barradas, Carlos. "Descolonizando enunciados: a quem serve objectivamente a fotografia?." In *O Império da Visão: Fotografia no contexto colonial português (1860-1960)*, edited by Filipa Lowndes Vicente, 447-460. Lisbon: Edições 70, 2014.

Barradas, Carlos. "Poder ver, poder saber. A fotografia nos meandros do colonialismo e pós-colonialismo." *Arquivos da Memória* 5-6 (2009): 59-79.

Bindman, David, Suzanne Preston Blier, and Henry Louis Gates Jr., eds. *The Image of the Black in African and Asian Art*. Cambridge, Mass. and London: The Belknap Press of Harvard University Press, 2017.

Blanchard, Pascal, Gilles Boetsch, and Nanette Jacomijn Snoep, ed. *Human Zoos: the invention of the savage*. Arles and Paris: Actes Sud, Musée du Quai Branly, 2011.

*Botânica. Esculturas* by Vasco Araújo, Text by Emília Tavares (Lisbon: Documenta: 2014), Exhibition Catalogue.

Cabecinhas, Rosa, and João Feijó. "Collective Memories of Portuguese Colonial Action in Africa: Representations of the Colonial Past among Mozambicans and Portuguese Youths." In *International Journal of Conflict and Violence* 4, no. 1 (2010): 28-44.

Campos, Ângela. *An Oral History of the Portuguese Colonial War*. Basingstoke: Palgrave Macmillan, 2017.

Campt, Tina M. *Image Matters: Archive, Photography and the African Diaspora*. Durham: Duke University Press, 2012.

Campt, Tina M. *Listening to Images*. Durham: Duke University Press, 2017.

Campt, Tina M. *Other Germans: Black Germans and the Politics of Race, Gender and Memory in the Third Reich*. Ann Harbor: University of Michigan Press, 2004.

Castelo, Cláudia. *Passagens para África: O povoamento de Angola e Moçambique com naturais da Metrópole (1920-1974)*. Porto: Afrontamento, 2007.

Castro, Teresa. "In-Between Memory and History: Artists' Films and the Portuguese Colonial Archive." In *(Re)imagining African Independence: Film, Visual Arts and the Fall of the Portuguese Empire*, edited by Maria do Carmo Piçarra and Teresa Castro, 205-223. Oxford: Peter Lang, 2017.

Childs, Adrienne L., and Susan H. Libby. *Blacks and Blackness in European Art of the Long Nineteenth Century*. Farnham, Surrey and Burlington, VT: Ashgate, 2014.

Coly, Ayo Abiétou. "Housing and Homing the Black Female Body in France: Calixthe Beyala and the Legacy of Sarah Baartman and Josephine Baker." In *Black Womanhood: Images, Icons, and Ideologies of the African Body*, edited by Barbara Thompson, 259-277. Hanover, NH: Hood Museum of Art, Dartmouth College in association with University of Washington Press, 2008.

Costa, Catarina Alves. *Guia para os filmes realizados por Margot Dias em Moçambique 1957-1961*. Lisbon: National Ethnology Museum, 1997.

Costa, Elmano Cunha e. *Catálogo da exposição de penteados e adornos femininos das indígenas de Angola*. S.l.: Agência Geral das Colónias, 1951.

Doy, Gen. "More than meets the eye... Representations of black women in mid-19th-century French photography." In *Women's Studies International Forum* 21, no. 3 (1998): 305-319.

Edwards, Elizabeth. "Anthropology and Photography (1910-1940)." In *The Image of the Black in Western Art*, edited by David Bindman, Karen C. C. Dalton and Henry Louis Gates Jr., vol. V, pt. I, 47-62. Cambridge, Mass.: Belknap Press, 2014.

Garraio, Júlia, "Perdidas na exposição? Desafiar o imaginário colonial português através de fotografias de mulheres negras." In *Geometrias da memória: configurações pós-coloniais*, edited by António Sousa Ribeiro and Margarida Calafate Ribeiro, 279-303. Porto: Afrontamento, 2016.

Gates Jr., Henry Louis. "The Black Person in Art: How Should S/He Be Portrayed?" *Black American Literature Forum* 21, no. 1/2 (Spring-Summer 1987): 3-24.

Geary, Christraud M. "The Black Female Body, the Postcard, and the Archives." In *Black Womanhood: Images, Icons, and Ideologies of the African Body*, edited by Barbara Thompson, 143-160. Hanover, NH: Hood Museum of Art, Dartmouth College in association with University of Washington Press, 2008.

Geary, Christraud M. "The Image of the Black in Early African Photography." In *The Image of the Black in African and Asian Art*, edited by David Bindman, Suzanne Preston Blier, and Henry Louis Gates Jr., 141-166. Cambridge, Mass. and London: The Belknap Press of Harvard University Press, 2017.

Geary, Christraud M. "Through the Lenses of African Photographers: Depicting Foreigners and New Ways of Life, 1870-1950." In *The Image of the Black in Western Art. The Twentieth Century. The Impact of Africa*, edited by David Bindman and Henry Louis Gates Jr., Vol. V, 87-99. Cambridge, Mass.: The Belknap Press, 2014.

Geary, Christraud M., and Virginia-Lee Webb, eds. *Delivering Views: Distant Cultures in Early Postcards*. Washington: Smithosian Institution Press, 1998.

Haney, Erin. *Photography and Africa*. London: Reaktion Books, 2010.

Hartman, Saidiya. "Venus in two Acts." *Small Axe* 26, vol. 12(2) (June 2008): 1-14.

Hayes, Patricia. "'Cocky' Hahn and the 'Black Venus': The Making of a Native Commisioner in South West Africa, 1915-46." In *Cultures of Empire. A reader. Colonizers in Britain and the Empire in the Nineteenth and Twentieth centuries*, edited by Catherine Hall, 329-355. Manchester: Manchester University Press, 2000.

Hayes, Patricia. "Visual History in Photographs." Review of *The Face of the Country: A South African Family Album, 1860-1910*, by Karel Schoeman. *The Journal of African History* 39, no. 1 (1998): 168-170.

Heintze, Beatrix. "In pursuit of a Chameleon: Early ethnographic photography from Angola in context." *History in Africa* 17 (1990): 131-156.

hooks, bell, *Black Looks: Race and Representation*. Boston: South End Press, 1992.

*In/sight: African Photographers, 1940 to the present*. Exhibition Catalogue. New York, N.Y.: Guggenheim Museum, 1996.

Kossoy, Boris, and Lilia Moritz Schwarcz. *Um olhar sobre o Brasil: a fotografia na construção da imagem da Nação: 1833-2003*. Rio de Janeiro: Objetiva and Fundación Mapfre, 2012.

Marques, Ana Martins. "As casas pertencem aos vizinhos..." In *O Livro das Semelhanças*. São Paulo: Companhia das Letras, 2015.

Martins, Leonor Pires. *Um Império de Papel: imagens do colonialismo português na imprensa periódica ilustrada (1875-1940)*. Lisbon: Edições 70, 2012.

Morais, Isabel. "'Little Black Rose' at the 1934 Exposição Colonial Portuguesa." In *Gendering the Fair. Histories of Women and Gender at World's Fairs*, edited by T.J. Boisseau and Abigail M. Markwyn, foreword by Robert W. Rydell, 19-36. Urbana: University of Illinois Press, 2010.

Mulvey, Laura. "Visual Pleasure and Narrative Cinema." *Screen* 16, no. 3 (Autumn 1975): 6–18.

Piçarra, Maria do Carmo, and Teresa Castro, ed. *(Re)imagining African Independence: Film, Visual Arts and the Fall of the Portuguese Empire*. Oxford: Peter Lang, 2017.

Pimentel, Joana. "La Collection Coloniale de la Cinemateca Portuguesa." *Journal of Film Preservation* 64 (2002): 22-30.

Pinney, Christopher. "What's Photography Got to Do with It?." In *Photography's Orientalism. New Essays on Colonial Representation*, edited by Ali Behdad and Luke Gartlan. Los Angeles: Getty Research Institute, 2013.

Raiford, Leigh. "Photography and the Practices of Critical Black Memory." *History and Theory* 48, no. 4 (December 2009): 112-129.

Ramos, Afonso Dias. "'Rarely penetrated by camera or film': NBC's Angola: Journey to a War (1961)." In *(Re)imagining African Independence: Film, Visual Arts and the Fall of the Portuguese Empire*, edited by Maria do Carmo Piçarra and Teresa Castro, 111-130. Oxford: Peter Lang, 2017.

Ramos, Afonso Dias. "Angola 1961, o horror das imagens." In *O Império da Visão: fotografia no contexto colonial português (1860-1960)*, edited by Filipa Lowndes Vicente, 397-432. Lisbon: Edições 70, 2014.

Rassool, Ciraj, and Patricia Hayes. "Science and Spectacle: /Khanako's South Africa, 1936-1937." In *Deep Histories: Gender and Colonialism in Southern Africa*, edited by Wendy Woodward, Patricia Hayes, and Gary Minkley, 117-161. Amsterdam and New York: Rodopi, 2002.

Ribeiro, Margarida Calafate and António Sousa Ribeiro, eds. *Geometrias da Memória: configurações pós-coloniais*. Oporto: Afrontamento 2016.

Ripert, Aline, and Claude Frère. *La Carte postale: son histoire, sa fonction sociale*. Lyon: Presses Universitaires de Lyon; Paris: Editions du CNRS, 1983.

Sanches, Manuela Ribeiro, ed. *"Portugal não é um país pequeno": contar o "Império" na pós-colonialidade*. Lisbon: Cotovia, 2006.

Sanches, Manuela Ribeiro, ed. *Deslocalizar a "Europa": Antropologia, arte, literatura e história na pós-colonialidade*. Lisbon: Cotovia, 2005.

Sanches, Manuela Ribeiro, ed. *Malhas que os impérios tecem: textos anti-coloniais, contextos pós-coloniais*. Lisbon: Edições 70, 2011.

Santos, Boaventura de Sousa. *Epistemologies of the South: Justice Against Epistemicide*. New York: Routledge, 2016.

Schwarcz, Lilia Moritz. "Black Nannies: Hidden and Open Images in the Paintings of Nicolas-Antoine Taunay." *Women's History Review* (2017): 1-18.

Seabra, Jorge. *África Nossa: o Império colonial na ficção cinematográfica portuguesa 1945-1974*. Coimbra: Imprensa da Universidade de Coimbra, 2011.

Serén, Maria do Carmo, ed. *A Porta do Meio: a Exposição Colonial de 1934. Fotografias da casa Alvão*. Oporto: Centro Português de Fotografia, 2001.

Thompson, Barbara, ed. *Black Womanhood: Images, Icons, and Ideologies of the African Body*. Hanover, NH: Hood Museum of Art, Dartmouth College in association with University of Washington Press, 2008.

Thompson, Barbara. "Decolonizing Black Bodies: Personal Journeys in the Contemporary Voice." In *Black Womanhood: Images, Icons, and Ideologies of the African Body*, edited by Barbara Thompson, 279-311. Hanover, NH: Hood Museum of Art, Dartmouth College in association with University of Washington Press, 2008.

Thompson, Krista. "The Evidence of Things Not Photographed: Slavery and Historical Memory in the British west Indies." *Representations* 113, no. 1 (Winter 2011): 39-71.

Vacchi, Dante. *Penteados de Angola*. Lisbon: Author's Edition printed at Litografia de Portugal, 1965.

Vargavtig, Nadia. *Des Empires en carton: Les expositions coloniales au Portugal et en Italie*. Madrid: Casa de Velazquez, 2016.

Vicente, Filipa Lowndes and Inês Vieira Gomes. "Inequalities on Trial: Conflict, Violence and Dissent in the Making of Colonial Angola (1907-1920)." In *Inequality in the Portuguese-Speaking World*, edited by Francisco Bethencourt. Brighton: Sussex Academic Press, 2018 pp. 217-242.

Vicente, Filipa Lowndes. "Introduction." In *O Império da Visão: fotografia no contexto colonial português (1860-1960)*, edited by Filipa Lowndes Vicente, 11-29. Lisbon: Edições 70, 2014.

Vicente, Filipa Lowndes. "Retornar não é possível: Fotografia nas partidas, nos regressos e na distância." In *Retornar: Traços de memória do fim do Império*, edited by Elsa Peralta, Bruno Góis, and Joana Gonçalo Oliveira, 197-212. Lisbon: Edições 70, 2017.

Vicente, Filipa Lowndes. "Rosita ou o Império como um objecto de desejo." *Público*, August 25, 2013.

Vicente, Filipa Lowndes. "Rosita. La Vénus noire de Porto." *Books.fr: livres & idées du monde entier*, March 2014.

Vicente, Filipa Lowndes. Review of *Zoos Humains: de la Vénus Hottentote aux Reality Shows*, by Nicolas Bancel, Pascal Blanchard, Gilles Boetsch, Éric Deroo and, Sandrine Lemaire, eds. *Estudos do Século xx*, no. 3, 2003.

Wallace-Sanders, Kimberly. "The Body of a Myth: Embodying the Black Mammy Figure in Visual Culture." In *Black Womanhood: Images, Icons, and Ideologies of the African Body*, edited by Barbara Thompson, 163-179. Hanover, NH: Hood Museum of Art, Dartmouth College in association with University of Washington Press, 2008.

Willis, Deborah, and Carla Williams. *The Black Female Body: A Photographic History*. Philadelphia: Temple University Press, 2002.

Willis, Deborah. "Picturing the New Negro Woman." In *Black Womanhood: Images, Icons, and Ideologies of the African Body*, edited by Barbara Thompson, 227-245. Hanover, NH: Hood Museum of Art, Dartmouth College in association with University of Washington Press, 2008.

FILIPA LOWNDES VICENTE, a historian, is a researcher at the Institute of Social Sciences of the University of Lisbon (ICS-ULisboa). In 2015 she was a Visiting Scholar at King's College, University of London and in 2016, at Brown University, Providence, USA. She completed her Ph.D. at the University of London (Goldsmiths College, 2000). Her Ph.D. thesis was the origin for the book *Viagens e Exposições: D. Pedro V na Europa do Século xix* (Lisbon: Gótica, 2003), winner of the "Victor de Sá" Prize in Contemporary History in Portugal (2004). She has also published *Other Orientalisms. India between Florence and Bombay, 1860-1900* (published in Lisbon 2009, and in India and Italy in 2012) and *Entre Dois Impérios. Viajantes Britânicos em Goa (1800-1940)*. Her publications on women artists and feminist art history include *A Arte sem História. Mulheres e cultura artística (séculos xvi-xx)* (Lisbon: Athena, 2012) and the exhibition catalogue, *Aurélia de Sousa, Mulher Artista, 1866-1922* (Lisbon: Tinta da China, 2016). She coordinated the research project *Knowledge and Vision. Photography in the Portuguese Colonial Archive and Museum (1850-1950)*, which resulted in the book, *O Império da Visão. Fotografia no contexto colonial português (1860-1960)*, published in 2014. Her work has concentrated on intellectual, visual, exhibition and cultural history in different spaces in the nineteenth and twentieth centuries, from Europe to India. Her approach is mainly historical, but her research also draws from other areas, from visual culture to anthropology.

1. *Beleza Bijagoz, Guiné, 1ª Exposição Colonial Portuguesa, Portugal, Porto, 1934.* Black and white photographic postcard. Photograph by Domingos Alvão. Uncirculated. (Collection of the author).

2. *Indígenas Balantas-Guiné. 1ª Exposição Colonial Portuguesa. Portugal. Porto, 1934.* "Rosinha" is standing on the right side. Black and white photographic postcard. Photograph by Domingos Alvão. Uncirculated. (Collection of the author).

3. *Guia Oficial. Secção Colonial da Exposição do Mundo Português.* [Official Guide. Colonial Section. Exhibition of the Portuguese World]. With a black and white photograph of two women. Lisbon. 1940. (Collection of the author).

4. *Como se deve ver a Exposição* [How one should see the Exhibition]. Inside page of the cover of the leaflet *Official Guide. Colonial Section. Exhibition of the Portuguese World.* Caption under the black and white photograph reads *Indígenas de Bijagós* [Indigenous from the Bijagós]. Lisbon. 1940. (Collection of the author).

1.

2.

3.

4.

5.

6.

7.

8.

5. *Portugal. Lisboa. Exposição do Mundo Português*. [Portugal. Lisbon. Exhibition of the Portuguese World]. Photograph with a printed caption under the image; no writing on the back (probably a commercial photograph on sale at the exhibition site). Uncirculated. (Collection of the author).

6. *Angola. Penteado de Noiva. Secção Colonial da Exposição do Mundo Português. 1140—Duplo Centenário—1940.* Neogravura, Lda , Lisboa. Photograph by Cunha e Costa. Circulated. Manuscript text begins on the back of the postcard and ends on the front. The text is written in an almost illegible, humorous mixture of badly written Spanish and French. (Collection of the author).

7. *Jardin d'Acclimatation. Deux soeurs* [Two Sisters]. Black and white photographic postcard. "ND Phot". Circulated. Paris. 12, 1918 sent to Le Havre. (Collection of the author).

8. *Tipos de Angola*. Black and white photographic postcard published by "Foto-Sport". Circulated. The postcard was sent from Luanda on October 30, 1953, to Lisbon, to the civil servants of one of the departments of the Instituto Nacional de Estatística in Lisbon [National Institute of Statistics]: *"Queridos Ex-colegas. Enriqueçui o vosso simpático album com a foto da "miss Angola" que em nada fica atrás da Silvana Mangano como podereis constatar. Que tal, Hei???? Abraça-vos o ex-colega e amigo [assinado]"*. [Dear Ex-Coleagues. Enrich your nice album with the photograph of "miss Angola" who, as you can see, could be compared with Silvana Mangano. What do you think???? Your ex-colleague and friend embraces you [signed]. (Collection of the author).

9. *Grupo Étnico "Umbundo". Mulher "Kaconda". Distrito da Huíla. Angola* [Ethnic Group "Umbundo". "Kaconda Woman". Huíla District-Angola]. Photographic Colored Postcard. Edition "Foto-Polo", Luanda. Uncirculated. (Collection of the author).

10. *Beleza Negra. Tipo Índigena* [Black Beauty. Indigineous type]. Photographic Colored Postcard. Printed in Belgium. Uncirculated. (Collection of the author).

11. *Lesotho. Southern Africa. Perfect balance and poise is necessary when strolling with babe and clay pot*. Photographic Colored Postcard. Publishers (PTY) LTD, Durban, South Africa. Circulated. The back of the postcard is occupied entirely by a manuscript text written in Portuguese: "JHB [Johanesbourg], 4/6/76 "*Mãezinha, Hoje é esta encantadora selvagem! Repare bem no olhar dela e, veja lá, se é ou não, o que lhe tenho dito. Um olhar mau e um ar insolente, não é? Esta gente é toda ruim e odeia todos os brancos. Eles, além de pretos, invejam tudo o que branco tem. Isto daqui a uns tempos, vai ser uma tragédia, por causa destes tipos. Pronto. Aqui tem mais uma postal para a sua coleção e olhe que há muita gente,* [sic] *têm coleções destes postais que são uma maravilha. Beijinhos e saudades [assinado].*" [Mummy, Today this lovely wild woman! Look at her gaze and tell me if she isn't as I have been telling you? An evil gaze and an insolent look, isn't it? These people are all mean and hate all whites. They, apart from being black, envy everything the white has. Soon this will be a tragedy, because of these guys. There. Here you have another postcard for your collection and remember there are many people with these kinds of postcard collections that are wonderful. (...) [signed]". (Collection of the author).

12. *Rapariga fula (Bissau). Guiné Portuguesa* [young Fula woman (Bissau). Portuguese Guinea]. "Fotografia verdadeira. Reprodução proibida. Edition "FOTO SERRA"—C.P. 239—Bissau. Impresso em Portugal". Uncirculated. (Collection of the author).

TRANSNATIONAL AFRICAS    Filipa Lowndes Vicente

9.

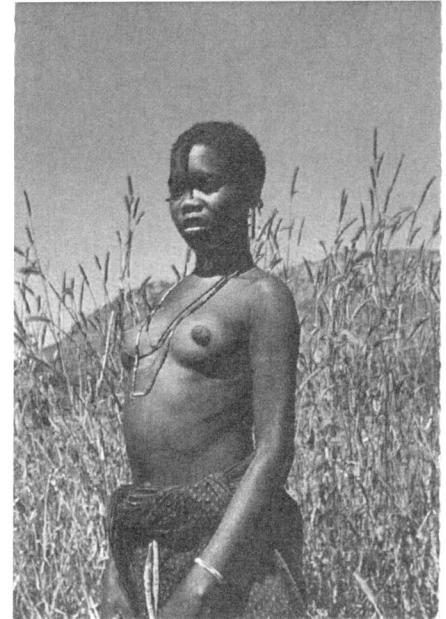

10.

11.

12.

13.

14.

15.

16.

17.

13. *Lourenço Marques. Mulher Indígena. A Kafir Woman*. Photographic Colored Postcard with printed caption in Portuguese and English. Published in Lourenço Marques. Circulated. Postcard sent from Lourenço Marques 7/4/1922 to a woman in Abrantes, Portugal. Manuscript text on the back: *"Cristina, Envio-te uma das figuras mais atraentes que aqui há a não serem as inglesas e algumas portuguesas o resto é tudo isto, e não são más, em breve tenho casamento feito com uma como esta, não achas que esta é interessante? A cidade não é feia mas ainda não é Lisboa; (...) [assinado]"* [Cristina, I send you one of the most attractive figures one can find here as beyond the English women and a few Portuguese the rest is like this, and they are not bad, soon I will have an arranged marriage with one like this, don't you think this one is interesting? The city is not ugly but it is not yet Lisbon; (...) [signed]". (Collection of the author).

14. *Pescadora (papel)—Guiné Portuguesa. Agência-Geral do Ultramar-Lisboa.* Colored picture postcard. Uncirculated. (Collection of the author).

15. *Campune (Bijagós)—Guiné Portuguesa. Agência-Geral do Ultramar-Lisboa.* Colored picture postcard. Uncirculated. (Collection of the author).

16. *Mulher Fula—Guiné Portuguesa. Agência-Geral do Ultramar-Lisboa.* Colored picture postcard. Uncirculated. (Collection of the author).

17. "O Banco de Angola na Exposição Colonial [1934]" [The Bank of Angola at the Colonial Exhibition [1934], in *A Província de Angola. Número extraordinário dedicado à Exposição Colonial Portuguesa Portuguesa e em honra da Restauração de Angola* (15 Ag. 1934) (Luanda: Empresa Gráfica de Angola, 1934), p. [18], Cortesia da Biblioteca Pública Municipal do Porto.

18. [Woman carrying a baby]. Black and white photograph with manuscript text on the back. Dated 15/11/61 [Angola]. *"Esta preta é do Norte de Angola (...) estas mulheres do norte não parece mas são mais estúpidas e selvagens que as do Sul, esta é a mulher dum "Soba" da região do "Dembe" é lá muito para o norte e muito no interior do mato. [assinado]"* [This black woman is from the North of Angola (...) these women from the North do not seem so but are more stupid and wild than those of the South, this is the wife of a "Soba" from the "Dembe" region which is in the farthest north and very much in the jungle interior. [signed]". (Collection of the author).

19. Photograph. Black and white. No written reference on the photograph. Portuguese soldier and a Guinean woman. Guinea. Undated (1960s-1970s). Private Collection (in the family of the photographed soldier).

20. Photograph. Black and white. No written reference on the photograph. Portuguese soldier with a group of Guinean people, mostly women and children. Guinea. Undated (1960s-1970s). Private Collection (in the family of the photographed soldier).

21. Photograph. Black and white. No written reference on the photograph. Portuguese soldier with a Guinean woman and baby. Guinea. Undated (1960s-1970s). Private Collection (in the family of the photographed soldier).

TRANSNATIONAL AFRICAS   Filipa Lowndes Vicente

18.

19.

20.

21.

22.

23.

24.

25.

22. Photographic album where figs. 19-21 are mounted with metal corners. On this page six photographs of the same dimensions (including figs. 19 and 21) are placed next to each other. In all of them, the Portuguese soldier appears next to a young woman. Guinea. Undated [1960s-1970s]. Private collection (in the family of the photographed soldier). Photograph taken in January 2018.

23. Photographic album where figs. 19-21 are mounted with metal corners. On this page fig. 20 is placed next to another photograph where the Portuguese soldier is photographed in the same pose and gesture as seen in other images, but he is here surrounded by children. Guinea. Undated (1960s-1970s). Private collection (in the family of the photographed soldier). Photograph taken in January 2018.

24. Photographic album where figs. 19-21 are mounted with metal corners. On this page two photographs are placed next to two postcards. The one on the left belongs to the same postcard series as fig. 12: "*Dançarino mandinga (Farim). Guiné Portuguesa* [Mandinga dancer (Farim). Portuguese Guinea], "Fotografia verdadeira. Reprodução proibida. Edition "FOTO SERRA"—C.P. 239—Bissau". Private collection (in the family of the photographed soldier). Photograph taken in January 2018.

25. Plastic box with photographs on sale at the Feira da Ladra maket in Lisbon. Photograph taken by the author in December 2017.

FERNANDO ARENAS

# The Filmography of Guinea-Bissau's Sana Na N'Hada: From the Return of Amílcar Cabral to the Threat of Global Drug Trafficking[1]

ABSTRACT: This essay offers a critical assessment of the work of Sana Na N'Hada, one of the most important cultural producers of Guinea-Bissau, centering on his documentaries, *The Return of Amílcar Cabral* (1976) and *Bissau d'Isabel* (2005), as well as the feature films, *Xime* (1994) e *Kadjike* (2013). Through his feature films and documentaries, Sana has been creating an audiovisual archive spanning the late colonial and early postcolonial periods that is key for understanding Guinea-Bissau's trajectory as a nation.

KEYWORDS: Lusophone African cinema, Guinea-Bissau, Sana Na N'Hada, documentary, feature film, Amílcar Cabral

RESUMO: O presente ensaio oferece uma abordagem crítica da obra do cineasta Sana Na N'Hada, um dos maiores vultos culturais da Guiné-Bissau, centrando-se nos documentários *O regresso de Amílcar Cabral* (1976) e *Bissau d'Isabel* (2005) e nos longa-metragens *Xime* (1994) e *Kadjike* (2013). Através da sua carreira, Sana tem construído um arquivo vital abrangendo os períodos colonial tardio e pós-colonial. Este artigo examina as dimensões éticas, etnográficas e históricas deste importante arquivo audiovisual para um conhecimento alargado da Guiné-Bissau enquanto nação.

PALAVRAS-CHAVE: Cinema da África lusófona, Guiné-Bissau, Sana Na N'Hada, documentário, longa metragam, Amílcar Cabral

This essay offers a critical assessment of the cinematic work of Sana Na N'Hada,[2] the first filmmaker of Guinea-Bissau[3], together with world-renowned filmmaker Flora Gomes, one of the most important cultural producers from the West African nation. Both have been key figures in documenting the history of their nation to the point of establishing its cinematic meta-text. Whereas Flora has received wide critical attention for many years, Sana has rarely been the object of analysis that his work deserves.⁴ This essay focuses on the greater part of Sana's filmography, including the documentary *O regresso de Amílcar Cabral* (The Return of Amílcar Cabral) (1976), the feature film *Xime* (1994), the documentary *Bissau d'Isabel* (2005), and his most recent feature film *Kadjike* (Sacred Bush) (2013), in order to examine its historical, ethical, aesthetic, cultural, and geopolitical dimensions.

Sana Na N'Hada belongs to the generation of Africans whose consciousness was shaped by the leaders of the anti-colonial movement. He was born in 1950 in the predominantly Balanta village of Enxalé, near the majestic Geba River that slices the country's central coast in half. He attended a Franciscan primary school for "indigenous" students against the will of his father, who preferred that he work the land. During Sana's early school years, he was taught by professors who were active in the emerging liberation movement. In the 1960s, he joined the guerrillas for five years to work as a medical assistant. At age 17 he was sent by Amílcar Cabral to Cuba in order to finish high school and pursue film studies, together with three other young men and women (including Flora Gomes). In an interview, Sana states: "I discovered the outside world in Cuba."⁵ The film careers of both Sana Na N'Hada and Flora Gomes were indelibly marked by their experiences in Guinea-Bissau's liberation struggle against Portuguese colonialism, as well as their formative education in Cuba.

Cinema throughout Portuguese or Portuguese Creole-speaking Africa, like cinema in Francophone Africa, has tended to be author driven and highly attentive to social, political, and historical issues pertaining to the nation, while offering a variety of aesthetic, formal, and entertainment approaches. The memory of colonialism and its legacy, as well as the failures and promises of postcoloniality, remain a constant theme in the work of the two towering figures of Bissau-Guinean cinema, Flora Gomes and Sana Na N'Hada. On the other hand, the volume of cinematic production throughout Lusophone Africa as a whole remains quite small in comparison to production in Francophone and Anglophone areas of sub-Saharan Africa. It also continues to be heavily dependent on co-productions with European nations, especially in the case of Guinea-Bissau.⁶ By the same token, as of 2017 there are signs that the Lusophone African cinematic sphere is seeing the emergence of low-budget video films, following in the footsteps of Nollywood, unbeholden to state-funding, whether national or international.⁷

The reigning economic, material, and geopolitical conditions at the time of birth and subsequent development of cinema in the former Portuguese colonies were, as I argue in *Lusophone Africa: Beyond Independence* (2011, 108), much more precarious than those in the rest of Africa. Yet, the experience of armed struggle that marked the origins of cinema in Angola, Mozambique, and Guinea-Bissau during the 1960s and 1970s significantly contrasts with the cinema produced in other African nations during their early independence years. The lack of training in filmmaking and of infrastructure, on the one hand, and the cohesion and unity of purpose within the MPLA in Angola, FRELIMO in Mozambique, and PAIGC in Guinea-Bissau, on the other hand, inspired such a wave of international solidarity that filmmakers and activists from France, Sweden, Yugoslavia, Cuba, Italy, the US, and other countries were involved in the production of numerous documentaries as well as in training filmmakers (Andrade-Watkins, 181; Cunha & Laranjeiro, 9-12). They committed their talent and resources to the liberation movements' emancipatory vision, advancing an ideologically complex strategy: the use of film as a tool or even as a strategic weapon in order to document and disseminate information about the war, making it possible to educate the African public about their own historical condition, while informing the international community about the anti-colonial wars in Africa.[8] It is also crucial to note that the emergence of anti-colonial and postcolonial cinema in Angola, Mozambique, and Guinea-Bissau, coincided with the modernization and revitalization of the cinematic medium that was underway in the 1960s and 1970s, as pointed out by Marcus Power (272). In this way, cinema became a key representational vehicle for the advancement of the national liberation cause, which galvanized international support.

The foundational filmic text for independent Guinea-Bissau is the documentary *O regresso de Amílcar Cabral* (The Return of Amílcar Cabral) (1976), co-directed by five Bissau-Guinean filmmakers, including Sana Na N'Hada and Florentino "Flora" Gomes.[9] It is based on a series of news reports that Sana edited in Sweden in order to create a coherent filmic whole. The documentary, mixing live footage mostly in muted color with black and white still photos, features the return to Bissau of the slain liberation leader's corpse in 1976 from Conakry, the capital of Francophone Guinea (where he was assassinated in 1973). A significant portion of the film focuses on the emotionally charged procession through the streets of Bissau that was witnessed by tens of thousands of mourners (military, civilians, diplomats, elderly, young), in addition to the official state funeral. (Sana Na N'Hada filmed the scenes from Conakry to Bissau and Flora Gomes filmed the airport scenes.) The solemnity pervading the 30-minute "hagiographic" documentary, underscored by the musical soundtrack of the mythical band Super Mama Djombo, "Amílcar Cabral bu mori sedu" (Amílcar Cabral You Died Too Soon),[10] is interspersed with beautiful black and white still images and film clips of the charismatic leader smiling, in action on the battlefield, as well as educating, training, and warmly commingling with liberation fighters. In addition, there are film clips of speeches—either in Guinean Kriol or in Portuguese. In one speech, Cabral admonishes soldiers not to fall prey to colonialist propaganda against the PAIGC liberation movement.[11] In another speech that he gave shortly before his assassination, Cabral commemorates the ten years of the armed struggle, unilaterally declaring independence on behalf of Guinea-Bissau and Cabo Verde. In another speech to villagers, Cabral extols the importance of liberation from fear and of the struggle for education. He adds that "educators are fighters too" and are "crucial for the country's future." This foundational film mourns the beloved pan-African leader, but also celebrates independence and the realization of Cabral's utopian dream of the bi-national state of Cabo Verde and Guinea-Bissau, now retrospectively ephemeral. The film ends with an iconic still image of the beloved hero (Fig. 1).[12] As described by Cunha and Laranjeiro, Cabral emerges as a messianic figure "onde reside toda a força política e anímica da construção do novo país soberano e independente" (15).[13] (Film clip 1)

Amílcar Cabral was fully aware of the power of cinema as an educational and propaganda tool. Therefore, he sent several young men and women to study filmmaking in Cuba at the ICAIC (or Cuban Film Institute[14]) under the mentorship of legendary director Santiago Alvarez.[15] These were José Bolama Cubumba, Josefina Lopes Crato, Sana Na N'Hada, and Flora Gomes (the first two now deceased). This would be a seminal moment in the history of Bissau-Guinean cinema, according to Filipa César.[16] Years later, in 1978, shortly after independence, Sana, together with the Angolan Mário Pinto de Andrade, founded the National Film Institute of Guinea-Bissau, which he directed until 1989. Between the 1970s and 1990s, Sana co-directed and directed several short documentaries and a short feature film.[17] Sana was also assistant director to Flora Gomes in his pioneering feature film, *Mortu Nega* (Those Whom Death Refused) (1988), and in *Po di sangui* (Blood Tree) (1996). In addition, Sana collaborated with French maverick film director Chris Marker in the outstanding mixed-genre experimental essay-film *Sans soleil* (Sunless) (1982), recently voted one of the five best documentaries ever made.[18] Chris Marker borrowed from Sana footage of Bissau Carnival—one of the most extraordinary in Africa—for a film that explores by contrast and analogy experiences of time and spiritual belief systems, particularly between Japan and West Africa. Marker returned several times to Guinea-Bissau, taking on the role of mentor and film professor to the four founding directors of the country's national cinema. According to Sana, they would all watch films together and subsequently discuss them (including Marker's own movies). Years later, when Sana was visiting Paris, Marker made a list of films for him to see so that they could afterwards discuss them. This particular relationship became significant in the history of cinema in Guinea-Bissau.

Sana Na N'Hada's first feature film, Xime (1994), was distinguished at the Cannes Film Festival under the rubric "Un certain regard" and is Sana's most remarkable work both formally and aesthetically. A Bissau-Guinean-Dutch co-production, Xime, co-written by Sana and Joop van Wijk, is a historical film set in 1962—the year before the beginning of Guinea-Bissau's liberation war.[19] The opening scene, interspersed with the credits, takes place at dawn in old Bissau where a young man is painting graffiti on the wall with the word "Independência." His paint brush playfully moves from the wall to the camera lens by splashing it, as if extending the graffiti wall onto the screen and thereby imbuing it with the euphoric political desire that propels the film as a whole.

Xime posits some of Amílcar Cabral's dilemmas in the attempt to rally a budding nation across many ethnic and cultural differences and beyond traditional belief systems and customs. (Film clip 2) In fact, the second scene (also interspersed between the opening credits) depicts the silhouettes of young liberation fighters projected against the wall. The silhouettes show headwear indicating ethnicity (Fulani or Balanta, for instance), while they discuss in Kriol Cabral's exhortation to speak the various vernacular languages and return to the villages (or tabankas in Guinean Kriol) of their respective ethnic groups to convince the elders of the importance of the fight for independence. Cabral was fully aware of the enormous ethnic and linguistic diversity of Guinea-Bissau,[20] where Kriol was not yet as widespread as it would eventually become in the course of the liberation struggle.[21] As a result, young activists were sent to their respective ethnically-based villages (Tomás, 148). In the case of the Balanta people, who are the centerpiece of the film Xime (an actual Balanta village), the character Raul (activist-guerrilla) is forced to contend with a strict age-based hierarchical power system, which proves challenging, as the film contends. Nonetheless, the Balanta people became the engine that would propel the PAIGC revolution, given their long history of opposition to Portuguese colonialism (161). According to Temudo (52, cited by Green,

28), Amílcar Cabral was particularly struck by the level of Balanta support toward the anti-colonial struggle; they were in fact the first ethnic group to fully support the armed struggle in the 1960s. Patrick Chabal argues that because of the group's age-grade system it was only until the elders were convinced that they should support the nationalists that "the relevant age-group leaders could easily recruit among their peers" (70). Eventually, all ethnic groups rallied around the liberation cause. Indeed, there is general consensus around the claim that the nation of Guinea-Bissau emerged through the anti-colonial war.[22]

The narrative structure of Xime is built around two parallel stories that eventually intersect. The first one takes place in the film's eponymous village, featuring Iala, a widower and father of Bedan and Raul. The younger son, Bedan, will soon be initiated into adulthood, while the elder son, Raul, is a seminarian in Bissau. Following tradition, Iala is offered a young woman, N'Dai, as a bride, even though she and Iala's son Bedan are far more interested in each other. Both youngsters are against the arranged marriage, but they feel powerless under the weight of tradition.[23] While N'Dai sings her sorrows, Bedan continues to flirt with her. In the meantime, Raul has mysteriously disappeared since joining the anti-colonial movement. Raul eventually becomes a crucial figure in Xime in his attempt to bring the village over to the liberation cause, and because of that, he also emerges as a lightning rod that unleashes the ire of colonial authorities against the village.

The second main storyline is anchored in Portuguese colonial society, featuring the regional administrator Cunha, businessman Silva, Lieutenant Borges, and priest Vittorio. The first three men appear as one-dimensional caricatures representing key aspects of the Portuguese colonial state. These men are vessels of colonialist and racist ideologies. Administrator Cunha's black servant and interpreter, José Manuel, for instance, is the object of some of the film's most injurious comments. By the same token, Cunha is the object of the film director's derision and humor. Close-ups of Cunha's face are often juxtaposed with close-up images of a frog, a lizard, or an insect. One scene depicts Cunha as he films locals harvesting rice patties. His gaze exoticizes them at the same time that the director critiques the colonial gaze in a metafilmic way. While the administrator and lieutenant defend the interests of a Portuguese colonial state that barely controls its West African territory, the businessman defends his own personal interests as he rails against the utter incompetence of the colonial government. He mockingly asks the administrator, "What is happening in Bissau?" But Cunha appears to be clueless. The administrator states that the governor wants to exert more control over the "indigenous people" and is planning to conduct a census, but this plan has been inexplicably delayed.

In contrast, the priest Vittorio emerges as the most complex character in the film. The only white character who speaks fluent Kriol, Vittorio has a foothold in both Portuguese and Guinean worlds, being able to see both sides of the colonial and anti-colonial divide. (According to Sana Na N'Hada, Vittorio is inspired by his own elementary school teacher who sympathized with the liberation cause.) In one of the more important scenes of *Xime*, administrator Cunha and Vittorio discuss in a very slow, cartoonish enunciation one of the priest's former students, Raul, who is wanted by the colonial authorities as a "subversive." The priest defends opening students' eyes through education, while taking no responsibility for what their eyes see. In another important scene, Vittorio and Raul walk through a bucolic setting across the rice fields. A discussion takes place in which the priest expresses skepticism vis-à-vis the liberation war. He believes that even if liberation forces are victorious, post-independence power may nevertheless fall into the hands of unscrupulous middlemen, represented by the figure of the African colonial soldier, who is given the generic name of *Cipaio*.[24] While the priest takes refuge in his religious faith, Raul's faith resides within the struggle. At the end, Vittorio confesses that one day he may ultimately understand the struggle.

*Xime* not only underscores the chasm between a weak and ineffective Portuguese colonial power structure and an overwhelmingly rural native population steeped in traditional culture, virtually untouched by the West, but it also highlights the chasm between different generations of Guineans as well as between tradition and modernity—the latter articulated in Cabral's vision of the future nation to emerge from the liberation struggle.[25] Tensions mount when the colonial administration intrudes into the lives of villagers in the hinterland, while a son of the villagers who has been educated by a Catholic order attempts to raise awareness of the oppressed condition of Africans under colonialism. Tensions escalate to the point of rupture, thus unleashing the war for independence.

The specific conflict in *Xime* is caused by road construction plans overseen by the lieutenant, who delegates the task to *Cipaio*. The armed *Cipaio*, who is portrayed to a large extent as an inept buffoon, orders villagers to build the road, even though they are in the midst of harvesting rice at the height of the dry season, which is ideal for such critical activity. This situation stirs anger among villagers and is reminiscent of the classic film *Emitai* (1971) by Ousmane Sembene, in which the arrogance on the part of the French colonial authorities, as well as their obliviousness toward the livelihood of Africans, leads to a state of rebellion. In the cases of the Casamance region in southern Senegal (where *Emitai* takes place) and of Guinea-Bissau, rice is the most important staple, thus playing a pivotal role in the lives of the rural population.

Meanwhile, Raul, the wayward son who is plotting revolution, arrives near the village wearing a beanie (or *sumbia*) similar to that worn by Amílcar Cabral. He asks wary fishermen why they acquiesce to whites who dictate the price of fish. Later on, Raul and his message of liberation are rejected by his father Iala and the elders. In the interim, administrator Cunha arrives at the village demanding that Iala pay a fine on behalf of his son Raul for his subversive activities. Subsequently, tensions escalate to the point of rupture when in the middle of Iala's wedding to the young bride N'Dai, *Cipaio* shoots Raul dead, and, in turn, *Cipaio* is killed by the young villagers. Lieutenant Borges arrives at this turning point and threatens to shoot the whole village. Instead, he throws a firebomb at Iala's house. This chaotic climatic sequence entails the beginning of the liberation war. Bedan has the last word: "É bias, é guera" (It's time for war). The final scene depicts the house, which metonymically encapsulates the village and the country as a whole, engulfed in flames.

*Xime* stands out for its superlative aesthetic qualities, particularly the camera work and lighting (by the talented Melle van Essen). Maria do Carmo Piçarra argues that the beauty of the images softens the hardship of the villagers' lives (123). The film, in fact, exudes charisma and warmth, thanks especially to the framing that privileges close-ups of characters' faces, which are enhanced by the exquisite chiaroscuro lighting to the point of constituting the film's stylistic mark. Sana Na N'Hada's film exemplifies the Deleuzian notion (via Eisenstein) of the close-up encompassing the face and vice-versa, while together being the equivalent of the concept of affection-image, comprising a combination of the "immobile unity" of the face with "intensive expressive movements" (Deleuze, 87). *Xime*, in fact, exhibits a preponderance of medium-to-extreme close-ups that punctuate a wide spectrum of emotional instances ranging from foreboding, fear, and secretive complicity to joy, compassion, and defiance, among many others. One could argue, along with philosopher Emmanuel Levinas,[26] who wrote extensively on the ethics of responsibility toward the other and the encounter of the other's face that "L'épiphanie du visage comme visage ouvre l'humanité" (the epiphany of the face as face, opens humanity) (30). This particular insight is most apt in thinking about the power of the close-up and its relevance for understanding the ethical-aesthetic strategy on the part of director Sana Na N'Hada and his politics of representation in *Xime*. The close-ups grant most of his characters a sense of uniqueness and grace, eliciting the audience's interest, empathy, and identification with the black Guinean subjects represented on-screen in a film about the beginning of the most successful African liberation war against European colonialism.

The close-up as affective representational strategy is also featured in the opening scene of *Bissau d'Isabel* (2005).[27] It is a powerful documentary that encompasses poetic, ethical, and educational elements in connection to the multicultural mosaic of the country's capital city—as a microcosm of the nation—centered on the life experience of its eponymous subject. From the start, the documentary establishes a pact of empathy and regard on the part of the audience toward Isabel in a deeply moving scene featuring a long take (35 seconds) and extreme close-up of her teary-eyed face staring into space with the constant sound of small waves breaking against the riverbank. This particular scene synthesizes the film's emotional force while effectively drawing the audience visually and sonically into Isabel's innermost emotional sphere, as well as into the collective universe of Guinea-Bissau. (Film clip 3) While the film is intimate in scale as it follows Isabel's everyday routine and as the audience becomes privy to her life story, Isabel also becomes the axis through which the country is portrayed at a macro-level in myriad historical, political, social, and cultural details.

The following scene features a high angle shot above a shipping container with hundreds of sacks of cashew nuts (which are the primary export product of Guinea-Bissau to the world) and dozens of workers loading the sacks as well as the containers onto the ships anchored at the port. At the same time we hear the song "Nha mame" (My Mother) by legendary singer-songwriter Zé Manel honoring hard-working Guinean women as the foundation of daily life, along with the children who help out their mothers by selling peanuts or beans in the streets. The subsequent scene features a large canoe carrying numerous passengers and stacks of straw arriving at the port of Bissau. Simultaneously, with the sound of the kora playing in the background, a narrator in voice-off tells the story in Portuguese of the first inhabitants who landed in what would later become "Ulau, Ussau, Bissau." There is an implosion of temporalities between past and present; while the narrator tells the foundational story of Bissau centuries ago, we see the images of its contemporary inhabitants. What may appear as a cinematic narrative disjuncture is ultimately a strategy to establish a link between the long historical continuum[28] and the present of the land and its people.

*Bissau d'Isabel* offers a strong ethnographic dimension featuring many prominent facets of everyday life, such as the city's lively informal economy, with scenes of the fish market at Pindjiguiti port and the main market of Bandim, highlighting the *djilas* (or itinerant male traders, many of them Muslim from Guinea-Conakry)[29] and the *bideras* (female street vendors). *Bideras* (which means literally in Kriol, "women of life") are inveterate saleswomen, omnipresent throughout the African continent, who depend on small transactions to support their families. Raul Fernandes argues that *bideras* operate within a territory where boundaries between domestic space and public market space collapse. *Bideras* struggle for life in order to provide sustenance to themselves and their families; their profession in the public sphere is in fact an extension of their domestic domain (110-111). Most *bideras* are the head of their households, in many cases single mothers. Some have college degrees. Isabel, who has a vegetable garden plot to supplement the family's food supply, works as a *bidera* on the side, selling surplus vegetables at the local market for extra income. Her children help her out with the family garden plot.

*Bissau d'Isabel* features two major Bissau-Guinean paradigmatic collective rituals in which people of all ethnic groups and religions participate: carnival and *toka txur* ("mourning"). Both scenes are framed as emblematic of the nation's multiethnic and ecumenical character. The brief carnival scene depicts massive crowds milling around the heart of the city with people playing drums, dancing, or watching carnival groups parade. There is a transition toward black-and-white footage of Amílcar Cabral speaking in French about the relationship between politics and culture. In the film clip he articulates his well-known belief that the liberation struggle is not only political but also cultural. Cabral states that there is and isn't a tribal/ethnic problem in Guinea-Bissau. He believes that "tribalism" is used by political opportunists, adding that colonial powers have historically taken advantage of tribal differences or divisions. He warns his people that they must remain vigilant about such problems in Guinea-Bissau. Later, a *bombo lom* player emerges as an intra-diegetic narrator describing the Bissau-Guinean animistic ritual of *toka txur*. It is a collective celebration that commemorates a loved one who has passed away. It involves music based on the rhythms of the *bombolom* (a large hollow tree trunk with an opening at the top played horizontally with sticks), dancing, chanting, the killing of cows, pigs and/or goats, with a feast including food and drink shared by all. The *bombolom* player, facing the camera, describes *toka txur* as a ritual to ensure that the deceased one finds peace on his or her way to reincarnation (in the animistic belief system of Guinea-Bissau, each newborn is the reincarnation of another being). He states further that there are different rhythmic patterns of playing the *bombolom* in accordance with age and/or gender of the deceased person. Subsequently, the extra diegetic narrator returns, asserting that the *toka txur* is an occasion in which social, cultural, political, religious, and ethnic differences are set aside. Forgiveness and reconciliation prevail. Ultimately, *toka txur* is one of Guinea-Bissau's key unifying rituals at a time when politics have become "ethnicisized" to a certain degree, and pose a threat to the nation's unity—a concern that was voiced by the nation's founder (as described earlier) and fully shared by director Sana Na N'Hada.

As the documentary moves from the macrological to the micrological levels, Isabel Nabalí Nhaga emerges as a figure that is emblematic of the nation as a whole; her life story is in many ways the story of Guinea-Bissau. Isabel is primarily a nurse at the country's main hospital. Similarly to Sana, she joined the PAIGC forces and worked as a medical aid. Later on, she was sent to Cuba to become a nurse. After returning to Guinea-Bissau she worked in the liberated zones during the war's final years. Isabel and her companions (including Sana) embodied the hopes and dreams of the generation of Amílcar Cabral. Yet, ever since independence her life has been an endless struggle in which her salary, when paid, is insufficient to support her family (including her unemployed Cuba-educated agronomist husband and several college-age children). Sana's documentary celebrates Isabel's strength, kindness, intelligence, and determination. Her values are those of Cabral, i.e. the overarching importance of education and an ethos of egalitarianism across genders, ethnicities, religions, etc. Nevertheless, the film also laments the personal and historical tragedy that has befallen Isabel and her country. Isabel is a paragon of hard work, honesty, and resilience, but her country has been unfair, corrupt, and, at times, violent and hateful toward its own people. The film elicits a great deal of admiration from the audience toward Isabel, and through her, toward the country as a whole.

Sana Na N'Hada and Flora Gomes, as well as countless other African intellectuals, writers, artists, and filmmakers, bemoan the insurmountable gap between the dreams and hopes of a fair and egalitarian post-independence society and the reality of greed, venality, and injustice that has prevailed in numerous postcolonial African nations. Given the heroic circumstances of Guinea-Bissau's independence, which was seen as a "hope-filled harbinger of Africa's potential," in the words of Toby Green (229), this reality is particularly stinging. Postcolonial critic Albert

Memmi lucidly wonders, "Why, if the colonial tree produced bitter fruit, has the tree of independence provided us only with stunted and shriveled crops?" (21).

Sana Na N'Hada's most recent feature film, *Kadjike* (Sacred Bush) (2013), presents a dramatic confrontation between tradition and one of the most perverse manifestations of global modernity. It was shot almost entirely on the Bijagós archipelago off the coast of Guinea-Bissau and focuses on the clash between traditional Bijagó culture and the global drug trafficking network as it intrudes upon the lives of the inhabitants of this pristine corner of the planet. The remote and largely unknown Bijagós archipelago comprises eighty-eight islands off the coast of Guinea-Bissau with a high diversity of ecosystems from mangroves, mudflats, and palm forests to coastal savanna, sandbanks, and aquatic zones, with a unique fauna, including the salt water hippopotamus, the African manatee, the Atlantic hump-backed dolphin, and marine turtles. The Bijagós constitute one of the most important destination points for migratory birds in Africa.[30] In 1996 UNESCO declared this unique region a Biosphere Reserve.

Visually, the film *Kadjike* capitalizes on this stunning location with sweeping wide-angle landscape shots of beach and ocean views, along with island tropical forests, including the majestic kapok trees. According to Anne Laerke Roefoed, "The poignancy of this film lies in the juxtaposition between the natural beauty of the archipelago and the imminent dangers that lurk in the shadows of this fragile world" (4). In fact, the natural landscape and the environment play a key role throughout the film, becoming a character in and of themselves in the defense of the symbiotic relationship between traditional society and culture and the archipelago itself against the intrusion of destructive forces of modernity. In the film *Kadjike* the Bijagós archipelago emerges as a powerful example of the notion of "natureculture," as conceptualized by Donna Haraway (2003), to emphasize the intrinsic interdependence between both dimensions.

*Kadjike*'s story is framed in an atemporal place in harmony with God Nindo's creation, according to Bijagó animistic cosmogony, where time moves at a slow pace following the cycles of nature. In fact, the opening scene features an extraordinary shot of the starry sky, followed by a long take with close-up images of a crab emerging from a hole on the sandy beach. The voice-off narrator in Kriol (Sana himself) tells the Bijagó creation myth. Acapacama, the original female inhabitant, founded the first village of Nocau. Before it was time for her to leave the world, she charged her four daughters with the care of tradition, the ocean, the forest, and the wind. Acapacama's heritage was to be protected by her descendants.

The Bijagó society at the center of *Kadjike* not only lives in harmony with its natural ecosystem, but is also portrayed as an egalitarian society in terms of gender relations and roles. According to Álvaro Nóbrega, the geographic isolation of the Bijagó archipelago and the general lack of modern infrastructure have contributed to the preservation of traditional social structures on the islands, including its matrifocal configuration (84). However, in the film *Kadjike*, Bijagó society is descending into conflict.

There are two narrative coming-of-age threads that run parallel in *Kadjike* involving the young men Ankina and Toh. Ankina has been chosen to be initiated into becoming a medicine man and he struggles to live up to the task. Meanwhile, Omi, his girlfriend, is interested in marrying him despite a prohibition against marrying a would-be-initiate. Toh, on the other hand, is restless and rebellious. He is tired of living on the islands under the rule of the elders and is eager to explore the world. Both stories become entangled through the intrusion of a couple of outsiders from the capital city, Togon and Assumé, who bribe the local state authorities so that they may purchase a strategic piece of land on a sacred island in order to run a cocaine transshipment operation. While Ankina must learn the secret power of the snake, Toh becomes involved with the drug trafficking couple. He is seduced with promises of traveling the world, but in reality the couple is more interested in using him as a mule. In the meantime, Ankina, as he emerges as a new community leader after being initiated, discovers the drug trafficking operation and becomes determined to mobilize his people to oust the intruders so as to save Nocau. As a Bijagó man tells Ankina, all islands are being desecrated by "foreigners" and that there is no more room for traditions.

As the action unfolds, *Kadjike* also offers cultural, ethnographic, and ecological insights into the everyday life of Bijagó society, featuring, for instance, a ceremony in honor of the first mother Acapacama and her four daughters, scenes of women and boys crushing palm fruit for palm oil, young men picking oysters, women fishing with nets, the elders deliberating and consulting with the village priestess. Basic ecological insights offered by the film include: planting several trees in order to replace the majestic kapok that is to be cut for a canoe; not cutting the root of mangrove trees where oysters grow and are later harvested; leaving the land fallow so that the soil may regenerate; and the notion of itinerant agriculture, where the land is collectively owned based on customary law.

During the mid-2000 decade the Bijagós archipelago became a nodal point in the international drug trafficking network between Latin America and Europe, as

Guinea-Bissau emerged as a transshipment depot along the West African coast. Given the island territory's remote location and defenselessness in the context of a weak nation-state, with little control over its borders and where government has been prone to corruption, Guinea-Bissau offered an ideal platform for drug traffickers. As Joshua Forrest points out, this transnational threat underscores "the strong links among political instability, economic vulnerability, and state fragility" (197). Hassoum Ceesay remarks that Guinea-Bissau's fragility has, in fact, made it a "hunting ground for drug traffickers, a fragility which their presence has since exacerbated" (219). Indeed, Guinea-Bissau remains a weak democracy due to on-going cycles of chronic political unpredictability and economic stagnation, alongside continued dependence on foreign aid. Forrest argues that the history of post-liberation Guinea-Bissau has been characterized by a tendency toward an authoritarian centralization of executive power, punctuated by multiple coup attempts, in addition to the short civil war that took place between 1998-99 (171). More recently, the cycles of institutional crises and political violence in connection to the internal struggle for power have become exacerbated by drug trafficking and its close proximity to circles of power (Ceesay, 220). After a brief period of political and economic stabilization, as well as generalized optimism in 2014, the country appears to be once again undergoing a period of political stalemate at the executive level and economic stagnation as of 2017. In the meantime, drug trafficking appears to have become less conspicuous in Guinea-Bissau since the mid-2010 decade, with foreign traffickers driven away. Nevertheless, Davin O'Regan states that there remain local operators tied to the drug trade, and that the phenomenon of drug trafficking should be understood within a larger regional context that is constantly in flux (2014).[31] The independent weekly newspaper Última Hora reported on a United Nations study conducted in 2015, concluding that Guinea-Bissau remains at the mercy of organized crime due to weaknesses in the judicial system, corruption, and political instability.[32]

Through the film *Kadjike* Sana Na N'Hada not only deploys a "cautionary pedagogy" for the people of Guinea-Bissau,[33] but also sends an "alarm signal" to the world, offering a fictionalized story based on numerous anecdotal accounts about the increase in drug consumption among youth, as well as incidents involving drug trafficking throughout the islands. For instance, a mysterious airplane stuck on the runway of Bubaque airport (Bubaque is the economic center of the Bijagó archipelago), where the local youth were asked to help free the plane from the mud; a local fisherman who discovered bags of white powder being thrown into the sea from small airplanes; or locals discovering bags of white powder on the islands, not quite knowing what the "white powder" was.

Kadjike posits the Bijagós islands as a microcosm of what the nation should be: an ideal society living in harmony with nature and the environment, while preserving to a large extent its customs and traditions, including a shared power structure between men and women. At the same time, Sana Na N'Hada's filmic narrative revolves around the binary opposing tradition and modernity that has been vastly explored in the context of African cinema, for example in Ousmane Sembene's Emitai (1971), mentioned earlier in connection to Sana's film Xime.[34] In Sembene's paradigmatic Emitai a village in the region of Casamance, bordering Guinea-Bissau, must unite to confront the French colonial government, which, during World War II, forces the village to provide fifty tons of rice for the war effort, against the traditional custom of using excess rice for religious rituals. Even though traditional belief system and customs are ultimately insufficient in overcoming the cruelty and injustice of the colonial authorities as agents of Western modernity, collective mobilization, especially among women, in defiance of the colonial oppressor, is symbolically potent and politically empowering in and of itself. Sana's Kadjike, for its part, presents a diffuse globalized force that suddenly emerges in the remote Bijagó islands through urban middlemen who, in turn, entice and corrupt naïve or gullible members of the island community. Here, Sana asserts the ability of traditional society to overcome drug trafficking, even though, in reality, as the case of Guinea-Bissau has demonstrated, only the concerted effort of the national and international communities, governmental and nongovernmental forces, can effectively deal with global drug trafficking. Yet, Sana prefers to offer Kadjike as an allegory of national unity through the plight of the Bijagó as a counterforce against the threat of malevolent forces. The film asserts the centrality of collective action as well as unity in purpose, identity, and preservation of the land's culture, values, and livelihood, in order to vanquish or, at least, deter the perverted intrusion of global modernity in the form of drug trafficking. The Bijagós are seen as vulnerable to forces that may overwhelm it, and Sana's film demands its defense and protection, but it argues that such efforts should emerge from the people themselves. By the same token, Kadjike offers a strong contemporary ecological message that is elicited in the film's title "Sacred Bush" and the profusion of extraordinary shots of the Bijagó natural landscape, where traditional spirituality and nature remain inextricably intertwined, thus complicating the binary between modernity and tradition. (Film clip 4)

Through documentary and feature films Sana Na H'Nada has been making a pivotal contribution to the archive of Guinea-Bissau spanning the late colonial and early postcolonial periods[35] by tracing the birth of the nation along with its hopes and achievements, as well as its challenges and travails. Sana's artistic vision and ethos, and those of Flora Gomes, have been influenced by their experiences as protagonists in the nation's liberation saga. For both Bissau-Guinean film directors, as well as for numerous founding figures in the history of African cinema—which coincided with the dawn of independence—film has not only been put at the service of nation-building, but has also been used to serve against all odds as a bastion of critical consciousness in postcolonial societies where individualized political and economic agendas have often superseded the national collective well-being, while mortgaging its future indefinitely.

## NOTES

1. I would like to thank the Department of Afro-American and African Studies and the African Studies Center at the University of Michigan for their generous support that made possible my research trips to Guinea-Bissau in 2014 and 2016.

2. I would like to warmly thank director Sana Na N'Hada for his kind generosity in providing me with copies of all his films discussed throughout this essay and for the extensive interview I conducted with him during my visit to Bissau in 2016.

3. See the essay by Filomena Embaló, "O cinema da Guiné-Bissau" featured in the volume, *Flora Gomes: o cineasta visionário* (19).

4. See the page written by Filomena Embaló, "Cinema da Guiné-Bissau," https://misosoafricapt.wordpress.com/cinema-da-guine-bissau-filomena-embalo/ and the article by Anne Laerke Koefoed's, "Under the Radar: Sana Na N'Hada is one of Africa's Most Important Filmmakers Today," http://africasacountry.com/2015/03/sana-na-nhada-guinea-bissaus-revolutionary-filmmaker-is-one-of-africas-most-important-directors-today/

5. Interview with filmmaker at Hotel Coimbra (Bissau) in June, 2016.

6. The mega-production *Njinga: Rainha de Angola* (Njinga, Queen of Angola) (2013) directed by Portuguese Sérgio Graciano is a major exception to the co-production model with Portugal, Brazil, or France, in that it was entirely funded by Angolan public and private sources and produced by Semba Comunicação. Angola is also becoming a TV power house in Lusophone Africa through highly sophisticated *novelas* that have been exported to Brazil and Portugal (*Windeck* (2013) and *Jikulumessu* (2014)), both nominated for Emmy awards. These are currently being dubbed into English and French for their distribution throughout the African continent, as evidenced by Semba's presence at FESPACO (Ouagadougou) in 2017. It is uncertain whether the Angolan government will continue to invest

in audiovisual production due to the severe economic crisis caused by declining oil prices. Angola is almost exclusively dependent on revenues from oil exports.

7. For a discussion on the emerging amateur or semi-professional digital production of film series, documentaries, or short films in Guinea-Bissau, see Paulo Cunha and Catarina Laranjeiro (2016).

8. For more information on the early history of film production in post-independent Lusophone Africa, see José Mena Abrantes (1986), Manthia Diawara (1992a), Frank Ukadike (1994), Claire Andrade-Watkins (1995), José Matos-Cruz and José Maria Abrantes (2002), Ros Gray (2011) and Mohamed Bamba (2011).

9. The five directors of *O regresso de Amílcar Cabral* were: Sana Na N'Hada, Florentino "Flora" Gomes, José Bolama Cubumba, Djalma Martins Fetterman, and Josefina Lopes Crato.

10. The song "Amílcar Cabral bu mori sedu" was written/composed by Tony Lima. Today, it is also a sample of a rap song from 2011 featuring Chullage, LBC, and Kaya (available on YouTube), signaling the continued political and cultural relevance, as well as iconic power of Cabral for younger generations of Bissau-Guineans, Cabo Verdeans, diasporic Africans in Portugal, and Afro-Portuguese.

11. PAIGC (Partido Africano para a Independência da Guiné Bissau e Cabo Verde) was the founding party of independent Guinea-Bissau and Cabo Verde. Both countries became a bi-national state between 1975-80. Since the end of the bi-national experiment, the party has retained the acronym in Guinea-Bissau while in Cabo Verde it changed to PAICV.

12. Flora Gomes is currently at the pre-production phase of a documentary on the life of Amílcar Cabral.

13. "who galvanizes the full political and emotional force behind the newly sovereign and independent nation."

14. Instituto Cubano de Artes e Industrias Cinematográficas.

15. See Anne Laerke Koefoed.

16. See description of Filipa César's archival film project focusing on the history of militant cinema in Guinea-Bissau, "Luta ca caba inda" (The Struggle is not Over Yet): http://www.jeudepaume.org/index.php?page=article&idArt=1639

See her 30-minute documentary essay titled, *Transmission from the Liberated Zones* (2016), based on statements and documents that are presented by a young boy through a low fidelity channel. Also, see Filipa César's remarkable short experimental film, *Conakry* (2013), based on forgotten raw video footage from the Bissau-Guinean liberation struggle and early post-independence from 1972-80 as a poetic exercise in memory recovery, in collaboration with San Tomean-Portuguese writer and artist Grada Kilomba and US radio activist Diana McCarty.

The collective film *Spell Reel* (2017) assembled by Filipa César, together with Anita Fernandez, Flora Gomes, and Sana Na N'Hada, further develops her on-going meditation on the ruins of a film archive that was crucial to the decolonization of Guinea-Bissau and what it may portend for the future.

17. Sana co-directed with Florentino "Flora" Gomes, Josefina Lopes Crato, and José Bolama Cubumba, *Anos no osa luta* (We Dare to Struggle), a 15' documentary released in 1976. Sana also directed *Os dias de Anconó* (The Days of Anconó), a 26-minute documentary commissioned by UNESCO and *Fanado* (Initiation), a 26-minute documentary, currently available at the Arsenal Film Archive in Berlin.

18. See Laerke Roefoed's article.

19. Flora Gomes was assistant director of *Xime*, in addition to António Reis, Suleimane Biai, and Juan Carlos Tajes.

20. Robert J. C. Young points out that Cabral's detailed knowledge of the cultural diversity in Guinea-Bissau was largely based on his extensive agricultural survey for the colonial Forestry Department (285). Antonio Tomás argues that this experience enabled Cabral to interact with the most influential leaders of various ethnic groups across the land (91). Also, see Cabral's essay, "Brief Analysis of the Social Structure in Guinea," (published in English in 1969) for a comparative discussion of the power structure within Balanta and Fulani societies, arguably, Guinea-Bissau's two most influential ethnic groups.

21. The foremost linguistic authority on Guinean Kriol, Luigi Scantamburlo, argues that through the national liberation struggle Kriol became the country's lingua franca, and that the capital city of Bissau today, as the nation's largest urban area, as well as its economic, political, and media center, has become the bastion of Kriol, where most of its native speakers are concentrated (30). (Also, based on conversations with Scantamburlo and Sana Na N'Hada).

22. Sana Na N'Hada states that Amílcar Cabral was a unifying figure of all ethnic groups in Guinea-Bissau that Portuguese colonialism was keen on dividing. He argues further that the nation was forged through the liberation war. In his pioneering biography of Cabral, Patrick Chabal argues that, in fact, Bissau-Guinean society was transformed during the liberation struggle rather than after it (10).

23. Arranged marriages crossing generational lines leading to conflict between elderly parents and adult children are the centerpiece of the classic African film, *Tilai* (1990), directed by the late Idrissa Ouedraogo from Burkina Faso. In this particular case, the marriage in question eventually leads to the downfall of the whole community.

24. The term *Cipaio*, derived from Hindi, signifies "soldier." In the Portuguese colonial context in Africa it meant a (black) "African colonial soldier." In Sana's film *Xime* the use of the term is generic for the character in question, who becomes objectified as a "colonial soldier type."

25. For Cabral's own discussion on the role of culture as a factor of resistance to colonialism, as well as the relationship of culture to power and its social and economic effects, see "National Liberation and Culture" (1973).

26. I would like to thank Charlie Sugnet for reminding me of the relevance of Levinas' phenomenology of the face-to-face encounter with the other in thinking of Sana's privileging of the close-up in his cinematography.

27. The assistant director of *Bissau d'Isabel* is Suleimane Biai.

28. Term used by Toby Green (3).

29. See Raul Mendes Fernandes (111).

30. See *The Protected Areas of Guinea-Bissau: Guide to Ecotourism*.

31. For one of the most lucid and exhaustive accounts on Guinea-Bissau, see "Anatomy of State Fragility: The Case of Guinea-Bissau" by Joshua B. Forrest (2010). For a detailed analysis of the drug trafficking situation in Guinea-Bissau and West Africa, see "The Evolving Drug Trade in Guinea-Bissau and West Africa" by Davin O'Regan (2014). For an incisive analysis of drug trafficking and the responses by civil society, particularly rappers, see "Les conséquences du narcotrafic sur un État fragile: le cas de la Guinée-Bissau" by Miguel de Barros, Patrícia Godinho Gomes and Domingo Correia (2013).

32. "Relatório da ONU diz que a Guiné-Bissau está a mercê do crime organizado" (2016).

33. The concept of "cautionary pedagogy" is used by critic Stefan Sereda in describing "a common convention in African Cinema that cuts across the political ideologies of filmmakers" (196). He argues that African cinema has been used for educational and instructional purposes since its beginning (194).

34. I would like to thank Charlie Sugnet for his generosity and invaluable insights regarding the work of Ousmane Sembene within the context of African cinema and its resonance in the work of Sana Na N'Hada.

35. Other major filmic projects from or related to Guinea-Bissau include: the documentary *José Carlos Schwarz: A voz do povo* (José Carlos Schwarz: The People's Voice) (2006) by Abdulai Jamanca, focusing on the country's musical founding figure; the feature film *Clara di Sabura* (Clara, The Party Girl) (2011) by José Lopes, a cautionary tale of a young woman who is lured by the temptations of a leisurely life in a social context of material scarcity and struggle; the documentary *Bafatá Cine Clube* (2012) by San Tomean director Silas Tiny, focusing on the ruins of a movie theater and the memories of those who experienced it during colonial times in the interior city of Bafata; and the feature film *A batalha de Tabató* (The Battle of Tabató) (2013) by Portuguese director João Viana, a haunting allegory that brings together colonialism and postcolonialism, tradition and modernity, where music (particularly the *balafon* instrument of Mandinka roots) plays a pivotal mediating role. *O espinho da rosa* (The Thorn of the Rose) (2013), a debut feature by Bissau-Guinean director Filipe Henriques, is a daring thriller that focuses on pedophilia mixed with paranormal and fantastic elements set in Portugal with an African cast.

## WORKS CITED

Abrantes, José Mena. 1986. *Cinema angolano: um passado a merecer melhor presente.* Luanda: Cinemateca Nacional.

Andrade-Watkins, Claire. 1999. "Portuguese African Cinema: Historical and Contemporary Perspectives—1969 to 1993." In *African Cinema: Post-Colonial and Feminist Readings,* ed. Kenneth Harrow. Trenton NJ: Africa World Press. 177-200.

Bamba, Mohamed. 2011. "In the Name of 'Cinema-Action' and Third World: The Intervention of Foreign Film-Makers in Mozambican Cinema in the 1970s and 1980s" *Journal of African Cinemas.* 3: 2 173-185.

Barros, Miguel de, Patrícia Godinho Gomes e Domingo Correia. (2013). "Les conséquences du narcotrafic sur un État fragile: le cas de la Guinée-Bissau." *Alternatives Sud* 20: 145-158.

Cabral, Amílcar. 1969. "Brief Analysis of the Social Structure in Guinea." In *Revolution in Guinea: An African People's Struggle.* London: Stage 1. 46-61.

———. 1973. "National Liberation and Culture." In *Colonial Discourse and Post-Colonial Theory: A Reader,* eds. Patrick Williams and Laura Chrisman. New York: Columbia University Press. 1994. 53-65.

César, Filipa. 2013. *Conakry.* n.d.

———. 2016. *Transmission from the Liberated Zones.* France: Spectre Productions.

César, Filipa and Anita Fernandez, Flora Gomes, and Sana Na N'Hada. 2017. *Spell Reel.* Germany, Guinea-Bissau, France, and Portugal: Spectre Productions.

Chabal, Patrick. 2002. *Amilcar Cabral: Revolutionary Leadership and People's War.* London: C. Hurst &. Co. Reprint.

Cunha, Paulo and Catarina Laranjeiro. 2016. "Guiné-Bissau: do cinema de Estado ao cinema fora do Estado." *Rebeca: Revista Brasileira de Estudos de Cinema e Áudiovisual.* 5:2. 1-23.

Deleuze, Gilles. 1986. *Cinema 1: The Movement-Image.* Trans. Hugh Tomlinson and Barbara Habberjam. Minneapolis: University of Minnesota Press.

Diawara, Manthia. 1992. *African Cinema.* Bloomington & Indianapolis: Indiana University Press.

Embaló, Filomena. 2015. "O cinema da Guiné-Bissau." In *Flora Gomes: o cineasta visionário.* Bissau: Corubal. 19-23.

———. "Cinema da Guiné-Bissau," misosoafricapt.wordpress.com/cinema-da-guine-bissau-filomena-embalo/ . Access July 18 2016.

Fernandes, Raul Mendes. 2012. "O informal e o artesanal: Pescadores e revendedeiras de peixe na Guiné-Bissau (fronteiras pós-coloniais—rigidez, heterogeneidade e mobilidade)." PhD diss. Universidade de Coimbra.

"Filipa César: "Luta ca caba inda" ("The Struggle is Not Over Yet"). 2012. http://www.jeudepaume.org/index.php?page=article&idArt=1639. Access 20 Aug 2016.

Forrest, Joshua B. 2010. "Anatomy of State Fragility: The Case of Guinea-Bissau." In *Security and Development: Searching for Critical Connections*, eds. Neclâ Tschirgi, Michael S. Lund and Francesco Mancini. Boulder and London: Lynne Rienner Publishers. 171-210.

Graciano, Sérgio. 2012. *Windeck*. Luanda: Semba Comunicação.

———. 2013. *Njinga: Rainha de Angola*. Luanda: Semba Comunicação.

———. 2014. *Jikulumessu*. Luanda: Semba Comunicação.

Gray, Ros. 2011. "Cinema on the Cultural Front: Film-Making and the Mozambican Revolution." *Journal of African Cinemas*. 3: 2 139-160.

Green, Toby. 2016. "Introduction." In *Guinea-Bissau: Micro-State to 'Narco-State'*, eds. Patrick Chabal and Toby Green. London: C. Hurst & Co. 1-16.

———. 2016. "Dimensions of Historical Ethnicity in the Guinea-Bissau Region." In *Guinea-Bissau: Micro-State to 'Narco-State'*, eds. Patrick Chabal and Toby Green. London: C. Hurst & Co. 19-36.

———. 2016. "Conclusion." In *Guinea-Bissau: Micro-State to 'Narco-State'*, eds. Patrick Chabal and Toby Green. London: C. Hurst & Co. 229-234.

Haraway, Donna. 2003. *The Companion Species Manifesto: Dogs, People, and Significant Otherness*. Chicago: Prickly Paradigm Press.

Henriques, Filipe. 2013. *O espinho da rosa*. Lisboa: Duxilian Filmes & Plural Entertainment.

Jamanca, Adulai. 2006. *José Carlos Schwarz: A voz do povo*. Lisboa: Lx Filmes.

Laerke Roefoed, Anne. 2015. "Under the Radar: Sana Na N'Hada is One of Africa's Most Important Filmmakers Today." *Africa is a Country*. http://africasacountry.com/2015/03/sana-na-nhada-guinea-bissaus-revolutionary-filmmaker-is-one-of-africas-most-important-directors-today/. Access 20 Aug 2016.

Lévinas, Emmanuel. 2001. *La visage de l'autre*. Paris: Éditions du Seuil.

Lopes, José. 2011. *Clara di Sabura*. Bissau: Gapro Audiovisual & Cabos Internacional Venture.

Marker, Chris. 1983. *Sunless*. France: Argos Films.

Matos-Cruz, José de and José Mena Abrantes. 2002. *Cinema em Angola*. Luanda: Chá de Caxinde.

Memmi, Albert. 2006. *Decolonization and the Decolonized*. Trans. Robert Bononno. Minneapolis: University of Minnesota Press.

N'Hada, Sana na, Florentino "Flora" Gomes, José Bolama Cubumba, Djalma Martins Fetterman, and Josefina Lopes Crato. 1976. *O regresso de Amílcar Cabral*. Bissau: Instituto Nacional de Cinema e Audiovisual.

N'Hada, Sana na. 1994. *Xime*. Netherlands, Guinea-Bissau, France, and Senegal: Molenwiek Film BV, Arco-Íris, Les Matins Films, Cap Vert.

———. 2005. *Bissau d'Isabel*. Portugal & Guinea-Bissau: Lx Filmes.

———. 2013. *Kadjike*. Portugal & Guinea-Bissau: Lx Filmes.

Nóbrega, Álvaro. 2003. *A luta pelo poder na Guiné Bissau*. Lisboa: Instituto Superior de Ciências Sociais e Políticas.

Ouedraogo, Idrissa. 1990. *Tilai*. Switzerland, UK, France, Burkina Faso, and Germany: BBC, COF, Evangelisch Reformierte Kirche, Filmcooperative, Ministère Français de Coopération et Développement, La Fondation Gan pour le Cinéma, Les Films de l'Avenir, Ministère de la Culture de la République Française, Rhea Films, Stanley Thomas Johnson Stiftung, UTA, Waca Films.

O'Regan, Davin. 2014. "The Evolving Drug Trade in Guinea-Bissau and West Africa." *Center for Security Studies*. http://www.css.ethz.ch/content/specialinterest/gess/cis/center-for-securities-studies/en/services/digital-library/articles/article.html/182200. Access 20 Aug 2016.

Piçarra, Maria do Carmo. 2016. "Um olhar sobre a libertação (através do cinema) de uma nação a partir da tabanca de Xime." In *África(s): cinema e revolução*, ed. Lúcia Ramos Monteiro. São Paulo: Caixa Cultural. 121-124.

Power, Marcus. 2004. "Post-colonial Cinema and the Reconfiguration of *Moçambicanidade*." *Lusotopie* 11: 261-278.

"Relatório da ONU diz que a Guiné-Bissau está a mercê do crime organizado." 2016. *Últimas notícias*, June 16.

Scantamburlo, Luigi. 1999. *Dicionário do Guineense*. Lisboa: Colibri.

Sembene, Ousmane. 1971. *Emitai*. Senegal: Filmi Domirev.

Sereda, Stefan. 2010. "Curses, Nightmares, and Realities: Cautionary Pedagogy in FESPACO Films and Igbo Videos." In *Viewing African Cinema in the 21st Century*, eds. Mahir Saul and Ralph A. Austin. Athens: Ohio University Press. 194-208.

Temudo, M. P. 2009. "From the Margins of the State to the Presidential Palace: The Balanta Case in Guinea-Bissau." *African Studies Review* 52 (2) : 47-67.

*The Protected Areas of Guinea-Bissau: Guide to Ecotourism*. 2016. Bissau: Institute for Biodiversity and Protected Areas (IBAP)

Tiny, Silas. 2012. *Bafatá Cine Clube*. Lisboa & Bissau: Real Ficção, TeleCine Bissau, and Filmes do Mundo.

Tomás, António. 2007. *O fazedor de utopias: uma biografia de Amílcar Cabral*. Lisboa: Tinta da China.

Ukadike, Nwachukwu Frank. 1994. *Black African Cinema*. Berkeley: University of California Press.

Viana, João. 2013. *Batalha de Tabató*. Lisboa: Papaveronoir.

Young, Robert J.C. 2001. *Postcolonialism: An Historical Introduction*. Oxford: Blackwell.

FERNANDO ARENAS is Professor of Lusophone Cultural Studies (including Portuguese-speaking Africa, Portugal, and Brazil) at the University of Michigan with a dual appointment in the departments of Afro-American and African Studies and Romance Languages and Literatures. His book *Lusophone Africa: Beyond Independence* (University of Minnesota Press, 2011) is forthcoming in 2018 in an expanded and updated version in Portuguese by Edusp (University of São Paulo Press).

Figure 1. Still image from the film *O regresso de Amílcar Cabral*.

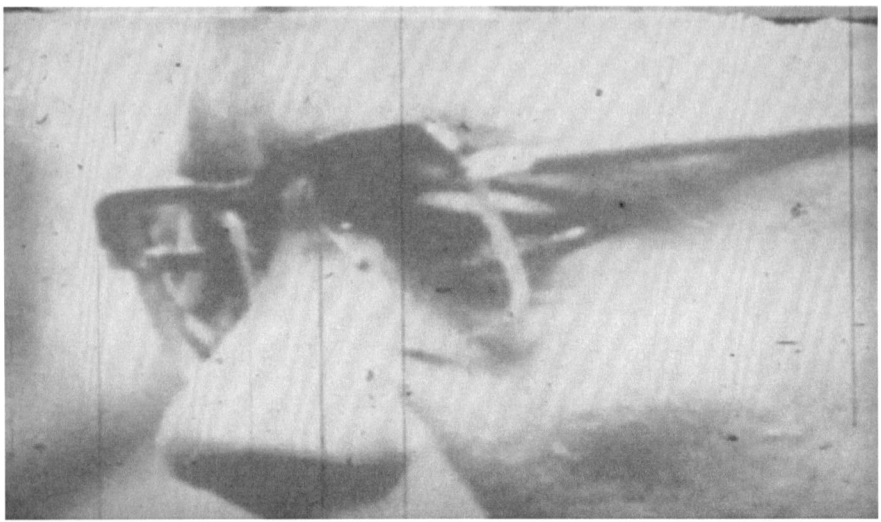

Film clip 1. *O regresso de Amílcar Cabral* (The Return of Amílcar Cabral) (1976)
(Courtesy of Sana Na N'Hada)

Film clip 2. *Xime* (1994)
(Courtesy of Hillie Molenaar & Joop van Wijk, Molenwiek Film, Amsterdam)

TRANSNATIONAL AFRICAS   Fernando Arenas

Film clip 3. *Bissau d'Isabel* (2005)
(With permission by LX Filmes)

Film clip 4. *Kadjike* (2013)
(Courtesy of Sana Na N'Hada)

JOSÉ MANUEL FERNANDES

# Arquitetura Moderna Portuguesa na África Subsaariana

RESUMO: Apresenta-se o tema da arquitetura e urbanismo modernos na África Portuguesa dos anos 1950-1970. Os seus antecedentes e contextualização. Os valores coletivos e humanos dessa arquitetura moderna. Dão-se exemplos de obras e autores, nos cinco territórios coloniais luso-africanos. Faz-se reflexão sobre a herança patrimonial atual dessas arquiteturas e cidades, nos PALOP.

PALAVRAS-CHAVE: Arquitetura Moderna / África Subsaariana / África Portuguesa

ABSTRACT: This article discusses the theme of modern Portuguese architecture in Sub-Saharan Africa with a focus on architecture and urbanism from the 1950s to the 1970s. The collective and human values of this architecture is referenced. Examples of buildings, projects and authors from the five ex-colonial areas, now independent countries, are presented. General thoughts on the heritage of architectural and urban modernism in these countries are likewise expressed.

KEYWORDS: Modern architecture / Sub-Saharan Africa / Portuguese Africa

## 1. Antecedentes e Contexto Africano: Anos 1950-70

No dealbar da década de 1950, no Portugal Ibérico, havia uma situação difícil, em termos políticos e sociais, para que pudesse acontecer uma afirmação livre da nova geração de arquitetos no retrógrado e repressivo ambiente, nos aspetos culturais e profissionais, do país. Para os novos técnicos era inevitável pensar na "saída," como solução de recurso para a abertura de vida que aqui lhes era negada. Porém, a mobilidade profissional para a Europa ou América era ainda restrita na época—sendo que a terra das oportunidades era a propagandeada África Portuguesa do Regime Salazarista.

Portanto, para a geração então recém-formada reforçava-se a ideia de escape e aventura, associada à ida para África—facilitada a afirmação profissional pela língua comum e pelo funcionamento social e institucional das comunidades luso-africanas, muito próximas e dependentes das da Metrópole. Repare-se que as outras e pequenas colónias lusitanas se situavam demasiado longe (o Estado da Índia, Macau, Timor), não potenciando tantas possibilidades.

Foi também na década de 1950 que se sentiu, nas práticas da arquitetura e no urbanismo (sobretudo em Angola e Moçambique), uma profunda diferença com as fases anteriores, pelo abandono crescente dos modelos neo-tradicionalistas, iniciando-se, em termos sócio-económico-culturais, uma fase mais dinâmica e virada para a modernidade—apoiada pelas novas escalas tecnológicas, de planeamento e de construção.

Se, por um lado, se transpunha culturalmente o conflito "moderno-tradicional" da Europa para África—com a nova geração de arquitetos portugueses aqui fixados, de formação mais informada e atualizada, produzindo no quadro da ação estruturante dos poderes públicos—, por outro lado, a ativa iniciativa privada, com dinâmica económica e social, também eclodiu, procurando afirmar-se por novos espaços, estruturas e símbolos.

Assim, nos anos 1950, a via conservadora da "Arquitetura do Estado Novo" (desenvolvida nos anos 1930-40) entrou em conflito direto com a procura de afirmação da "Arquitetura Moderna." Em consequência, os arquitetos mais tradicionalistas opuseram-se claramente aos arquitetos modernos. Então, a iniciativa mais liberta e a grandiosa escala de intervenção em territórios vastos e virgens constituíram um desafio com apelo à modernidade—ditando a vitória rápida dos defensores das práticas mais inovadoras. Sem esquecer a ação dos arquitetos "oficiais," adstritos ao centralizante Gabinete de Urbanização do Ultramar (GUU)—que procuraram exercer uma arquitetura de consenso, de sentido equipamental e público, nela mediando entre a expressão radicalmente moderna e o desenho mais conformista—, esta afirmação moderna foi geral, poderosa, clara e abrangente.

A fase da transição das décadas de 1950-60 refletiu a relativa abertura política, no Portugal da época, entre as sequelas do Movimento de Unidade Democrática e a ressaca da euforia da candidatura de Humberto Delgado à Presidência da República (1958). De facto, a segunda metade dos anos 1950 foi—também internacionalmente—de desanuviamento, sobretudo desde 1957-58, após o final da guerra da Coreia e da caça às bruxas norte-americana. As nuvens só voltariam com o fatídico ano de 1961 (início da Guerra Colonial em Angola). Estes anos foram assim o tempo de algum debate cultural em Angola, sobretudo em Luanda, pela afirmação da cultura de esquerda (dentro das limitações fortes do regime luso-colonial), com intervenções por arquitetos como Francisco Silva Dias, Francisco Castro Rodrigues e José Pinto da Cunha.

A participação dos arquitetos portugueses radicados em Angola e Moçambique nos encontros e conferências internacionais africanas, com clara preocupação social e modernizadora, foi efetiva, embora irregular e pontual. Os temas eram sobretudo os da habitação coletiva e do urbanismo, no quadro dos países ainda colonizados ou em vias de descolonização. A título exemplificativo, refere-se a *Conference Interafricaine / Logement et Urbanization*, na sua segunda sessão, realizada em Nairobi em Janeiro de 1959, onde estiveram presentes dezasseis arquitetos de Moçambique, dois de Angola e dois do Portugal europeu.

Em Moçambique deve mencionar-se igualmente a gradual emergência de um debate cultural autónomo, centrado sobretudo na capital Lourenço Marques, e servido por associações locais, como o Núcleo de Arte ou o Cineclube. A isso ajudava a proximidade da África anglófona, com a sua capacidade informativa e atualizada, quebrando o isolamento, bem como a tradição de elite culta que a cidade cultivava. Destacavam-se arquitetos com consciência social e política amadurecida, como João José Tinoco e o seu grupo.

Também outros arquitetos, não tanto pela politização mas pela sua cultura aberta e de sentido participativo, como Pancho Miranda Guedes, contribuíram para o fortalecer do debate cultural. Como exemplo, no quadro da gradual tomada de consciência coletiva do problema das más condições de habitação e de vida da população africana negra nos arredores de Lourenço Marques, refira-se o artigo daquele arquiteto, no jornal progressista A Tribuna (nº 228 de 9 de Junho de 1963), "A Cidade Doente—Várias Receitas para Curar o Mal do Caniço e o Manual do Vogal sem Mestre," onde o autor, em estilo irónico e humorado, propunha uma série de medidas para a recuperação e qualificação urbana dos "caniços," designação local para bairro de barracas.

Na viragem dos anos de 1960-1970, em paralelo e decorrente da guerra colonial, acentuou-se pelo Estado a tentativa tardia da ideia de Nação Plurirracial, com ela surgindo um novo surto de investimento público na criação de fontes de energia e de bases industriais, para uma escala mais global (as grandes barragens hidroelétricas, os povoamentos agrícolas de irrigação)—e assistiu-se a uma aceleração da explosão urbana e da expansão das cidades, com renovação de equipamentos e serviços, bem como a construção privada de imóveis de porte.

Atingiu-se nesta fase o auge da consolidação das nascentes redes urbanas, sobretudo em Angola e em Moçambique, num processo geral de construção das cidades, que decorreu em várias frentes, paralelas entre si: pelo maior desenvolvimento das urbes já existentes; pela elevação a cidade de vilas e povoações de menores, mas com importância estratégica e/ou administrativa; e pela implantação de novos povoados, mesmo que ainda embrionários.

Foi nestas décadas que, correspondendo ao surto urbanizador, se incrementou uma nova linguagem arquitetónica, mais dinâmica do que a anterior e primeira Arquitetura Moderna, e dela nascida: a do Movimento Moderno Internacional, com uma maior escala de realização e sofisticação, assente em novas tecnologias construtivas, que o acesso ao betão (com produção local de cimento e a importação do aço e do vidro) prodigalizavam cada vez mais. Novas construções, e sobretudo com uma ampla dimensão—nas cidades e vilas, mas também nos centros industriais e energéticos adentro dos territórios—, exprimiam a crença no progresso acelerado que o súbito desenlace político-militar das independências suspendeu, em 1975.

## 2. Lições e Valores, Coletivos e Humanos, na Fase da Arquitetura Moderna da África Luso-Colonial: Anos 1950-75

Em síntese, podem destacar-se aqui quatro características que decorrem de uma comum, sólida e contemporânea formação profissional, cultural e política, da que designamos por geração moderna dos arquitetos portugueses—informada e atualizada, apesar das limitações referidas, de teor político-social. Trata-se de uma generalização, havendo autores que de algum modo praticaram mais coerentemente estes aspetos, e outros de atuação mais irregular, ou menos identificada com eles. Vejamos então essas características, de atitude e de atuação, próprias desta renovada geração de arquitetos:

1) Ética da funcionalidade: esteve patente nos programas, espaços e conceções da grande maioria das intervenções arquitetónicas; ou seja, nos projetos houve, em geral, o entendimento da importância fulcral dos aspetos da utilidade das respetivas obras (privilegiando com isso a sua dimensão social para as comunidades afetas)—o qual se considerou dever conduzir, ou nortear, os outros fatores, classicamente primaciais, da conceção dos espaços arquitetónicos (a tecnologia, a dimensão estética).

2) Abertura à tecnologia: em todo o caso, a dimensão técnica da profissão da arquitetura também foi considerada (talvez num plano imediatamente a seguir ao funcional), pois os arquitetos-autores sempre introduziram por princípio os novos materiais e conceções tecnológicas inovadoras, sem as relevarem como

protagonistas, mas também sem lhes recusar papel importante nas suas obras. Sobre este aspeto referia Vasco Vieira da Costa que (no mundo da construção ainda sem os sistemas generalizados de ar condicionado), só um bom arquiteto saberia construir eficazmente no contexto climático tropical—pois uma obra deficiente simplesmente não seria habitável (respirável) num clima deste tipo (conforme depoimento ao autor pelo arquiteto Troufa Real).

3) Visão global: soube integrar as áreas ou disciplinas do planeamento e urbanismo com as da arquitetura e desenho; isto é, os arquitetos praticantes nestes territórios e nesta fase histórica compreendiam bem, na sua atuação, a necessidade de ordenar o espaço numa perspetiva de conjunto, relacionando os vários níveis e escalas necessariamente interdependentes (do território, das cidades e povoações, das edificações e espaços arquitetónicos); trabalharam por isso, com igual abertura, em planos e estudos urbanísticos, em projetos de desenho urbano e paisagístico, além dos temas do projeto arquitetónico específico—o que ainda mais se entendia nesta fase, que foi de uma primeira estruturação urbana em muitas regiões africanas.

4) Ideia do serviço à sociedade: tema muito comum nos autores desta geração; considerando-se como fazendo parte de um corpo profissional, treinado e preparado para intervir nos vários níveis exigidos pela sociedade, quer nos programas públicos quer nos privados, o seu norte e referência para uma atuação (também aqui do ponto de vista ético ou, mais propriamente, deontológico) foi sempre o de dar primazia/protagonismo ao trabalho produzido, e dar muito menos valor, ou nenhum, à questão da autoria individual do mesmo; houve portanto uma prática de autoapagamento dos autores enquanto tal, os quais se consideravam agentes e impulsionadores, ao serviço da causa (preferencialmente pública) mas não reivindicando (em postura não individualista) por essa via a sua condição de operadores-criadores estéticos.

Numa leitura conjunta, tratou-se afinal de uma época e geração, no que toca à arquitetura, de claros sentidos dentro dos temas do concretizador-utilitarista, do coletivo-socializante, do funcional-tecnicista—em articulação com uma geral visão da Modernidade, ativa e atuante, plena de confiança no futuro.

## 3. Exemplificações—Obras, Autores e Realizações Marcantes do Terceiro Quartel do Século XX, Território a Território

Nos cinco espaços coloniais luso-africanos dos meados de novecentos, as manifestações e realizações da arquitetura moderna tiveram registos diferentes, em função da escala e dimensão de cada área. O contraste maior estabeleceu-se entre os pequenos arquipélagos do Atlântico Norte (Cabo Verde, Bijagós e a costa da Guiné-Bissau) e do Golfo da Guiné (São Tomé e Príncipe)—e os vastos espaços continentais de Angola e Moçambique, a sul de África, com milhões de quilómetros quadrados. Em breves referências e exemplos, seguem-se os casos mais relevantes.

1) Cabo Verde. O arquipélago ficou marcado, nesta fase, pelo crescimento (embora moderado) das duas maiores cidades, da Praia (ilha de Santiago) e do Mindelo (ilha de São Vicente)—através da renovação ou construção de equipamentos públicos, bem como pela implantação de novas infraestruturas e a execução de planos de ordenamento urbanístico. Na Praia, implantaram-se sobretudo obras na linguagem arquitetónica oficial do Estado Novo (o Liceu da Praia/Liceu Adriano Moreira, com o Monumento Henriquino fronteiro, de 1960; a antiga gare do aeroporto Gago Coutinho, de linhas modernistas sóbrias). Pelo contrário, no Mindelo, as novas construções públicas e privadas, embora escassas, afirmaram de modo qualificado as formas e espaços da modernidade: o edifício do Comando Naval, na baía (de 1962, pelo GUU, a que terá estado ligado Lucínio Cruz (1914-99), sendo o projeto de António Saragga Seabra (cf. Milheiro, *Construir em África 1944-1974*); o Hotel Porto Novo, na central Praça Nova.

2) Guiné-Bissau. As cidades da então Guiné Portuguesa tiveram algum crescimento, ao longo de meados de novecentos, havendo na colónia 544.000 habitantes em 1960. Como na Praia cabo-verdiana, foram os modelos arquitetónicos de transição ou mestiçagem moderno-tradicional que pontificaram na arquitetura pública da urbe: em Bissau, veja-se o edifício dos CTT, na avenida da República, com cobertura em telha e eixo de simetria na composição, e pórtico com fachada de linhas modernizantes (por Lucínio Cruz, de 1950-55); o hospital de Bissau, com pavilhões de cobertura telhada e fachadas com pórticos e colunatas, obra também por Lucínio Cruz, com Mário de Oliveira (1914-2013), de 1951-53, ampliado por Eurico Pinto Lopes em 1961-63; a Associação Comercial, atual sede do PAIGC, por Jorge Chaves (1920-1981), de 1949-53, talvez a mais elegante e moderna das edificações locais; a Alfândega, ao cais da urbe, com longo corpo horizontal e torre cilíndrica moderna, de betão e vidro. Exemplo de uma arquitetura moderna e pragmática de raiz portuguesa é o edifício da Administração do

Porto de Bissau—construção ligeira mas procurando a adaptação climática ao trópico, por Carlos Tojal, Manuel Moreira e Carlos Roxo (de 1967-68).

3) São Tomé e Príncipe. A arquitetura destes dois reduzidos espaços territoriais foi em geral, nesta época, mais discreta e simples do que nos vastos territórios afro-lusos a sul do Equador. Na cidade de São Tomé, edificadas ao longo da baía (ao lado dos edifícios tradicionais, sucessivamente alterados e modernizados, da Sé e do Palácio do Governo), encontram-se algumas arquiteturas representativas da Arquitetura Moderna, de iniciativa pública. Com linhas modernizantes (mas pórtico central) e eficácia funcional, o Liceu (antiga Escola Técnica Silva Cunha), por Mário de Oliveira, dos anos 1960, foi só inaugurado em 1969. O mais notável é, sem dúvida, o atual edifício das Telecomunicações Santomenses, virando a sua fachada, protegida por uma larga retícula de *brise-soleil*, em betão armado, às águas equatoriais, uma obra por José Pinto da Cunha (1921-2007) e Pereira da Costa (1923-1976), de 1957-1962, inaugurada em 1965.

4) Angola—Luanda e Lobito. Com a transição para as décadas de 1950-60, surgiram finalmente os exemplos modernos, de uma arquitetura mais geométrica, próxima das formas industriais e moduladas—mudança que, de resto, sucedia igualmente na Metrópole. Refiram-se, neste registo estético, em Luanda: a aerogare General Craveiro Lopes, por Keil Amaral (1910-75), com volumes baixos, horizontais, encastrados, e interior com escadaria e decoração mural a fresco por Neves e Sousa, dos inícios dos anos 1950; o volumoso Palácio de Vidro, bloco com galeria e varandas em caixa, ao lado da Alfândega (por Luís Amaral, João Américo e António Campino); e, fruto da iniciativa privada e do ciclo do café, a sede cafeeira da firma Cirilo e Irmão, pelo arquiteto Pereira da Costa, de 1958, com sólida volumetria e desenho corbusiano.

Nesta época, e já que a ênfase deste texto se colocou na ação da nova geração de autores e na sua capacidade individual de contribuir para a afirmação moderna, podem destacar-se alguns autores e obras, trabalhando em Luanda:

— João Garcia de Castilho (1915-2007) e o irmão Luís Garcia de Castilho, dos primeiros arquitetos modernos fixados na capital angolana, autores do antigo cinema Restauração—que depois da independência, serviu como Assembleia Nacional—com torre fina e abstrata rematando um denso corpo horizontal, de 1946-51; e do cinema-esplanada ao ar livre Miramar, de 1964, sobre a encosta, com ampla vista para a baía, de palas em consola, em betão e madeira;

— Vasco Vieira da Costa (1911-1982), um dos grandes autores de Luanda, criador de um poderoso Bloco habitacional para os Servidores do Estado, com galerias e sábia adaptação ao terreno em declive, de 1965; da moradia Casa Inglesa, no paisagístico morro da Alta da cidade / rua do Balão; e do fortíssimo edifício do largo da Mutamba, já de 1968-69 (atual Ministério de Habitação e Obras Públicas), com dois volumes ao alto justapostos e uso de grelhagens corbusianas, em obra a um tempo monumental e moderna (ver fig. 1. Edifício Mutamba);

— José Pinto da Cunha (1921-2007), qualificado autor (com Simões de Carvalho) da Instalação da Radiodifusão de Angola (ou Rádio Nacional de Luanda, edifício a lembrar um pouco a obra em La Tourette por Corbusier)—de 1963-67; e, no sector assistencial, do hospital de Lubango / Sá da Bandeira, com poderosa volumetria moderna;

— Fernão Lopes Simões de Carvalho (1929-), que trabalhou em Paris na equipa de Le Corbusier, com André Wogenscky, até 1959. Foi, desde 1961, chefe do Gabinete de Urbanização da Câmara Municipal de Luanda, e autor dos blocos de habitação coletiva da PRECOL na Unidade de Vizinhança nº1 do bairro Prenda (1963-65, com José Pinto da Cunha e Fernando Alfredo Pereira); com Lopo de Carvalho, construiu os blocos de habitação coletiva para os funcionários dos CTT de Luanda, obra expressiva em betão aparente (1968-69);

— António Nunes e Silva Campino (1917-1997), formado no Porto (tese sobre *Arranjo Turístico para a Ilha de Luanda*, 1953), trabalhou para a Câmara Municipal de Luanda (no Plano Diretor, em 1961-62), e nesta cidade projetou e construiu obras como o edifício da Auto-Avenida (ao lado do Banco de Angola), o Colégio dos Maristas, o Prédio Totobola, o Comando Naval de Luanda, além do qualificado hotel Presidente de Luanda, nos anos 1960-70 (na praça da Alfândega, à avenida Marginal, o atual Presidente Mériden, para o qual cursou uma formação especial de seis meses em Barcelona).

De referir ainda Luís Taquelim (1928-), natural de Lagos, Algarve, que, radicado em Luanda (1958-71), trabalhou sucessivamente como professor (1958-59), na Câmara Municipal (até 1964) e para a JAEA-Junta Autónoma de Estradas de Angola, indo depois para o Lubango / Sá da Bandeira (1971-75). Taquelim, também artista plástico (pintor), erigiu obras como, em Luanda, o Prédio Cuca, no Quinaxixe, e um prédio na rua Brito Godins; e, pelo território, projetou e construiu estações de correios (na Estrada do Catete e no Lubango), a Igreja de São Pedro em Mocâmedes / Namibe, o Hotel do Luso em Luena/Vila Luso. Executou os centros rodoviários da JAEA em várias sedes distritais (Benguela, Lubango e Namibe/Moçâmedes). No Lubango / Sá da Bandeira executou o Monumento a Sá da Bandeira, um vasto cineteatro (por inaugurar, 1975), a fábrica de cerveja, a estação de caminhos-de-ferro (e habitações para os funcionários), o edifício da Câmara Municipal (inacabado) e diversas moradias.

Na cidade do Lobito, a segunda mais importante em Angola (em articulação com a vizinha Benguela) durante largo período do século XX, destaca-se a figura ativa de Francisco Castro Rodrigues (1920-2015), ali trabalhando entre 1953 e 1988, com continuada e decisiva participação nas áreas municipal, urbanística, infraestrutural e arquitetónica. De 1953, quando se radicou em Angola, é o projeto do Prédio do Sol, bloco residencial sobre pilotis, com painel mural de azulejos (por Manuel Ribeiro de Pavia, 1907-1957). Foi autor do mercado municipal (de delicada escala, 1963), do cine-esplanada Flamingo (entre mangais e praia, com elegante pala em betão, tensionada por cabos, 1963), da nova Aerogare (volume transparente, com extensos panos de grelhagem para ventilação, 1964), e do liceu (sóbrio e bem adaptado ao clima, com fachada ventiladora, de grelhas, de 1966) (ver fig. 2. Prédio Universal; fig. 3. Jardim no Lobito).

5) Moçambique—Lourenço Marques e Beira. Tal como em Angola, a arquitetura moderna afirmou-se aqui gradualmente ao longo dos anos de 1950-60. O Banco Nacional Ultramarino (atual Banco de Moçambique), projeto dos anos de 1956-60, na avenida 25 de Setembro (antiga avenida da República), é obra marcante da afirmação do moderno na área central da cidade, pela dimensão, qualidade e função (por José Gomes Bastos, 1914-91); o Prédio TAP (ou Montepio de Moçambique), na avenida de Dom Luís I (atual Samora Machel), é uma obra muito afirmativa na sua arquitetura alegre e de volumetrias soltas (por Alberto Soeiro, de 1960); o aeroporto de Gago Coutinho, agregado à gare mais antiga, é também uma obra de linhas modernas a assinalar (de 1962-65, com projeto de Cândido Palma de Melo (1922-2003). Refira-se ainda a igreja da Polana, por Nuno Craveiro Lopes (1921-72), de 1962, de característica forma circular de expressão estrutural.

A estruturação do trabalho e do investimento, num território amplo como Moçambique, levou à fixação e afirmação de dois grupos principais de arquitetos, respetivamente na capital, Lourenço Marques, (atual Maputo) e na Beira, segunda cidade em importância. Refiram-se os mais destacados, sem prejuízo de outros com valor, em Lourenço Marques:

— Pancho Guedes (1925-2015), de nome completo Amâncio D'Alpoim Miranda Guedes, tem obra extensa, numa linha profundamente original, mostrando influências mistas corbusianas, da Arte Nova e dos temas da cultura vernácula africana: o edifício de habitação, sobre pilotis, Leão Que Ri (de 1956-58); a Padaria Saipal (1952-54), no bairro do Alto-Maé (avenida General Machado/Guerra

Popular), com uma complexa estrutura curvilínea; fora de Lourenço Marques, assinale-se ainda o prédio Nauticus (ou Hotel Portugal), explorando um gaveto urbano de Nampula, dos meados dos anos 1950, obra influenciada por Frank Lloyd Wright (ver fig. 4. Cooperativa de Habitação);

— João José Tinoco (1924-1983), autor fluente, criativo e claramente seguidor do Movimento Moderno, tem obra pública realizada um pouco por todo o território moçambicano, como o Palácio das Repartições (atual sede do Governo Provincial do Niassa), em Lichinga / Vila Cabral, no norte do país, de cerca de 1962-68, com um delicado corpo de dominante horizontal, avarandado e com grelhas, assente em *pilotis*; na área da capital Tinoco projetou obras como o Hospital de Tuberculosos da Machava (com Alberto Soeiro), ou, de cariz privado, a Fábrica de Relógios "A Reguladora de Moçambique," com interessante modulação em corpos distintos, de ritmada silhueta triangular, e o Entreposto Comercial de Moçambique (com António Matos Veloso, 1921-2013) (Ver fig. 5. Hotel Inhaca; fig. 6. Loja TAP; fig. 7. Aerogare; fig. 8. Prédio em LM).

Na Beira, a Arquitetura Moderna contou com outros autores, fixados na cidade:
— Francisco de Castro (1923-), que aqui trabalhou até 1961 (Hotel Embaixador, de 1956-57, no centro da Beira; Banco Nacional Ultramarino de Quelimane, de 1961-73). A obra mais importante de Francisco de Castro foi projetada em colaboração com Paulo de Melo Sampaio e João Garizo do Carmo: a notável Estação de Caminhos de Ferro da Beira (de 1958-66), obra poderosa, com três componentes volumétricas—um bloco retangular de escritórios, articulado com o elegante corpo curvilíneo de entrada, em abóbada de betão, de ampla transparência, e o sector dos cais;

— Bernardino Ramalhete (1921-), com a elegante e original igreja de Macúti, com grandiosa frontaria revestida por uma grelha modulada, enquadrando a vasta cobertura ligeira e curva, de estrutura metálica, e a torre sineira, destacada do conjunto (de 1961); e o edifício Lopes Duarte, de volumetria fragmentada, dentro das influências *neo-liberty* da arquitetura italiana de então (1968);

— Paulo de Melo Sampaio (1926-1968), com a sede da Associação Comercial da Beira, edificada num gaveto da praça central da cidade, em afirmação de modernidade (1956-57); com o Motel Estoril, com fachada longa e ondulada, na praia do Macúti (de 1959); e, na região de influência, o Cinema Montalto, também em Vila Pery (atual Chimoio), inaugurado em 1963 (ver fig. 9. Cinema Montalto);

— João Afonso Garizo do Carmo (1917-1974), com o cinema São Jorge, na Beira (na praça Almirante Reis, término da avenida da República / Eduardo Mondlane), de longa fachada curva com *brise-soleils* verticais (e painel decorativo por Jorge Garizo do Carmo, artista plástico e irmão), obra de 1953-54; a igreja matriz da Manga, ao estilo Niemeyer, com casca de betão em parábola, e geométrica torre (de 1957); e o inventivo Paço Episcopal de Quelimane (após 1954).

De entre as obras realizadas por autores portugueses não radicados na cidade da Beira, além da aerogare já referida, destaque-se o esplêndido edifício misto de comércio, indústria e habitação, Montegiro, em Quelimane (por Arménio Losa, 1908-88, e Cassiano Barbosa, 1911-98, ambos do Porto, projeto de 1954).

## 4. A Atual Questão do "Património Moderno" na África dos PALOP (Países Africanos de Língua Oficial Portuguesa)

O legado material da fase 1950-75 é vasto, do ponto de vista da organização territorial e urbana, da construção de sistemas edificados, e do desenho dos núcleos construídos. A infraestruturação do conjunto dos espaços dominados e ocupados/urbanizados foi enorme: nunca se construiu na chamada África Portuguesa como nesta fase, de modo tão encadeado, coerente e consistente, tanta infraestrutura, equipamentos, espaços de habitação e de mobiliário, urbano e arquitectónico.

Tal legado de urbanização e edificação dos PALOP, apesar de desfocado e desatualizado em parte pela nova dimensão e conteúdos nacionais dos vários estados independentes (bem como pelo novo surto de expansão urbana acelerada de algumas cidades, como Luanda), não deixa de ser ainda hoje o suporte fundamental da vida conjunta das suas cidades, vilas e demais povoados, para além de sustentar o essencial da sua global estruturação viária, ferroviária e aeroportuária.

Apesar desta realidade, porém, não está ainda plenamente assumida—quer pelos poderes públicos e políticos, quer pelas dimensões sociais e culturais vigentes nos PALOP (aspeto ditado por fatores vários, que não vem ao caso descrever em detalhe)—, a importância e os valores perenes deste legado que é por vezes erroneamente confundido, numa visão ideológica retrógrada, com o seu papel, circunstancial e passado, como agente da colonização.

É igualmente curioso (sobretudo em Angola) que, em termos de conservação e restauro, tem-se por vezes dado mais valor e importância às obras da chamada Arquitetura do Estado Novo, neoclássica, neo-regional e/ou historicista, do que ao legado funcional-racionalista, internacionalista, da Arquitetura Moderna (que tem um fundo conceptual de índole progressista, socializante e igualitário)—numa curiosa inversão identitária (assumindo que os paises atuais devem privilegiar a dimensão da modernidade). Assim, a título de exemplo, em Luanda, enquanto o excessivo e neobarroco Banco de Angola, por Vasco Regaleira (1897-1968), de 1953-56, permanece intacto e aparentemente intocável, o soberbo Mercado Kinaxixe (de 1950-52) foi simplesmente demolido, como "coisa velha, inútil e decadente."

Em todo o caso, um bom sinal de começo de mudança nesta questão da consciência nacional, e cultural-pedagógica, quanto aos valores reais da arquitetura moderna anterior às independências, foi dado em Julho de 2015, pela realização em Luanda, promovido pelo Instituto Nacional de Planeamento e Gestão Urbana de Luanda / IPGUL, de um colóquio internacional dedicado ao tema: "Jornadas de Reflexão sobre Arquitetura do Movimento Moderno—O Movimento Moderno em Angola e no Mundo. Contemporaneidade e os Mecanismos para a sua Preservação."

É de facto necessário e urgente encetar todo um processo de debate e discussão cultural, nas comunidades dos PALOP, nos vários níveis profissionais correlatos e ativos no terreno (arquitetos, investidores, classe política e dirigente, instituições patrimoniais, etc.) para clarificar este conjunto dos valores do passado próximo, mais significativos para o futuro das suas sociedades, as quais estão hoje em profunda mutação e (nova) modernização. No fundo, simplesmente, é necessário saber olhar, aproveitar, trabalhar e aprender—sem falsas peias e iludidos complexos—a partir deste passado-presente material e bem consistente, mas tão próximo como ignorado.

(adaptado do texto publicado em tradução castelhana in *La Modernidad Ignorada. Arquitectura Moderna de Luanda*, coord. Roberto Goycoolea Prado e Paz Núñez Martí, 2011, Madrid, pp.45-63, que por sua vez se baseou no texto "Arquitetura Moderna na África Colonial de Expressão Portuguesa—Algumas Reflexões Aplicadas ao Século XXI—O Contexto, os Valores e a Produção Realizada; Alguns Temas e Conclusões," escrito para o catálogo *Cinco Áfricas—Cinco Escolas* da Representação Portuguesa Oficial à Bienal Internacional de Arquitetura de São Paulo, BIA 2009)

## BIBLIOGRAFIA

campino, José. Entrevista pessoal sobre António Campino. 9 Outubro 2014.

Fernandes, José Manuel. *Geração Africana* [2002]. 2ª ed., Livros Horizonte, 2009.

———, coordenação. *Património de Origem Portuguesa no Mundo—Arquitetura e Urbanismo—África Subsaariana*. Fundação Calouste Gulbenkian, 2010 (edição em inglês *Portuguese Heritage Around The World—Architecture and Urbanism—Subsaharian Africa*, FCG, 2012).

———. "Some Thoughts on the Portuguese Colonial City and Architecture in Post-Colonial Times." *Sociology Study*, vol. 4, nº 10, 2014, pp. 881-890.

———, et al. *Angola no Século XX—Cidades, Território e Arquiteturas, 1925-1975*. Ed. Autores, 2010.

———, et al. *Cabo Verde—Cidades, Território e Arquiteturas*. Ed. Autores, 2014.

———, et al. *João José Tinoco Arquiteturas em África*. Livros Horizonte, 2008.

———, et al. *Moçambique 1875-1975—Cidades, Território e Arquiteturas*. Ed. Autores, 2008.

———, et al. *São Tomé e Príncipe—Cidades, Território e Arquiteturas*. Ed. Autores, 2013.

Milheiro, Ana Vaz, coordenação. *Construir em África 1944-1974. A Arquitetura do Gabinete de Urbanização Colonial em Cabo Verde, Guiné-Bissau, São Tomé e Príncipe, Angola e Moçambique*. ISCTE-IUL, 2013.

———. *Nos Trópicos sem Le Corbusier. Arquitetura Luso-Africana do Estado Novo*. Relógio D´Água, 2012.

Taquelim, Luís. Entrevista pessoal com CV impresso. 24 Março 2015.

JOSÉ MANUEL FERNANDES é Professor Catedrático da Faculdade de Arquitetura da Universidade de Lisboa. José Manuel Fernandes nasceu em Lisboa, em 1953. Formou-se em Arquitetura pela Escola Superior de Belas-Artes de Lisboa (1977) e doutorou-se em História da Arquitetura e Urbanismo pela Faculdade de Arquitetura de Lisboa (1993). Membro do Conselho Editorial da revista Monumentos desde 1994. Primeiro Presidente do DOCOMOMO Ibérico, 1993-97. Conferencista convidado no Departamento de Arquitetura da Universidade Autónoma de Lisboa, e seu Diretor no período 1998/2000. Diretor do Instituto de Arte Contemporânea do Ministério da Cultura em 2001/2003. Coordenador da área da África Subsaariana no estudo *Património de Origem Portuguesa no Mundo—Arquitetura e Urbanismo*, sob orientação de José Mattoso, para a Fundação Calouste Gulbenkian (2007-2010), editado em livro em 2010-2012 (versão em português e em inglês, e disponível online (www.HPIP.org, 2012). Investiga, escreve e publica regularmente sobre temas de História, Arquitetura e Urbanismo.

1. Edifício Mutamba, atual Ministério das Obras Públicas /MOP, Luanda, Angola, pelo arquiteto Vasco Vieira da Costa, 1968 (foto Alexandre Alves Costa, anos 1980)

TRANSNATIONAL AFRICAS    José Manuel Fernandes

2. Prédio Universal, Lobito, Angola, pelo arquiteto Francisco Castro Rodrigues, 1967 (foto arquivo Castro Rodrigues)

3. Jardim no Lobito, Angola, pelo F. Castro Rodrigues (foto arquivo Castro Rodrigues)

4. Cooperativa de Habitação, em Lourenço Marques / Maputo, pelo arquiteto Pancho Guedes, 1975 (foto arquivo Pancho Guedes)

TRANSNATIONAL AFRICAS  José Manuel Fernandes

5. Hotel na Ilha da Inhaca, Moçambique, pelo arquiteto João José Tinoco (foto arquivo José Luís Tinoco)

6. Loja TAP /Transportes Aéreos Portugueses em Lourenço Marques / Maputo, pelo arquiteto João José Tinoco (foto arquivo José Luís Tinoco)

7. Aerogare de Vila Cabral / Lichinga, Moçambique, pelo arquiteto João José Tinoco
(foto arquivo José Luís Tinoco)

8. Cinema Montalto, em Vila Pery / Chimoio, Moçambique, pelo arquiteto Paulo Sampaio, de 1963
(foto bilhete postal, colecção João Loureiro)

9. Prédio Fervereiro e Rocha, de escritórios e com Teatro Avenida, Lourenço Marques / Maputo, pelo arquiteto João José Tinoco (foto arquivo José Luís Tinoco)

## Malangatana: *Viagem Salvadora*, Where Blood and Tears Run

It was mid-August and winter in Mozambique when I called Malangatana on the telephone from Maputo. "Yes, come tomorrow," he said, "between 4:00 and 5:00." I was surprised at how easy it was to talk to him, how he immediately made time for an interview, and then, the near impossibility of finding my way to his house and studio in the Bairro do Aeroporto on the outskirts of the city.[1]

We were driving a rented car with South African plates and were oddly out of place as we pulled into a petrol station to ask for directions. "Malangatana?" Oh yes, they knew him. The artist. A great man. So important, you know, as an artist and during the revolution. We will tell you where. "That way, over there, down that dirt road, turn left, you'll find him. A big red house." And there he was, with his assistant, kind, imposing, generous, ready to answer questions. We sat among his paintings and books, his volumes of poems and prints rolled up in the corner of the room. Everywhere there was evidence of his work and the importance that it has had in defining a particular language of Mozambican art and culture: a mural on the façade of the house, inside on the walls and the ceiling. "You've come at a good time," he said. "I'll show you what I've been doing, and we'll walk through the house so that you can see everything." From the doorway, his assistant nodded his head and then disappeared. After we had sat together for a while, we wandered through the house, opening trunks, looking at his books, entering his studio and talking about his family, of his daughter in Rome. He was thoughtful and laughed easily, open and ready to answer everything that I asked.

Long before his political beliefs during the revolution and the role he played in it were known, Malangatana was recognized as an artist. He began as a ball boy at the Clube de Tênis in Lourenço Marques, where he met mentors who gave him materials and space where he could work. Augusto Cabral, a scientist and artist, gave him paint, brushes and plywood and advised him to "paint what is in your head." This meant the myths that he knew, a spirit world, and an early blend of Western and African imagery. In the early 1960s, Pancho Guedes, the architect who collected his work, was the architect of his house, and with whom Malangatana had a lifelong friendship, gave him a garage to use as his studio with the promise of buying two pictures a month at good prices. Before long, Malangatana had planned an exhibition, and in 1961 he held his first solo exhibition in Lourenço Marques. He had received no academic training, and as a commentator remarked, revealed a genuinely original and creative form in which he featured familiar African themes.[2] From his earliest works, he used the intensity of color, and later red and blue specifically, to show the violence of colonialism and war. In our conversation, he emphasized this: that the traditions of the people among whom he lived, their sorcery, their monsters, and their healers were at the basis of what he felt, saw and put on canvas.

One of the ways to judge the talents and abilities of an artist is to observe the development from the early work to that of maturity. Broadly speaking, Malangatana's work can be divided into four phases. In the first, as a young painter in his twenties in the early 1960s, he painted expressionistic nudes that played with European culture. In some there are religious symbols and attributes of crosses and Bibles, Adam and Eve and the snake, or sleeping figures in blue surrounded by clocks, chairs and windows. These were experiments that extended to surrealistic-like narrative: secret voyages (*A Viagem Secreta*), lost women (*A Menina Perdida*), a note in *Historia da Carta no Chapeu* that ends with 'goodbye forever.'

In an early interview, Betty Schneider, who spoke with Malangatana in 1972, describes this early work as vivid and violent, displayed in heavily carved frames.[3] Claws, sharp teeth and blood are everywhere. In one of his early paintings, a man sits in a dentist's chair pulling a bloody tooth, Malangatana himself. His mother was the village expert at sharpening teeth, a tradition of the time. He watched her as she worked, and later in his paintings embedded sharp aggressive teeth that bite and threaten. From this early experience of pain, and his mother's profession, Malangatana unfurled paintings in which bared teeth of animals and humans repeatedly appear. In some paintings only the teeth are bared, stripped from the body and face.

Hair, too, has its place in these pictures. He likens the long black hair of women to the strings of a guitar, a trope that also appears in his poetry.

"This is your hair,
strings of Xitende
strings of the Xipendane
that Harossi and Tshinguele
play."

Some of his poetry was published in *Black Orpheus*. From his earliest work, Malangatana was quick to experiment in various media: in painting and drawing, poetry and sculpture. He writes:

> "When she dies I shall cut off her
> hair to deliver me from sin
> Woman's hair shall be the blanket
> Over my coffin when another artist
> Calls me to Heaven to paint me…"[4]

Almost immediately, in the second phase in the mid to late 1960s, he made pictures of workers, wizards and diviners. Even his final judgments (*Juizo Final*) are invaded by the monsters from local mythology that became a trademark of his work and increased during the revolution. There are paintings of what he saw before him in the streets: women carrying water, densely packed men in forced labor (*O Trabalho Forçado*). He experienced firsthand the effects of physical repression and, by 1964, as a result of his imprisonment by the PIDE, there are drawings of men leaving for war and inmates packed into prison cells: *Cela 4, Cela Disciplinar I* and *Julgamento de Militantes da Frente de Liberação de Moçambique*; the last, a picture where the accused sit in court surrounded by lawyers and wives. His later paintings and etchings are different from the more Europeanized works of the early 1960s, many of them in the collection of Pancho Guedes. The work that followed, first in the 1970s and after in the third phase, more fully incorporated African mythologies and burst with the energy of creatures that recall birds, crocodiles, and pigs. They lean towards a world of fantasy, a world populated with animals that create a disquieting and ominous cosmology. "A cosmology," writes Júlio Navarro, "from popular culture, animals who move in the night in the secrecy of nocturnal darkness."[5] There is a return to the fire pit, to a blending of the real and unreal. With his use of magical ritual, so familiar to him, Malangatana relied on stories long known, the songs that he had learned as a child, the dances that he and others performed. He took what was familiar from his people and from the tradition that sustained them. This, Malangatana says in our conversation, this reference to his people was just a simple dialogue, full of life, "worth making as an expression of ourselves." But this art, with its African references and its representation of the struggle of Mozambicans, was seen as a threat by the colonial administration.

Finally, from the 1980s until his death, the artist's work retained its densely packed space populated by monsters with sharp teeth, but it was now painted almost entirely in red and blue, with surfaces that by the 1990s were layered with scumbled dry paint: *Relatos do Tempo da Guerra dos 15 Anos* (1992), *Primavera Radiosa* (1995), and *Ritual Nocturna* (1995). These are the works that he showed in retrospectives in Lisbon and around the world. Some of them are stacked against the walls in his house; some are in the Museu Nacional de Arte. Many of the heads in these pictures look like Malangatana himself, his hooded eyes, lips divided into four parts, vertically and horizontally.[6]

By this time he had secured his subject matter and the dense manipulation of space in which figures are jammed together, much as one might see in an urban crowd, or in earlier pictures, in a teeming prison cell. Now the paintings are more freely drawn. They are more erotic, more explicit. Men and women kiss, embrace and copulate; there are erect phalluses, enlarged breasts, bellies and bodies sensually drawn with curving, wandering lines. (*Carta a Gelita* II, 1981). He repeatedly emphasizes ritual and magic, the *missanga* (beadwork) and the importance that family has for him.

Malangatana has always consistently used whatever came to mind, along with personal experience that included the faces of friends and family, birds, especially the owls they feared, lovers, ritual, dance. All of these have fed his work.

When I asked him about his work during the revolution, he replied: "Ah, yes, the revolution," and looked away, though after awhile he began to talk about the cell where he had been imprisoned, densely packed with too many men, a jar used for a toilet. He was quiet. He remembered some of those with whom he had been held, and mentioned that he'd been questioned for seventeen hours at the PIDE headquarters at the Vila Algarve before being hauled off to Sommershild prison.[7] And then he went on to another topic. It was time, he said, to go upstairs, time to look at the enormous collection of his own work that he had retained, along with pieces of Ronga sculpture that are all over the house.[8] Malangatana was, and still is, known for his participation in the revolution as an artist, and he was taken by the PIDE, imprisoned in 1964 and again in 1965. He has spoken about this period at length in an interview recorded in Maputo in 2000 and published online in 2016 after his death. In the interview, he was explicit about his involvement with FRELIMO, his jail sentence, the conditions there and those he knew as part of the movement.[9]

He told the interviewer that he became politically aware at the end of the 1950s through reading the writings of Kwame Nkrumah[10] and the work of Jomo Kenyatta of Kenya on his education. As a participant in the Núcleo de Arte, the local gallery in Lourenço Marques, Malangatana began to exhibit and continued to paint. At about the same time, he met José Craveirinha with whom he began to talk politics.[11] Malangatana had cared for the children of Portuguese colonials, and through them, was exposed to intellectuals whose conversations he heard, but whose ideas he didn't yet fully understand. Some of his friends had already been taken by the PIDE.[12] By 1962, Malangatana was already involved with FRELIMO, and remembers those that he knew: José Craveirinha, Daniel Tomé Magaia, Cristina Tembe with whom he was taken prisoner and others. "We were called to the Vila Algarve," he remembers. "This included Ebenizario Guambo whom I never saw again and many others, many part of the Centro Associativo dos Negros de Moçambique." Although Malangatana couldn't remember the name of the interrogator, he says that he remembers perfectly the three days from June 1 when they were taken prisoner, when he was questioned, how they were removed from the interrogation room, and, after three days, taken in a car that waited for them in the garage and sent to the jail. By this time, Ebenizario Guambo had already been murdered during the interrogation.

He remembers that the reasons for his being questioned had to do with his links to the Quarta Região Militar, and to the fact that he spent some time with the poet Craveirinha in Swaziland, out of Mozambique. Most tellingly, he describes the conditions of the cells, recalling that he was in Cell Four, so called after state mine Number Four where some of the prisoners had worked, the prisoners placed in a cell too small for so many, crawling with bedbugs, fed with bread and oranges thrown onto the cell floor covered with urine, and water provided according to the will of the jailer. His most telling record of this are the drawings that he did of these conditions: *Cell 4* of June 27, 1965; *Calcinados* 1965; *Cela Disciplinar I*, 1965.

Six months later, he was taken prisoner a second time when the lawyers appeared to defend all prisoners. Finally, the PIDE had no further reason to detain them, and Malangatana and the others, who been well represented, were sent home from Machava, the second prison. Because of these lawyers, he says, "we were more or less untouchable." While there was no interrogation, the accused had to wait for six months for a final judgment. "Our work had been to sweep because we were political prisoners who also did some carpentry."

"I never stopped being a part of FRELIMO," he says. "I am honored to say this. None of our group left FRELIMO, the three hundred of us." From this time and after independence, Malangatana worked for various ministers in the government: as head of the department of Artesanatos for the Secretaria de Estado da Cultura, and one of the teachers at the Escola de Estudos Culturais. He was consistently dedicated to teaching young artists, and collaborated with instructors who taught African art history and art at Eduardo Mondlane University where he demonstrated his belief in creating work with links to traditional culture, in his lectures, and by encouraging students to look at the designs used in beadwork and cloth as a basis for their work. In 1984, he established a small school in Matalana for children where they could sing, make pictures in the sand and improvise with the few materials they had.

During all of those years, from the Lisbon coup in 1974 through the formation of the new government in 1975, he painted and drew, and in the aftermath dedicated himself to educating the young. His late work done in the 1990s shows a greater technical skill and a fluency in conveying his message. But it was Malangatana's service to the revolution as an equal, a comrade and an artist who was known internationally that brought him focus and acclaim. The revolution provided him with ways to serve, with searing pictures of a nation under the thumb of oppression, but the exchange went both ways: the revolution elevated his work to an international audience and Malangatana provided the revolution with official designs that the new nation needed: with others, he worked on the flag, a stamp series with reproductions of his work, and his murals.

Malangatana has always drawn from his African roots, his people's personal lives, their resilience in the face of political struggle and violence and repression. The revolution, and those he met during and afterwards, gave his work a distinct focus, one useful for a new African nation and in this sense, his art was in service to a political idea. But the revolution also provided Malangatana with a greater sense of himself as an artist whose work had significance beyond the personal, and a sense of his place in his community. From his earliest work in 1957 to the work that he showed me as we walked through his house, there was development both with and through the revolution. The prison drawings done during his incarceration are reflections from 1965 on a period of hardship. His drawings from the 1970s, even after his Gulbenkian fellowship in Lisbon, continue to show what he had developed earlier in his concerns for ritual and tradition, and the murals that he did in 1985 continue to fill his canvases with what was his signature: many figures, rendered in shorthand, biting, and with widened eyes that look back at the observer. Although he was fully aware of the Western tradition of art, he did not waver from his initial impulse and revealed in his own visual and African inspired language a genuinely creative and African perspective.

To gain a sense of the range and diversity of Malangatana's expression and of the artist as a person, one has to look further. To see him dancing, singing, speaking with his neighbors and family gives an insight into the content and power of his work. In 2007, four years before he died, Isabel Noronha made Ngwenya, o crocodilo, a ninety-minute film that shows his formation in the mythical universe of the Ronga, with comments on his work by the writer Mia Couto. As spectators, we are given an intimate view of his daily life as we see him through the guiding eye of the camera with Noronha as guide. Noronha, a friend of Malangatana's daughter, had seen his drawings and paintings as a child and asks Malangatana why he draws so many bloody monsters, to which the artist replies, "they are my friends and magical beings."

Structurally, the film is a series of fragments that lacks a distinct narrative. The artist appears among the sun and trees, watches children at play, feeds the pigs and goats, and sings for his ancestors. He teaches children to paint and tells us through song how to court a Ronga woman from within the region in which Malangatana grew up. There is *curandismo* and magic in the appearance of chicken feathers, ashes and symbols of wizards. There is the legend of how the Ngwenya came to Maputo as crocodile eaters and the origin of his ancestors. Early in the film we walk through his studio, see his books and sculpture, and the murals high on the walls of the house. He reads from his poems, and goes outside where we see more murals on the red exterior of the house.

At the center of the film are comments by those who have shared the artist's life and those who know him best as they locate him in the close circle who recount his past: his brother, family members and teachers comment on how he learned to play the guitar, what he was like as a child, how he drew flowers and monsters from an early age. As he listens to these personal stories, Malangatana laughs in agreement and looks on as they continue.

In an interview on camera, Mia Couto relates the effects that Malangatana's work had on his writing, how each trace of color prompted him to think, to dream and to describe *mestiçagem*. He reads from his own work, *O beijo da palavrinha* (*The Kiss of the Word*), which was published in 2006 with illustrations by Malangatana, and one that links the writer and artist in a search for distinct aspects of Mozambican culture, the desire for well-being among the diversity of the country formulated with a dreamlike language.[13] Both, Couto says, seek a language that is their own, a Mozambican idiom specific to the African myths of the country. Malangatana's cover for the text is not just an illustration of the story. "Metam a menina no barco numa viagem salvadora," it reads. Put the girl in the boat on a voyage that will save her, a metaphor itself for Malangtana's life, a voyage that began in his immersion in Ronga culture that took him far away, to Lisbon and other cities where he exhibited his work.

(Elsewhere, and years earlier in an interview in *Jornal de Letras*, Couto observed that in the work those tortured figures with their infinite bitterness are images created by us, and finally against us. "The monsters, that we thought were extinct, are reactivated by Malangatana's pencil. A fear that we thought was asleep resurges. We are at the mercy of these visions, assaulted by the fragility of our visual representation of the universe." This artist who invokes chaos, he says, undoes our certainties and calls for us to find order beyond the picture.) [14]

In the final scene of the film, Malangatana opens a suitcase filled with magical things used to call up the spirits. He holds each object carefully and turns each one over in his hand. As he does so, he thanks his ancestors who have provided him with imagination and ability, and those, along with his friend and patron Pancho Guedes, who have made it possible for him to find himself among other artists. Those ancestors have inspired him, and he closes by saying: Kanimambo! Thank you in Malangatana's native tongue. He could as easily close his story and my questions about his life and work by referring to the 'viagem salvadora,' the title that he gave to the illustration to Mia Couto's story, and the objective that he held close, both for himself and all Mozambicans who traveled with him on the road to independence and nationhood.

NOTES

1. The visit to Malangatana's studio and the interview took place on August 11, 2008.

2. Eugenio Lemos. *Retrospectiva de Malangatana Valente* Ngwenya. (Maputo: Secretaria de Estado de Cultura, 1986).

3. Betty Schneider, "Malangatana of Mozambique," African Arts. 5, no. 2 (1972): 40-45.

4. Schneider notes that while African women generally cover their hair, Malangatana painted whatever entered his imagination, even though this was not in keeping with the realism of women's practice. Betty Schneider "Malangatana of Mozambique," *African Arts*," African Arts. 5, no. 2 (1972): 40-45. The lines of poetry are from *Black Orpheus*, in Ulli Beier. *Contemporary Art in Africa* (London: Pall Mall Press, 1968).

5. Júlio Navarro. *Malangatana* (Lisbon: Lisboa: Caminho, 1998), 206.

6. Other artists, such as Inácio Matsinhe, use the same division of the lips. He claims that the swollen lips of his paintings are divided in four parts which means that the people in those territories [Mozambique, Angola and Guinea, that is, the people oppressed

by the Portuguese] for five hundred years would not speak out, "so I portray their suffering, their inability of speaking out in those lips divided into four." In Inácio Matsinhe. *Transformei-me em Tartaruga para Resistir* (Lisbon: Coleccão Artistas de Moçambique, 1975)1. Edward Alpers argues that this was an image shared with Malangatana and the sculptor Chissano. In Edward A. Alpers,"Representation and Historical Conscious in the Art of Modern Mozambique. *Canadian Journal of African Studies* 22. No. 1 (1988): 88.

7. My information here comes from the interview with Malangatana. As a political prisoner during colonialism, he was an object of various actions meant to 'reconcile and purify' those who had been active in Frelimo. The trial has not been well studied, although Malangatana mentions it here. He was sent to the northern province of Nampula to work on various social and cultural projects in some of the villages there.

8. Ronga (or XiRonga) is a south-eastern Bantu language spoken south of Maputo, and the dialect spoken by Malangatana. Ronga is also used to describe the form of sculpture made in the area. Both Malangatana and Craveirinha speak of Ronga as part of their local culture, and a source of the meanings of their work.

9. See Batalho de Caçadores 1891 http://bcac1891.blogspot.com/2016/01/entrevista-malangatana-valente-ngwenya.html. Accessed May 30, 2017.

10. Kwame N'krumah was the first prime minister and president of Ghana and led the country to independence from Britain in 1957. Malangatana may be referring to Nkrumah's book *Africa Must Unite* (New York: Praeger, 1963). Nkrumah's administration was socialist and nationalist.

11. For an analysis of the links between Malangatana and Craveirinha see Carmen Lucia Tindo Ribeiro Secco, "Craveirinha e Malangatana: cumplicidade e correspondência entre as artes." *Scripta* 6, no 12 (2003): 350-68.

12. The PIDE, (Polícia Internacional e de Defesa do Estado) was the secret police under Salazar's Estado Novo. In Mozambique the PIDE was housed at the Vila Algarve in Lourenço Marques, and was used by the regime as a repressive force against any opposition considered to be enemies of the Portuguese colonial administration.

13. For a critical review of the narrative of O beijo da palavrinha as an example of the preservation of culture and a diverse society see: http://ricardoriso.blogspot.com/2008/01/mia-couto-o-beijo-da-palavrinha.html. He notes that "Mia Couto conduz-nos ao interior de sua Moçambique, a um lugar onde *vivia* uma menina que nunca vira o mar, e para enfatizar a distância da localidade do litoral, afirma: viviam numa aldeia tão interior que acreditavam que o rio que ali passava não tinha nem fim nem foz." Accessed May 1, 2017.

14. Mia Couto, Depoimento inserido na reportagem "Malangatana Valente Ngwenya: Relação Fiel e Verdadeira", organizada por Rodrigues da Silva. (*Jornal de Letras* 663 13 a 26 de março de 1996):12-13.

MEMORY HOLLOWAY is a member of the Executive Board of the Center for Portuguese Studies and Culture at the University of Massachusetts Dartmouth where she has taught modern and contemporary art, including the art and architecture of Portugal and Brazil. She has organized exhibitions, has worked as an art critic for *The Australian* and the Melbourne *Age,* and was commissioner for Australia at the São Paulo Biennial. She has published on Iberian art, including *Making Time: Picasso's Suite 347* and *Open Secrets: Paula Rego.* She has delivered papers at conferences in Lisbon, Bahia and the UK, and holds a Ph.D. in art history from the Courtauld Institute, London University.

Malangatana and the author at his studio, Bairro de Aeroporto, Mozambique, August 11, 2008.

MARIO PEREIRA

# Malangatana, Nationalist Movements and Modern African Art in Mozambique: An Introduction to "Artes Plásticas e Movimento Nacionalista em Moçambique"

Malangatana Ngwenya (1936-2011) was the most important painter from Mozambique and one of the most prominent artists of his generation from Africa. His celebrated artistic career, beginning in the late 1950s, spanned six decades in a country that experienced constant, intense and profound historical change. Malangatana and the arresting, colorful images he created were integral, active participants in these transformations. Indeed, the figure of Malangatana and the power of his art, especially his paintings, enjoyed the rare ability to communicate ideas, dreams, emotions and meanings far beyond the studio space and international art galleries. He touched so many so deeply that Mia Couto could describe him, after his death, as the soul of the country.

Despite (or perhaps because of) his artistic greatness, which was recognized almost immediately in Mozambique, his instant fame, which quickly spread to a number of other African countries, his prolific artistic production in a variety of media over the course of a lifetime, which was collected and exhibited throughout Africa, Europe and America, critical art historical and theoretical scholarship on Malangatana and his images remains relatively underdeveloped.[1] When the David Winton Bell Gallery at Brown University held a major retrospective exhibition of his work in 2002, it provided visitors with the unique experience of viewing in the United States representative works from throughout Malangatana's career.[2] The breathtaking exhibition featured canonical early works, such as *25 de Setembro*, *Juízo Final* and *Monstros Grandes Devorando Monstros Pequenos*, and the presence of the charismatic artist at the opening. (Figs. 1 & 2) But a lack of critical scholarship on the artist, and on twentieth-century art in Mozambique in general, meant that a number of complex issues could only be indicated, not interrogated.[3]

The transcription, editing and publication of "Artes Plásticas e Movimento Nacionalista em Moçambique" is intended to make available the kind of documentation necessary for the writing of a critical, theoretical history of art in Mozambique.[4] This essay likewise facilitates a new approach to some of Malangatana's more difficult work, such as his prison notebooks, which have been neglected in favor of his more celebratory decorative and mural works. It also provides a new understanding of the internationalism he practiced in workshops in Africa, the United States and elsewhere.

This study was completed by Malangatana and Paulo Soares in 1982 for the Centro de Estudos Africanos (CEA) of the Universidade Eduardo Mondlane, but was never published.[5] The CEA was one of the principal centers of intellectual activity in Mozambique in the 1970s and 1980s, and its research director, Ruth First, was brutally killed by a letter bomb in her office there on August 17, 1982. The research activities of the CEA were often inspired by political ideas and undertaken in the pursuit of political goals. The article might have been undertaken soon after Malangatana returned from Nampula to Maputo in the early 1980s when he began a new period in his life. The valuable study was later copied by the Angolan intellectual and nationalist, Mário Pinto de Andrade, who was an affiliated researcher of the CEA and who taught a course there with Maria do Céu Carmo Reis on "Ideologias de Libertação Nacional" in 1985. Mário Pinto de Andrade was committed to collecting and preserving historical documents related to the nationalist and liberation movements of Lusophone Africa, and it was in his remarkable archive, now housed in the Fundação Mário Soares in Lisbon, that I came across the article by Malangatana and Paulo Soares.[6]

The typescript study published here for the first time focuses on the conditions of artistic production in colonial Mozambique and the relation of this art to anticolonial sentiment, nationalist ideas and liberation movements during the 1950s and 1960s. We learn much about the working conditions of artists in rural and urban settings; the training and exploitation of artists; the role of patrons, the market, cultural associations, exhibition practices and cultural expression as a form of anticolonial resistance. But the most important passages are those that address the relationship between art and nationalism, modern art and colonialism, and the emergence of modern African art. The essay is a valuable source for understanding how modern African art in Mozambique emerged in the 1960s as a self-consciously national culture that was galvanized by anticolonial resistance, nationalist aspirations and liberation movements. It likewise provides evidence that integrates the history of art in Mozambique into broader art historical developments throughout Africa during this crucial period of African independence and liberation.

Throughout the 1960s Malangatana's paintings were celebrated as exemplary of modern African art by an influential group of critics, curators and patrons—Ulli Beier in Nigeria, Julian Beinart in South Africa, Pancho Guedes in Mozambique and Frank McEwen in Southern Rhodesia—who pioneered theoretical approaches to contemporary African art.[7] This study, however, looks at this extraordinarily rich artistic production from a different perspective. It documents the cultural, intellectual, political and social considerations behind the artistic and aesthetic choices made by artists as they critically engaged with colonialism, modernity and tradition to create powerful images which "profoundly shocked the entire ideology and values of colonialism."[8] The authors are careful to emphasize the political implications of these kinds of choices and the very real dangers involved in making them. These were artists who endured brutal fascist repression because they were committed to fulfilling their role as the "'collective voice [of the people],' mobilizing anticolonial consciousness, denouncing racist exploitation and oppression, and maintaining a continuous clandestine political activity."[9]

Indeed, this essay features a number of the critical and theoretical categories that would later be used to define modern African art in the scholarly literature.[10] For instance, in this essay, we see how art emerged as an independent cultural practice through the activities of the Núcleo de Arte, artistic workshops and private patronage, and how this nascent artistic freedom, so vividly expressed in the works by Malangatana, Abdias Muchanga, and Alberto Chissano, resulted in the expression of individual subjectivity and critical self-awareness. These developments led to the rapid appearance of an incisive, critical voice that analyzed and condemned colonialism; rehabilitated and affirmed African subjectivity, culture and identity; and assessed and commented on the current social, political and economic situation in Mozambique and throughout Africa. This was achieved by selectively appropriating techniques, expressive strategies and media associated with European modernism and intentionally rejecting Western artistic values and aesthetic principles in order to fashion new models of cultural and artistic expression that arose from within African culture, history and subjectivity and would come to constitute a national culture.

NOTES

I would like to thank Alda Costa, Delinda Collier and Drew Thompson for their helpful comments on the text. I would also like to thank the David Winton Bell Gallery at Brown University for generous permission to reproduce the two photographs of the exhibition installation and opening and the Visual Resource Center at the University of Massachusetts Dartmouth for kindly scanning the negatives.

1. However, see Memory Holloway, "Malangatana: *Viagem Salvadora*, Where Blood and Tears Run," in this issue.

2. *Malangatana: A 40-Year Survey of a Contemporary Mozambican Artist*, David Winton Bell Gallery, Brown University, curated by Vesela Sretenovic, April 13, 2002—May 27, 2002.

3. In 1982, when Malangatana and Paulo Soares wrote this essay, there were no museums to collect art and no culture of museum curatorship in Mozambique. At the time, socially-conscious art and artists were to be integrated with the life of the people and, by extension, art was considered property of the nation. However, Malangatana would participate in the creation of the Museu Nacional de Arte, which would be opened to the public in 1989.

4. For the development of art in Mozambique, see Alda Costa, *Arte em Moçambique: entre a construção da nação e o mundo sem fronteiras* (1932-2004), Lisbon: Verbo, 2013; Alda Costa, *Arte e artistas em Moçambique: diferentes gerações e modernidades*, Maputo: Marimbique, 2014.

5. The essay was written during a difficult period in the history of post-independence Mozambique. In the early 1980s Mozambique would be engaged in a series of costly and damaging wars against Rhodesia (Zimbabwe) and then South Africa, which would be followed by a protracted civil war against RENAMO. These conflicts helped undermine FRELIMO's economic, political and social policies, which included the controversial re-education camps and the forced removal of people from urban centers. However, FRELIMO likewise attempted during these years to define a national culture that would align with its practices, policies and strategies and this essay must be situated within this intellectual and political climate. See Edward Alpers, "Representation and Historical Consciousness in the Art of Modern Mozambique," *Canadian Journal of African Studies / Revue Canadienne des Études Africaines*, Vol. 22, No. 1 (1988), pp. 73-94.

6. Malangatana Ngwenya and Paulo Soares, "Artes Plásticas e Movimento Nacionalista em Moçambique," typescript dated 1982, Fundação Mário Soares, Arquivo Mário Pinto de Andrade, 04331.008.004.

7. See, Ulli Beier, *Contemporary Art in Africa*, London: Pall Mall Press, 1968. For brief discussion of these figures, see Chika Okeke-Agulu, *Postcolonial Modernism: Art and Decolonization in Twentieth-Century Nigeria*, Durham: Duke University Press, 2015.

8. Paulo Soares, "Biografia de Malangatana Valente Ngwenya," typescript dated January 8, 1984, Fundação Mário Soares, Arquivo Mário Pinto de Andrade, 04331.008.001.

9. Malangatana Ngwenya and Paulo Soares, "Artes Plásticas e Movimento Nacionalista em Moçambique," p. 145

10. See, for example, the landmark exhibition catalogue, *The Short Century: Independence and Liberation Movements in Africa, 1945-1994*, edited by Okwui Enwezor, New York: Prestel, 2001.

MARIO PEREIRA (Ph.D., Brown University) is Editor of *Portuguese Literary & Cultural Studies* and Executive Editor of Tagus Press in the Center for Portuguese Studies and Culture at the University of Massachusetts Dartmouth.

Fig. 1. Gallery Installation, Malangatana: A 40-Year Survey of a Contemporary Mozambican Artist, David Winton Bell Gallery, Brown University, April, 2002
(Courtesy of the David Winton Bell Gallery, Brown University).

Fig. 2. Malangatana at the opening of Malangatana: A 40-Year Survey of a Contemporary Mozambican Artist, David Winton Bell Gallery, Brown University, April, 2002
(Courtesy of the David Winton Bell Gallery, Brown University).

```
ARTES PLÁSTICAS E

MOVIMENTO NACIONALISTA

EM MOÇAMBIQUE
```

1. BREVES INDICADORES DOS ANOS '50
2. RESISTÊNCIA E LUTA CULTURAL
3. A ALTERAÇÃO DO ESTATUTO DO ARTESÃO
    o artesão rural
    o artesão nos centros urbanos
4. LUTA POLITICA E CONSCIÊNCIA NACIONAL
            NO MOVIMENTO URBANO
5. ACÇÃO CULTURAL E ARTES PLÁSTICAS
            EM LOURENÇO MARQUES
6. AS ARTES PLÁSTICAS NO DESENVOLVIMENTO
            SOCIAL

MALANGATANA NGWENYA
PAULO SOARES

MAPUTO - 1982
U.E.M.

## Artes Plásticas e Movimento Nacionalista em Moçambique (Contribuição para uma reflexão dos anos '50 e '60 em Moçambique)[*]

Do cartão de indígena ao Bilhete de Identidade da Província de Moçambique, ocorrem inúmeras mudanças políticas e sociais, e decerto económicas, que demarcam duas práticas coloniais diversas, embora na evolução do mesmo sistema de exploração colonial.

Do Moçambique do indígena ao Moçambique do autóctone, houve toda uma luta passada entre reivindicações, greves e manifestações, reivindicando iguais direitos para a força principal, como se considerava então o indígena, o mais numeroso e explorado grupo, de uma sociedade que lhe negava o mais elementar direito cívico.

As mudanças ocorridas depois da abolição do Estatuto do Indígena operam-se já sob pressão do início da luta armada, mas subordinadas aos mesmos princípios políticos do colonial-fascismo português, de integração de Moçambique no Espaço Português.

A integração do indígena no estatuto de assimilado começa a ser tónica dominante da política colonial, particularmente depois de 1956, preparando a abolição do trabalho forçado como modo de produção dominante do Estado Colonial. Este processo veio polarizar o desenvolvimento da consciência nacionalista, pela promoção de novos sectores sociais à classe intermédia de assimilados, já então reivindicando a independência nacional. Tratava-se, no entanto, para o Estado Colonial, de travar essa tomada de consciência, passando da política de despersonalização cultural para a de integração ou passagem do indígena a português.

Em 1955, Silva Cunha, Ministro do Ultramar de Salazar, afirmava: "[d]ado o primeiro passo no caminho da evolução, o africano deve ser cuidadosamente amparado e guiado, carinhosamente protegido, no moral e no físico, até ao termo da evolução que tem de ser o seu completo aportuguesamento."[1]

O primeiro passo teria sido a prossecução de uma sistemática política de despersonalização, levada a cabo nas décadas anteriores de implantação de trabalho forçado em toda a colónia. A integração, ou assimilação progressiva das

---

[*] Fundação Mário Soares, Arquivo Mário Pinto de Andrade, 04331.008.004

populações colonizadas, não passou sempre, como diria Amílcar Cabral, de uma tentativa, mais ou menos violenta, de negar a cultura dos povos em questão.[2]

Como é que as mudanças efectuadas na década de '50 se fizeram sentir ao nível do estatuto social do artesão e artista produtor de imagens?—Nota-se com efeito, desde esta altura, um esforço do Estado Colonial em promover indígenas ao estatuo de "artistas;"—Como trabalhava o artista subordinado ao chibalo e o que na mesma altura colocava as suas obras nos salões de exposição da burguesia colonial? Como era explorado o artesão rural e o urbano? Estas são algumas questões que procuraremos abordar, tendo presente o movimento nacionalista em curso, e que se enraíza historicamente na secular resistência à ocupação estrangeira, opondo-se não só a ela, como às diferentes formas de apoio que o colonialismo obteve de diversas forças sociais internas. Até que ponto a política de despersonalização cultural se fez sentir entre os artistas de então? Como neles se mantiveram acesos os ideais de independência cultural negados e combatidos pelo colonialismo? Como se manifestaram como voz colectiva do povo?

A necessidade de compreensão global do fenómeno artístico à escala nacional levou-nos a ter de fazer uma pequena reflexão sobre os aspectos económicos e sociais mais relevantes dos anos '50 em Moçambique, apresentando alguns indicadores de âmbito geral, que nos apontam para a necessidade de estudos mais aprofundados caracterizarem este período fundamental na história recente de Moçambique.

### 1. Breves Indicadores dos Anos '50

Muito embora nos demais países africanos e vizinhos de Moçambique o direito à independência política dos povos colonizados fosse uma reivindicação tornada comum e reconhecida nos fóruns internacionais após a II Guerra Mundial, o projecto colonial português mantinha-se determinado a desenvolver-se contra o movimento da história.

Com efeito, em 1951, a fim de alcançar um estatuto jurídico que lhe permitisse o acesso à Organização das Nações Unidas, o Governo de Salazar opera a mudança nominal de Colónia para Província Ultramarina. Procurava assim escamotear a luta interna e internacional contra a continuidade do colonialismo e manutenção institucionalizada do trabalho forçado.

Beneficiando em relação às demais potências coloniais de uma estabilidade económica e social interna que lhe advinha do facto de não ter participado na Grande Guerra, o regime de Salazar vai então começar a desenvolver, de uma forma concertada e em todo o espaço territorial da colónia, a sua acção política assente na racionalização máxima da exploração da força de trabalho pelo meio compulsivo do chibalo, trabalho forçado ou migratório, como forma principal de obter a mais-valia absoluta da pilhagem colonial.

Se, até 1940, Moçambique não constituía um espaço económico coeso, em que a manutenção da Companhia Majestática de Moçambique, com sede na Beira, era um testemunho da antiga incapacidade de exploração de toda a colónia pelo capitalismo português, o fim do contrato desta Companhia coincide com a realização no mesmo ano da Exposição do Império Colonial Português, em que foram estudados em pormenor os recursos naturais e humanos das colónias, com vista à sua máxima exploração.

Muito embora a Guerra fizesse adiar a concretização dos planos coloniais, a estabilidade do regime de Salazar do pós-guerra vai permitir que então ele se lance em novas formas de colonização.

Até final dos anos '50, a presença de capital estrangeiro é relativamente reduzida em Moçambique, o capital português é fraco, e o recurso aos capitais acumulados e investidos localmente é insuficiente para se garantir altos índices de exploração assentes quase que exclusivamente na exploração da força de trabalho compulsivamente integrada na economia de mercado, produtora de bens exportados em bruto ou semi-elaborados.

Procura-se, no decorrer da década, a par da manutenção do modo de exploração tradicional do chibalo, alterar a natureza do sistema colonial, de colónia de exploração simples dos recursos naturais, para colónia de povoamento, que permitisse a continuidade da dominação colonial. O número de colonos duplica durante a década para cerca de 100 mil, acelerando-se o desenvolvimento urbano e os grandes projectos dos colonatos agrícolas e concessões a grandes proprietários e latifundiários colonos, das melhores terras retiradas aos camponeses colonizados.

Com fraca capacidade de investimento em infra-estruturas que elevassem os índices de exploração, o Estado Colonial chamava a si a responsabilidade de assegurar racionalmente a utilização da força de trabalho indígena, como mediador entre os vários interesses internos e regionais do desenvolvimento capitalista da zona, determinando reservas de grandes áreas populacionais não só para as culturas obrigatórias, como para grandes companhias e para exportação de mão-de-obra para países vizinhos, mantendo internamente o trabalho compulsivo com ordenados irrisórios e um constante fluxo de migração que atingia então a cifra de cerca de 250 mil emigrantes (mais de 1/10 da população masculina activa),[3] permitido pela violência e elevada exploração operada debaixo do regime da palmatória e chibalo.

As importações, compostas em grande parte pelos produtos manufacturados, passavam sempre o valor da exportação e, no fim de 1958, o défice da balança comercial era compensada pela entrada invisível proveniente do comércio em trânsito, pelos retornos dos trabalhadores migrantes e pelo turismo.

A produção agrícola e a fraca indústria de transformação eram dominadas por um pequeno número de grandes sociedades, centradas na zona norte de Moçambique, que produziam a quase totalidade dos produtos comerciais agrícolas e que era, contudo, a mais pobre. Somente as grandes sociedades estavam em posição de se defrontarem com os fortes investimentos iniciais requeridos para a economia de plantação.[4]

As alterações políticas e económicas introduzidas no decorrer da década, cujo aprofundamento não cabe no âmbito deste trabalho, são significativas não só por se oporem a uma constante luta reivindicativa, económica, social e política nacionalista, entremeada de greves e massacres como o de 1956 no porto de Lourenço Marques, como também porque testemunham a forma como o sistema colonial fez participar diversos sectores sociais internos, antes nacionalistas e hostis ao regime de Salazar, no "novo" projecto colonial.

Conseguindo o apoio activo de toda a burguesia colonial, silenciando pela repressão fascista os sectores coloniais adversos ao regime, como democratas, liberais e colonos pobres, proporcionando-lhes estatuto privilegiado e discriminatório pelo simples facto de serem brancos, o Estado Colonial procurou ainda o apoio da então diminuta classe média (intermédia) de mulatos e assimilados, que exercem, desde o início do século, um inegável papel de liderança política e representatividade dos largos sectores sociais de indígenas.

Colocada à prova a consciência nacionalista e independentista das diversas camadas sociais moçambicanas, perante as regalias obtidas da exploração colonial sobre a grande massa populacional, continuam elementos provenientes desta, despersonalizados pelo processo de integração como assimilados, a integrar-se no escalão "civilizado" como elementos servis do sistema.

É neste contexto de promoção do estatuto de indígena a assimilado, que se mantém como uma constante em vários séculos de colonização, embora operado de forma diversa desde o tráfico mercantil, e que representa uma luta que no decorrer deste século se manteve acesa nos órgãos de informação africanos "em prol dos interesses dos naturais das colónias," que salientamos a estratégia da colonização na década de '50, com vista a aumentar a classe média que comportava, em 1950, menos de cinco mil assimilados para seis milhões de habitantes.

Estratégia global de integração de Moçambique no Espaço Português, realizado ao nível económico na prossecução dos Planos de Fomento, a integração opera-se ao nível cultural de forma bastante contraditória, porque assentando em métodos despersonalizantes do fascismo, apoiados pela acção evangelizadora da missão cristã, em especial a católica, que por Concordata de 1940 recebeu a função de educar os indígenas.

Preparando a inevitável abolição do Estatuto do Indígena, que viria a acontecer em 1962, o Estado Colonial provoca o crescimento social dos assimilados, bem como a sua importância relativa no quadro dos servidores do regime, de forma a criar um grupo intermediário maior, que se opusesse à grande massa da população, promovendo os que mais servis apoiavam o regime.

1956 será talvez o ano de viragem daquilo que poderemos considerar política de despersonalização, à de integração com vista ao completo aportuguesamento. Ao nível cultural, a agudização da luta de classes é acompanhada por diversas realizações que culminam na visita do Presidente Craveiro Lopes, que vem testemunhar as realizações operadas no quadro da colonização, dando realce à promoção do indígena, posto que estava concluída a "pacificação;" pela integração maciça de todos os indígenas na economia de mercado colonial, através da força coerciva e tentativa de destruição de todas as formas populares de expressão cultural, em que assentou a política de despersonalização, porque eram tidas como formas de resistência ao colonialismo.

## 2. Resistência e Luta Cultural

Com uma incidência progressivamente mais forte que nas décadas anteriores, o final dos anos '40 no Sul até meio dos anos '50 no Norte, são marcados por ondas sucessivas de repressão contra as mais significativas manifestações culturais tradicionais. Considerava-se que elas interditavam a participação voluntária dos indígenas no contrato ou na cultura obrigatória.

Estado de violência institucionalizada, através do trabalho forçado, o regime colonial fascista tudo faz por destruir toda a manifestação cultural e social que se desenvolva fora da sua tutela paternalista, porque, de qualquer forma, exprimem a vitalidade de valores de culturas que se opõem aos princípios da colonização, que se nega a existência, para serem considerados por usos e costumes de povos selvagens que era necessário evangelizar.

Administração Colonial, Missão, Cabo de Terra e Sipaio, tornam-se uma intricada rede contra todas as manifestações culturais populares, para se imporem os valores da civilização ocidental-cristã. Das cerimónias de casamento às fúnebres, passando pelos ritos de iniciação ou qualquer tipo de prece religiosa, todas as instituições são alvo de uma luta cerrada, tendente à destruição pelo completo aportuguesamento.

O saque e a destruição dos valores culturais materiais de mais significação histórica e social, a destruição de máscaras, trajes rituais e cerimoniosos, utensílios diversos, de instrumentos de caça, a forjas, utensílios musicais ou cabaças de curandeiros, visava não só a eliminação dos valores materiais em si, mas dos valores mais profundos que eles representavam.

No vazio cultural aberto pela violência fascista de tal repressão instalam-se os valores de submissão das missões. Em 1956, faz-se a alteração dos programas do ensino rudimentar, para ensino de adaptação, já no quadro da promoção do indígena a assimilado.

Com os cursos orientados para Portugal, a função da igreja era "doutrinar os filhos dos nativos moçambicanos negros, assegurando assim ao governo uma população dócil e leal a Portugal,"[5] e "todo o sistema do ensino africano é delineado para produzir não cidadãos, mas servos de Portugal."[6]

Em 1960, porém, somente 3/100 das crianças frequentavam a escola, e o número de assimilados era ainda de poucos milhares. O Estatuto do Indígena demarcava então claramente o sector social "moderno" do "tradicional." A prática anti-cultural do Estado Colonial operava-se no quadro da arregimentação de trabalhadores forçados e, amiúde, a prática de manifestações culturais era o pretexto para se fazer a contratação forçada de mais um grupo de indígenas para o chibalo.

A viagem do Presidente Craveiro Lopes a Moçambique, em 1956, é acompanhada de uma série de reformas administrativas e acções políticas de indubitável alcance no quadro colonial e social. Procurando consolidar o poder colonial, em altura de grande movimentação internacional anticolonial (Cimeira de Bandung, etc.), procurando agradar ao capital ocidental, pela apresentação de uma pretensa acção civilizatória preocupada na promoção do indígena mais do que na exploração económica. O poder colonial defrontava-se, porém, com profundos conflitos sociais derivados da maciça expulsão de camponeses, para as melhores terras serem entregues aos colonos recém-chegados, tentando reter a força de trabalho no campo subordinada aos régulos, que actuavam como intermediários directos do poder colonial. Através da sua acção conseguia-se envolver toda a força de trabalho masculina em seis meses de contrato ou à cultura obrigatória, restando aos demais a emigração e o retorno de bens e capital para na colónia pagarem o imposto ou a cantina.

Nos centros urbanos, a repressão é patenteada pelo massacre do porto de Lourenço Marques, para além de inúmeros outros casos dispersos de formas individuais de resistência perante o patrão e a ocupação estrangeira. Não podemos deixar de referir a acção associativista de várias instituições de carácter cultural e recreativo onde se desenvolviam acções políticas e de consciencialização anticolonial, pela sua acção no campo cultural, de onde sobressaiu *a voz colectiva dos poetas*, que decerto não deixou de ter influência ao nível das artes plásticas.

É significativo que tal viagem seja anunciada pelo *Diário da Manhã* de Lisboa, nos seguintes termos de título:[7] "Craveiro Lopes—anunciada ida a Moçambique e acção cultural com exposição de artes plásticas," e indicando que "a próxima visita do chefe de Estado à Província Ultramarina de Moçambique vai certamente dar ensejo à efectivação de vários actos da vida espiritual, significativos das manifestações próprias daquela parcela de Portugal, ou expressivas das realizações metropolitanas."

Outras realizações de "acção cultural" marcam a referida visita, como a inauguração do "Palácio da Rádio e Emissor de 10 Quilovátios"—apresentado como então o mais potente de África,[8] ou do Museu de Nampula, concebido para projectar uma imagem internacional de preocupação e interesse "científico" pela promoção cultural do indígena, e de facto repositório de alguns dos bens materiais, de indubitável importância cultural, objecto de saque violento pelas administrações coloniais, na sua política despersonalizante.[9] Se o primeiro representa a utilização de um potente meio de difusão da ideologia e valores da colonização, o segundo significa os resultados da luta cultural travada para impor o cristianismo, em que a oferta do "cofre de prata" na Ilha de Moçambique, pela Comunidade Maometana, é a outra face local da submissão alcançada.

De facto, em 1955/56, passa-se no norte de Moçambique o que acontecera em 1949 no sul: com violência são retirados os restantes bens culturais materiais, que mais profundamente ligavam os povos colonizados às suas raízes históricas e culturais. Todas as povoações foram percorridas, na altura do imposto, pelos administradores e seus sipaios, extorquindo tais bens para o Museu de Nampula e venda a coleccionadores de todo o mundo capitalista.

A importância que salientamos para a exposição de artes plásticas realizada então em Lourenço Marques é a de aí se ter imposto a presença de "artistas" recém-promovidos do estatuto de indígena para tal efeito. Todos eles haviam frequentado missões na aldeia, confluído para a cidade (Maputo ou Beira) à procura de serviço doméstico e aí revelado interesse por desenho. Importante o facto de o "mecenas" que lhes pagou aulas com o mestre Frederico Aires ter sido o próprio Governador Geral da Colónia.

## 3. A Alteração do Estatuto do Artesão

### 3.1. O Artesão Rural

No meio camponês colonizado, o artesão é o próprio camponês produtor de bens materiais diversos, muitos deles de indubitável valor artístico e cultural. É o camponês que é levado para o chibalo ou contrato e as suas "qualidades são descobertas" por algum administrador, missionário, comerciante ou simples colono, que o contrata para realizar, no pátio do quintal, trabalhos diversos para utilização doméstica (peças de mobiliário ou de cozinha), decorativa (estatuetas de madeira, peças de torno, figuras humanas ou animais e miniaturas diversas), ou mesmo obras de propaganda ideológica (bustos de dirigentes fascistas ou personalidades portuguesas, cristãs, terços religiosos, etc.).

O primor técnico e estético alcançado amiúde nessas obras, se testemunha um desenvolvimento técnico e artístico secular em tradições culturais ricas, deve-se também à especialização progressiva dos artesãos em determinados modelos preferidos pelos coleccionadores e patrões coloniais, bem como à canalização das capacidades criativas sufocadas, para o recurso único do aperfeiçoamento de técnicas de produção de imagens padronizadas, transformando a sua arte em artesanato.

Se as normas religiosas e étnicas, e os respectivos princípios estéticos, dominavam a produção artística anterior, agora tomam peso as normas e princípios estéticos do colonizador, na produção de imagens, sobretudo ao nível da escultura.

Arte produzida para as elites colonizadoras, turistas das colónias vizinhas ou marinheiros, debaixo de relações de trabalho forçado, mesmo que o seu trabalho fosse menos violento que o do comum trabalhador rural, não representava de alguma forma a exclusão de uma continuidade cultural de antigas realizações de arte sagrada ou profana. Muitas delas constituem até peças de particular rigor técnico estético dentro da simbologia tradicional.

Outras, porém, vão assumir um velado tom de crítica ou de caracterização social, e conservam-se hoje como símbolos bem evidentes de dignidade cultural na resistência anticolonial, mantida por muitos escultores com uma perspicaz criatividade. A sua integração no mercado colonial irá no entanto fazer-se sempre como artesãos inferiorizados pelo racismo colonial, e as suas obras vendidas a preços irrisórios, para grande lucro dos intermediários colonos ou coleccionadores de outros países.

### 3.2. O Artesão nos Centros Urbanos

O crescente afluxo de camponeses para as cidades, apesar das medidas restritivas impostas, faz com que se desenvolva um processo, particularmente em Lourenço Marques, de criação de exércitos de mão-de-obra desempregada, de onde, nesse *lúmpen*, emergem alguns a ganhar a vida como vendedores de "artesanato indígena."

Enquanto uns se dedicam a utensílios domésticos diversos, outros realizam trabalhos decorativos, tantas vezes mais ao gosto da burguesia colonial e pelas necessidades de sobrevivência, do que por pertencerem a realizações que tivessem alguma tradição artístico-cultural anterior, ou fossem fruto de uma visualização própria do produtor. Realmente encontravam-se mais preocupados com a sobrevivência material do que com outras preocupações espirituais mais profundas.

Como exemplo, destaca-se, em Lourenço Marques, nos inícios dos anos '50, a acção de um taxidermista que contratou vários serviçais para produzirem máscaras de madeira a partir de modelos de fotografias e desenhos de livros e revistas diversos e referentes à "arte de povos primitivos." O negócio não deu para o taxidermista, pois depressa os assalariados-artesãos o deixaram, para sós se lançarem à venda de seus produtos no porto, aos marinheiros e turistas que então abundavam vindos principalmente da África do Sul, ou por entre as ruas e cafés da baixa vendendo aos colonos, e mesmo aventurando-se nos seus bairros residenciais. A tradição de máscaras que nunca houvera passou a ser referenciada em catálogos como tradicional de Lourenço Marques.

Destes, alguns abandonarão esses modelos, entrando na produção de esculturas, com um melhor aproveitamento tridimensional da madeira, representando figuras sociais com um realismo particularmente expressivo como arte popular.[10]

A grande procura que então passou a haver pelo "artesanato indígena" não deixou, decerto, de ter influência no despertar de uma grande criatividade entre estes artesãos, desenvolvendo-se trabalhos com materiais dos mais diversos, em especial madeira, produzindo-se pirogravuras, baixos-relevos, obras de artesanato popular, pinturas de paisagens e temas africanos, etc.

Expressão dessa criatividade é a forma como em 1956, ao serem distribuídas pelos subúrbios de Lourenço Marques tintas para as pessoas pintarem as casas preparando-se a visita do Presidente Craveiro Lopes, estas são aproveitadas em murais de indubitável valor artístico e com uma temática popular bastante expressiva, de que se conservam somente fotografias.

Todo este artesanato e arte popular continuavam, porém, a ser considerados racistamente como de "primitivo," pela maioria dos colonos que o adquiriam a preços irrisórios, que a própria abundância e concorrência entre os artesãos mantinha. Eram "ainda" realizações de indígenas, muito embora a maioria deles já tivesse passado pelas missões. A promoção do indígena tinha de se fazer pelo seu aportuguesamento, e a sua arte como assimilados tinha de se desenvolver subordinada aos valores e princípios da civilização ocidental cristã.

A participação e promoção de indígenas a artistas, feita na exposição de 1956, realizou-se já dentro destes princípios. Por "descoberta" de talento e indicação do Governador Geral, desde 1954, a Secretaria dos Negócios Indígenas pagava a esses pintores (irmãos Jacob e Campira) bolsas como estudantes de Mestre Frederico Aires, e posterior estágio em Portugal. Ensinados a reproduzirem paisagens com materiais, técnicas e formas de visualização consideradas "clássicas" da cultura ocidental, vão-se especializar na reprodução de "paisagens africanas," com variações entre a visão bucólica e a "queimada." No entanto, embora beneficiem do prestígio de acesso aos salões de exposição coloniais, depressa se juntam nas ruas ao conjunto de vendedores ambulantes de "artesanato indígena," embora procurando manter as características "evoluídas" da sua arte.

### 4. Luta Política e Consciência Nacional no Movimento Urbano

É importante determo-nos nas características do desenvolvimento urbano de Lourenço Marques, dos seus profundos e contraditórios conflitos sociais, ao longo das várias décadas que nos separam da corrida internacional para o ouro do Rand, que é quando este porto começa a ser estratégico para o desenvolvimento da região.

Tomando, no final do século passado, o lugar à Ilha de Moçambique como capital da colónia, após a ocupação efectiva do sul da mesma, veio a ter um agitado desenvolvimento político e social próprio da implantação capitalista e colonial. Se salientamos estes primórdios é para localizarmos as origens de algumas classes e camadas sociais moçambicanas, que desde o início do século começam organizadamente a lutar "em prol dos interesses dos naturais das colónias," envolvendo sectores sociais tão diversos como colonos da terra, mulatos descendendo de antigas famílias ligadas ao tráfico mercantil, professores de missões, operários dos portos e caminhos-de-ferro, mineiros e mesmo camponeses, que desenvolvem uma luta que revela uma consciência social contra o Estado Colonial, em forma de primeiras formulações nacionalistas.

Começa-se então a desenvolver uma organização em moldes associativistas, dirigida por uma classe média local que integra os "filhos da terra" discriminados pelo sistema colonial. A implantação do fascismo e do Acto Colonial em 1930 provocam um golpe violento nas formações sociais internas, silenciando todas as oposições internas, em particular depois da década de '50, quando a burguesia colonial, que estava dividida no seu apoio ao Estado Colonial, passa a apoiar resolutamente o regime de Salazar.

São os "filhos da terra," integrando brancos, pretos e mulatos, que se destacam também no princípio desta década, dando novo alento aos ideais nacionalistas e de reafricanização, típicos desse período precursor das independências africanas, e que assumem forma artística, em particular no domínio da poesia. Este fenómeno de polarização social, reflexo da intensidade da luta política vivida então em Moçambique, é que atingia mais violentamente as camadas sociais do "indígena," rural ou urbanizado.

Sem querermos aprofundar a conjuntura então vivida, é sintomático que nas eleições presidenciais de Humberto Delgado, que tinha no seu programa a autodeterminação das colónias, em 1958, um largo sector da sociedade colonial com direito a voto tenha votado a seu favor.

A discriminação social e racial imposta na sociedade criara, porém, um profundo distanciamento entre esta classe média e a grande massa de "indígenas," tornando a permeável aos aliciamentos da burguesia e poder colonial. Esta divisão entre os que se iam aliando ao sistema colonial para usufruto de benefícios individuais, e os que optavam pela continuidade da luta, aliando-se aos sectores mais explorados da sociedade, mantém-se até ao desenvolvimento da luta armada e clandestina nos anos posteriores.

Estudos mais detalhados sobre os crescimentos do poder de compra das várias camadas sociais privilegiadas em relação aos "indígenas," até à abolição deste estatuto e nos anos posteriores, indicar-nos-iam, com mais precisão, a sua evolução em termos económicos. De qualquer forma, a alteração do sistema do trabalho forçado na década de '60 veio a modificar profundamente a estrutura interna do mercado colonial e a situação de oferta e procura de trabalho, dados importantes para um desenvolvimento capitalista.

Na década de '50, porém, a compartimentação da sociedade em duas camadas bem demarcadas culturalmente, ocupando posições económicas, políticas e sociais distintas no sistema colonial, cria condições para que uma abertura à promoção social, através do estudo e revelação de qualidades individuais, seja aproveitada por um largo sector de "indígenas," para se integrarem como assimilados, nos vários campos de actividade económica e social abertos pelo regime.

O individualismo imposto pelo sistema capitalista, a ambição pessoal, as necessidades familiares, a possibilidade de acesso a um escalão social e economicamente superior e o processo assimilatório despersonalizante, estão na base das formas contraditórias como este sector reage a respeito da questão nacional. De facto, a sua atitude é amiúde de alheamento total. O servilismo com que se relacionam com os patrões torna-os subservientes dóceis do sistema colonial, em particular no período de ascensão.

Destacamos no movimento urbano esta promoção social, porque consideramos importante o seu papel como travão no desenvolvimento da consciência nacional então em curso, debaixo da repressão colonial fascista. Por outro lado, ampliando o número de intermediários internos na exploração colonial, o governo de Salazar diluía as contradições sociais que opunha o seu poder à grande massa colonizada, e assegurava de alguma forma a sua continuidade de dominação directa.

Nesta política de promoção social, os pintores que se formaram com o Mestre Frederico Aires foram utilizados como instrumentos de propaganda interna e internacional das possibilidades de abertura e desenvolvimento do regime no quadro de uma política colonial, que visava o completo aportuguesamento do africano.

A acção nacionalista mantém-se constante na sua ligação com os vários movimentos sociais e políticos que ocorriam no âmbito colonial, regional ou internacional, apesar da censura, repressão e interdição de organização política, impostas pelo fascismo colonial. Se as antigas organizações urbanas tinham as direcções infiltradas de elementos dóceis ao regime e o seu âmbito geral não permitia a discussão política, é de destacar a fundação da NESAM (Núcleo dos Estudantes Secundários Africanos de Moçambique), cuja eficácia assentava, como a de todas as organizações dos primeiros tempos, no ser estritamente limitada a um pequeno número de membros (conforme Eduardo Mondlane. *Lutar por Moçambique*. Sá da Costa, 1977, p. 121).

Há a considerar também como o movimento anticolonial se articula com o antifascista conduzido por democratas portugueses residentes, pois ao nível cultural a sua acção converge em diversos momentos, contra as realizações programadas pelo regime. Ao nível das artes plásticas, música, palestras, saraus de poesia e outras realizações culturais, não deixou de ter importância em certos momentos mais agudos de luta, particularmente os que precediam períodos eleitorais fascistas, a acção desenvolvida no seio do Núcleo de Arte.

## 5. Acção Cultural e Artes Plásticas em Lourenço Marques

Desde o século passado, desenvolveram-se no seio da sociedade colonial associações de interesse recreativo, cultural e literário. É, porém, após a implantação do fascismo em Portugal, que este tipo de associações passam a cumprir funções políticas mais amplas, face à interdição de qualquer outra organização política que não a de Salazar.

Ao nível da cidade de Lourenço Marques, surge na primeira metade deste século o Núcleo de Arte, que viria a ter um papel de realce no movimento cultural, primeiro ao nível das artes plásticas, e depois alargando a sua acção para outras expressões artísticas.

O Núcleo de Arte nascera através do esforço de alguns artistas portugueses, e com uma noção de Academia, à semelhança de instituições congéneres existentes em Portugal. Servindo nas primeiras décadas só a comunidade de colonos portugueses, irá mais tarde alargar a sua acção para outros sectores sociais moçambicanos.

Congregando o trabalho de vários artistas e pessoas associadas, irá promover cursos diversos, palestras, exposições e outras actividades culturais. No início dos anos '50, alguns membros vão polarizar uma destacada actividade antifascista, que é reprimida pela polícia de Salazar.

A luta política nacionalista desenvolvida no decorrer da década no meio urbano, e exprimindo-se principalmente ao nível cultural através da poesia, não deixa de ter o seu equivalente ao nível das artes plásticas, onde no movimento de "reafricanização" nos surge Bertina Lopes, a "pintora revoltada," como era então considerada nos salões de exposição da burguesia colonial. Mulata, o pai pagara-lhe os estudos na Escola de Belas-Artes, em Portugal, regressando como professora de desenho, e desenvolvendo uma acção cultural junto de Craveirinha e Nogar, e uma actividade de pesquisa ao nível da pintura, combatendo os padrões clássicos ocidentais, para afirmar as suas raízes africanas.

O movimento de promoção do estatuto do indígena, iniciado ao nível da pintura com os três pupilos de Frederico Aires, o desenvolvimento da actividade de produção e procura de artesanato, a promoção da padronização que o mercado colonial impunha a esta actividade para melhor explorar o artesão, não deixam também de ter influência na actividade que, no decorrer da década, se vai desenvolver à volta do Núcleo de Arte, como a entrada para os seus cursos de alguns estudantes negros e empregados domésticos.

O confronto realiza-se então entre a sujeição a padrões e valores estéticos coloniais e "clássicos" na cultura ocidental, e a apreensão de técnicas e utilização de materiais diversos, para a libertação da criatividade individual. Durante esta década e a de '60, muitas acções se desenvolvem neste âmbito, não só ao nível de cursos proporcionados pelo Núcleo de Arte, e alguns artistas individualmente, como também na sua acção junto de artesãos com vista a incrementarem a sua criatividade. Destaca-se a acção do Arquitecto "Pancho" Guedes, não só como mecenas do pintor Malangatana Valente, como também incentivando e adquirindo de todos artesãos obras que se distinguissem dos padrões dominantes.

Na exposição de 1959, organizada aquando da vinda do então Ministro do Ultramar, estreia-se Malangatana em actos públicos desta natureza, e é sujeito a fortes críticas, mesmo da parte dos alunos de Frederico Aires, que como ele provinham do estrato indígena. Com efeito, a visualização imprimida nas suas obras, nada tinha a ver com os padrões "aceitáveis" pela sociedade colonial. No mesmo ano, volta a expor na Associação dos Naturais de Moçambique, onde "A mulher na Cidade" ganha uma menção honrosa.

Os primeiros anos da década de '60 são marcados por uma intensa actividade cultural e política, e sem dúvida a abolição do estatuto do Indígena veio sobrepor-se a um forte movimento de libertação da criatividade individual em vários domínios artísticos. Ao nível das artes plásticas, é notório o aparecimento de diversos artistas populares fazendo escultura, como Chachuaio e Paulo Come, ou pirogravura como Nhaca e Fumo.

Chachuaio é sem dúvida o artista popular que então mais se destaca, mas

> começa a ser aproveitado por alguns espertalhões, de maneira que não o deixavam acabar as suas obras. Um era o Senhor Fernando Rosa de Oliveira, que andava à volta dele e não o deixava acabar, queria logo sacar-lhe as coisas para vender. O que o Rosa de Oliveira fez com ele, foi o mesmo que fez em Nampula com os escultores macondes; pegou neles, tu agora vais fazer isto!—Ah! O.K., pronto, está bem!
>
> O Chachuaio está para a escultura, como o Malangatana está para a pintura.[11]

Em Novembro de 1962, o jornal *Tribuna*[12] publica uma entrevista com este artista, onde ele afirma nunca ter tido mestre, que a escultura nasceu com ele, que esculpe e entalha desde pequeno. Diz não ter tradição de escultores na sua família, embora considere a escultura uma arte muito divulgada entre os seus de Chongoene.

Além de fazer arte "absolutamente cônscio da importância e da dignidade que ela assume, com um orgulho franco, mas despido de vaidades supérfluas," conforme o articulista, salientamos a publicação de fotografias de sua casa na Matola, onde numa tabuleta se lia: "Escultura Moçambicana por Alberto Chachuaio—Artista A.T.C.—Matola—L.M." e de uma sua obra intitulada "O Milando," composta por três expressivas figuras típicas do colonialismo—o sipaio, o queixoso e o administrador.

Alberto Chachuaio é posteriormente preso, sujeito aos "tratamentos" da polícia de Salazar e, depois de ficar tuberculoso, deportado para fora da cidade onde acaba por morrer tísico. A sua curta trajectória não deixou, porém, de influenciar o movimento artístico e cultural de então, existente a nível popular.

A primeira exposição individual de Malangatana em 1961, o prémio de pintura que recebeu no "2º Concurso de Artes Plásticas" em 1962, a participação de mais moçambicanos nas exposições e concursos artísticos coloniais, o "Concurso para o Cartaz das Comemorações de Lourenço Marques" ganho por Abdias Muchanga no mesmo ano, são indícios de uma intensa actividade de afirmação cultural nacionalista, neste período de fundação da Frente de Libertação de Moçambique, em que ainda se considerava viável a independência sem recurso à luta armada.

A implantação da PIDE na colónia, o reforço da repressão fascista contra qualquer manifestação de descontentamento ou de qualquer forma que transparecesse o nacionalismo, a onda de prisões que caiu sobre activistas nacionalistas, e a ida de muitos outros para junto da FRELIMO, não deixaram de corresponder a um posterior período de grande repressão com implicações no movimento cultural popular.

Vários artistas moçambicanos continuam, no entanto, a cumprir a sua função de "voz colectiva," mobilizando a consciência anti-colonial, denunciando a exploração e opressão racista, e mantendo clandestinamente uma actividade política constante. A nova onda de repressão que o regime colonial-fascista impõe no final de 1964 irá conduzir à prisão, por alguns anos, os artistas que então mais se destacavam, como José Craveirinha, Rui Nogar, Luis Bernardo Honwana, Malangatana Ngwenya e Abdias Muchanga.

Silenciada a expressão artística denunciadora do sistema, o mercado colonial impõe de forma dominadora os seus valores, desenvolvendo-se um período de produção para consumo, quer ao nível de artesanato, quer do considerado artes plásticas, principalmente servindo o cada vez mais vasto turismo sul-africano.

Acompanhando a implantação do "mercado de artesanato," em 1967/68 são abertas diversas lojas de artesanato africano, que impõem cada vez mais os seus padrões aos artesãos, para melhor baixarem os seus preços de compra. À estereotipação dominante continuam a opor-se artistas e antifascistas portugueses, procurando fomentar, entre os artesãos que melhores qualidades revelassem, a libertação da sua criatividade na aquisição de tais obras.

De assinalar o novo movimento que começa a ressurgir no Núcleo de Arte, neste âmbito, tomando novo vigor a abertura de cursos para jovens trabalhadores ou estudantes negros. Só então é que novos artistas começam a surgir, como Alberto Chissano e Mankeu. A acção de António Quadros, Bronze e irmãos Mealha torna-se importante na direcção do Núcleo de Arte, promovendo actividades nas mais diversas expressões artísticas e culturais, e desempenhando um importante papel para a unidade de acção cultural de diversas associações culturais e recreativas, que actuavam no campo artístico, isoladamente conforme a própria estratificação social e racial. Ligando-se à Associação Africana, à Associação dos Naturais de Moçambique, aos Cine-clubes e outras associações similares, o Núcleo de Arte veio a elaborar um trabalho ambicioso que permitiu uma ligação dinâmica entre as diversas formas de expressão artística e cultural desenvolvidas na sociedade, e a realização de cursos e actividades culturais, nos diversos domínios artísticos.

Nesta altura, é elaborado um projecto, com financiamento da Fundação Calouste Gulbenkian, de construção de um complexo arquitectónico para a promoção e desenvolvimento de várias manifestações artísticas e culturais, oficinas, *ateliers*, auditórios, salas de exposição, para aulas de música, canto e dança e salas de espectáculos, a ser edificado na barreira da Maxaquene.

O regime colonial não viria, porém, a autorizar a execução de tal projecto, temendo a amplitude da sua acção cultural a nível social. Mais tarde, a mesma Fundação viria a subsidiar a construção do auditório galeria da Beira, a "Casa dos Bicos," um projecto bem mais modesto e virado exclusivamente para a burguesia colonial do centro de Moçambique.

O desenvolvimento da luta armada provando ser a única forma de alcançar politicamente a independência nacional, o reforço constante da repressão fascista a nível interno, a acção de aliciamento a que foram submetidos os artistas nacionalistas depois de saírem das prisões, não deixam de ter influência no desenvolvimento do movimento artístico nacional. A burguesia colonial, entretanto, passa a aceitar a existência de expressões culturais reivindicando fortes raízes africanas, diluindo-se por completo as pretensões colonialistas de alcançarem o aportuguesamento dos povos submetidos. Para o poder colonial, tratava-se entretanto de acelerar o processo de criação de uma classe média nacional, que permitisse a continuidade da dominação de forma neocolonial. Acções de âmbito diverso continuam, porém, a ser conduzidas por vários artistas, estabelecendo ligações a nível popular e continuando a denunciar a falta de Liberdade e Justiça Social.

## 6. As Artes Plásticas no Desenvolvimento Social

Sem sobrevalorizarmos o papel das artes plásticas no desenvolvimento social, notamos que a importância que lhes é dada pelo poder colonial não deixa de estar ligada às próprias necessidades de desenvolvimento capitalista que caracterizou a colónia e a sobrevivência do regime, durante a década de '60 e até 1974.

A promoção artística, iniciada em 1954 e tomando forma em '56, ganha uma dimensão mais ampla entre 1959 e 1962, altura de intensa luta política e social, envolvendo a realização de cursos diversos, concursos, exposições, palestras e debates, incrementados pelo próprio estado colonial, numa política que visava a alteração da estrutura social e superestrutura ideológica.

Correspondendo a uma mudança "orgânica" do regime social assente no Estatuto do Indígena e trabalho compulsivo, a sua abolição é acompanhada por um alargamento do "bloco no poder," de forma a integrar todas as camadas sociais "privilegiadas," desde o nível de "assimilado" que vai sendo alargado aos "aspirantes a burgueses."

O fim do chibalo e a eminência da luta armada compreendem uma alteração profunda das relações sociais, impondo-se progressivamente as capitalistas às do antigo regime de trabalho forçado, introduzindo-se alterações diversas que permitissem um desenvolvimento económico e social de acordo com as teorias da economia política burguesa.

Tratava-se no entanto de activar o desenvolvimento capitalista e sufocar as aspirações nacionalistas, cada vez mais activas, através de um regime de terror fascista. Promover o crescimento de uma classe média nacional, que não fosse nacionalista, formando-a desenraizada culturalmente, em atitude de desprezo pelos valores antepassados e seus próprios familiares, e submissão perante os valores da metrópole colonial e da exploração capitalista, passa a ser uma estratégia fundamental para a continuidade da dominação estrangeira.

A promoção artística visava estimular o desenvolvimento das qualidades individuais e da liberdade burguesa, necessária para promover o desenvolvimento capitalista da colónia. A liberdade criativa de expressão individual através da arte não pode, porém, deixar de exprimir os conflitos sociais gerados pelo sistema colonial-fascista e as aspirações nacionalistas, pelo que a repressão se impõe violenta, no então pequeno e dinâmico grupo de artistas nacionalistas.

Das ondas de prisões e de terror social conduzidas em '62 e '64/'65, à prisão de inúmeros nacionalistas, e entre eles artistas, corresponderam ao silenciamento de toda a expressão interna que reivindicasse a independência. Em nome de todo o povo oprimido, a FRELIMO inicia então a luta armada, como único recurso de obter a independência, e a liberdade de expressão cultural que era negada ao povo moçambicano.

O desenvolvimento crescente da luta armada obriga o poder colonial e o imperialismo a multiplicar os investimentos económicos e sociais e a efectuar reformas em diversos aspectos não fundamentais à sobrevivência do sistema, e mesmo a ter de aceitar, volvidos mais de dois anos, que os artistas presos continuassem a exprimir os seus valores culturais, embora de forma velada, amiúde. As tentativas de aliciamento posteriores procuravam mais o seu isolamento em relação às massas, e serem elementos de propaganda política do regime, a nível interno e internacional, do que em silenciarem a afirmação da sua identidade cultural. Os artistas nacionalistas passam então a ser voz de esperança de uma certeza que a FRELIMO começara a construir, e a unidade de acção que conseguem alcançar no fim dos anos '60, envolvendo diversos clubes e associações, divididas pela segregação racial e social imposta pelo regime, revela o carácter de luta então desenvolvida, em conjunto com os sectores antifascistas portugueses, e em torno do Núcleo de Arte.

Correspondendo a novo período de abertura do regime, as medidas demagógicas de Caetano não deixaram de ter influência, porque visavam acelerar o crescimento cada vez maior da classe média de aspiração burguesa e submissa aos valores coloniais, e também porque permitiram em reverso desenvolver-se novos valores artísticos.

A reflexão exposta, não tem outro objectivo que abrir um quadro de referências históricas e sociais que permitam compreender o contexto em que se desenvolveram as artes plásticas moçambicanas nas últimas décadas, como passaram a existir, da negação da sua existência.

Tema para debate, consideramos ter omitido dados importantes e, decerto, valorizado outros não tanto. Dados de uma história presente, que se faz hoje, precisam de ser enriquecidos para melhor valorização das experiências acumuladas na luta anticolonial, no desenvolvimento artístico popular. Decerto ainda subsistem inúmeras concepções e valores culturais impostos pelo sistema colonial e derivados principalmente da criação de um mercado de consumo internacional, que se continua impondo sobre Moçambique.

Hoje, não é a necessidade de sobrevivência que determina a afirmação cultural, mas a necessidade de desenvolvimento económico e social, possibilitado por uma ampla participação popular.

MN/PS

NOTES

* This article is published with the kind permission of the Fundação Mário Soares. The formatting of the typescript in the Fundação Mário Soares has been retained. The text has been edited for publication. Minor mistakes and errors in spelling, grammar and punctuation have been corrected.

1. Silva Cunha. *Questões Ultramarinas e Internacionais (Direito e Política)*. Colecção Jurídica Portuguesa, Edições Ática, 1956, p. 64.

2. Cf. Amílcar Cabral. *Libertação Nacional e Cultura*. UNESCO, 1970.

3. Anderson, Perry. "Portugal and the end of Ultra-colonialism." *New Left Review*, vol 15, 1962, pp. 83-102; e vol. 16, 1962, pp. 88-123.

4. Veige Coutinho, et al. *La transformation idéologique de la couche intermediaire autoctone colonial du Mozambique, (1962-1968): études des lettres des lecteurs du journal Catholique 'Voz Africana'*. Université Catholique de Louvain, Institute de Sociologie, 1978, p. 47.

5. Eduardo Mondlane. *Lutar por Moçambique*. 3º ed, Livraria Sá da Costa Editora, 1977, p. 71.

6. Idem, p. 76.

7. Citação do *Diário de Lourenço Marques*, 23 de Fevereiro de 1956.

8. Idem, de 17 de Março de 1956.

9. Cf. *Tempo de Maputo*, nº 518, pp. 58-63.

10. Paulo Come é um artista que, em 1961, foi para o "negócio de máscaras," e depois passou a esculpir figuras humanas.

11. Transcrição de entrevista gravida por Paulo Soares, com Júlio Navarro, em 8 de Outubro de 1981.

12. *Tribuna de Lourenço Marques*, 9 de Novembro de 1962.

NADINE SIEGERT

# Art Topples Monuments: Artistic Practice and Colonial/Postcolonial Relations in the Public Space of Luanda

ABSTRACT: Even though there have been very few modern and contemporary artworks in the urban space of Luanda in the years after independence in 1975—and especially after the end of the civil war in 2002—there are two works by Angolan artists that are of particular interest: the sculpture *Mitologias II* (1984) by António Ole (b. 1951) and the photographic series *Redefining the Power* (2011) by Kiluanji Kia Henda (b. 1978). Both works address the possibility of using contemporary art as a symbolic form of the replacement of power, since both are built on pedestals that had previously supported monuments of Portuguese colonial power. They might, therefore, be read as a form of substitution for monuments that would commemorate and celebrate independence or the end of colonialism. This article also discusses whether these two artworks can also be regarded as counter-monuments and this contributes to the discourse on the visual and material culture of Lusophone Africa.

KEYWORDS: Angola, Luanda, Contemporary Art, Urban Space, Memory, Monument

RESUME: No espaço publico em Luanda, há dois trabalhos de artistas angolanos particularmente interessantes: a escultura *Mitologias II* (1984) de António Ole (n. 1951) e a série das fotografias *Redefining the Power* (2011) por Kiluanji Kia Henda (n. 1977). Ambos os trabalhos falam sobre a possibilidade de usar a arte contemporânea como uma forma de substituição aos símbolos de poder colonial—como uma forma de substituição de monumentos que comemorariam a independência (1975) ou o fim do colonialismo. Este artigo pergunta se as duas obras também podem ser consideradas como uma forma de "contra-monumento" e contribuem para o discurso sobre a cultura visual e material da África lusófona.

PALAVRAS-CHAVE: Angola, Luanda, arte contemporânea, espaço urbano, memoria, monumento

## Introduction

The engagement with public space on the African continent is part of the recognition of the role of the environment on social processes that entered the humanities within the context of the spatial turn.[1] Within art studies specifically, the relationship of artists with place and space is of increasing interest.[2] Research on art in public space not only deals with commemorative sites that carry official history or sculptural works that, often commissioned, are designed to sit within the public space and are therefore site-specific, but also considers more temporal, often performative, artistic interventions in the public environment. These have the potential to raise questions by testing the limits of normativity and of the social boundaries of the private and the public.[3] In these practices, the city is more than just a neutral stage for artistic engagement. It is rather the specific history inscribed into the urban space and its architecture that is often the main focus of the artists' attention. The city is conceptualized as a script, an archive of collective memory, a palimpsestic carrier of the layers of history.[4]

The artistic strategies dealing with this shared memory space may use documentary approaches to depict the specificities of urban space, such as in the recent photographic series by the 2013 Venice Golden Lyon Award winner Edson Chagas (b. 1977) and his artwork *Found Not Taken* (2009), where, in a sort of fieldwork, the urban space is mapped.[5] In this project, Edson Chagas took found objects from the streets of Luanda, London and Newport, and photographed them at new, carefully chosen sites. His perspective offers another view of these abandoned objects that have a very short life in the consumeristic societies in which he worked. Other artists fictionalize the space and use it as a setting for narratives that intervene in the reality script. One such work is the photographic series *Redefining the Power* by Kiluanji Kia Henda, which will be discussed below. Here, the city is seen as imaginative, a space that gives place for staging and performing different realities.[6] The urban space is, therefore, not a given reality, but one that is actively created by the artists' imagination. These imaginative aspects can be utopian, phantasmagorical or even irrational.[7]

In this article, I question both whether and how art offers forms and practices that deal with the public space in Angola's capital, Luanda, in ways which are different from official commemorative practices. This study is based on extended research visits to Luanda over the past ten years and a number of conversations with artists and academics in the field of art and memory studies. Building upon studies that deal with the so-called archival turn in the visual arts, I am interested in investigating how collective memory is rendered through contemporary art and in the relationship between the ethics and aesthetics of postcolonial thought.[8] How do artists seek to subvert the colonial archive—also manifest in the urban space—and the historical order it implies? Sometimes in this process, those who deploy such practices might be seen to be imagining alternative futures. A close reading, analysis and interpretation of two selected artworks from two different generations of artists will explore these questions from a visual culture perspective.

In the examples discussed, contemporary art is used as a form of physical replacement, since both are built on pedestals that had previously supported monuments of Portuguese colonial power. Can we consider them as a substitution that would perhaps commemorate independence or the end of colonialism? Can these two works be regarded as counter-monuments for an alternative commemoration of the colonial history of the Angolan capital? I will first present the urban space in Luanda, specifically, in relation to art and aesthetic practice since independence. I will then introduce the history of some colonial monuments and their toppling in the context of the decolonisation of the urban space. An in-depth analysis and interpretation of the artworks—*Mitologias II* (1984) by António Ole and *Redefining the Power* (2011) by Kiluanji Kia Henda—will be the focus of the final part of this article.

## Art and Urban Space in Luanda

In Luanda, engagement with the urban space is mostly a phenomenon of the post-civil war era, beginning in 2002. The history of over forty years of armed conflict—first against the Portuguese colonial power, then, after independence in 1975, between several independence movements—is engraved into the city, even though Luanda has only rarely been the actual stage for hostilities.[9] Until the late colonial period in the 1970s, there had been several urban planning initiatives, which remain visible in the modern architecture still dominating the city center. During the 1950s and 1960s, the city was growing rapidly. These new buildings were mainly the work of Portuguese architects, such as Vieira da Costa (1911—1982) and Fernão Simões de Carvalho (b. 1929), who, following the modernist ideas of Le Corbusier, shaped the city at that time. During the war decades—with a growing urban population—city planning was neglected, but so was the development of an infrastructure to support the arts and culture. Facilities, such as studio spaces for artists and gallery spaces, were scarce, and there were no art museums. Except for support from the national artist union UNAP,[10] there were no other state-funded fine arts projects.[11] After 2002, a new wave of reconstruction tried to create a Dubai-like face with the "Marginal," a restored and altered road that runs along the coast, which showcases rows of palm trees shipped from Florida. This trend also led to the demolition of several buildings from the early 1900s as well as others from the late colonial period in order to create space for shopping malls, hotels and car parks. The new cosmopolitan metropolis is based on the booming economic sectors.[12]

Nevertheless, in spite of these challenging conditions, there has never been no artistic practice. The first generation of artists after independence consisted of a cosmopolitan urban elite, but their main point of reference were the rural areas in their nostalgic motivation to (re)connect to what was believed to be the lost authentic arts of the pre-colonial period.[13] It was only after the end of the civil war that walking in the city became a common public practice, which today is also seen in the appropriation of the urban environment through open-air sports and other spare time practices. Nevertheless, contrary to other African cites such as Douala, Kampala and Dakar, contemporary art in the public space of Luanda is virtually non-existent. For many years after 2002, the urban space was not considered a space for the arts, regardless of whether these were state-sponsored public sculptures or ephemeral sub-cultural manifestations in the form of graffiti or street art. The city's significance as a space for contemporary art increased with the establishment of the Luanda Triennial in 2005/6, an art event with an international outreach that has been directed by the Angolan artist and curator Fernando Alvim.[14] The organization reconstructed empty spaces into artspaces, and content-wise young artists such as Yonamine, Kiluanji Kia Henda and Ihosvanny worked with and within the urban space.[15] Luanda has not only been "acted on," but, since 2002, it has also provided space for art that created new spheres of action through the temporary establishment of galleries and workshops. In addition, artistic media related to subversive and popular practices, such as street art and graffiti, became visible in the early 2000s, though still in comparatively small quantities. Nevertheless, a young post-war generation of artists came together at UNAP, the Teatro Elinga[16] and in the new spaces of the Luanda Triennal, and they began to formulate their visions of the future and the role of the artist in it. Art practice in early post-war art started to be re-invented in the context of the re-structuring of the local art world. The Luanda Triennial and an increasing internationalization of the art-scene through the participation of artists such as António Ole, Fernando Alvim, Kiluanji Kia Henda, Yonamine and Edson Chagas in events such as the Biennials of Venice, São Paulo and Guangzhou were part of this process.

In this context, art was seen as a tool of social action and as a means to deal with abandoned or invisible places in the center of Luanda. Action was mainly taken by the curators and artists themselves; despite some nominal support the government has not yet seriously invested in the cultural infrastructure. Therefore, artists depend on private donors and collectors as well as local industries and the bank sector as sponsors. Still, the relationship of Luanda's artists with their city is today one of hate and love—"odio e amor." This ambivalence is expressed in art works, including nostalgic reflections on the city's past and the significance of its peripheries, as in António Ole's *Township Walls* (a series of installations that began in 2003).

One of the first major events in the public space was the art exhibition *Pela Paz (For the Peace)* by the young artist collective *Os Nacionalistas*[17] in 2003 on the streets in front of the *Teatro Elinga* and the headquarters of UNAP on the occasion of the commemoration of the birthday of Angola's first president, Agostinho Neto.[18] Despite the fact that the government typically monopolizes this date to perform commemorative events, *Pela Paz* successfully staged what was probably the first self-organized art exhibition after the official end of the civil war in 2002. Although the artworks had no political content, the exhibition itself made a political statement by being held on the same day as the government's commemoration. What the artists did was to explore a new format: a collaborative public space exhibition where they displayed the variety of their aesthetic practices. This event was something new for the art world in Luanda and reflected the urge to re-appropriate the city, which was once a quite hostile space, and to invent new, unexpected spaces for art in the urban expanse. The partly collaborative artworks shown in the streets of Luanda have been path-breaking for the artistic practices of the years that followed, which have been more process-oriented and experimental than previous practices.

**A Journey to the Sun**

Art in the urban space of Luanda is directly connected to colonial and post-colonial histories and their manifestations in the cityscape. The creation of official sites for commemoration is commonplace. But instead of actively engaging with history, it has often "been stopped" here by official images that provide a fixed version of the event. The engagement by artists with sites of the aftermath of colonialism can be considered a form of "memory work" that is fundamentally different from official sites of commemoration. Reference points in the cityscape, such as the omnipresent *Mausoleum of Agostinho Neto* (1980/2011), are re-interpreted in works of art and this enables an alternative reading of their possible meanings, as in, for example, Kiluanji Kia Henda's *Icarus 13: The First Journey to the Sun* (2007). (Fig. 1) Here, the mausoleum—a monument and, as such, part of the cityscape—not only becomes a spacecraft, but is connected to a (post)socialist and even Afro-futuristic imaginary space—an imaginary city. In this work the artist plays with the heroic past and its political icons—in this case the mausoleum of Angola's first president, Agostinho Neto (1922-1979). Construction began on it in the 1980s with financial support from the Soviet Union, but the building was never completed. Nevertheless, it epitomizes the material concreteness and imaginative power of the utopia of socialism. When Neto died in Moscow in 1979, the USSR decided to offer the new Republic a monumental mausoleum that would, according to Marxist-Leninist tradition, host the embalmed body of Angola's first president and symbolize his greatness. In 1980 a team of now-unknown Soviet designers from the Design Institute of the Union of Soviet Socialist Republics started work on the conception of the building, which was to be erected in Luanda. Two years later, in 1982, the laying of the cornerstone took place, but due to the fall of the USSR, the long-lasting civil war, and the economic and political crisis in Angola, the completion of the Mausoleum was postponed for more than twenty years. In 1998 the Angolan government decided to restart the project and intended to transform the Mausoleum into a cultural center. In 2005 construction of the project was taken over by the North Korean company MANSUDAE, which completed work in 2011. One year later, in 2012 the building opened to the public, and today the 120 meter-high concrete structure of the Mausoleum is a public venue and one of the most visible landmarks of Angola's capital, Luanda. The sarcophagus of the former Angolan president is stored, as is Lenin's sarcophagus in his mausoleum in Moscow, in a central block, which also serves as the pyramidal base of the constructivist tower which is composed of concrete juxtaposed plastic elements. The contrast between the rough and brutal elegance of the Mausoleum's exterior, the airport-like interiors and the Dubai-like design of the surrounding area reveals the long building history of the project and the shifting paradigms between the early independent government and the current one. Neto's Mausoleum represents a specific

Eastern European constructivist tradition of monuments. The bright socialist future embedded in Neto's engraved words, and in the beauty of the original design of the monumental building, clashes with the current social issues that are evident in Luanda and throughout the country. At the present moment, the building could be seen as an architectural metaphor of a failed utopia, or of the modernist melancholia of this late socialism, when the architecture of the present has been monumentalized in order to project itself into the future. Moreover, it could be interpreted as part of Soviet Modernism with its references to space travel and hyperbolic modernity. Surprisingly, the most popular nickname for the futurist building is not the 'space rocket' (*o foguetão*) which can be found not only in public discourses, but also in contemporary artworks, such as Kiluanji Kia Henda's *Icarus 13*.

**The Empty Pedestal**

An important reference point in the city, the memorial is unique in its architectural design. The rest of the inner city offers insights into other historical layers of the urban space. Apart from the late colonial modern architecture from the 1940s to the 1970s which still dominates the city center, very few houses from the earlier colonial period remain visible in the urban space. The ones that are standing consist of some pre-modernist buildings, which were falling apart and which were removed to make space for the real estate boom of the early 2000s. Today, few of them have been renovated. This includes the structure, built by a rich Portuguese family at the end of the nineteenth century, that since 1976 has housed the Museu Nacional de Anthropologia in Coqueiros and the former Grand Hotel, which was transformed into the Brazilian Cultural Center after it had nearly completely deteriorated.[19]

In addition, some artworks from the late colonial period, such as a mural by the colonial artist Neves e Sousa at the international airport *4 de Fevereiro*, have survived in the ever-changing cityscape.[20] But the absence of direct markers of coloniality is quite evident. During the colonial period, monuments to historic Portuguese personalities had been scattered all over the inner city. These included, among others, sculptures of the voyager Diogo Cão, who arrived on the Angolan coast in 1485, created by António Duarte in 1948 and of Paulo Dias de Novais, who founded the city of Luanda in 1576. Former colonial monuments were toppled by the new political power during the course of independence in 1975/6 with the iconoclastic motivation to make the old regime invisible.[21] In contrast to many European countries, where former colonialists still have visibility in the urban spaces as equestrian sculptures, the toppling of monuments outside the West is a strategy that is often employed to mark political change. This happened with the colonial statues in the city-space of Luanda. Some of the pedestals have been given new figures. Perhaps the most radical toppling took place on Kinaxixi Square, then called Largo Maria da Fonte, when the Victory monument by Portuguese artist Henrique Moreira dating from 1937 was dynamited in 1974 and replaced by a Soviet tanker. It is said that this was the very tanker on which Angola's first president Agostinho Neto entered the city to proclaim independence with his revolutionary movement MPLA.[22] The tanker was later replaced by the sculpture of the historical heroine Queen Njinga (1582-1663) that was also intednd to mark victory over the colonial power. Njinga is perhaps the most important symbol of the anti-colonial struggle in Angola. Throughout her life she refused to acknowledge the imperial power of Portugal. From her local queendom of Ndongo and Matamba, she fought the colonial power from the interior. After independence, she started to become a national heroine. This sculpture was removed from Kinaxixi Square in 2008 as part of the demolition of the modernist market building (1950-52) in order to make space for a new shopping center, and it was then transported to the Military Museum at the old colonial fort. (Fig. 2)

The works by António Ole and Kiluanji Kia Henda that are discussed in this article are erected on pedestals that had previously supported monuments of Portuguese colonial power, and these had been toppled in the context of the independence process as an anti-colonial gesture. They form a counter-visuality to the official commemorative monuments of the colonial and socialist past by working with traces of the aftermath of colonialism and the ways in which it marked the urban landscape of Luanda.

## Mitologias II

Next to the official monuments of the socialist era, such as the statues of Rainha Njinga and Agostinho Neto—both produced in bronze at the North Korean artcraft factory of Mansudae,[23] and both, therefore, epitomizing a "socialist realist" style[24]—the metal sculpture *Mitologias II* by António Ole from 1985 can, as of 2018, be considered the only state-sponsored modern artwork in the public space of Luanda. It is positioned in front of the German embassy situated along the coastal avenue known as the Marginal. The sculpture was commissioned by the Angolan state-owned petrol company *Petromar* for the city of Luanda. This new contemporary artwork replaced the colonial sculpture of the Portuguese seaman Vasco da Gama. (Figs. 3 & 4)

The sculpture consists of four vertical figurative elements, two of them anthropomorphic, one zoomorphic and one abstract. On the bottom, between the four figures, is another element in the form of a snake. The metal figures are painted in bright colors, such as yellow, red, blue and white, and one of the anthropomorphic elements is brown. They are distributed equally over the pedestal, with the yellow and orange bird-like figure and the brown human-like figure facing outward on the two narrow sides. Between them is the smaller human-like figure in yellow and brown and the abstract figure that resembles a striped tower with a half-round top in blue. There are also step-like elements that lead to some of the figures. The work resembles not only the pop-art style of a number of António Ole's paintings from the 1980s, but also the surrealist art of the Portuguese artist José de Guimarães with its clearly distinct color fields and simple forms. Guimarães served in the Portuguese military in Luanda in the late 1960s and curated António Ole's first exhibition at the Museu de Angola in 1968. The sculpture also anticipates the colorful installation of his later *Township Walls* that earned him popularity in the international art world.[25] However, the sculpture plays a rather minor role in Luanda's profile as a cosmopolitan African city.[26] Instead, it serves to underline the absence and not the presence of art in the public space. Nevertheless, *Mitologias II* can be seen as a late modern response to the colonial city by replacing an empty pedestal with a new work embedded in the nationalist discourse on modern art in Angola that was circulating around definitions of "authenticity." "Angolanidade" was a key term in the formation of the modernist aesthetics of the post-independence period as late as the 1980s.[27] The partly nostalgic motivation to reconstruct Angolan identity also had an impact on fine arts practice. Socialist modernity was combined with the idea of a rooted African culture, fuelling the artistic imagination in the late 1970s and early 1980s. *Mitologias II* is one of the last manifestations of this period in Angolan art-making and an important work that embraces this aesthetic discourse both formally and in its positioning in the public space.

**Redefining the Power**

The monuments by the young artist Kiluanji Kia Henda[28] create alternative narratives of the past. In his photographic series *Redefining the Power* (2011) he works performatively with the pedestals of historic monuments in Luanda's cityscape. (Fig.

5) Some of them have been re-appropriated by socialist monuments. Others have remained empty and almost invisible—a dysfunctional architecture in the space of the city. The photographs form part of the series *Homem Novo* (New Man), which is a reference to the Angolan national anthem and reflects the nation's aspiration to reinvent its national identity following independence in 1975. The socialist notion of the "New Man" conceptualized a modern "wo_man" on the way to a communist society.[29] Based on the Soviet model, the concept has also been applied to the post-revolutionary cultural politics of the former Portuguese colonies.[30]

This work may be interpreted as the next step for Angolan artists who not only work with the visual/material traces of history, but who also creatively redefine it. The ephemeral performances are later translated into high-quality photographic work, and enter distribution within the art world and art market. The issue of monuments as a form of official commemoration of historical events or personalities comes into play in this work. Monuments reveal the complexity of official commemorations: on the one hand, they manifest a will to remember, while, on the other, they freeze memory in stone. Kiluanji Kia Henda is tracing this frozen history of the colonial monuments in Luanda—an archive in itself—by working both with the empty pedestals in the city-space, from where the former colonial statues had been removed during the moment of liberation, and with the removed statues themselves. In *Redefining the Power*, the artist stages new images with new "figures"—his "cultural heroes"[31]—on top of the pedestals, thereby filling the gap, the void left on top of the pedestals. He has collaborated with other artists from the local cultural scene who work in different genres, such as the fashion designers Shunnuz Fiel and Didi Fernandes and the dancer Miguel Prince, and who have posed as living sculptures on the pedestals in various costumes. These costumes partly resemble wedding dresses (designed by Mwamby Wassaki) or ball gowns, and they add in this way a queer aesthetic to the work—an aspect that Kiluanji Kia Henda has also explored in his photograph *Poderosa de Bom Jesus* (2006).[32]

The aspect of performance as ephemeral aesthetic strategy, which is enacted only in a certain moment is crucial here. It creates a specific relationship with space and time, and this is still visible in the photographs. In this work, Kiluanji Kia Henda chooses one of the most ephemeral of media: fashion. By working with the textile creations of Angolan contemporary fashion designers, he proposes a new form and medium for the manifestation of power: a bright, moving and queer body representing the new Luanda, the new post-war, post-socialist and post-colonial Angola. He is also blurring the line between bodies as living human media and lifeless mediating objects. The "new wo_men" on top of the pedestal are consciously ephemeral, fluid and queer, but at the same time they *perform* an act of world-making[33]—or even future-making. The optimistic hopes for a new future become reality in the very moment of the staged performance on top of the pedestals.

Kiluanji Kia Henda uses the body to hint at an absence, a part of history, which had to be made unseen in the course of the implementation of a new state and its ideology. His new men on top of the pedestals are performing the optimism of the post-war period and the artist argues, that "[...] every city should have empty pedestals that could be customized regarding our passions, instead of having representations in cold stone of dead people that no one really cares about today and most of them are connected with wars or political power."[34] In one photograph from the series, the artist reveals this history and his intervention. The new image with the staged living sculpture is juxtaposed with a picture of the empty pedestal but also with a historical photograph of the colonial monuments with the respective historical figure on top, the founder of the city, Paulo Dias de Novais. (Fig. 6)

A related work, based on the toppled monuments themselves, is *Bulumuka* (Ambush) (2010). (Fig. 7) Here, the artists depicted the dismantled, partly fragmented colonial statues depicting Luis Vaz de Camões, Dom Afonso Henriques and Pedro Ànvadres Cabral, among others, which were gathered together next to tanks and cannons in an almost theatrical way, recalling a cemetery, at the Fortress of São Miguel (build by the Portuguese in the fifteenth century). The formally and aesthetically diverse sculptures not only represent different periods in colonial art history, but they also, in the way the artist depicts them, seem to be engaged in a silent dialogue that crosses time and space and even holds the flow of time for a while. Kiluanji Kia Henda considers "those monuments [as] clandestine citizens with expired visas: they should be deported to their place of origin after paying the fine for illegal permanence."[35] After the reopening of the Military Museum in 2013, the abandoned figures, led by the bronze statue of Rainha Ginga, were lined up in the courtyard without any further explanation, thus silencing the history of oppression and power relations of the colonial period.

Kiluanji Kia Henda's artworks can be understood as the creation of new images and narratives that speak about Luanda's heterogeneous present. At the same time, they provide a critical rereading of the past through a performative intervention. He is questioning the symbolic power of monuments by introducing the possibility to break it, commenting on the post-war society in transit. Furthermore, the work is also a transmission into the future, for the new, staged figures speak about a queer Luanda yet to come. Posing in the clothes and fabrics of emergent Angolan fashion designers, the artist constructs his models as the incarnation of a new Luandan: a bright, queer and moving body.

Future is regarded as something to be envisioned, a process which is, at the same time, rewriting the past by toppling monuments and anticipating new heroes. Through this juxtapositioning, Kiluanji Kia Henda uses the imaginary to reflect on numerous moments and perhaps versions of the history of the country, and in so doing, could be seen to be projecting a future for Angola. He provides an alternative to how history is perceived and comments on the (non)permanence, significance and historical heritage of objects of history.

**Intervention in the Urban Script**

In the interpretation of the works above I understand the city as an urban archive[36]—as a knowledge base that can be reactivated and redefined through artistic enactment. The artworks question the relationships between colonial memory and public space. Through the performative act, the symbolic system is re-actualized, which makes it possible to inscribe new meanings.

Artistic practice offers manifold means of questioning the archive and, in the process, redefining the power. These new artworks filled a gap—not only a spatial one, but also a temporal one—because they were created by the erasure of a historical marker, the colonial monument—with new images and narratives that address Luanda's heterogeneous present.

The works of both António Ole and Kiluanji Kia Henda are redefinitions of colonial power structures embedded in the urban landscape by intervening into the urban script. The need for this kind of artistic intervention can be compared to similar initiatives on the African continent, such as the Rhodes Must Fall movement in South Africa, where monuments are toppled and streets are renamed.[37] In the seamless connections between fiction and non-fiction, history is told anew and thereby redefined. New heroes and new power structures are defined and the old narratives are questioned by working on monumental places that are carriers of history. Their works—whether a metal modernist sculpture or an ephemeral performance translated onto photographic paper—fill a void at the core of the urban archive—with new images and narratives that address Luanda's heterogeneous present. They creatively redefine (a certain) history's visual traces, bringing them into the here and now and imagining a future with new aesthetics and heroes for the city yet to come that stands in radical contradistinction to the old "heroes" carved in stone.

NOTES

1. See e.g. Ana Balona de Oliveira and Edson Chagas, *Found Not Taken* (Heidelberg: Kehrer Verlag, 2016).

2. cf. Okwui Enwezor, *Under Siege, Four African Cities Freetown, Johannesburg, Kinshasa, Lagos* (Ostfildern: Hatje Cantz, 2002).

3. Akinbode Akinbiyi, et al., *Africas: The Artist and the City: A Journey and an Exhibition* (Actar, 2002).

4. cf. Sarah Nuttall and J.-A. Mbembé, *Johannesburg: The Elusive Metropolis* (Durham: Duke University Press, 2008), 8.

5. Ana Balona de Oliveira and Edson Chagas, *Found Not Taken*, (Heidelberg: Kehrer Verlag, 2016).

6. cf. Murray und Myers, *Cities in Contemporary Africa*, 27.

7. cf. Filip de Boeck and Marie-Françoise Plissart, *Kinshasa* (Antwerp: Ludion, 2004); James Donald, *Imagining the Modern City* (Continuum International Publishing Group, 2005).

8. Hall Foster, "An Archival Impulse," *October*, vol. 110, 2004, p. 3.

9. The city of Luanda itself has rarely been the site of violent armed struggle. One occasion was the failure of the Bicesse Accord and the first presidential elections in 1991, when government troops attacked the oppositional party UNITA. See, Fernando Batalha, *Angola: arquitectura e história* (Vega, 2006); Patrick Chabal and Nuno Vidal, *Angola: The Weight of History* (New York: Columbia University Press, 2007); Silvia Baptista Leiria Viegas, "Luanda, cidade (im)previsível?" February 2015, https://www.repository.utl.pt/handle/10400.5/10063.

10. The National Artists Union (*União Nacional dos Artistas Plásticos*) was founded with a strong socialist impetus in 1979 to support artistic practice and education. It offered courses in different techniques, access to studio space, and opened a gallery in the city center. The union still exists, but has only very limited financial resources. Its headquarters and gallery is situated in an old, deteriorating building from the early twentieth century in the city center.

11. Nadine Siegert, *(Re)Mapping Luanda: Utopische und nostalgische Zugänge zu einem kollektiven Bildarchiv* (LIT Verlag, 2016), 55ff.

12. Fabio Vanin, "Physical and Ephemeral Devices for Urban Security: the Case of Luanda," in *Urban Safety and Security*, edited by Emanuela Bonini Lessing (Milano: FrancoAngeli, 2015), 82.

13. Siegert, (Re)Mapping Luanda.

14. Christian Hanussek, *Memórias Íntimas Marcas. Interview mit dem Künstler Fernando Alvim über den Aufbau eines afrikanischen Kunstnetzwerkes*, Bd. x, 2 (Springerin: Hefte für Gegenwartskunst, 2004); Sue Williamson, "The Trienal de Luanda is coming: a new vision for art events in Africa," *Artthrob*, N. 97 (September 2005); Delinda Collier, *Repainting the Walls of Lunda: Information Colonialism and Angolan Art* (Minneapolis: University of Minnesota Press, 2016); Siegert, (Re)Mapping Luanda.

15. Nadine Siegert and Ulf Vierke, "Urban Memories and Utopias—Contemporary Art in Luanda and Nairobi," in *Living the City in Africa: Processes of Invention and Intervention*, edited by Veit Arlt, Birgit Obrist, and Elisio Macamo (LIT Verlag Münster, 2013), 135–52.

16. The theater is located in one of the old colonial buildings in the city centre and is one of the most important cultural venues in Luanda with a program of theater and music, and a nightclub. Some artists such as António Ole also (temporarily) use it as their studio space.

17. The loose artist collective consisted of mainly young contemporary artists and had been founded in 1999. They explored experimental formats and events over the previous years, mostly at *Teatro Elinga*. The core group was active until 2005. With the name *Nacionalistas* the group refers to the cultural patriotism of the Angolan art-scene, sometimes they also used the addition *Os Nacionalistas / Internacionalistas*.

18. Siegert, (Re)Mapping Luanda, 217.

19. Nilsa Massango, "Grande Hotel de Luanda é futura Casa do Brasil," *Jornal de Angola*, March 1, 2014, http://jornaldeangola.sapo.ao/sociedade/grande_hotel_de_luanda_e_futura_casa_do_brasil; Pedro Cardoso, "Museu de Antropologia," *Rede Angola —Notícias independentes sobre Angola*, July 17, 2014, http://www.redeangola.info/roteiros/museu-de-antropologia/.

20. The green and white graphite mural measures 345 square meters and shows linear human figures. It features an exoticizing scene of different ethnic groups of Angola, depicting them in their everyday work and social life.

21. Berta Maria Oliveira Jacob, "A toponímia de Luanda: das memórias coloniais às pós-coloniais," 2011, http://repositorioaberto.uab.pt/handle/10400.2/1866; Vera Mariz, "The Understanding of the Touristic Value of Portuguese Overseas Monuments: The Case of Angola (1959-1974)," *Journal of Spatial and Organizational Dynamics* 4, Nr. 2 (2016): 157–68.

22. The MPLA (Movimento Popular Libertação de Angola) was a former independence movement that became the governing party after independence in 1975. Until 1991, it was ideologically informed by Marxism-Leninism and acted as single political party. After 1991, the state officially became a multi-party system, but the MPLA has remained ruling party until today.

23. The Mansudae Overseas Project manufactured a number of bronze statues for the African continent and also built commemorative sites. All of these works were state-commissions; a recent one was the *African Renaissance Monument* in Dakar. The socialist aesthetics that dominate these works seems to fit the ideals of beauty of states with a totalitarian tendency.

24. Ferdinand de Jong and Vincent Foucher, "La tragédie du roi Abdoulaye? Néomodernisme et Renaissance africaine dans le Sénégal contemporain," *Politique africaine*, N. 118 (November 15, 2012): 187–204; Paul van Riel, Luca Faccio, and Martin Sasse, "All official portraiture of North Korea's reigning Kim family is made by Mansudae Art Studio," COLORS Magazine, January 10, 2013, http://www.colorsmagazine.com/stories/magazine/87/story/all-official-portraiture-of-north-koreas-reigning-kim-family-is-made-by-man.

25. António Ole has exhibited widely at the Biennials of São Paulo, Havanna, Johannesburg and Venice, and has had solo shows in Lisbon, Luanda, Salvador, Washington and Bayreuth.

26. Vanin, "Physical and Ephemeral Devices for Urban Security: the Case of Luanda," 84.

27. cf. Marissa Jean Moorman, *Intonations: A Social History of Music and Nation in Luanda, Angola, from 1945 to Recent Times*, New African Histories Series (Athens, Ohio: Ohio University Press, 2008).

28. Kiluanji Kia Henda is one of the most prominent Angolan artists today. He started to work professionally during the first Luanda Triennial in 2005/6 and has had a number of solo and group exhibitions since then, including the Biennials of Venice, São Paulo and Guangzhou.

29. Yinghong Cheng, *Creating the "New Man": From Enlightenment Ideals to Socialist Realities* (Honolulu: University of Hawaii Press, 2009).

30. The concept has also been applied in former French colonies, such as the Republic of Congo (Greani 2013).

31. Kim Knoppers, "Interview with Kiluanji Kia Henda," Foam Fotografiemuseum Amsterdam, accessed May 9, 2016, http://www.foam.org/talent/spotlight/interview-with-kiluanji-kia-henda.

32. In this work, Kiluanji Kia Henda confronts the colonial gaze with a staged portrait of a transgender person who is dressed in a female dress of an ethnic group from southern Angola. Nadine Siegert, "The archive as construction site—Collective memory and trauma in contemporary art from Angola," *World Art*, April 2016, 103–23.

33. Nelson Goodman, *Ways of Worldmaking* (Hackett Publishing, 1978), 106.

34. Knoppers, "Interview with Kiluanji Kia Henda."

35. Knoppers.

36. Vyjayanthi Rao, "Embracing Urbanism: The City as Archive," *New Literary History* 40, n. 2 (22. November 2009): 371–83, https://doi.org/10.1353/nlh.0.0085; Michael Sheringham and Richard Wentworth, "City as Archive: A Dialogue between Theory and Practice," *Cultural Geographies* 23, Nr. 3 (July 1, 2016): 517–23.

37. Minesh Parekh, "On #RhodesMustFall and what it means," *History Matters* (blog), January 29, 2016, http://www.historymatters.group.shef.ac.uk/rhodesmustfall-means/.

## BIBLIOGRAPHY

Akinbiyi, Akinbode, Kan-Si, Bodys Isek Kingelez, Yacouba Konate, Simon Njami, Pep Subiros, Anapa, et al. *Africas: The Artist and the City: A Journey and an Exhibition*. Actar, 2002.

Amin, Ash, and N. J Thrift. *Cities: Reimagining the Urban*. Cambridge: Polity, 2002.

Batalha, Fernando. *Angola: arquitectura e história*. Vega, 2006.

Boeck, Filip de, and Marie-Françoise Plissart. *Kinshasa*. Antwerp: Ludion, 2004.

Cardoso, Pedro. „Museu de Antropologia." Rede Angola—Notícias independentes sobre Angola, 17. Juli 2014. http://www.redeangola.info/roteiros/museu-de-antropologia/.

Chabal, Patrick, and Nuno Vidal. *Angola: The Weight of History*. New York: Columbia University Press, 2007.

Cheng, Yinghong. *Creating the „New Man": from Enlightenment Ideals to Socialist Realities*. Honolulu: University of Hawaii Press, 2009.

Collier, Delinda. *Repainting the Walls of Lunda: Information Colonialism and Angolan Art*. Minneapolis: University of Minnesota Press, 2016.

Donald, James. *Imagining The Modern City*. Continuum International Publishing Group, 2005.

Enwezor, Okwui. *Under Siege, Four African Cities, Freetown, Johannesburg, Kinshasa, Lagos*. Ostfildern: Hatje Cantz, 2002.

Hall Foster, "An Archival Impulse," October, vol. 110, 2004, p. 3.

Freund, Bill. *The African City*. Cambridge: Cambridge University Press, 2007.

Goodman, Nelson. *Ways of Worldmaking*. Hackett Publishing, 1978.

Hanussek, Christian. *Memórias Íntimas Marcas. Interview mit dem Künstler Fernando Alvim über den Aufbau eines afrikanischen Kunstnetzwerkes*. Bd. x. 2. Springerin: Hefte für Gegenwartskunst, 2004.

Jacob, Berta Maria Oliveira. „A toponímia de Luanda: das memórias coloniais às pós-coloniais," 2011. http://repositorioaberto.uab.pt/handle/10400.2/1866.

Jong, Ferdinand de, and Vincent Foucher. „La tragédie du roi Abdoulaye? Néomodernisme et Renaissance africaine dans le Sénégal contemporain." *Politique africaine*, N. 118 (November 15, 2012): 187–204.

Knoppers, Kim. „Interview with Kiluanji Kia Henda." Foam Fotografiemuseum Amsterdam. Zugegriffen May 9, 2016. http://www.foam.org/talent/spotlight/interview-with-kiluanji-kia-henda.

Mariz, Vera. „The Understanding of the Touristic Value of Portuguese Overseas Monuments: The Case of Angola (1959-1974)." *Journal of Spatial and Organizational Dynamics* 4, N. 2 (2016): 157–68.

Massango, Nilsa. „Grande Hotel de Luanda é futura Casa do Brasil." *Jornal de Angola*, March 1, 2014. http://jornaldeangola.sapo.ao/sociedade/grande_hotel_de_luanda_e_futura_casa_do_brasil.

Moorman, Marissa Jean. *Intonations: A Social History of Music and Nation in Luanda, Angola, from 1945 to Recent Times*. New African Histories Series. Athens, Ohio: Ohio University Press, 2008.

Murray, Martin J., and Garth Andrew Myers. *Cities in contemporary Africa*. Palgrave Macmillian, 2007.

Nuttall, Sarah, and J.-A. Mbembé. *Johannesburg: The Elusive Metropolis*. Durham: Duke University Press, 2008.

Oliveira, Ana Balona de, and Edson Chagas. *Found Not Taken*. 01. Heidelberg: Kehrer Verlag, 2016.

Parekh, Minesh. „On #RhodesMustFall and what it means." *History Matters* (blog), January 29, 2016. http://www.historymatters.group.shef.ac.uk/rhodesmustfall-means/.

Rao, Vyjayanthi. „Embracing Urbanism: The City as Archive." *New Literary History* 40, N. 2 (November 22, 2009): 371–83. https://doi.org/10.1353/nlh.0.0085.

Riel, Paul van, Luca Faccio, and Martin Sasse. „All official portraiture of North Korea's reigning Kim family is made by Mansudae Art Studio." COLORS Magazine, January 10, 2013. http://www.colorsmagazine.com/stories/magazine/87/story/all-official-portraiture-of-north-koreas-reigning-kim-family-is-made-by-man.

Salm, Steven J., and Toyin Falola. *African Urban Spaces in Historical Perspective*. University Rochester Press, 2009.

Sheringham, Michael, and Richard Wentworth. „City as Archive: A Dialogue between Theory and Practice." *Cultural Geographies* 23, N. 3 (July 1, 2016): 517–23.

Siegert, Nadine. *(Re)Mapping Luanda: Utopische und nostalgische Zugänge zu einem kollektiven Bildarchiv*. LIT Verlag, 2016.

———. „The archive as construction site—Collective memory and trauma in contemporary art from Angola." *World Art*, April 2016, 103–23.

Siegert, Nadine, and Ulf Vierke. „Urban Memories and Utopias—Contemporary Art in Luanda and Nairobi." In *Living the City in Africa: Processes of Invention and Intervention*, edited by Veit Arlt, Birgit Obrist, and Elisio Macamo, 135–52. LIT Verlag Münster, 2013.

Simone, Abdou Maliqalim. *For the City Yet to Come*. Durham: Duke University Press, 2004.

Soja, Edward W. *Postmetropolis*. Wiley-Blackwell, 2000.

Vanin, Fabio. „Physical and Ephemeral Devices for Urban Security: the Case of Luanda." In *Urban Safety and Security*, edited by Emanuela Bonini Lessing, 81–92. Milano: FrancoAngeli, 2015.

Viegas, Silvia Baptista Leiria. „Luanda, cidade (im)previsivel?" February 2015. https://www.repository.utl.pt/handle/10400.5/10063.

Williamson, Sue. „The Trienal de Luanda is coming: a new vision for art events in Africa." *Artthrob*, N. 97 (September 2005).

DR. NADINE SIEGERT is Deputy Director of Iwalewahaus at the University of Bayreuth, and member of the research project *Revolution 3.0* at the Bayreuth Academy of Advanced African Studies. She teaches modern and contemporary African arts and curatorial studies. She published her Ph.D. thesis *(Re)mapping Luanda* on nostalgic and utopian aesthetic strategies in contemporary art in Angola (LIT 2016). Her current research project is on socialist aesthetics in Africa. She has also worked on a number of exhibitions such as António Ole—*Contrary Alignment* (Nairobi, 2010), GhostBusters I & II (Berlin, 2011 & 2013), Mashup (Bayreuth 2015), FAVT: Future Africa Visions in Time (Bayreuth 2015, Nairobi and Salvador de Bahia 2017). Since 2015, Siegert has led the project *African Art History and the Formation of a Modernist Aesthetics*, which explores the history of the art collections at Iwalewahaus, the Museum of World Cultures (Frankfurt) and the Makerere Art Gallery (Kampala).

TRANSNATIONAL AFRICAS   Nadine Siegert

Fig. 1 Kiluanji Kia Henda, Icarus 13: The First Journey to the Sun, 2007,
Eight photographs on aluminium, 80 × 120 cm each. Model, 100 × 50 cm.

Fig. 2 Queen Njinga, late 1970s, Bronze. (Photograph by Nadine Siegert)

Fig. 3 António Ole, Mitologias II, 1985, painted metal. (Photograph by Nadine Siegert)

Fig. 4 António Ole, Mitologias II, 1985, painted metal. (Photograph by Nadine Siegert)

Fig. 5 Kiluanji Kia Henda, Redefining the Power IV
(with Miguel Prince), from the series Homem Novo, 2011,
photographic print mounted on aluminium, 120 × 80 cm.

Fig. 6 Kiluanji Kia Henda, Redefining the Power III
(Series 75 with Miguel Prince), 2013, Triptych,
photographic print mounted on aluminium, 120 × 80 cm each.

Fig. 7 Kiluanji Kia Henda, Balumuka—Ambush, 2010,
photographic print mounted on aluminium, 30 x 40 cm each.

MARCOS CARDÃO

# "Muamba, Banana e Cola."
# O Duo Ouro Negro e o Tropicalismo Desnacionalizador[1]

RESUMO: O Duo Ouro Negro foi um dos conjuntos portugueses com maior projeção e reconhecimento internacional na década de 1960. O mediatismo na imprensa e a integração numa indústria fonográfica em expansão transformou o conjunto num caso raro de sucesso internacional. Ao estabelecer um diálogo com as noções de diáspora e hibridismo, o percurso musical do Duo Ouro Negro escapou à fixidez identitária, nacional e étnica, e traduziu uma história de deslocamentos e reinscrições. Não obstante a sua dimensão internacional e cosmopolita, o Duo Ouro Negro foi também objeto de discursos nacionalistas, nomeadamente quando se tentou converter as suas práticas expressivas numa expressão idealizada da nacionalidade, de modo a criar e manter a ideia de unidade do império português. Neste artigo pretendo analisar as formas de traduzir o percurso artístico do Duo Ouro Negro e comentar como as narrativas nacionalistas procuraram, por um lado, impor um sentido único às práticas expressivas do conjunto e, por outro lado, como estas se revelaram insuficientes para as explicar.

PALAVRAS-CHAVE: Duo Ouro Negro, música popular, luso-tropicalismo, colonialismo, hibridismo

ABSTRACT: Duo Ouro Negro was one of the most prominent and internationally recognized Portuguese groups in the 1960s. Their integration into an expanding music industry, medialization and international tours turned them into a rare case of international success. Establishing a dialogue with the notions of diaspora and hybridism, the musical career of Duo Ouro Negro escaped from the identitary fixation, national and ethnic, and translated a history of displacements and reinscriptions. Despite their international and urban dimension, the Duo Ouro Negro was also subjected to nationalist discourses, especially when diverse agents of Portuguese colonialism tried to convert their music into an idealized expression of nationality, in order to create and maintain the idea of unity and integrity of the late Portuguese empire. In this article I will try to analyze the ways of translating Duo Ouro Negro's music, mentioning how the nationalist discourses sought, on one hand, to impose a national sense to their music and, on the other hand, how such imposition was limited to explain them.

KEYWORDS: Duo Ouro Negro, popular music, luso-tropicalism, colonialism, hybridism

## 1. Formas de Mediar

O Duo Ouro Negro foi provavelmente o conjunto musical português com maior projeção e reconhecimento internacional na década de 1960. O mediatismo na imprensa, a integração numa indústria fonográfica em expansão e as sucessivas digressões internacionais transformaram o conjunto num caso raro de sucesso internacional. Fundado em Vila Carmona (atual Uíge) em 1957, o conjunto era constituído por Raul Indipwo (Raul Cruz) e Milo Macmahon (Emílio Pereira), tendo sido por um breve período Trio Ouro Negro entre 1961 e 1963, com a integração de José Alves Monteiro. O Duo Ouro Negro distinguiu-se por fazer uma síntese de domínios musicais que até então eram mantidos em separado, optando por cruzar ritmos angolanos, como a *rebita* ou o *semba*, com o *funk*, o R&B e a música pop, e interpretar temas em Português, Francês, Inglês e nas diversas línguas de Angola (Umbundu, Tchokwe, Massongo, Conhama e Kimbundu). A criatividade musical do conjunto granjeou-lhe uma aura de cosmopolitismo, que se manifestou nas colaborações com músicos de outros países, na circulação universal dos seus discos, nas sucessivas digressões internacionais e nos prémios recebidos.

A música molda a memória popular e organiza um sentido do tempo (Frith 40). Ela é simultaneamente uma *performance* e as histórias, experiências e sociabilidades, que se contam a partir dela, bem como um terreno discursivo marcado por relações de poder e interpretações diversas. Nesse sentido, requer que se atente às "ligações entre a música enquanto expressão cultural, o desejo das audiências, as expectativas governamentais e os inescapáveis imperativos mercantis" (McCann 6). É a capacidade de articular campos aparentemente dispersos, como o ideológico, mercantil ou cultural, que permite evitar interpretações reducionistas ou essencialistas. Segundo Stuart Hall, articulação é um processo de fazer conecções e uma forma de compreender como diversos elementos ideológicos podem, em determinadas condições, coexistir dentro de uma formação discursiva e ser articulados dentro de uma conjuntura específica (Hall 141).

Ao estabelecer um diálogo com as noções de diáspora e hibridismo, tanto histórica como culturalmente, o percurso musical do Duo Ouro Negro parece escapar à fixidez identitária, nacional ou racial/étnica, e traduzir uma história de transformações, deslocamentos e reinscrições. Não obstante a sua dimensão cosmopolita, multilinguística e estereofónica (Gilroy, Jaji), o Duo Ouro Negro foi também objeto de discursos de índole nacionalista, nomeadamente quando se tentou converter as suas práticas expressivas numa expressão idealizada da nacionalidade, de modo a criar e manter a ideia de unidade do império português. A fim de consagrar e justificar a chamada viragem luso-tropical do regime autoritário—que se caracterizaria pela generalização de um discurso "humanista," respeitoso da diferença e diversidade cultural africana, ajustado a uma caracterização complacente da colonização portuguesa—, a música do Duo Ouro Negro foi convertida num emblema da fusão e interpenetração de culturas (Cardão).

Partindo do princípio de que as formas de mediar o Duo Ouro Negro construíram significados sobre a sua obra, e que estes foram sujeitos a processos de negociação e relações de poder, neste artigo pretende-se analisar as formas de traduzir o percurso artístico do Duo Ouro Negro, estabelecendo conexões entre domínios aparentemente dispersos, e comentar como as narrativas nacionalistas procuraram, por um lado, impor um sentido único às práticas expressivas do conjunto e, por outro lado, como estas se revelaram insuficientes para as explicar. Através da imagem avançada por Paul Gilroy de um navio enquanto "sistema vivo, microcultural e micropolítico" (4), que constituiu e reflete uma cultura marcada pelo movimento e trânsito, e não tanto pela pureza e autenticidade, procurar-se-á argumentar que o Duo Ouro Negro se aproximou de sensibilidades transnacionais e cosmopolitas e foi precursor de uma música moderna, híbrida, instável, em constante transformação e pouco compatível com idealizações nacionalistas.

## 2. Na Rota da Internacionalização

O primeiro espetáculo ao vivo do Duo Ouro Negro realizou-se no Cinema Restauração em Luanda, em 1957. Depois de várias atuações ao vivo em Angola e Moçambique, o conjunto rumou a Lisboa em 1959 para se apresentar ao vivo no Cinema Roma, Casino do Estoril, mas também no salão da Casa dos Estudantes do Império (CEI). O conjunto chegou a ser notícia no Boletim da CEI, *Mensagem*, em que se mencionava a sua importância, juntamente com conjuntos, como os Ngola Ritmos e Fogo Negro, no âmbito da "moderna música popular angolana."[2]

A capacidade do Duo Ouro Negro realizar espetáculos em várias salas e para diversos públicos revelava a elasticidade do conjunto e o seu desejo de não ficar confinado a um público fixo ou salas de espetáculo previsíveis. A ênfase dada aos espetáculos ao vivo implicava a existência de repertórios atualizados, *performances* inovadoras e sentido coreográfico. O profissionalismo dos membros do conjunto não descurou essas dimensões, nem impediu que a internacionalização atrapalhasse a gestão da sua carreira artística. A gravação de temas como "I Wanna Hold Your Hand" dos The Beatles, renomeado "Agora Vou Ser Feliz;" êxitos brasileiros, como "A Banda," de Chico Buarque; temas franceses, como "La Mamma" de Charles Aznavour; mas também temas de Miriam Makeba, como "Jikele Mauenhi" ou "Click Song," demonstrava a versatilidade do conjunto.

A emergência de novos públicos urbanos, o desejo de formas de consumo modernas e a capacidade do Duo Ouro Negro adaptar e renovar o seu repertório musical terá contribuído para o sucesso internacional do conjunto. Depois do sucesso no mercado discográfico português, e das digressões bem sucedidas em Angola, Portugal e Moçambique, o conjunto apostou em internacionalizar a sua carreira, passando a integrá-la em circuitos transnacionais. A França foi um dos locais de eleição, com o conjunto a efetuar diversos espetáculos no Olympia de Paris e a editar oito Ep's na editora francesa Pathé Marconi. A aposta na internacionalização era verbalizada pelos membros do conjunto que, a propósito do lançamento do Ep *La Kwela* (Ep—Columbia, 1965), diziam que o disco era "muito angolano, muito ié-ié e muito bonito. Estamos a cantar em francês para conquistar o público, dar-lhes coisas novas que perceba."[3]

Na tentativa de ir ao encontro de sensibilidades próximas da música ligeira, o Duo Ouro Negro participou por três vezes no Festival RTP da Canção (1967, 1969 e 1974); bem como em festivais internacionais, como o II Festival Internacional de Música Popular do Rio de Janeiro; foi convidado para participar no espetáculo "Rendez-Vous avec Danny Kaye," por ocasião do vigésimo aniversário da UNICEF; participou no espetáculo musical de celebração do Dia de Portugal na Exposição Internacional de Osaka em 1970; ou a presença no Festival Vilar de Mouros em 1971, onde apresentou o álbum conceptual *Blackground*. O conjunto produziu ainda a opereta *A Rua d'Eliza*, com texto e coreografia de sua autoria, na qual participaram a cantora Lilly Tchiumba (que participaria também no Festival RTP da Canção de 1969) e o conjunto Os Sheiks. Semelhante aos espetáculos da Broadway, a opereta contemplava vários estilos musicais e coreografias, e o seu tema principal era "Eliza (Gomara Saia)," uma adaptação de um tema tradicional de marrabenta. O programa foi transmitido pela RTP em 1968 e foi posteriormente selecionado para representar a televisão portuguesa no Festival de Milão.

A fama e o reconhecimento internacional foram assinalados na imprensa, com o Duo Ouro Negro a figurar na capa de diversas publicações periódicas (*Flama*, *Rádio & Televisão*, *Século Ilustrado*, *Álbum da Canção*, *Notícia*, *Revista de Angola*, etc.). A propósito do seu sucesso comercial e internacionalização, a revista *Álbum da Canção*, que editou um número especial dedicado integralmente ao conjunto, comentou:

> Bem se pode dizer que Milo e Raul se viram guindados, de um momento para outro, de simples desconhecidos, à condição de vedetas internacionais. . . . Paris, Madrid, Barcelona, Estocolmo, Londres, Roma, Atenas escutaram e aplaudiram as estranhas melopeias destes dois jovens que lhes ofereciam algo de novo, algo que não entendiam, mas que lhes tocava a alma, emocionando-os.[4]

As digressões internacionais levaram o conjunto a percorrer três continentes (África, Europa e América) e a experimentar uma sensação de trânsito que extravasava o local de origem e o exclusivismo identitário. As sucessivas digressões terão dado origem a formas de redesenhar a cultura viajante e perspetivá-la a partir de uma experiência enriquecedora de trocas culturais, estéticas e políticas. Estas tiveram um papel fundamental na formação de novas expressões e estilos musicais e abriram espaço para a emergência de códigos interpretativos diferentes das generalizações nacionalistas que acompanharam o conjunto ao longo da sua carreira, sobretudo quando gravou temas da música popular angolana, o que terá contribuído para marginalizar a sua relevância cultural e política.

### 3. As Fronteiras do Nacionalismo

Há várias zonas cinzentas no percurso do Duo Ouro Negro e desconhece-se, em pormenor, quais foram as suas simpatias políticas. A investigação recente aponta para a ligação do conjunto ao MPLA (Movimento pela Libertação de Angola), para o qual chegaram a financiar "a expatriação e exílio de estudantes a partir de Lisboa e da Argélia para países europeus, sobretudo França e países do então bloco de leste" (Cidra 389). Em 1975, o Duo gravou inclusivamente o single "Poema para Allende" (Ep—Emi, 1975), uma homenagem ao Presidente Salvador Allende, deposto pelo golpe militar no Chile em 1973, bem como os longas durações, *Blackground* (Lp—Columbia/ Valentim de Carvalho, 1971) e *Epopeia*

(Lp—Emi/ Valentim de Carvalho, 1975), ambos os álbuns marcados por um discurso crítico da colonização.

Porventura desconhecida da maioria, a aproximação do conjunto aos movimentos de libertação desarruma lugares pré-definidos que os associava à falta de engajamento político antes da independência, ou mesmo conivência com o regime colonial, e ao saudosismo colonial da população "retornada" após a descolonização. A inexistência de estudos sobre a receção do Duo Ouro Negro impossibilita respostas conclusivas, mas a releitura da sua obra num contexto pós-colonial, em que a dimensão festiva estava fortemente investida pelo sentimento de saudade, e o sucesso comercial de temas, como "Vou Levar-te Comigo" (editada em Lp em 1979 e reeditada em single pela editora Rádio Triunfo em 1985), que abordava a guerra civil em Angola, mas com um título polissémico sujeito a diferentes usos e reinterpretações, terá alimentado a aura de nostalgia pós-colonial.

Com músicas assentes em arranjos para duas vozes, acompanhadas por violas, orquestra e instrumentos tradicionais africanos, um dos primeiros álbuns intitulado *Africaníssimo* (Lp—Columbia, 1959), que foi objeto de várias reedições, evidenciava a propensão do Duo ouro Negro para abordar diversas linguagens musicais. Parte do álbum inspirava-se nas raízes da música tradicional angolana, incluindo o primeiro êxito do conjunto, "Kurikutela," o tema popular "Muxima," uma canção tradicional goesa, "Deknni," o tema "Singing My Song" e uma versão do tema brasileiro "Upa Neguinho," da autoria de Edu Lobo. Com arranjos e direção musical do maestro Jorge Machado e Thilo Krassman, e participação do coro feminino da Emissora Nacional, o álbum contou ainda com a participação do músico brasileiro Sivuca. A contracapa do álbum continha uma nota escrita pelo Dou Ouro Negro que traduzia a vontade do conjunto não se confinar a um único lugar:

> Quando em 1959 saímos de Angola rumo à Europa trazíamos na nossa bagagem um lote de canções lindas. Umas eram estilizações do nosso folclore, outras eram de nossa autoria, traduzindo a cor mulata da nossa terra. Para o Edu Lobo, além da admiração, um cordial *kuala peka* dos mulatos que lhe pedem para ele dar uma olhada e ver com a música do Brasil é igual à nossa. (*Africaníssimo*)

Animados desde o início por uma ideia de trânsitos tropicais e sincronismos musicais, a música do Duo Ouro Negro dificilmente se encaixaria nos discursos purificadores da autenticidade local, nem no carácter normativo do luso-tropicalismo. Porém, o conjunto foi objeto de vários discursos que pretendiam fixar a sua diferença musical e caracterizar o seu significado segundo convenções nacionalistas.[5]

O impacto do nacionalismo depende mais da sua circulação discursiva e banalização na vida quotidiana (Billig), do que das ideias mais ou menos concisas que abrange e transmite. Os discursos nacionalistas fizeram parte dos exercícios de mediação de vários intérpretes africanos, foram transversais a vários agentes e recriados por protagonistas culturais, jornalistas e editoras discográficas ocupadas em comercializar a diferença cultural africana. Por exemplo, a Valentim de Carvalho tinha a coleção "Ngola," um selo exclusivo para comercializar artistas angolanos, e a editora Alvorada, propriedade da empresa portuense Rádio Triunfo, lançou uma coleção dedicada exclusivamente à música folclórica africana em meados da década de 1960, onde comercializou fonogramas de Alba Clyngton, cognominada a "embaixatriz do folclore angolano", Ngola Ritmos, Ngola Melodias, entre outros. A editora Alvorada dispunha inclusivamente de uma publicação oficial na qual anunciava as novidades do seu catálogo. Por ocasião da edição de fonogramas dos conjuntos Negoleiros e Ngomas dizia-se: "O folclore de Angola é riquíssimo. A sua importância é extraordinária na medida em que nos ajuda a conhecer melhor a nossa africana província ultramarina. Os tambores da África negra sempre excitaram a imaginação dos ocidentais. Os tambores serviram para transmitir mensagens, servem para nos oferecer ritmos inebriantes."[6]

Apoiado numa fantasia primitivista, a comercialização de fonogramas de folclore africano recorria a uma linguagem da alteridade através da qual se associava o outro cultural e étnico quase unicamente ao ritmo e à dança. Esta forma paternalista de codificar o folclore nas colónias reenviava os intérpretes para um estado natural onde predominavam as sensações, as emoções e raramente o discernimento, elaboração e a autonomia musical. Fora do âmbito da produção e comercialização de objetos musicais exóticos, parecia não haver espaço para uma valorização autónoma das práticas expressivas africanas. Nesse sentido, o trabalho de tradução da música africana realizada pelas editoras não se conseguia libertar das representações coloniais, uma vez que negava a possibilidade de a conceber enquanto uma expressão musical legítima e independente, sem que esta passasse pelo crivo da autenticidade atribuído pelos folcloristas. Mesmo submetido a uma lógica comercial, fosse enquanto objeto de consumo pitoresco e exótico destinado a algumas camadas da população urbana, ou símbolo da diversidade regional destinado a uma indústria do turismo colonial emergente,[7] mantinha-se a ideia de uma africanidade intocada, consentânea com os discursos nacionalistas integradores, que infantilizavam e, simultaneamente, estilizavam a diferença africana.

A popularização do folclore africano enquanto género inerente à cultura africana terá condicionado a carreira artística de vários conjuntos provenientes das colónias. Nomeadamente a carreira do Duo Ouro Negro, que chegou a ser criticado na imprensa por interpretar temas de música ligeira, o que evidenciava a transversalidade de agentes ocupados na salvaguarda da integridade das práticas expressivas africanas. Num artigo publicado na revista Plateia criticava-se as alterações que o Duo Ouro Negro tinha introduzido no seu repertório, dizendo que as características do conjunto eram "diferentes, muito nossas, da nossa música, em particular da província-irmã. Essa base, a do folclore português, deveria constituir o seu espetáculo total entre nós, principalmente entre nós."[8] Ao mesmo tempo que zelava pela defesa de um ideal de pureza e autenticidade musical, o jornalista da Plateia afirmava que era empobrecedor ver o Duo Ouro Negro a imitar grupos de música ligeira, como os Los Panchos, ou Los Paraguaios, ambos citados no artigo. No fundo, pretendia-se que o Duo Ouro Negro não fizesse concessões comerciais e continuasse a seguir a via da música tradicional que havia caracterizado a sua carreira até então. Implícito nestas críticas estava a ideia de que a aposta na comercialização poderia destruir a integridade artística do conjunto, por se entender que o comércio discográfico era incompatível com uma conceção fundacional e preservacionista da música popular africana, que deveria ser autêntica e representativa da diversidade cultural do império português.

A gravação de diversos fonogramas de música tradicional, como *Duo Ouro Negro Canta Canções do Folclore de Angola* (Ep—Columbia, 1960); as declarações do conjunto afirmando que "o folclore de Angola é a nossa face, o nosso ineditismo;"[9] ou as capas de discos que incluíam a justaposição de signos associados à portugalidade, favoreciam as interpretações de cariz nacionalista. Por exemplo, na capa do Ep *Maria Rita* (Ep—Columbia, 1969) surgia uma fotografia do conjunto com um galo de Barcelos sob pano de fundo, numa sobreposição de elementos reconhecidos da portugalidade que contribuía para o pretendido efeito pitoresco e convertia o conjunto num alegado paradigma da lusotropicalidade. Porém, o galo de Barcelos impresso na capa era um dos vários adereços criados propositadamente para o filme *Hammerhead* (1968—Columbia Pictures), realizado por David Miller, que foi rodado parcialmente em Lisboa e Cascais. O galo de Barcelos serviu, aliás, de cenário a uma sequência do filme onde se vê cerca de trezentos *hippies* numa "festa psicadélica em Cascais."[10] O Duo Ouro Negro terá inclusivamente aproveitado a sessão fotográfica em Cascais para fazer várias capas para os seus discos, desfazendo assim a ideia de que havia uma intenção de alegorizar as representações da portugalidade na capa do referido Ep.

Para tornar os discos de folclore africano comercialmente apelativos, as indústrias fonográficas imprimiam capas de discos que reforçavam o exotismo e que, no caso português, procuravam caucionar a ideia de diversidade regional do império colonial português e, assim, provar a originalidade dos encontros culturais no espaço sob soberania portuguesa. Invariavelmente previsíveis e estereotipadas, era comum as editoras optarem por capas com imagens de músicos negros vestidos com trajes regionais, pés descalços e a ensaiar passos de dança sob cenários tropicais.[11] Enquanto propostas de consumo exótico, que obedeciam a um princípio de absolutização das diferenças étnicas e raciais, a comercialização do outro musical parecia generalizar um modo de olhar para as práticas expressivas africanas, algures entre a curiosidade estética e a admiração (Huggan).

### 4. O Tropicalismo Desnacionalizador

As tentativas de colocar a etnicidade como categoria fundamental para explicar a "diferença" das práticas expressivas africanas foi criticada por diversos autores. Designadamente por Paul Gilroy, que alertou para os equívocos dos absolutismos étnicos na crítica cultural, sobretudo quando estes são convocados para justificar formas de pertença, identidades ou nacionalismos. No entender de Paul Gilroy, os "absolutismos étnicos" podem ser desafiados através da música e dos seus rituais, que permitem "criar um modelo onde a identidade possa ser entendida como algo diferente de uma essência fixa" (102). Como sugere a música do Duo Ouro Negro, não por qualquer desígnio teórico, ou forma de ilustrar conceitos pré-existentes, mas porque o conjunto convocou diversos elementos expressivos e articulou dimensões políticas, ideológicas e culturais. Com efeito, o conjunto animou uma utopia transnacional, que permitiu deslocar os conceitos de tropicalismo e hibridismo de uma leitura essencialmente nacional e colocou em evidência as inconsistências e fraquezas das formas de mediação nacionais.

No final da década de 1960, o Duo Ouro Negro introduziu uma série de inovações formais no seu repertório, realizando álbuns mais coesos nos quais transparecia uma ideia de hibridismo e modernidade. A edição dos álbuns *Mulowa Afrika* (Lp—Columbia, 1967)—provavelmente o disco mais internacional do Duo, com edições no Brasil, França, Israel, Alemanha, Argentina e nos Estados Unidos, onde se intitulou "The Music of Africa Today"—, BlackgrounId (Lp—Columbia/ Valentim de Carvalho, 1971) e *Epopeia* (Lp—Emi/ Valentim de Carvalho, 1975) marcaram uma viragem na carreira do conjunto. Explorando novas tipologias musicais, estes álbuns aproximavam-se dos padrões de consumo de públicos cosmopolitas, predispostos à chamada música de fusão, um subgénero em voga no início da década de 1970, e assinalavam a importância que as alegorias políticas tinham adquirido no seu discurso. Por exemplo, o álbum *Epopeia*, talvez o longa duração menos conhecido do conjunto, enunciava claramente sensibilidades e ideias anticoloniais. Nomeadamente no tema "Muinda Kwateni, Chegou o Homem Branco," que alegorizava o processo de colonização europeia, salientando a indiferença dos europeus em relação às culturas locais e o carácter violento e devastador do estabelecimento europeu.

Contrariamente ao projeto de mistura e interpenetração de culturas associado ao luso-tropicalismo, integrado na noção de "mística luso-cristã de integração,"[12] e nas concepções essencialistas do nacionalismo cultural, a propensão do Duo Ouro Negro para sobrepor diferentes domínios musicais e alegorizar o processo de colonização sugeria uma conceção desterritorializada de tropicalismo e uma desvinculação das políticas coloniais.[13] As identificações políticas terão sido importantes para as experiências musicais realizadas pelo conjunto no início da década de 1970, mas não terão sido o único fator a determinar a sua criatividade e expressão artística. Como indicava o álbum *Blackground*, que abarcava a fusão de diversos elementos sonoros, políticos, poéticos e coreográficos (os espetáculos de promoção do álbum tinham cerca de duas horas de duração e reuniam cerca de trinta e cinco participantes, entre músicos e bailarinos). Com a ambição de um projeto conceptual, o disco inventava uma narrativa sobre o continente africano e as suas ramificações extracontinentais. O seu primeiro tema, intitulado "Iemenjá," contava a história de *Iemenjá* e do seu filho, Rio, que cresceu, atravessou o continente africano e se ramificou, e "cada ramificação foi um filho novo, com o de nome: Missouri, Amazonas, Mississippi e Rio de La Plata," como se referia na letra. A celebração das raízes africanas e suas ramificações, bem como uma ideia de angolanidade, traduzia-se na capa do disco, que continha uma ilustração do artista angolano Eleutério Sanches.

Em oposição a uma ideia de cultura territorial fechada e codificada, no álbum *Blackground* recorria-se à mitologia do princípio fundador de África e dos rios africanos para tematizar as transformações que ocorreram na música levada pelos escravos na viagem transatlântica. Sem pretensões de um regresso às origens primordiais africanas, privilegiando antes o poder transformador das rotas em detrimento das raízes, o álbum aproximava-se da noção de "passagem do meio," sugerida por Paul Gilroy, que representava tanto os "vários projetos redentores de regresso a uma pátria-africana, a circulação de ideias e ativistas, bem como a circulação de artefactos culturais e políticos chave: panfletos, livros, discos e coros" (4).

Ao ampliar e desnacionalizar a noção de tropicalismo, que extravasa o espaço geográfico do chamado "mundo português"[14] e se desdobrava na alusão aos caudais e ramificações dos rios do continente americano (ver nota 14), o álbum *Blackground* convocava metáforas que sinalizavam a fluidez, movimento, trânsito, dispersão e a vitalidade de uma cultura de diáspora. O trânsito entre três continentes—África, Europa e América—reportava-se a um espaço imaginário de uma viagem substancialmente diferente da efetuada (e celebrada) pelos colonizadores nas suas rotas de expansão e conquista e traduzia a agência e autonomia artística do Duo Ouro Negro. Ao evocar a geografia imaginária da diáspora africana, o conjunto distanciava-se dos absolutismos étnicos, afastando-se também das exigências de autenticidade musical. Sugerindo uma genealogia alternativa da categoria "negro" (Mbembe), o Duo Ouro Negro ensaiava novas configurações identitárias "não delimitadas por fronteiras em sentido clássico, mas sim pela imbricação de espaços múltiplos, constantemente produzidos, desfeitos e refeitos tanto através de guerras e conquistas como através do movimento de bens e pessoas" (Mbembe 99). A desvalorização do local tornava possível negociar o cruzamento entre vários espaços, privilegiando o deslocamento em vez de uma territorialidade fixa ou identidade orgânica.

Nos antípodas das imagens pastorais de uma pretensa tradição africana, que deveria ser preservada e embalsamada para conter o poder corrosivo da modernidade, o Duo Ouro Negro enveredava pelos processos dinâmicos do hibridismo, itinerância e mistura. A preferência pela amálgama de elementos musicais heterogéneos traduzia-se musicalmente num álbum que continha passagens e trechos musicais, instrumentais e cantados, que combinavam estilos musicais afro-americanos, como o *funk, soul, rhythm n' blues*, com espirituais negros, ritmos latinos, africanos e música pop. Esta opção, musical e política, era assumida em diversas ocasiões, por exemplo, numa entrevista os membros do conjunto diziam:

> Um dos caudais do *Blackground* é precisamente o rio brasileiro; outro é o ramo europeu, mas só no que diz respeito ao ritmo, a pop-music; outro, ainda, um dos mais importantes, aliás, é o ramo americano, a música dita branca: a junção,

por exemplo, do espiritual-folk, soul-music, etc. Como sabe, há muito que se processa um retrocesso da música americana para África, chamado o afro.[15]

A referência e o uso de vários subgéneros musicais confirmavam a dificuldade em converter o Duo Ouro Negro num baluarte da música tradicional, ou signo de pureza identitária. Faltava ao conjunto os requisitos da cultura tradicional, que era idealmente rural, fixa e imutável, as especificidades do "carácter nacional," imaginado enquanto presença tangível, e uma conceção rígida das fronteiras entre géneros musicais. Produto da expansão das indústrias discográficas, renovação dos gostos musicais e renegociação dos géneros urbanos, o Duo Ouro Negro não dispunha do elemento de autenticidade, que seria uma condição fundamental para a sua nacionalização. Nesse sentido, o conjunto terá contribuído para a redefinição e expansão do conceito de (música) popular—híbrida, urbana e transversal a públicos. Paralelamente, o conjunto introduziu uma forma de tematizar a identidade segundo um princípio de diferença e rutura em vez de unidade, semelhança e continuidade, aproximando-se assim de uma "conceção mais cultural e processual de identidade do que essencialista" (Hall 225). Em vez de completa e acabada, ou tradutora de uma ideia de plenitude, a identidade do Duo Ouro Negro permanecia incompleta, estando sempre num processo de ser formada e preenchida com novos referentes.

### 5. "Muamba, Banana e Cola"

Talvez por não se ajustar ao paradigma interpretativo da textualidade, a produção musical é normalmente negligenciada nos debates sobre a modernidade. Porém, ela integra as novas tecnologias da informação, comunicação e difusão e articula uma série de ansiedades e fantasias que permitem identificar a emergência de noções compósitas de modernidade feitas de empréstimos e encontros. Como se se tratasse de uma esfera pública alternativa, a produção musical oferece uma multiplicidade de materiais expressivos massificados, que transcendem os lugares de origem, bem como conceções unívocas de modernidade, que tendem a equivaler modernidade a ocidente, entendendo que esta pode ser inclusivamente exportada para as áreas de colonização e/ou é incompatível com os paradigmas da governamentalidade colonial (Chakrabarty).

A obra do Duo Ouro Negro oferece um retrato vivo, ainda que parcial, de um local e um tempo histórico. Mesmo não elegendo a denúncia da guerra colonial, nem as assimetrias e hierarquias do colonialismo como tema principal, o Duo

Ouro Negro não deixou de se referir às contradições de um território colonial onde se sentiu o impacto da modernidade e que foi igualmente marcado por grandes transformações no tecido urbano, pelo aparecimento de classes médias, pela generalização de novas formas de consumo e lazer e o surgimento de estilos de vida sinalizadores de uma vivência moderna. No âmbito da produção discográfica, a iniciativa económica em Angola conduziu à constituição de novas editoras, como a Fadiang (Fábrica de Discos de Angola), a Fonográfica (Companhia de Discos de Angola) e uma sucursal da Valentim de Carvalho (subdividida nas etiquetas *Decca* e *Ngola*, esta especificamente para a edição de música angolana) a operar em Angola. A proliferação de editoras evidenciava o vigor do mercado interno, que levou a Valentim de Carvalho a inaugurar uma loja de discos em Luanda em 1968.

Há uma diversidade de lugares onde a modernidade é realizada e constantemente traduzida. Um dos marcadores de modernidade em Angola foi o aparecimento de bens de consumo internacionais, entre os quais várias marcas americanas, como a *Coca-Cola*, cuja comercialização se tornou um fator de distinção simbólica no território. Alegadamente proibida em Portugal continental, a comercialização da *Coca-Cola* em Angola e Moçambique indicava, por um lado, as promessas de liberdade associadas à cultura de consumo americana e, por outro lado, abria espaço à afirmação de proto-identidades nas colónias, em que a imaginação da modernidade era fundamental.

Incluída no álbum *Sob o Signo de Iemanjá* (Lp—Columbia/ Valentim de Carvalho, 1970), a canção "Muamba, Banana e Cola" tinha um padrão rítmico sincopado e traços estilísticos distintivos dos géneros performativos de Angola, como o *semba*. A letra era constituída por poucos versos, repetidos várias vezes ao longo da canção, que diziam: "Que vontade chorar quando eu me lembro de Angola. Muamba, banana e Cola isso se come em Angola." Ao mencionar três produtos consumidos em Angola—um prato regional,[16] um fruto tropical e um refrigerante americano de consumo global—, o tema inventava e performativizava uma nova identidade angolana, colocando-a fora do nacionalismo integrador e da ideologia integracionista ou assimiladora. E fazia-o combinando realidades locais com produtos globais, uma combinação que sugeria a existência de uma versão de modernidade atualizada.

Em vez de ser considerado um símbolo nefasto do imperialismo americano, que ameaçaria a cultura local, a *Coca-Cola* era um ingrediente da modernidade que poderia ser articulado com uma ideia de angolanidade. Ou seja, a angolanidade não passava por um processo de depuração nacional dos artefactos de consumo, no qual se excluíam os artefactos que não fossem realmente nacionais ou angolanos, nem pela rejeição da cultura de massas. Pelo contrário, a cultura de massas era incorporada e permitia renovar os discursos identitários, colocando na imaginação popular produtos globais cujo valor e poder de atração eram reconhecidos. Como refere Victoria de Grazia, "a sociabilidade da sociedade de consumo apresentava-se como uma alternativa progressista à tacanhez do exclusivismo, provincialismo ou, pior, às solidariedades reacionárias" (8). Além de sugerir a aceitação do processo de americanização cultural, a atitude em relação à *Coca-Cola* parecia admitir a existência de um elemento democratizador no consumo de produtos internacionais. Nesta visão simultaneamente complacente e utópica das oportunidades de consumo, a marca tinha um poder persuasor de criar estilos de vida modernos e cosmopolitas.

### 6. "Política(s) da Transfiguração"
A tensão entre o nacional e o internacional é um dos terrenos mais produtivos para discutir os significados da música popular. O Duo Ouro Negro dramatizou essa discussão e introduziu novas categorias para a mapear, estas não se enquadravam nas definições exíguas de resistência cultural. Com efeito, a alusão metafórica a uma cultura de diáspora, marcada por fluxos e trocas culturais, e aos aspectos transnacionais da modernidade, não cabia nas descrições heroicizadas de resistência anticolonial ou combate cultural, invariavelmente imaginadas num quadro nacional, nem numa versão idealizada de identidade negra, identificada exclusivamente por pertença étnica ou autenticidade cultural, muito menos nos discursos nacionalistas do regime colonial. Próxima da cultura do "Atlântico Negro," que pelo seu carácter híbrido não se encontrava circunscrita às fronteiras nacionais, a música do Duo Ouro Negro promoveu uma "política da transfiguração" (Gilroy 37) desvinculada da ideologia colonial. A vontade de incorporar e reconfigurar aquilo que era estrangeiro, renovando constantemente a sua música, não se ajustava aos essencialismos autossuficientes da singularidade luso-tropical nem a uma ideia de identidade enraizada, supostamente estável e natural, que fundamentaria uma "história de encontros." Ao quebrar com os nós explicativos entre lugar, cultura e identidade, o Duo Ouro Negro deslocou o debate para um campo transnacional, anulou o poder do território na determinação da sua música e contribuiu para ressignificar as noções de resistência política e luta anticolonial, apartando-as de uma moldura nacional.

## NOTES

1. Marcos Cardão, investigador de Pós-Doutoramento no Centro de Estudos Comparatistas da Faculdade de Letras da Universidade de Lisboa. Este artigo foi desenvolvido no âmbito das atividades de investigação avançada do Projeto UID/ELT/00509/2013, no Grupo CITCOM do Centro de Estudos Comparatistas da Faculdade de Letras da Universidade de Lisboa. Todas as traduções são da minha responsabilidade.

2. Ver Carlos Eduardo. "A Propósito da Moderna Música Popular Angolana." *Mensagem*. Boletim da Casa dos Estudantes do Império, nº 3, ano XIV, Agosto, 1962. Organização de Manuel Ferreira. *Mensagem*. Boletim da Casa dos Estudantes do Império, vol. 2, ALAC, 1996, s/p.

3. Beça Múrias. "Ouro Negro." *Flama*. 19 de Março de 1965, s/p. A denominada "Kwela" era inspirada numa dança ritual da tradição sul-africana, apropriada pelo Duo Ouro Negro, que inventara uma nova coreografia com grande popularidade na época. A revista *Flama* chegou a publicar reportagens ilustradas sobre o novo estilo de dança, onde se viam os elementos do Duo Ouro Negro a ensinar as artistas Tonicha e Maria da Glória a dançar o novo o ritmo. Embora fosse uma dança híbrida e internacional, na revista *Flama* o articulista regozijava-se pelo facto do novo ritmo ter origem portuguesa: "E se os jornais de todo o mundo deram caixa-alta aos novos ritmos, chegou agora a nossa vez de 'ditar a moda.' Não se trata de mais um ritmo importado, já rotulado de êxito e que se ensaia a preceito para fazer furor no próximo baile em cada da 'Milá.' Agora o ritmo é nosso, é estreia e chama-se 'kwela!' Os seus criadores são o nacionalíssimo duo Ouro Negro." Manuel Vieira. "Ouro Negro: O ritmo é kwela." *Flama*. 5 de Fevereiro de 1965, s/p.

4. S/a. "Nota de Abertura." *Álbum da Canção*, 50, 1 de Abril de 1967, p. 1.

5. Homi Bhabha refere que "a fixidez, enquanto signo de uma diferença cultural/ histórica/ racial no discurso do colonialismo, constitui um modo paradoxal de representação: conota rigidez e uma ordem imutável, bem como desordem, degeneração e repetição compulsiva" (143).

6. S/a. "Negoleiros e Ngomas. Mensagem musical de Angola." *Alvorada*. Setembro/Outubro, 1964, s/p.

7. A estilização e o embelezamento da cultura popular africana faziam parte das iniciativas do Centro de Informação e Turismo de Angola (CITA), que estava incumbido de promover a expansão do turismo em Angola através da elaboração de planos turísticos gerais, promoção de festas, espetáculos, concursos literários e efetuar a recolha do folclore musical, "no sentido de defender e conservar na sua possível pureza, as tradições e costumes locais que o mereçam," como se referia no diploma legal que promulgou a criação do CITA em 1959. S/a. *Boletim Geral do Ultramar*, vol. 35, Agência Geral do Ultramar, 1959, s/p.

8. S/a. "Ouro Verdadeiro nas Vozes do 'Ouro Negro'." *Plateia*, 1 de Abril de 1964, p. 13.

9. S/a. "Duo Ouro Negro: Confissão a Dois." *Magazine*, 17 de Dezembro de 1966, p. 13

10. A sequência do filme *Hammerhead* está disponível em: https://www.youtube.com/watch?v=RwzKWeg3I3U (Acedido em Maio de 2017).

11. Segundo Marissa Moorman: "The album covers of Angolan music produced in the late 1950s and early 1960s are particularly useful for demonstrating how Portuguese companies marketed Angolan music as folklore. Images of *assimilado* musicians like the three young men of Ngola Melodias—one black, one white, one mixed-race, holding acoustic guitars and a local drum, all shirtless in rolled-up khakis and bare feet—were meant to represent the truth of lusotropicalism" (114).

12. "Uma Mística Luso-Cristã de Integração" é o título de um dos capítulos do livro de Gilberto Freyre, *O Luso e o Trópico* (225-242).

13. Por economia de espaço não foi possível apreciar os desdobramentos do conceito de luso-tropicalismo introduzidos por Gilberto Freyre no final da década de 1960, que procurou retirar peso político-ideológico a um conceito ligado historicamente ao colonialismo português. A introdução do conceito de tropicologia e a supressão definitiva do prefixo "luso" visava alegadamente inaugurar uma ciência "pós-colonial" que estudaria os fatores ecológicos e culturais dos grupos humanos situados nos espaços tropicais. Paralelamente seria interessante encetar uma análise comparativa entre o "tropicalismo desnacionalizador" do Duo Ouro Negro e o potencial alegórico, urbano e transfigurador, do movimento Tropicália no Brasil. Este introduziu uma linguagem crítica do exclusivismo identitário, visando especificamente as várias formas de nacionalismo brasileiro, quer o nacionalismo redentor de inspiração marxista, quer o nacionalismo paternalista e essencializador dos discursos oficiais. Distanciando-se da designação de "tropicalismo," porque esta se reduzia a um repertório de clichés sobre a vida nos trópicos e evocava remotamente o conceito introduzido por Gilberto Freyre, o movimento Tropicália privilegiou a indefinição e o fragmento e encontrou na cultura de massas internacional um campo aberto de possibilidades para redefinir a imagem do Brasil, parodiar alguns dos seus aspetos e exponenciar as suas contradições (Dunn).

14. *O Mundo Português* foi o nome dado a uma das primeiras revistas de propaganda colonial publicada na primeira metade do século xx e editada conjuntamente pela Secretaria para a Propaganda Nacional (SPN) e pela Agência Geral das Colónias (AGU). O primeiro número da revista foi publicado a 26 de Janeiro de 1934 e último em 1946. A publicação pretendia construir uma imagem positiva sobre o império português e fazer das colónias grandes escolas do nacionalismo português. Embora o último número da revista tivesse sido publicado em 1946, a designação "mundo português" continuou a ser largamente utilizada durante a vigência do regime autoritário. Nomeadamente na Exposição do Mundo Português, no título do livro de Gilberto Freyre, *O Mundo que o Português Criou*, no subtítulo do jornal *Diário Popular*, que se intitulava "o jornal de maior expansão no mundo português," no subtítulo da revista publicada em Angola, *Jornal Magazine*, que se intitulava "Um Jornal

de Angola para o Mundo Português," etc. A designação "mundo português" converteu-se assim numa espécie de significante instrumental para descrever a área de colonização portuguesa e passou a ser um descritor banal da pluricontinentalidade do império português.

Duo Ouro Negro (entrevista a). "Blackground. O Velho e Novo Testamento da Música Africana segundo o Duo Ouro Negro." *Nova Antena*, 2 de Outubro de 1970, p. 22.

A valorização das gastronomias regionais constituiu uma forma de elevar os produtos étnicos/regionais a produtos nacionais, como se verificou com o prato regional angolano, "Muamba," que foi incluído num livro de cozinha português. Os livros de cozinha tiveram um papel constitutivo na edificação de um corpo culinário nacional, tornando-se indissociáveis de um esforço nacionalizador. Ver, por exemplo, M. A. M, edição. *Cozinha do Mundo Português*. Livraria Tavares Martins, 1962. Numa outra publicação sobre a cozinha nas colónias dizia-se: "Pode-se julgar uma civilização pela cozinha. Ora nas nossas províncias ultramarinas vamos encontrar manjares dos mais requintados e depois de dados a conhecer muito apreciados pelos mais exigentes." S/a. *Cozinha e Doçaria do Ultramar Português*. AGU, 1969, p. 9.

15. Duo Ouro Negro (entrevista a). "Blackground. O Velho e Novo Testamento da Música Africana segundo o Duo Ouro Negro." *Nova Antena*, 2 de Outubro de 1970, p. 22.

16. A valorização das gastronomias regionais constituiu uma forma de elevar os produtos étnicos/regionais a produtos nacionais, como se verificou com o prato regional angolano, "Muamba," que foi incluído num livro de cozinha português. Os livros de cozinha tiveram um papel constitutivo na edificação de um corpo culinário nacional, tornando-se indissociáveis de um esforço nacionalizador. Ver, por exemplo, M. A. M, edição. *Cozinha do Mundo Português*. Livraria Tavares Martins, 1962. Numa outra publicação sobre a cozinha nas colónias dizia-se: "Pode-se julgar uma civilização pela cozinha. Ora nas nossas províncias ultramarinas vamos encontrar manjares dos mais requintados e depois de dados a conhecer muito apreciados pelos mais exigentes." S/a. *Cozinha e Doçaria do Ultramar Português*. AGU, 1969, p. 9.

OBRAS CITADAS

Bhabha, Homi. "A questão Outra. Estereótipo, discriminação e o discurso do colonialismo." Organização de Manuela Ribeiro Sanches. *Deslocalizar a Europa: Antropologia, Arte, Literatura e História na Pós-Colonialidade*. Edições Cotovia, 2005, pp. 143-166.

Billig, Michael. *Banal Nationalism*. Sage Publications, 1991.

Cardão, Marcos. *Fado Tropical. O Luso-Tropicalismo na Cultura de Massas (1960-1974)*. Edições Unipop, 2014.

Chakrabarty, Dipesh. *Provincializing Europe: Postcolonial Thought and Historical Difference*. Princeton University Press, 2000.

Cidra, Rui. "Duo Ouro Negro." Edição de Castelo-Branco Salwa. *Enciclopédia da Música em Portugal no Século xx, c-l*. Temas e Debates/ Círculo de Leitores, 2010, pp. 387-390.

Dunn, Christopher. *Brutality Garden: Tropicalia and the Emergence of a Brazilian Counterculture*. University of North Carolina Press, 2001.

Ferreira, Manuel, organização. *Mensagem. Boletim da Casa dos Estudantes do Império*. Vol.2, ALAC, 1996.

Freyre, Gilberto. *O Luso e o Trópico: Sugestões em Torno dos Métodos Portugueses de Integração de Povos Autóctones e de Culturas Diferentes da Europeia num Complexo Novo de Civilização: o Luso-Tropical*. Comissão Executiva das Comemorações do V Centenário da Morte do Infanta D. Henrique, 1961.

Frith, Simon. "Towards an Aesthetic of Popular Music." Edição de Simon Frith. *Popular Music. Critical Concepts in Media and Cultural Studies, Volume IV, Music and Identity*. Routledge, 2004, pp. 32-45.

Gilroy, Paul. *The Black Atlantic: Modernity and Double Consciousness*. Verso, 1993.

Grazia, Victoria. *Irresistible Empire: America's Advance through Twentieth-Century Europe*. The Belknap Press of Harvard University Press, 2005.

Hall, Stuart. "Notes on Deconstructing the Popular." John Storey. *Cultural Theory and Popular Culture: A reader*. Harvester—Wheatsheaf, 1998, pp. 442-453.

———. "On Postmodernism and Articulation: An Interview with Stuart Hall" (editado por Lawrence Grossberg). Organização de David Morley, Kuan-Hsing Chen, e Stuart Hall. *Critical Dialogues in Cultural Studies*. Routledge, 1996, pp. 131-150.

Huggan, Graham. *The Postcolonial Exotic: Marketing the Margins*. Routledge, 2001.

Jaji, Ella Tsitsi. *Africa in Stereo: Modernism, Music, and Pan-African Solidarity*. Oxford University Press, 2004.

Mbembe, Achille. *Critique of Black Reason*. Duke University Press, 2017.

Mccann, Bryan. *Hello, Hello Brazil. Popular Music in the Making of Modern Brazil*. Duke University Press, 2004.

Moorman, Marissa Jean. *Intonations: A Social History of Music and Nation in Luanda, Angola, from 1945 to Recent Times*. Ohio University Press, 2008.

MARCOS CARDÃO é doutorado em História Moderna e Contemporânea pelo ISCTE - Instituto Universitário de Lisboa (2013); investigador de Pós-doutoramento no Centro de Estudos Comparatistas da Faculdade de Letras da Universidade de Lisboa (CEC—FLUL); autor do livro *Fado Tropical. O luso-tropicalismo na cultura de massas 1960-1974* (Lisboa: Edições Unipop, 2014), e coautor de *Gilberto Freyre: novas leituras, do outro lado do Atlântico* (São Paulo: Edusp, 2015).

# Dez perguntas para Ondjaki
# Em conversa com Christopher Larkosh

No outono de 2016, aqui na UMass Dartmouth, tivemos a oportunidade singular de receber o autor angolano Ondjaki como Hélio and Amélia Pedroso/Luso-American Foundation Endowed Chair in Portuguese Studies. Com estas perguntas para Ondjaki, eu queria não só deixar um documento da sua estadia entre nós, mas também avaliar, ou talvez até interrogar, o papel atual da língua portuguesa que naturalmente marcou a nossa discussão de temas literários e culturais, com as perguntas adicionais—sobre cultura visual, material e sónica—talvez um exemplo da tarefa quase impossível, e talvez por isso tão necessária, de seguir indo ao encontro do outro, com o outro. Hoje continuamos estes diálogos culturais entre comunidades globais em vários continentes (em África desde logo, mas na América do Norte também), utilizando a língua portuguesa e outros sistemas simbólicos não só para comunicação entre si, mas também para "irem (ou irmos) além": de colonialismos europeus ou os limites culturais das comunidades diaspóricas locais, e de reconfigurações desta Lusofonia tão dispersa que frequentemente continua a privilegiar os mesmos centros literários tradicionais. Portanto, como é que estes diálogos, desde uma série de pontos alternativos de referência cultural, podem descentrar ou aumentar as formas de compreensão convencionais deste espaço linguístico transnacional, ou até propor um leque mais amplo de paradigmas culturais?

1. **Para começar: Qual é a importância da cultura visual para si como autor? Como é que se integra na sua obra, seja nos romances, as obras infantis ou nas peças de teatro?**

Há uma vasta dimensão a considerar se falarmos na cultura visual. Desde a natural, como as paisagens geográficas e humanas; até às culturas visuais pictóricas, na pele ou na areia, passando também pela cinematográfica. Tudo isso contribui aos poucos para as impressões visuais que se interiorizam e que, mais tarde, chegam aos livros. Eu gosto muito de paisagens humanas, onde quero englobar não só as estéticas mas alguns conteúdos, as estórias, as memórias e as saudades do futuro.

Portanto, penso que sim, há muito dessas impressões que chega aos meus livros. A medida exata, eu não saberia calcular nem expor.

2. Quais são os elementos visuais, materiais e sónicos (seja de Luanda, Angola ou doutros lugares em África) que mais inspiram a sua produção literária?

Não sei precisar. Lembro-me de vastas paisagens do Sul de Angola que me ficaram nos olhos de dentro, e nas noites de sonhar. São esses materiais que mais tarde regressam a mim e chegam à escrita. Também os lagos na Itália, um intenso carnaval de cheiros na ilha de Zanzibar, o verde da Huíla, mas também os verdes da Irlanda. Não posso deixar que as cores se fiquem pelo continente africano, há tons e cores belíssimos que vivem no México ou na Argentina.

3. Certo, nessa altura quase todos somos, sejamos autores ou leitores ou ambos, não só locais, mas ao mesmo tempo cada vez mais globais (e talvez ainda um pouco nacionais). Com isso em mente, há determinadas estéticas visuais ou materiais desse leque amplo de lugares no mundo que têm deixado uma marca na sua obra? Penso na estética da cultura material soviética, ou outras da época dos 70-80, ou talvez haja outras que têm a sua origem na África da mesma época da pós-independência.

Acho que há materiais estéticos que nos acompanharam, em Luanda, no nosso quotidiano. É difícil listá-los em detalhe, ou identificá-los com a facilidade que me pede. Tudo isso me chegou na altura de modo espontâneo, à medida que os dias iam desenrolando a infância. Mais tarde, quando me pus a escrever sobre os anos 80, os restos dessas impressões afectivas invadiram os livros e os intervalos da escrita. Não é algo que eu possa pensar na perspectiva de uma lógica expositiva. São antes uma espécie de "lugares" a que a infância convida e a memória permite, quando permite. São esconderijos semi-arejados…

4. Compreendo que nem é sempre fácil separar e identificar estes elementos… mas talvez se pode falar de uma cultura visual do texto; por exemplo, uma que se revela de maneira mais marcante através do uso de palavras angolanas num texto em português? Até que ponto identifica-se com este conceito de estética visual do texto?

Pouco sei sobre conceitos de estética visual, seja do texto ou outra. Não creio que o uso de palavras angolanas revele num texto uma cultura visual. E ainda que assim fosse, a quem causaria isso estranhamento? Certamente que não a um angolano ou moçambicano. Existem traços culturais que certamente chegam aos textos e à construção do pensamento. Esse pensamento, digamos assim, se for literário, pode ter um pendor acentuado que dialoga com a matriz cultural do lugar.

Acho isso normal. Também penso que um texto repleto de palavras angolanas é, em todo o caso, um texto em português. A língua portuguesa é uma das línguas faladas em Angola, senão mesmo a mais falada.

> 5. Estou percebendo… de qualquer maneira, para qualquer leitor que nunca visitou Angola este tipo de texto literário dá uma excelente introdução à paisagem linguística do país. Quando eu penso na estética visual da sua obra literária, lembro-me do formato visual do seu romance Os transparentes: sobretudo a intercalação de páginas pretas com a escrita em branco. Qual é a importância do livro material, ou seja, de papel, numa época cada vez mais digital?

Penso que ainda são duas coisas diferentes. Ambos são livros, mas ocupam lugares e dimensões distintas. Quase contêm em si os mesmos materiais, claro, mas acabam por ter usos diferentes. Por outro lado, é preciso considerar que são poucos os lugares do mundo onde já se viva uma época predominantemente digital. Há lugares onde se vive uma época cheia de livros de papel, e há lugares onde até os livros de papel escasseiam. É preciso considerar que o mundo está cheio de muitos lugares…

> 6. Sem dúvida; há lugares, tanto em África quanto aqui na América do Norte, onde o uso do telemóvel já virou mais essencial para a vida quotidiana de muitos do que a leitura de um livro. Mas voltando ao livro… Os transparentes trata da Luanda de hoje. Como é que a cultura sónica desta realidade contemporânea exerce uma influência sobre a sua obra? Ninguém pode negar que os sons dessa cidade, sobretudo os gêneros mais recentes de música popular, têm atingido uma popularidade transnacional.

Há um lado forte da sonoridade, também musical, da cidade e das pessoas nos "Transparentes". Luanda é uma cidade que respira um ritmo de dança no seu dia a dia, a música e a dança são muito importantes na construção do quotidiano dos luandenses, e penso que isso de certo modo entrou na obra. Mais do que a música, ou a dança, há uma lado de *performance* diária, quotidiana, que me interessa muito em Luanda. As pessoas, seja por que razão for, precisam dessa performance constante, teatral, as estórias, os modos de dizer e de viver a língua portuguesa. Isso é um material bom para a matriz do que depois vem a ser a literatura sobre e com Luanda.

7. Por isso é evidente para qualquer leitor que Luanda fica sendo importante para si e a sua obra. Há alguns elementos da estrutura material urbanística de Luanda que deixou, ou continua a deixar, uma marca na sua visão literária?

A ação de alguns dos meus livros acontece em Luanda. Mas não é em todos que isso acontece. Mas acho que nas obras Bom dia, camaradas, Quantas madrugadas tem a noite e Os transparentes, há um lado urbano que aparece e que é importante no desenrolar da narrativa.

8. Há outros elementos de cultural popular angolana que são importantes no seu processo de criação literária; por exemplo, a música da sua infância, o cinema, ou a rádio?

Quase todos os elementos que constituem a nossa infância, acabam por aparecer nos livros, mais ou menos explicitamente. Quando a ficção recorre à memória e ao país "real" é normal que essas coisas apareçam, como estrutura da própria narrativa ou como balizas que apontam direções subjetivas, seja dos personagens, seja do autor. Dos aspectos que citou, penso que a rádio seria o mais "popular" de todos.

9. Você já conhece outras partes de África, e até tem morado em lugares onde há uma presença importante da diáspora afrodescendente global (Brasil, Europa, e agora os Estados Unidos). Os pontos de referência continuam a expandir para nós todos, acho... então, até que ponto fica sendo importante sublinhar a sua identidade como um autor angolano ou africano, tomando em conta a difusão globalizada e traduzida da sua obra?

Eu de facto não dou importância a sublinhar identidades... Acho que a obra em primeiro lugar é minha, da minha pessoa, da minha sensibilidade. Assim também leio as obras dos outros, e por vezes encaro-as mesmo como obras autónomas. Interessa-me o livro, pouco me interessa o autor. E o mesmo penso do autor que eu sou. O que os editores, os tradutores, os livreiros, os jornalistas e os políticos fazem nos seus afazeres profissionais, isso é outra estória. Mas não passa por mim. Eu celebro traduções seja de quem for, as minhas e as dos outros. Penso realmente que a tradução é das mais lindas pontes que acontece entre culturas, mas isso não requer que sublinhemos identidades, fronteiras, etc. Os livros falam pela literatura, pela arte.

10. Mas às vezes os jornalistas são autores, e os autores também são políticos, tradutores ou editores... os nossos papéis profissionais também mudam com os nossos lugares no mundo e as nossas formas de pensar e interagir com os múltiplos rôles que transitamos. Portanto, na sua opinião, quais são as possibilidades de pensar numa cultura transnacional através da criação literária em português, no contexto mais amplo de cultura visual, material ou sónica?

Eu penso que existe uma coisa óbvia, que é esse território comum de Língua Portuguesa nas mais distintas geografias mundiais que foram afectadas por esta língua, e pelas culturas subjacentes a ela. O caso de Cabo Verde, Guiné Bissau, Timor Leste, Moçambique e Angola, têm a especificidade de conviver com outras línguas, que também abordam e afectam a língua portuguesa. Mas há um espaço comum, nalgumas partes do mundo, que é delimitado pelo uso (mais ou menos criativo) da Língua Portuguesa. Se isso vai criar uma cultura transnacional, eu não sou a pessoa indicada para dizer. Mas cria certamente um espaço de convívio, de intervenção, que não se reduz às fronteiras de cada nação. Penso que isso é bom e pode ser bonito, sobretudo se aproveitado pelos artistas e por intervenções que se pautam pela liberdade mais do que pelos conceitos políticos.

**Talvez seja por isso, que para nós, os lusófonos da Nova Inglaterra, onde o nosso uso quotidiano da língua portuguesa fica sendo menos óbvia, é tão importante poder partilhar este espaço transnacional e multilíngue de convívio e diálogo consigo através da Língua Portuguesa. Muito obrigado, Ondjaki.**

NDALU DE ALMEIDA is an Angolan author who writes under the pen name Ondjaki. His literary work ranges from novels, short stories and dramatic works to children's stories and poetry. He has received a number of prestigious literary prizes, including the 2010 Jabuti Prize for the novel *AvóDezanove e o Segredo do Soviético* (Eng. trans. *Granma Nineteen and the Soviet's Secrets*), and the 2013 José Saramago Prize for the novel *Os transparentes* (The Transparent Ones). In addition to English, his work has been translated into many other languages, including Spanish, French, Italian, German, Greek, Swedish, Serbian, Polish and Chinese. He currently lives in Rio de Janeiro.

# Essays

# Mário Pinto de Andrade and the Orders of Discourse: An Introduction

Mário Pinto de Andrade (1928-1990) has long been recognized as one of Africa's most important intellectuals as well as one of the leading anticolonial and nationalist militants of the twentieth century. He was, throughout his life, a prolific writer and tireless editor in French and in Portuguese and is best known for his critical writings on Lusophone African literature, especially poetry, and on movements of national liberation and independence in Lusophone Africa, particularly in Angola. Although Mário Pinto de Andrade was an active participant in the intellectual debates and political events about which he wrote, he nevertheless possessed the remarkable capacity to analyze them from a critical distance in history, sociology, criticism and theory.

Despite his pioneering work as an intellectual and as an anti-colonialist and nationalist, it was said that he considered his main contribution to Angolan nationalism, broadly understood in cultural and political terms, to be his documentation of its history.[1] He intended to achieve this goal in three ways: by collecting, preserving and archiving documents; by editing and publishing scholarly, theoretical and literary works by others; and by assiduously researching, writing and lecturing about it.

Mário Pinto de Andrade's attempt to document and understand the history of Lusophone African nationalism enhances his prominent intellectual and political legacy. His extensive archive is now housed at the Fundação Mário Soares in Lisbon and a significant portion of its contents have been made available online.[2] He was the official biographer of Amílcar Cabral and editor of his writings,[3] and he edited and published several groundbreaking anthologies of Lusophone African poetry related to anti-colonial and nationalist themes.[4] His seminal book-length study, *Origens do Nacionalismo Africano*, and landmark article, "As Ordens do Discurso do 'Clamor Africano': Continuidade e Ruptura na Ideologia do Nacionalismo Unitário," represent his principal historical and theoretical writings on the development and significance of nationalism in Lusophone Africa from the late nineteenth century to the unleashing of the armed struggle in Angola in 1961.⁵ Both of these publications, written in Portuguese, have until now remained inaccessible to the general Anglophone academic community. The present translation of "As Ordens do Discurso do 'Clamor Africano'"and the forthcoming translation of *Origens do Nacionalismo Africano* are intended not only to promote knowledge and advance research on the works of Mário Pinto de Andrade and on the history and theory of nationalism in Lusophone Africa. They also aim to better integrate Mário Pinto de Andrade as a writer, editor and lecturer into African, Francophone and Lusophone intellectual traditions, while highlighting his distinctive contributions to them, and to more easily facilitate incorporation of the study of anticolonial and nationalist movements in Lusophone Africa into mainstream scholarly conversations and university teaching. We feel this initiative honors the intention of Mário Pinto de Andrade's lifelong archival, editorial and scholarly efforts.

Mário Pinto de Andrade's article "As Ordens do Discurso do 'Clamor Africano'" provides a theoretical consideration of the ideologies and practices of movements of unitary nationalism in Lusophone Africa from nineteenth-century nativism, through the proto-nationalist period (first order of discourse, 1911-early 1930s) and subsequent transitional phase (discourse of rupture) to the emergence of modern nationalism (second order of discourse, 1957-1961), which was followed by the beginning of the armed struggle for national liberation and independence (Angola, 1961; Guinea-Bissau, 1963; and Mozambique, 1964).⁶

In his analysis of the lines of continuity and rupture in nationalist ideology and praxis, Mário Pinto de Andrade focuses on language and discourse. He also investigates the social background of the producers of texts and of their intended readers, and underscores the site and medium of that political enunciation. The "Orders of Discourse" of the title derives explicitly from the article by J. Achille Mbembé, from which he quotes, but also more distantly from *L'ordre du discours* by Michel Foucault.⁷ This theoretical framework enables Mário Pinto de Andrade to foreground the linguistic and demand research on a wide range of written, performative and oral texts, while reminding readers that the nationalist discourse must be understood amid pre-existing institutional power relations within an international context. Mário Pinto de Andrade here shows us the ways in which these relations were negotiated, challenged and refused in political enunciations and nationalist discourses through newspaper articles and editorials, political associations as well as class and cultural organizations, canticles and church songs, poetry and literary movements, academic lectures and research, and a theoretical body of writings composed of proceedings from meetings, letters, communications and resolutions.

However, what is not made explicit in the article is that fact that Mário Pinto de Andrade was himself one of the principal figures of the transitional period (1940s-1950s) and the emergence of modern nationalism (1957-1961) and the primary author of the texts he discusses from these years. This is concealed, in part, by the theoretical language of analysis he adeptly employs with such precision. In keeping with the argument of his article on the significance of language, certain word choices and phrasings were made to convey specific meanings and evoke particular associations, and their deliberate stiltedness has been retained in the translation. Mário Pinto de Andrade's strategic use of language in this text and others is itself worthy of investigation.

A brief biographical sketch of these years can help restore Mário Pinto de Andrade to the narrative and provide insight into the development of his thought and political activity as well as the role language played in it.[8] Mário Pinto de Andrade left Angola for Lisbon in 1948 to study classical philology and his interventions at the Casa dos Estudantes do Império and the Centro de Estudos Africanos (CEA) focused on language, linguistics and literary themes. The famous *Caderno de poesia negra de expressão portuguesa* (1953), which he edited with Francisco José Tenreiro, emerged out of his intellectual activity at the CEA, which he founded in 1951 with Amílcar Cabral and Agostinho Neto. Mário Pinto de Andrade was the critical and editorial champion of Lusophone African poetry during the 1940s and 1950s as well as one of the intellectual and organizational leaders of the period of transition.[9] Forced to leave Lisbon in 1954, he transferred to Paris and became an editor at *Présence Africaine*, where he worked with the major intellectuals of Francophone Africa, including Alioune Diop, Cheikh Anta Diop, Frantz Fanon, Léopold Sédar Senghor and Aimé Césaire, and enrolled in sociology at the École des Hautes Études en Sciences Sociales (EHESS), where he sharpened his skills of critical analysis with France's leading academics. His experience in Paris and exposure through *Présence Africaine* to figures associated with Pan-Africanism and the Négritude movement were transformative. The kinds of Pan-African connections Mário Pinto de Andrade forged in Paris and the intimate knowledge he gained of French and Francophone anti-colonial and nationalist thinking determined the shape and success of the period—and the language and substance of the theoretic corpus of writings—he here describes as the second order of discourse (1957-61) and which corresponds to the emergence of modern nationalism in Lusophone

Africa. The intellectual, political and geographical trajectory of these movements of unitary nationalism is incomprehensible without the apprenticeships first in Lisbon and then in Paris.

As one of the founders and first president of the MPLA (Movimento Popular de Libertação de Angola), Mário Pinto de Andrade would announce the decision for "direct action" in the press conference he held in the House of Commons in London and he would serve as president of the first conference of CONCP (Conferência das Organizações Nacionalistas das Colónias Portuguesas), an organization he would continue to oversee for many years. Although he would remain one of the leading figures of the movements of national liberation and independence, he would be forced to leave Angola in 1974 due to political disagreements with Agostinho Neto that led to the dissolution of the "Revolta Activa" and persecution of those involved in it.[10] While in permanent exile he would serve as minister in Guinea-Bissau until the coup of 1980.[11] However, he would continue to research, write and lecture, activities he indefatigably pursued throughout his life. He collaborated with UNESCO in Paris, worked with the government of Cabo Verde and eventually found a home for a brief period of time at the Centro de Estudos Africanos (CEA) at the Universidade Eduardo Mondlane (UEM) in Mozambique. The article translated here belongs to this phase. It was originally written on a notebook of the Conselho Nacional/Partido Africano da Independência de Cabo Verde (PAICV), to which he belonged; it is signed and dated "Centro de Estudos Africanos da Universidade Eduardo Mondlane/Maputo, 13 de Outubro de 1987/ Mário de Andrade"; and it is dedicated to Aquino de Bragança, his longtime friend and director of the CEA who died in the mysterious plane crash that also killed President Samora Machel on October 19, 1986.[12] The CEA/UEM was appropriately named after the Centro de Estudos Africanos founded by Mário Pinto de Andrade in Lisbon in 1951, and this connection draws attention to the continuity and rupture experienced in his own life. In many ways, the writing of the article "As Ordens do Discurso do 'Clamor Africano'" embodies the characteristics defining the transitional period and the emergence of modern nationalism, for it highlights the importance of personal relationships and sociability, the necessity of conceiving of Lusophone Africa as a whole in relation to broader international contexts, and the crucial role of unremitting intellectual activity and production for the future of Africa. But it also underscores Mário Pinto de Andrade's unwavering commitment to these principles and values and the uncompromising urgency of securing a space for praxis.

NOTES

I would like to thank Henda Ducados, Annouchka de Andrade, Jean-Michel Mabeko-Tali, Fernando Arenas, John Fobanjong and Memory Holloway for their support, comments and assistance.

1. "Obituary: Mario de Andrade, 62, a Founder of Angola's Governing Movement," *The New York Times*, August 27, 1990.

2. http://casacomum.org/cc/arquivos?set=e_3944#!e_3944

3. Mário Pinto de Andrade, *Amilcar Cabral, Essai de biographie politique*, Paris: François Maspero, 1980; Amílcar Cabral, *Unité et lute: 1. L'arme de la théorie. 2. La pratique révolutionnaire*, edited and introduced by Mário Pinto de Andrade, Paris: François Maspero, 2 vols., 1975; *Pour Cabral: Simpósio Internacional Amílcar Cabral*, Paris: Présence Africaine, 1987.

4. Mário Pinto de Andrade and Francisco José Tenreiro, eds., *Caderno de poesia negra de expressão portuguesa*, Lisbon, 1953; Mário Pinto de Andrade, *Antologia da poesia negra de expressão portuguesa*, Paris: Pierre Jean Oswald, 1958; Mário Pinto de Andrade, *La poésie africaine d'expression portugaise*, Paris: Pierre Jean Oswald, 1969; Mário Pinto de Andrade, *Antologia temática de poesia africana: 1. Na noite grávida de punhais. 2. O canto armado*, Lisbon: Sá da Costa Editora, 1975 & 1979. For his criticism, see Mário Pinto de Andrade, "Qu'est que c'est le Luso-Tropicalisme?," *Présence Africaine*, n. 4, 1955, pp. 24-25; Mário Pinto de Andrade, "Literautre et Nacionalisme en Angola," *Présence Africaine*, n. 41, 1962, pp. 91-99.

5. Mário Pinto de Andrade, *Origens do nacionalismo Africano*, Lisbon: Publicações Dom Quixote, 1997 (written in 1990); Mário Pinto de Andrade, "As Ordens do Discurso do 'Clamor Africano': Continuidade e Ruptura na Ideologia do Nacionalismo Unitário," *Estudos Moçambicanos*, v. 7, 1990 (written in 1987), pp. 9-27.

6. The article ends with the decision for direct action and first meeting of CONCP. For some of his main writings on movements of national liberation and independence after the beginning of the armed struggle, see Mário Pinto de Andrade, *Liberté pour l'Angola*, Paris: François Maspero, 1962; Mário Pinto de Andrade, "La Lutte de Libération Nationale dans les Colonies Portugaises: Fondements Unitaires" and with Amílcar Cabral, "L'Afrique et la Lutte de Libération Nationale dans les Colonies Portugaises" in *La Lutte de libération nationale dans les colonies portugaises: la conférence de Dar Es-Salaam* (1966), Hydra, Algiers: Information CONCP, 1968; Mário Pinto de Andrade and Marc Ollivier, *La guerre en Angola—Étude socio-économique*, Paris: François Maspero, 1971; Mário Pinto de Andrade, *A guerra do povo na Guiné-Bissau*, Lisbon: Sá da Costa Editora, 1974

7. J. Achille Mbembé, "La palabre de l'indépendance: les ordres du discours nationaliste au Cameroun (1948-1958)," *Revue française de science politique*, n. 3, 1985, pp. 459-487; Michel Foucault, *L'ordre du discours*, Paris: Gallimard, 1971.

8. See Michel Laban, *Mário Pinto de Andrade: Uma entrevista*, Lisbon: Edições João Sá da Costa, 1997.

9. This was the "nationalist nucleus" composed of Amílcar Cabral, Mário Pinto de Andrade, Agostinho Neto, Marcelino dos Santos, Francisco José Tenreiro, and, briefly, Eduardo Mondlane, among others.

10. For discussion of the "Revolta Activa," see Jean-Michel Mabeko Tali, *Dissidências e poder de estado: o MPLA perante si próprio (1962–1977): ensaio de história política*, Luanda: Nzila, vol. 1, 2001, pp. 247-288.

11. In 1978, during his tenure as Minister of Information and Culture, Mário Pinto de Andrade, along with Sana Na N'Hada, founded the Instituto Nacional de Cinema e Audiovisual (INCA). This was the result of a deep and active interest in cinema. He was married to the French-born militant filmmaker Sarah Maldoror and they had spent time with the Senegalese filmmaker Ousmane Sembène in China (1958) and in Moscow (1962). Although Mário Pinto de Andrade vigorously supported the cinematic production of Sarah Maldoror and others, his contributions in this realm of cultural production remain less well known.

12. For the original typescript study with hand-written emendations, see Fundação Mário Soares, Arquivo Mário Pinto de Andrade, 04356.007.001 (http://casacomum.org/cc/visualizador?pasta=04356.007.001).

MARIO PEREIRA (Ph.D., Brown University) is Editor of *Portuguese Literary & Cultural Studies* and Executive Editor of Tagus Press in the Center for Portuguese Studies and Culture at the University of Massachusetts Dartmouth.

MÁRIO PINTO DE ANDRADE

## The Orders of Discourse of *Clamor Africano*: Continuity and Rupture in the Ideology of Unitary Nationalism

*For Aquino de Bragança*
*In Memoriam*

When in May 1887 the "restless" and "irreverent" former second lieutenant from Angola, **Alfredo de Aguiar**, prepared himself in Quelimane (Mozambique) as editor for the launching of the weekly paper *Gazeta do Sul*,[1] he certainly could not have foreseen that a century later one of his future fellow countrymen would employ the evocative title of another newspaper of which he was the political editor—*Clamor Africano*—with the explicit purpose of using it to reconstruct the guiding ideological thread that was collectively elaborated by **elite** Africans.

Indeed, we intend in this presentation of the material under discussion to deconstruct the nationalist discursive system, in other words, to analyze the historical *processus* of continuity and rupture in the ideologies of movements of unity which emerged from the struggle against Portuguese colonial domination between 1911 and 1961.

Movements of unity, which brought together political groups presenting themselves as representatives of the oppressed masses in the Portuguese colonies, emerged during the beginning of the [twentieth] century, benefiting from a climate favorable to freedom of expression which was inaugurated with the proclamation of the First Republic in Portugal.

The first impulse for association came from the natives of São Tomé and Príncipe, who survived, economically, the relentless struggle for land possession unleashed during the course of the nineteenth century after the abolition of slave labor relations and the organization of an economic structure based on capital.

The African community resident principally in Lisbon expanded and included, in varying proportions, prominent personalities from throughout the "Empire."

Some members of this community, originating from the social class of agricultural property owners (this is the particular case of São Tomé and Príncipe), and the sons of public servants and businessmen, would come to practice the liberal professions and occupy administrative positions in colonial societies as well as in Portugal. This was a non-homogeneous **elite**, representative of a (rural and urban) petite bourgeoisie, whose natural vocation was the administration of autonomous or regional power in their own interest.

Influenced by the ideas disseminated by the theoreticians of the Portuguese Republic, the **proto-nationalists** unfurled the banner of protest against the "iniquitous laws of exception" and inscribed their action within the context of a greater Lusitanian fatherland. But, as blacks, it was their responsibility to defend, above all, the **race** from a counter-offensive position against the prevailing prejudice of the congenital inferiority of this human group.

For this reason, the foundation of the discourses rests essentially on two principal elements—the pride of belonging to the black world and the demand for the legal, social and political status of Portuguese Africans.

As often happens with political associations that form outside of the territory where their action is principally focused, the divisions that opposed the two African organizations in the **imperial** capital had a negative effect on the elaboration of their revendicatory project. However, the conflict between them, evident in the practical orientation of their programs, was not of a kind that would permanently divide the **Liga Africana** and the **Partido Nacional Africano** over the essential, which was their shared opposition to the colonial system.

The last attempt to overcome these divisions was the late merger of the two associations in 1931 with the **Movimento Nacionalista Africano**, at a time when the structure of the **Estado Novo** was taking shape in Portugal, but this would not produce anything of consequence.

The protagonists in this battle for unity were inspired by the ideas of their time. Though they transposed Monroe's maxim to the situation in Africa (but only during the early phase with the appearance of the paper *O Negro*), they did not reach the point of truly assimilating Wilson's precept and were even further from Lenin's ideas about the free determination of peoples and nations.

The dynamics of the Pan-African and Pan-Negro movements, centered respectively on the figures of W.E.B. Du Bois and of Marcus Garvey, constituted the integrating ideological connection for the "Afro-Portuguese" movement. Participation in these liberating currents (undertaken, incidentally, separately by the two organizations) was accompanied by their fascination with the experience of black Americans—the stages of a history that went from the horrors of slavery to the heights of knowledge, science and technology, letters and arts, and sports. This was an important point of reference for the **rebirth of Africa**.

Staying attuned to what was happening with the peoples of the "black world," the ideologues and journalists connected to these associations contributed to a universalization of the discourse on **race**. In this respect, they resembled their counterparts in France who participated in the "black movements" between the two World Wars.

Seen in its historical perspective, proto-nationalism was prisoner of a basic postulate that comprises the ideological matrix of its discourse: the demands of Portuguese Africans within a hypothetical space—**Greater Portugal**.

By taking Portugal's side regarding the cacao-slavery issue, which was raised by British philanthropists and chocolatiers, and, more generally, the issue of working conditions in the colonies, authoritative voices from the proto-nationalism movement joined the deliriously patriotic chorus in praise of Lusitanian glory.

Nevertheless, it remains true that despite the ambivalent language of the discourses, the interventions denouncing the **momentous questions** and the manifestation of popular protests in the **congress**, within the legal parameters established by the Republic, found a favorable response among broad sectors of opinion of the colonized society and gave rise to hope among them.

Similarly, the socio-political practice of the movement of unity had significant repercussions on certain glaring aspects of the despotism of local rulers.

## 1. The First Order of Discourse

Let us look at how the first order of discourse of *Clamor Africano* was expressed within the context of colonial legality. It is through the ambivalence of the language employed, through the analysis of content, through the identification of addressees—interlocutors—and, finally, through the sociological composition of the **actors-leaders** that we will understand the project of proto-nationalism.

The ideology implicit in the discourse under discussion, and this can likewise be inferred from its political categories, produces a language characterized by ambivalence. This ambivalence can now be grasped through a fundamental thematic unity—the identity of the actors as revealed by variable terminologies. The linguistic indicators used (the order and choice of words, the qualifiers and recurrences) help to uncover the social representations of the ideologues.

This analysis of content leads to the manifestation of the individual constituent of the **ego** of the social discourse and of its addressees. An understanding of the sociological composition of the protagonists is thereby facilitated.

## 1.1. Content Analysis

Let us take the textual **corpus** of the movements of unity, the editorials and theoretical articles, which, from the preface to the action exemplified by the paper *O Negro*, comprise the ideological fabric of proto-nationalism.

The definition of the actors involved in the movements of unity responds to a double positioning: a political position—in the face of the First Republic and of the regime of the **Estado Novo**—and a socio-cultural position—in front of the popular masses deprived of the benefit of education and of the enlightenment of "civilization."

The variables involved are the self-designations of **native**, **black**, **African**, **Portuguese** and associated qualifiers—**Portuguese African** or **Afro-Portuguese**.

Over the course of the brief preliminary phase of proto-nationalism (in 1911), the ideologues placed themselves in the terrain of the black.

Belonging to the "enslaved race par excellence," they endeavored to rehabilitate the race and save it from its state of misfortune.

They affirmed defending the "black race" and simultaneously advocated the abolition of the hierarchy established between "aristocrats" and "plebeians." The discourse on race adopted a prophetic style:

> "Blessed shall be every torrent of tears, every bead of sweat, and every drop of blood that you will spill for the realization of this ideal that will deliver a new and more refulgent inspiration to human consciousness."[2]

Using the terms **Blacks** and **Sons of Africa**, the editorialists of *O Negro* avoid explicit reference to the juridical category of **Portuguese**.

The period occupied by the **Junta de Defesa dos Direitos de África** (J.D.D.A.), the **Partido Nacional Africano** (P.N.A.) and the **Liga Africana** (L.A.), from 1912 to the end of the 1920s, saw an evolution in the way they referred to themselves.

They considered themselves, in the discourse they produced, **Africans** pledged to the organization of their fellow countrymen of the same **race** for the improvement of the moral, civil and social destiny of **black Africans**.

There is a metaphorical recourse to the **dominated-race** "that wakens from a centuries-long sleep" and to **dominated African peoples** "that cannot continue to live outside of the political constitution of the republic."

They clarify their existential situation in these terms:

"All of us, Africans, live in an oppressive and violent regime, crushed in our most legitimate aspirations, rejected from social contact, banished from civilization like ferocious animals."3

They are separated from the "brothers of Europe" by the fact of submission "to the tyranny of iniquitous laws," but at the same time they advocate the maintenance of the "integrity of the national soil" and fight against the existence of "two **castes** of Portuguese: the dominators and the dominated," of two **countries** (victors/vanquished, free men/slaves, colonials/metropolitans).

Within the heart of the formations of unity themselves, semantic changes to their self-designation can be observed. Thus, the **Liga Africana** claims to be composed of "individuals of the **African race** and of adherent associations," whereas the **Partido Nacional Africano** bases its legitimacy on the "organization of the **indigenous peoples** of the five provinces of Portuguese Africa into institutions of a civil, economic, social and political character."

The declaration of identity follows the progression **men of the African race**, **Africans**, and **Portuguese Africans**, this last becoming the most common. The expression **Portuguese Blacks** seems to be used less often, though **Afro-Portuguese** is used with more frequency in order to distinguish themselves from other members of the **African family** composed of "Afro-French, Afro-Belgians, Afro-English, Afro-Americans…"

If, at the end of the 1920s, the mouthpiece of the P.N.A., *A Voz d'África*, underlines the dual primordial origin—of **race** and of **Africa**—and gives prominence to the term **Africans**, the **Movimento Nacionalista Africano**, in contrast, at the time of its inception, leaves no room for equivocation in its collective designation:

> "…When we write **Africans**, we wish to refer principally to the group of Portuguese Africans, that is, to the populations of Angola, São Tomé and Príncipe, Guinea, Cabo Verde and Moçambique."4

## 1.2. The Interlocutors/Addressees

At the very beginning of the preliminary phase of the proto-nationalist battle, the role of "making the revendications of the enslaved race triumph" is assigned to the "most highly educated and cultured class of the black race" in association with the "least civilized." The signifier of the **elite**, in comparison with the indigenous populations, derives from the cultural acquisition that was made possible by colonial schooling, but it is necessary to resist the still dominant preconceptions regarding blacks, "the infamous stigma of the race":

> "Liberate in a word the black race from the shame of ignorant and slave, because it is known and demonstrated that it can elevate itself to the height of the white race through study, work and patriotism."[5]

From the same perspective, the arguments of those who deny intelligence and energy to the "African people," when success in elementary schools, secondary schools and universities as well as social organizations demonstrate the contrary, are refuted.

The ideologues who are the object of our study place themselves in an external relation to the indigenous peoples whom the Portuguese state should, in its role as guardian, instruct and civilize.

In the exposition of its objectives, the **Junta de Defesa dos Direitos de África** declares its blind faith in the "new era, rent by iron and fire in the darkness of the monarchy and the October 4 Revolution."

The statement continues:

> "It remains to be seen how the State will understand its redemptive mission in the face of this unexpected influx of an entire race which has already bitten the apple of Civilization and now wants to collaborate with it in the reform of national life."[6]

Juvenal Cabral, one of the protagonists of the period, is convinced of this "incontestable truth," according to which "we can make savage blacks into honest men, men citizens and citizens men of the State. These are successive transformations that can be obtained easily by the powerful machinery of instruction."[7]

The **Liga Africana**, for its part, emphasizes the "interest of the colonizing peoples" in producing "a sizeable intelligent, trained and professional black **elite**."

Since the **indigenous** peoples are deprived of any civil existence, the **ego** of the social discourse and its addressees are conflated into a single entity: the **men of letters** [letrados], the "African intellectuals." For this reason, one of the appeals made for electoral participation contains this injunction:

> "Give the example of unity, and honor our Race by having our most eminent compatriots draft our laws."[8]

## 1.3. The Sociological Composition

The social self-representation of the protagonists in the political discourse appeals to a "pleiad of our African **elite**" composed of students, school teachers, professors, journalists, publicists, lawyers, medical doctors, technicians, engineers, businessmen, industrialists, and property owners.

A significant portion of the "actors-leaders" who distinguish themselves in actions of unity, as we have mentioned, originally came from São Tomé. According to the analysis of Francisco José Tenreiro, "they are descendants of the relations between Europeans and black [female] slaves from the early period of sugar cane... It is they who constitute the social aristocracy of the *filhos da terra* [children of the land]."⁹

During the proto-nationalist period, this social group—"the Luso-descendants"—suffered the effects of the invasion of colonial capital with the irruption of new farmers supported by the Banco Ultramarino. But this group, the Luso-descendants, still included a sufficient number of "capitalists, industrialists, businessmen and farmers" to lead the executive committee of the "Sociedade Comercial Africana."

Other indicators provide some evidence of social class origins:

In the list of twelve candidates for senators and members of the Portuguese parliament proposed by the **Liga Africana**, there appear four property owners, two superior officers of the armed forces, two medical doctors, two lawyers, a publicist and a journalist. All of the issues of the newspaper *Tribuna d'África* for the years 1931-1932 carry the following notations on the frontispiece:

—Artur de Castro (from the class of African intellectuals);
—Luiz da Cunha Lisboa (from the class of African employers);
—Joaquim Ramos (representing indigenous workers);

But if the leadership of the organizations of unity is sociologically identified in this way, the same did not occur with the militants based in Portugal. Sources containing information that could be qualitatively and quantitatively evaluated are lacking.

There are brief, sporadic allusions to the "African colony" of Lisbon in which reference is made to "hundreds of blacks" living there and to the misery of numerous indigents, "legions of famished compatriots who extend their hand to charity."

Sometimes the socio-professional category of the adherents of the organizations is known. In the middle of 1922, the **Liga Africana** published a list with the names of thirty-nine of their new members, consisting of eighteen public sector employees, nine property owners, three business sector employees, two farmers, two farm employees, one civil servant, one elementary school teacher, one bookkeeper, one carpenter and one goldsmith.

Obvious reasons, which are apparent from the socio-political statute imposed by colonialism on the great mass of indigenous people, caused local formations to recruit their members from the civil milieu that was labeled "civilized." In this respect, the profession is a valuable indicator of colonial relations. We can take as an example the Grémio Africano de Lourenço Marques. Among its 150 associates registered in May 1921, one counts in order of frequency:

— business sector employees;
— public sector employees;
— salaried employees (mechanics and the press);
— office workers;
— junior-level workers of the railways;
— four property owners;
— three businessmen;
— three farmers;
— a journalist (the Chairman of the Board, João dos Santos Albasini);
— a single high-level civil servant, the top Treasury official, from Cabo Verde (Thomaz de Abreu Bastos).

One can raise the question of whether the proto-nationalists should be considered precursors of modern nationalism.

A response to this question comes from a global understanding of a movement of ideas and practices that it is useful to examine under the double perspective of continuity and rupture. The line of continuity is located on the level of the essential themes of the political discourse, considered in another context and invested with different meanings. In effect, the problematic inherent to the colonial system would be positioned for a long time in terms of the dichotomy indigenous/assimilated, the permanence of barely disguised obligatory work, the plundering of lands and access to education.

A recurring theme was the discourse of **race** recovered in the cultural context of the **Négritude** movement.

The sphere of practice offers a vast field to the enduring nature of the proto-nationalist message:

— At the **collective** level, future generations would retain the organizational will and the spirit of unity among the five countries under Portuguese domination, heralding further initiatives.
— At the **socio-political** level, the very survival of figures who were notable for the vertical coherence between their acts and nativist, emancipatory ideas would make the colonial powers designate them as potentially subversive elements. Such was the case with the agronomist engineer Salustino da Graça Espírito Santo who was implicated by the governor, Carlos Gorgulo, as a leader of the people of São Tomé in their resistance to recruitment for forced labor on plantations, a resistance that was crushed by the massacres of February 3 and 4, 1953.
— At the **familial and individual level**, oppositional socialization and conviviality would play a role in the options of certain singular figures who would mark the future course of history.

In short, the memory retained in this selective continuity of the determination of the proto-nationalists in elaborating a written protest against the collective fate of the indigenous populations contributed to the formation of new consciences of revolt.

But proto-nationalism, in its essence, produced a discourse with an illusory aim:

presenting themselves as **learned** blacks in the Western mold, **subjects** of the Portuguese nation and **legalists**, these ideologues had not, because of historical conditions leading to an immature analysis, reached the critical degree of understanding of the logic of the Portuguese colonial system.

And it is here, precisely on this point, that the rupture would be articulated by the generation that would make its entrance onto the stage of history in the years immediately following the Second World War.

## 2. Elaboration of the Discourse of Rupture

The gestation of nationalism originates from the colonial process of social restructuring of autochthonous communities and of urban proletarianization, from patterns of racial discrimination, as well as from the influence of inter-ethnic contact and inter-ethnic regroupings through forced labor and migrations.

Obviously, the elaboration of the discourse of rupture occurred during the "colonial time" when the African and international context was favorable to the affirmation of unitary nationalisms.

The sociological profile of the "actors-leaders," the producers of the written project, can be schematically organized in the following way:

— individuals from subaltern, autochthonous classes, whose formation occurred under the control of the colonial political power through the apparatuses of cultural hegemony (school, church); these classes are not in general directly connected to the apparatus of production—which makes explicit their **elite** status. This is a social group that was capable of assimilating into the **petite bourgeoisie.**

By arriving at criticism of the contradictions engendered by the colonial situation, these representatives of an embryonic **intelligentsia** refute the dichotomy between indigenous and civilized—something that characterizes the collective projects that were developed from within the colonial space.

In the years following the Second World War, nationalist **praxis** is marked by three phases: the coming together of men, and their cultural and political apprenticeship; followed by an explosion of organizations; and, finally, the definitive moment of deciding for armed struggle.

Nationalist **praxis** is observed in the legal associations, churches and literary groups.

Each one of these fields would merit an extensive analysis, if this were our intention here. Instead, we will indicate only some points of reference.

Seen from the perspective of continuity of the organic manifestations created in the wake of proto-nationalism, organized (and officially authorized) political expression in the Portuguese colonies presents the following characteristics in the period under investigation:

— the slow death of the operative character of the **legalism** advocated by the **ligas** [leagues] and **grémios** [clubs];
— the ambiguous position taken by the principal protagonists of these associations;
— the distortion of the message of the "African cause;"
— the use of certain African figures by the colonial power.

These traits stand out from among the ideas and practices that are particularly evident in Angola and Mozambique where one observes obvious analogies in the schisms and rivalries between associations: the **Liga Nacional Africana** (heir of the **Liga Angolana**) and the **Grémio Africano,** which gave way to the

Associação dos Naturais de Angola; the **Associação Africana da Colónia de Moçambique** (successor to the **Grémio Africano de Lourenço Marques**) and the **Instituto Negrófilo**, which would be called the **Centro Associativo dos Negros**.

By virtue of the racial and social composition of their members, there was a clear parallel between them: the **Liga Nacional Africana** in Angola corresponded to the **Centro Associativo dos Negros** in Mozambique, and the **Associação dos Naturais de Angola** maintained affinities with the **Associação Africana** (Mozambique).

The most visible break—the division between blacks and *mestiços*—reflected the socio-economic and cultural barriers upon which the colonial system based itself in order to prolong the "estatuto dos indígenas" [statute of indigenous peoples].

Within the ambiguity of the political position assumed by the social actors discussed above (that is, the leaders of associations), the kinds of behavior displayed vary: sometimes they take forms of dissimulation and at other times they reach the heights of compromise conveyed in the pro-colonial discourse.

The outcome of the confrontation provoked internally by elements of the new generation marks the division between the legalism then practiced and the nationalist dynamic.

The role of the "separatist" churches, as a movement of reaction against and rejection of the "established order," needs to be reevaluated from the perspective of the currents of protest that constituted the awaking of nationalism.

Appearing in the southern part of the continent almost a century ago (precisely in 1892) and in Central Africa, particularly in the ethnic areas of the **mukongo** after the First World War, the "black churches" embodied, according to Georges Balandier, the response of the group in the colonial situation "on the level on which they found themselves most threatened—on the level of fundamental beliefs and behaviors; on the only level on which emancipation was possible."[10]

As is well known, the manifestation of this phenomenon in Mozambique was integrated into the typology already established by the Lutheran missionary B.G.M. Sundkler, the so-called "Ethiopian" and "Zionist" churches.

However, it seems to us that a global understanding of this material in socio-cultural and politic terms requires critical comparison with the sources produced by the colonial administration. Despite the fact that the nature of these sources belongs inherently to the **sociology of policing**, the numerous reports dedicated to the "gentile sects" and "natives" contain information that was gathered from a vast network of informants and obtained from long interrogations, and these are extremely useful for knowledge about:

- churches (their origins, doctrines, codes of discipline, cults and rites);
- their organizational structure (hierarchies, decision-making bodies);
- "Identification of part of the governing staff spread throughout innumerable locations in the Districts of Lourenço Marques, Gaza, and Inhambane, and, in one or two cases, Manica and Sofala;"
- the identification of locations of centers of activity and areas of influence;
- estimates of the number of faithful and followers;
- confirmed or presumed connections to the **ANC (African National Congress)** in South Africa and, within Mozambique, to the Núcleo Negrófilo de Manica e Sofala;
- finally, subversive involvement in certain incidents (such as the Machanga riots).

These sources provide important information for the reconstruction of the historical affiliation of Mozambican nationalist sentiment through the numerous documents written in **bantu** and also in English: hymns, canticles (its theological mediation), conference proceedings, correspondence exchanged between leaders of African churches...[11] Thus, the contours of religious figures of political importance, such as **Elias Saúte Mucambe** and **Kamba Simango**, emerge with more clarity.[12]

As far as the literary groups are concerned, the role and function of the poetry of rupture [poesia de ruptura] in heightening political "awareness" ["consciencialização"] has already been sufficiently emphasized. A reading of the **corpus** of African writing in Portuguese, produced during the 1940s and 1950s, confirms this fact. At the head of this body of texts is the collection of poems published in 1942, entitled **Ilha de Nome Santo**, by the São Tomé author Francisco José Tenreiro whose singular and solitary *démarche* inaugurated the expression of **Négritude** within the context of Lusophone writing. After this came writings marked unequally by poetic inspiration and, concomitantly, critical writings (some of which remain unpublished).

These texts were written by authors living in urban centers (Luanda, Lourenço Marques) and also in Portugal, especially among university students in Coimbra and Lisbon. The first space, the urban centers, was the theater for attempts at organized literary movements (**Vamos descobrir Angola, Movimento dos Novos Intelectuais** and, less significantly, **Msaho**) and the launching of periodic publications dedicated to culture. The second space, in Portugal, was the home of the Centro de Estudos Africanos [Center of African Studies], which will be discussed below. Through correspondence exchanged between those involved a comparison and circulation of themes and ideas was established between them. The existing **corpus** of documentation, which is noteworthy for its will to testify, is relatively restricted, but the density and social range resulted from its integration into a significant and broader group of texts and from a reading, simultaneously, of texts and their intertextuality.

Poetry—exemplified by the poems of Agostinho Neto, Noémia de Sousa, José Craveirinha, Viriato da Cruz, Marcelino dos Santos, Gabriel Mariano, Ovídio Martins, and António Jacinto, among others—is organized, in our opinion, according to three principal themes:

a. the search for identity;
b. the search for African cultural models;
c. the expression of the social reality.

Some unpublished letters from this period reveal the premonitions of the poets—heralding the profound convulsion of the colonized society.

We can now return to what we had highlighted above—the phases that set the tempo of nationalist **praxis** during the years following the Second World War—but considered from the perspective of unity.

As had happened at the beginning of the twentieth century, it is in the capital of the "empire" that a group of Africans, which included university students and some mid-level civil servants of the state apparatus, engaged at the end of the 1940s in a peaceful battle for the revitalization of an association with the name of "Casa d'África Portuguesa" or, in the language of the period, for a society that would defend "the interests of the African masses." Ultimately, this was an attempt to seize the leadership that had been illegally controlled by a formerly prominent figure of proto-nationalism, Artur de Castro.

The **Comissão Reorganizadora** [Reorganizing Commission]—which included some of the future actors-leaders of the wars of national liberation, such as Amílcar Cabral, António Vasco Cabral, Marcelino dos Santos, Alda do Espírito Santo, and Mário Pinto de Andrade—finally lost the battle for compliance with the commission's statutory rules during the last, tumultuous meeting that took place on August 2, 1950.

A new field of activity then opened with the creation of the "Centro de Estudos Africanos" by a small group of young intellectuals in October 1951. The center was the mainspring of education and cultural information, of the "re-Africanization of spirits," where the denunciation of colonialism was forged. Parallel to this, the same nucleus of people developed initiatives with a nationalist character in the "class associations" and centers of cultural and political agitation—the **Clube Marítimo Africano** and the **Casa dos Estudantes do Império**.

It became increasingly necessary in the Portuguese political scene to act clandestinely.

The discourse of unity was formulated in step with the explosion of organizations that spread throughout the colonial space.

The originality of the phenomenon in relation to proto-nationalism can be seen on a number of different levels, such as:

- **concurrent leadership**, which is to say that the actors-leaders found themselves effectively in leadership positions of nationalist movements or in the process of assuming these roles;
- the multiplicity of external locations where the discourse was elaborated (expanding the spatial horizon) and, consequently, of the political praxis: Lisbon, Paris, Tunis, Conakry, Casablanca, Rabat;
- the appeal for a plurality of interlocutors-addressees:
  - Internally: manual laborers and intellectuals, from the countryside and from the cities, peasants, workers, students, soldiers obliged to serve in the colonial army;
  - Externally: colonial authorities, Portuguese and international public opinion, the United Nations.

## 3. The Second Order of Discourse

We are finally in a position to analyze the contents of the second order of discourse of *Clamor Africano*. We limit ourselves here to the period of its formulation, which occurred between the phase of organizational explosion and the constitutive meeting of C.O.N.C.P. [Conferência das Organizações Nacionalistas das Colónias Portuguesas], from 1957 to 1961. This corresponds to the emergence of the modern political process of unity in the historical context of the achievement of African independence and of **peaceful coexistence** and **positive neutrality**.

The theoretical **corpus** is composed of the following writings which would come to constitute the hegemonic statement:

1. The proceedings of the "consultation and study meeting for the development of the fight against Portuguese colonialism," which took place in Paris from November 15-18, **1957**.
2. The Manifesto of MAC (Movimento Anti-Colonialista) proclaimed on January 1, 1960, in Conakry.
3. The "Carta da F.R.A.I.N." (Frente Revolucionária Africana para a Independência Nacional das Colónias Portuguesas) released on January 28, 1960, in Tunis.
4. The statement in the press conference—the "Comunicado da Conferência de Imprensa dos dirigentes nacionalistas das colónias portugueses"—held in the House of Commons in London on December 6, 1960.
5. The resolutions of the "Conferência das Organizações Nacionalistas das Colónias Portuguesas" (C.O.N.C.P.) held in Casablanca from April 18-20, 1961.

We can identify the producers of these texts (those who were most involved): a restricted group of young intellectuals undergoing a **Jacobin** transformation into political professionalization.

How are the different political categories of the discourse presented through these texts?

Starting from the **unequivocal** affirmation of a cultural identity of **Africans** in the struggle for the advent of the nation, the nationalists express a line of thinking about the **enemy, violence, the organization and social base** that constitutes the chosen categories of our analysis.

### 3.1. The Enemy

In a concise formulation that leaves no margin for any doubt whatsoever, colonialism is defined as the **irreconcilable** enemy of the people of the Portuguese colonies in Africa. It is a system and an apparatus of oppression.

Guided by pedagogical purposes intended to clarify the notion of the enemy among the Africans and among the Portuguese, the MAC Manifesto refutes the juridical principles invoked by Portugal in defense of colonial domination—**the historical right, the effective occupation of territories, the need for progress and for the material and moral development of the colonies and their populations**; principles that were negated and destroyed, respectively, by the Berlin Conference, the League of Nations, and the United Nations.

In negative terms, "Salazarism," the Portuguese version of fascism, is not the principal enemy: "it is the virulent, but by nature transitory, instrument of the old and hateful Portuguese colonialism."

The reciprocity of the historical perspective, however, is affirmed:

> "But by fighting against Portuguese colonialism, our people are giving to the Portuguese people the best contribution to their fight against fascism. Because as long as the Portuguese colonial structure endures, it is certain that the Portuguese people will run the risk of becoming victims of fascist dictatorships."

Hence, the proposal for an **alliance** between the liberation movements and the Portuguese Opposition, for the formation of a **united front** against fascism and colonialism.

### 3.2. Violence

Even before Fanon's theorization of the liberating function of violence, the core group of nationalists had characterized the colonial situation as a permanent act of violence.

And because violence is inherent to the system of domination, the Portuguese government placed itself in a dilemma: either maintain the regime or, threatened at the foundations of its supremacy, pursue the colonial war. Violence was thus situated in the enemy's camp. The Portuguese government responded to the legitimate revolt of the people with bloody repression. Creator of a war psychosis, Portugal was accused of practicing genocide and of preparing the unleashing of a preventive war.

With its right to insurrection supported by international law, the nationalist movement establishes as an essential objective the response to violence, which, according to Fanon, is "a reality deriving from and mediated by the exploitative process of colonialism."

Hence the necessity of destroying the structure and the forces of Portuguese colonialism. But this destruction can be realized by peaceful and by violent means. Both options are referred to in the MAC manifesto.

As a last resort:

> "To unleash, under the most appropriate forms, the armed struggle against Portuguese colonialism, in a just war of national liberation, in response to the unjust colonial war imposed by the Portuguese colonialists."

A variation on this, which was adapted at the site of the political discourse given in the House of Commons, "this august house of democracy," on December 6, 1960, was the use of the expression—the only alternative of "direct action"—since the method was demanded by the peoples who "are now insisting with the maximum urgency for an organised plan of active self-defense."

The dominant language in this atmosphere of revendication and the defining of political principles focused on the **immediate** achievement of national sovereignty, **actual** independence, and the **total** liquidation of colonialism and of imperialism on the African continent.

### 3.3. The Organization and Social Base

The texts make clear the need for organization, the condition **sine qua non** for the achievement of the objective of liberation.

During the early moments, the appeal to organizational participation aimed to bring together **patriots, honest Africans** (in the anticolonial fight), though, at the time, the leadership of the struggle was assigned—illusorily—to the **proletariat**.

The meeting in which the core of nationalist ideologues intended to proceed to a **class** analysis of each one of the colonized societies ended with a mimetic exercise.

Thus, the adoption of the following principle:

> "The working classes of the Portuguese colonies of Africa are the most revolutionary. The role of mobilizing and organizing the masses and of the leadership of the struggle against colonialism belongs to the proletariat."

In 1960, F.R.A.I.N. defined itself as the "**alliance** of political parties and mass organizations of African countries under Portuguese colonial domination."

Finally, C.O.N.C.P. elevated the organizational quality of the movement by engaging "all of the patriots of the Portuguese colonies to mobilize themselves in their national organizations" and by inviting "the various nationalist movements to join forces in fighting fronts united around an immediate objective: the liquidation of Portuguese colonialism."

## 4. Conclusion

We have briefly seen the unfolding of the *processus* of expression of the protest writings, of the manifestations of unitary proto-nationalism in Portugal, and how this leads to the rupture provoked by the group of modern nationalists.

At the end of this ideological narrative, it is useful to question the epistemological limits of our **own démarche**.

1. The global understanding of the order of discourse of *Clamor Africano*, its nature, and the socio-cultural profile of its producers must proceed from a conception of history capable of capturing in the same movement the **social totality** of the African group under analysis—which explains the ideas and the formation of mentalities. Pierre Vilar encourages us "to think everything historically" as the essential line of Marxism. We took (**pro domo nostra**) social history as the guiding method of approach in the final writing of this research.

2. The nationalist political statement is not limited, obviously, to the "leadership cycle" of texts, but it is inter-related to the "popular cycle." It is for this reason that the historiography of nationalisms must base its ideological affiliation on the multiform and unremitting resistances that for centuries set the tempo of battle against foreign occupation—something which confers on this historiography the temporal breadth of the **long duration**. And it would not be possible to understand in any other way how the set of ideas of the original nationalist nucleus, which evolved progressively into the **Marxian** or **Marxist** leadership core of the wars of national liberation, took root in broad sectors of the colonized society, materializing collective aspirations for social change.

The importance of the oral and written testimonies of the protagonists of the "popular cycle" cannot be overemphasized.

The initiative of "Oficina de História," conceived and advanced by Aquino de Bragança, who remains present **here today** in our thoughts, should be seen as part of this attempt to understand the **lived experience** of the popular masses by the participants themselves.

We also wish to quote from the study undertaken by the historian Achille Mbembé on the nationalist discourse in Cameroon that takes the "Union of the Peoples of Cameroon" (UPC) as the paradigmatic example. The linguistic factor is relevant in all of this research on political expression. The author writes:

> What does it mean to say "enunciate the political" when "subaltern actors" decide to re-appropriate in their own language and organize word practices through which they define their space and their own logics? The "passage" or "non-passage" to the political is unintelligible if the mental, cultural, social and political structures within which the actors move, the understanding they possess from them and the modes by which they name them, are not taken into consideration.

...the sung or written text in the **basaà** language obliges the analyst to grasp the way in which the political actors enunciate political time, divide into periods, and articulate the calendar and the seasons, organize memory and accumulate motivations that authorize the radicalization of the struggle or the expulsion of this last to a kind of messianic waiting time. The same written or sung text allows us, then, to perceive the manner how, within a nationalist discursive structure, the monolithic and uniform appearance of the enunciation in French is enriched in the national language.[13]

It is in this context that the return to oral and written texts opens new possibilities for investigation.

3. The scope of the subject under discussion requires, finally, the incorporation of the entire African socio-cultural context beyond the borders in which the Portuguese colonies were artificially inserted.

These seem to us to be the necessary formulations that should guide the direction of the historiography of nationalism.

*Translated by Mario Pereira*

NOTES

\* Originally published as "As Ordens do Discurso do 'Clamor Africano': Continuidade e Ruptura na Ideologia do Nacionalismo Unitário" *Estudos Moçambicanos*, v. 7, 1990, pp. 9-27. This translation is published with the generous permission of the heirs of Mário Pinto de Andrade. The formatting, layout and typography of the original article have for the most part been retained in the translation. These strategic choices by the author do not conform to the recommendations of current style manuals, but they were intended to encourage a certain kind of critical reading experience. Section numbers have been added for clarity.

1. See, *Gazeta do Sul*, 1889-1892, weekly paper, Quelimane (Mozambique).
2. *O Negro*, n. 1, March 9, 1911.
3. *Tribuna d'África*, n. 7, v. 18, June 22, 1913.
4. "Para a união dos africanos de Lisboa e de toda a África! Para a união de todos os portugueses," *África*, November 11, 1931.
5. *A Voz d'África*, n. 15, April 1, 1913.
6. Ibid., n. 1, September 1, 1912.
7. *Correio de África*, n. 44, June 1, 1922.
8. Ibid., n. 2, June 7, 1921.
9. Cf. Tenreiro, Francisco José, *A Ilha de São Tomé*. Memórias da Junta de Investigação do Ultramar, v. 24, 1961.

10. See, George Balandier, "Messianismes et Natioanlismes en Afrique Noire," *Cahiers Internationaux de Sociologie*, v. 14, 1953, pp. 41-65.

11. Afonso Ivens Ferraz de Freitas, "Província de Moçambique: Seitas Religiosas Gentílicos (Confidencial)," *Arquivo Histórico de Moçambique*, v. 4, 1957.

12. See, Mário Pinto de Andrade, "Proto-Nacionalismo em Moçambique: Kamba Simango," *Boletim do Arquivo Histórico de Moçambique*, n. 6, 1989, pp. 127–148.

13. J. Achille Mbembé, "La palabre de l'indépendance: les ordres du discours nationaliste au Cameroun (1948-1958)," *Revue française de science politique*, n. 3, 1985, pp. 459-487.

MARIA MANUEL LISBOA

# De Onde Menos se Espera:
# A Disciplina do Terror em Lygia Fagundes Telles

> *O verdadeiro esforço ético não está apenas na decisão de salvar vítimas, mas também—e talvez muito mais—na dedicação impiedosa de aniquilar aqueles que fazem delas vítimas.*
> Slavoj Žižek, Bem-vindos ao Deserto do Real

> *Se não conseguir apaziguar os deuses poderosos comoverei os deuses infernais.*
> Virgílio, Eneida

RESUMO: Este ensaio considera a função do género do fantástico e de terror nas obras de ficção, crónica e pseudo-memórias de Lygia Fagundes Telles. Propõe a hipótese de utilizar a escritora um regime de incerteza e de recusa de verdade interpretativa como instrumentos de desestabilização de pre-supostas normas nas relações humanas, dando antes lugar ao desconhecido e ao pavor existencial.

PALAVRAS-CHAVE: Lygia Fagundes Telles/ fantástico/ terror/ incerteza

ABSTRACT: This essay explores the use of the genre of the fantastic and of terror as a recurring trope in the works of fiction and to a lesser extent the chronicles and would-be memorialistic writing of Lygia Fagundes Telles. It argues that the rule of uncertainty and the withholding from the reader of the possibility of interpretative truth is the tool whereby pre-supposed normality in human, familial and social relations gives way to the fearful unknown.

KEYWORDS: Lygia Fagundes Telles/fantastic/terror/uncertainty

Nunca se deve julgar um livro pela sua tampa? Pelo contrário, às vezes até é boa ideia. O que primeiro me levou, já faz mais de duas décadas, a pegar num livro de Lygia Fagundes Telles foi, não propriamente a sua tampa (ou capa), mas a estampa da escritora, numa fotografia na contracapa. Má razão? Talvez. Mas por vezes as Eríneas escrevem direito por linhas tortas. A tal fotografia mostrava um rosto feminino curiosamente parecido com um gato (gata, tigre, tigra, tigrela?), e especificamente com o gato que a escritora nesta—e como vim mais tarde a verificar, em muitas outras fotografias—acariciava ao colo: "Tenho um nome de gente na minha condição de gato. . . . Um gato que sonha com o homem assim como o homem sonha com Deus (HN, 81, 136);[1] "Um gato sem raça . . . e sem memória. . . . O que eu fiz, o quê?! para merecer esta forma. E não tenho fé, não acredito em nada. Um gato memorialista e agnóstico—existe? Memória que quase sempre é peçonha na qual me alimento. E me enveneno. . . . Agora tenho medo da liberdade" (HN, 111-15).

Assim fala Rahul, o herói felino de *As Horas Nuas*.[2] Gatos: felinos belos, encantadores (incluindo no sentido que este termo acarreta de feitiçarias, de bruxarias). Sedutores e perigosos, macios mas com garras, a espada de dois gumes que associamos também à figura da sereia a qual, como é sabido, usa o poder da palavra (cantiga) para aliciar os incautos à perdição. Como por exemplo aquela sereia escolhida pela autora para a capa de *Mistérios*, coletânea de alguns dos seus mais inquietantes contos: "uma capa da qual gosto muito, ilustrada com a gravura de uma pequena sereia sueca. Antiquíssima. Ao invés de um espelho ela tem na mão um livro."[3]

Ninguém se queixe que não foi avisado.

As sereias, felizmente (pelo menos do ponto de vista dos navegadores) não existem, mas os gatos sim, e em contos de fadas são o animal predileto de bruxas e outras pessoas parecidas: ser aveludado, ensimesmado, misterioso, carinhoso. Com garras. Contraditório e imponderável, tão inquietante e irresistível como as narrativas de uma escritora que ao longo das décadas nos tem vindo a montar armadilhas nas quais nós continuamos a cair com insistência e sem emenda. "Talvez desta vez ela não me apanhe?" Apanha sempre. E ainda bem. Que desapontamento se um dia o fruto proibido se transformasse em malga de caldinho caseiro e nutritivo.

Nada a dizer contra a sopa, está claro. Foi aliás com uma sopinha que, como é sabido, dá saúde e faz crescer, que tudo começou, no universo imaginário desta autora, em que, porém, como se verá, o que cresce nem sempre é o que se espera. Diz-nos Lygia que a arte de contar histórias começou, para ela, com escritos feitos com letrinhas de massa de alfabeto, a que se seguiram histórias contadas por si, ainda criança mas autonomeada substituta de uma rebelde foragida, a pequenos companheiros por aquela abandonados:

Na verdade, eu comecei a experimentar o gosto de narrar histórias um pouco depois. O sucesso dessa pajem contadora de histórias começou a atrair a criançada que vinha se sentar na escada de pedras do nosso quintal, depois do jantar, em meio da cachorrada, tínhamos muitos cachorros. Certa noite, ela não apareceu, tinha fugido com um trapezista do circo. Num impulso de audácia, resolvi substituí-la: foi quando descobri que sentia menos medo enquanto eu mesma falava porque se era excitante ouvir, mais excitante ainda era narrar e ver estampado nas caras em redor todo o horror que se esvaía de mim, transferia ao próximo a minha insegurança, o meu medo, mas não era extraordinário descobrir isso? Pensei e me senti independente, poderosa. Datam dessa idade de ouro os meus primeiros escritos, assim que comecei a escrever, isso depois do aprendizado com a sopa de letrinhas, tinha um macarrãozinho com todo o abecedário, eu ia alinhando as letras nas bordas do prato fundo, era muito difícil—me lembro—encontrar o "y" do meu nome. Então recorria ao caldeirão, onde as letras todas estavam lá no fundo, fervendo borbulhantes.[4]

O "y" é difícil de encontrar. Em matemática, a incógnita de uma equação é denotada pelas letras "x" ou "y." A descoberta do valor da incógnita leva à solução da equação. A solução da equação permite a enunciação de um axioma, e o axioma leva à prova do teorema: "Ele dizia *teorema* ao invés de *problema*, teorema é mais leve. E tem Deus na raiz. Teo" (HN, 14).

Nos contos de Lygia, a voz autoral (aquele "y" difícil de encontrar) frequentemente (quase sempre?) abandona-nos em terra incógnita. A equação verifica-se insolúvel, o axioma fugidio, o teorema improvável em ambos sentidos da palavra (implausível; impossível de provar). E a lei da implausibilidade/improbabilidade reina suprema no universo desta artista. A imagem de uma jovem bruxa, aprendiz de feiticeira assenhoreando-se do seu terror e exorcizando-o num caldeirão de signos devoráveis estabelece um padrão de regras de combate que permanecerá constante ao longo da obra futura. Decifrar o universo de Lygia requer o entendimento de qual é exatamente o alvo de ataque: no fim de um infernal banquete, quem sofreu, quem morreu, quem perdeu a razão de ser? A lista é inquietante, porque para além das vítimas e alvos facilmente identificáveis (amantes e amados, regras e leis, indivíduos e comunidades), encontramo-nos nós, os seus leitores, a quem é invariavelmente recusado um pressuposto direito básico a narrativas com moralidade, resolução ou pelo menos sentido. Quem passa ao ataque deve ter, no mínimo, a cortesia de explicar como, contra o quê e porquê esse ataque foi desencadeado. Da parte desta autora, porém, à partida, nada transparece para além da pergunta sibilina, "quem hei-de afligir hoje?"

As epígrafes de Slavoj Žižek e Virgílio acima providenciadas oferecem talvez (mas nunca mais que talvez) pontos de apoio para o entendimento do desafio que é Lygia: desafio impelido por uma cólera controlada contra prepotências poliformemente institucionalizadas, e contra tudo o que elas espezinham, mas que na obra desta escritora se volta a erguer, insurgindo-se em retaliação. Retaliação porém não desmedida mas pelo contrário, clinicamente medida. Amor com amor se paga? Em Lygia sim, quase sempre literalmente: ou, alternativamente, *amor com amor se mata*.

> "Quem hei-de afligir hoje" então? A resposta é poliforme, mas o critério é linear: o alvo de ataque é sempre quem quer que seja que, nessa específica conjuntura de tempo e situação detém as rédeas do poder, definido por classe, idade, sexo, posição pessoal, social, familiar ou política. Em Lygia, seja qual for a modalidade, essa única certeza permanece em narrativas em que a própria definição de realidade é frequentemente contestada.[5]

### Escrita Fora-da-lei

Este esboço define, em linhas gerais, o perfil da posição criativa, ética e ideológica desenvolvida em uma escrita que, ao longo de mais de sete décadas, tem abrangido os géneros do conto, romance, crónica e guião cinemático.[6] Os romances, (*Ciranda de Pedra*, 1954; *Verão no Aquário*, 1963; *As Meninas*, 1973;[7] *As Horas Nuas*, 1989) têm vindo, ao longo das décadas, a levantar lebres pelos prados de um *status quo* que, com maior ou menor firmeza (ou agressividade, ou violência) preferiria não as reconhecer: lesbianismo e impotência (*Ciranda de Pedra*); desconchavo existencial num contexto político e emocional conturbado, contra um pano de fundo de decadência e ditadura, em que uma sociedade rigidamente ordenada produz indivíduos psicologicamente à deriva numa narrativa semanticamente imponderável (*As Meninas*);[8] rivalidade amorosa entre mãe e filha durante um Verão concreta e metaforicamente quente, em que a realidade dá lugar a incertezas—políticas, amorosas, sexuais, religiosas—por fim sem solução (*Verão no Aquário*); e o devaneio *flâneur* de personagens cuja existência sem objetivo esborrata as linhas divisórias entre a fantasia e a realidade (*As Horas Nuas*).[9]

Uma das seduções de entre as muitas que nos aliciam ao universo escorregadio desta artista da palavra incerta é o próprio facto de ser o leitor (a leitora) por vezes transformado em joguete de artimanhas e artifícios que o reduzem a parceiro não do narrador omnisciente mas do protagonista involuntariamente agnóstico, em cenários em que porém a gnose vem a revelar-se ser ou o *sine qua non* da sobrevivência ou, alternativamente, o confrontamento com a morte inevitável. Para o leitor reduzido ao estatuto de títere de expetativas ambíguas relativamente a um conteúdo que se define, entre outros fatores, segundo género literário, há pelo menos duas formas de ser Lygia: romancista e contista, num universo em que a metamorfose é a arma(dilha)/arma(dela) predileta. O mundo difuso e inquietante dos romances alterna com o mundo inquietante mas incisivo e pungente dos contos, no final dos quais talvez nem nós nem os protagonistas saibamos o que se passou, mas sabemos, sem sombra de dúvidas, que algo nos/lhes aconteceu, numa indisciplinada disciplina de amor, rancor e dor.[10]

> Solução melhor é não enlouquecer mais do que já enlouquecemos, não tanto por virtude, mas por cálculo. Controlar essa loucura razoável: se formos razoavelmente loucos não precisaremos desses sanatórios porque é sabido que os saudáveis não entendem muito de loucura. O jeito é se virar em casa mesmo, sem testemunhas estranhas. Sem despesas. (DA, 28)[11]

"A beleza não está nem na luz da manhã nem na sombra da noite, está no crepúsculo, nesse meio tom, nessa incerteza" (ABV, 162).[12]

Na análise que se segue, a ênfase será concedida ao género do conto na obra desta autora, e ao panorama simultaneamente vasto, hermético e intenso que as obras nele inclusas abrangem. De dentro do casulo do conto, Lygia oferece ao espectador um espetáculo vertiginoso deste mundo e do outro, e das metamorfoses e incertezas que os atribulam, a esses mundos e a nós que dentro deles (graças a eles, apesar deles) existimos.

## I—ESTE MUNDO: FAMÍLIAS, AMANTES, ANIMAIS DOMÉSTICOS

> *As almas, não, as almas vão pairando,*
> *e, esquecendo a lição que já se esquiva,*
> *tornam amor humor, e vago e brando*
> *o que é de natureza corrosiva.*
> Carlos Drummond de Andrade

### Vítimas onde Menos se Espera

"Não há gente completamente boa nem gente completamente má, está tudo misturado e a separação é impossível. O mal está no próprio gênero humano, ninguém presta. Às vezes a gente melhora. Mas passa" (CP, 148-49).[13]

Quem ou que coisa é aniquilada no universo de Lygia Fagundes Telles? Quando articulamos esta questão e aceitamos o convite a ponderá-la, entramos no trilho de descobertas que porventura desvendarão, ainda que com limites, o que teria sido mais prudente desconhecermos. Mais prudente porque, tal como Eva, Pandora, Eurídice, Psique ou a desafortunada esposa de Lot descobriram a seu próprio custo, no imaginário greco-judaico-cristão a audácia de querer saber acarreta sempre castigo severo. Ficamos avisados? Ficamos avisadas?

### Sangue do Meu Sangue

Todos os jardins são potencialmente selvagens, e quanto mais propício o clima pior, ou melhor. A selva Amazónica começou obrigatoriamente com umas poucas ervinhas; um inofensivo parque citadino, sem a mais assídua vistoria, depressa reverte ao mato original; e no Jardim do Paraíso, mesmo sob a fiscalização do mais perito dos jardineiros, bastou um deslize ou dois para que o resultado fosse a paisagem muitíssimo pouco satisfatória que veio a ser o nosso pouco admirável mundo, novo e velho.

Para saber de quem é a culpa, está bem de ver, *cherchez la femme*. *Cherchez* e até *recherchez*, porque Eva foi a segunda esposa. Antes dela houve Lilith, tão perigosa que foi quase inteiramente elidida dos textos canónicos pelo Concílio de Trento: reduzida a um "l" minúsculo em Isaías 34:[14] ("*E as feras do deserto se encontrarão com hienas; e o sátiro clamará ao seu companheiro; e lilith pousará ali, e achará lugar de repouso para si*"); e apenas obliquamente recordada por via dos textos midráshicos de *Sepher Ben Sira* no século XI: "Depois que Deus criou Adão, que estava sozinho, Ele disse: "Não é bom que o homem esteja só" (Génesis 2:18).

> Ele então criou a mulher para Adão, da terra, como Ele havia criado o próprio Adão, e chamou-a de Lilith. Adão e Lilith imediatamente entraram em discórdia. Lilith disse: "Por que devo deitar-me embaixo de ti? Por que devo abrir-me sob teu corpo? Por que ser dominada por ti? Eu também fui feita de pó e por isso sou tua igual." E ele respondeu: "Eu não vou me deitar abaixo de ti, apenas por cima. Pois tu estás apta apenas para estar na posição inferior, enquanto eu sou um ser superior." Lilith respondeu: "Nós somos iguais um

ao outro, considerando que ambos fomos criados a partir da terra." Mas eles não deram ouvidos um ao outro. Quando Lilith percebeu isso, ela pronunciou o Nome Inefável e voou para o ar. Adão permaneceu em oração diante do seu Criador: "Senhor! A mulher que me deste fugiu!" Então Deus enviou três anjos para trazê-la de volta. Os três anjos encontraram-na numa caverna nas margens do Mar Vermelho, insistiram que ela voltasse e ameaçaram afogá-la, mas ela recusou." (Sepher Ben Sira)[14]

Na mitologia hebraica, suméria e mesopotâmica, Lilith (*Lylith*? O "y" é difícil de encontrar...) aparece variamente retratada como demónio, megera infanticida de bebés do sexo masculino, ou vampiro, e é a partir daí largamente esquecida. Esquecida, mas agora ressurgida no jardim selvagem que é o universo de Lygia.

## Home, Sweet Home

A caridade bem entendida começa por casa, e a crueldade também. A vasta maioria dos crimes violentos é cometida por um familiar ou pessoa conhecida da vítima. Em casos de violência doméstica, segundo dados fornecidos pela ONU, em números crus, a vastíssima maioria nomeia o homem no papel de agressor e a mulher no de vítima. Acerca do fenómeno oposto o silêncio é tão profundo e as estatísticas tão rarefeitas, que o crime se vem a assemelhar aos mais extremos tabus. No Brasil, por exemplo, a Lei Maria da Penha, referente a ataques contra mulheres no domicílio, só nos últimos cinco anos passou a incluir uma alínea referente ao homem enquanto vítima da mulher.[15]

No jardim selvagem que é o pelouro da família em Lygia Fagundes Telles, as permutações de perigo são múltiplas, multiformes e quase sempre inesperadas, em especial quando pensamos saber o que nos espera. O que, no caso desta escritora, não convém nunca pensar, porque nestes misteriosos universos, ninguém tem direito a nada, nem mesmo, ou muito menos, quem a lê. Quem pratica desportos perigosos, sabe que arrisca a pele. Nos contos de Lygia, todos estamos em perigo de vida, tanto protagonistas como leitores, cujos pontos de vista, aliás, por vezes inquietantemente se confundem. Quem sou eu? Onde estou eu? Já cá voltaremos.

Regressando para já ao terreno enganadoramente familiar da psicanálise, onde embora haja perigos, está-se a ver que todos pensamos que sabemos exatamente quais são, quando lemos Lygia descobrimos que afinal talvez não, porque nestes mundos fictícios nada é nunca o que se espera: a identidade e, de um modo geral, o sexo das vítimas, surpreende, o contexto alarma e a própria iconografia é inesperada (o verde, por exemplo, não é nunca a cor da esperança). Não o é, certamente, em "Antes do baile verde," em que uma filha desnaturada ajusta os últimos detalhes do reptilíneo traje recamado de lantejoulas verdes que vai exibir no baile de carnaval prestes a começar, e finge não saber que o pai há muito moribundo no quarto ao lado, inconvenientemente, talvez tenha agora morrido.

E não o é em "Verde Lagarto Amarelo," onde a cor verde também adquire conotações análogas de decomposição orgânica e moral. Para Rodolfo, gordo, desengraçado, vítima de glândulas sudoríparas excessivamente ativas, o pai castrador Freudiano não tem qualquer significado, nem sequer contracena no palco familiar, onde, tal como o pai moribundo em "Antes do Baile Verde," permanece invisível. Em seu lugar (e já mesmo essa eliminação do patriarca nos deveria dar que pensar), Rodolfo, socialmente inadequado desde a infância, é condenado ao espetáculo da sua própria vida repetidamente posta a saque por uma mãe não propriamente malévola, apenas indiferente, e por um irmão que ele inveja mas que (e é isso que é insuportável) o adora. Eduardo é tudo o que Rodolfo nunca será: "bonito, inteligente, amado" OMC, 17),[16] feliz dentro da sua própria pele, preferido primeiro pela mãe e depois por Ofélia—esta amada em silêncio por Rodolfo e em plena ventura conjugal por Eduardo, um "sweet prince" sem tragédia Hamletiana.

Neste conto a morte, terror supremo de qualquer animal, racional ou não, humano, humanoide ou reptilíneo (lagarto), não se manifesta, embora a cessação do direito à existência se torne de facto realidade. Rodolfo fantasia desde a infância a morte de um irmão o qual lhe reciproca ódio com amor ("desde menino eu já estava condenado ao seu fraterno amor," OMC, 17). Vítima de um resquício de dever fraterno que por fim não lhe permite ser o Caim deste formoso Abel, Rodolfo não sucumbe ao instinto atávico que a vida inteira o expôs à tentação. O réptil torna-se ele próprio o objeto das artimanhas do destino, e em adolescente defende o irmão de um perigo literalmente incalculável. Após um instante de tentação, o que nele há de bom bloqueia a tentação e leva-o a defender o irmão de um possível esfaqueamento às mãos de um bando de delinquentes, sendo que nunca saberemos se o perigo teria sido realmente de morte—física, para Eduardo, moral para Rodolfo.

Se o doce príncipe e a sua Ofélia contravêm o destino prescrito na tragédia precursora e vivem felizes para sempre, incluindo com muitos meninos, tal como na fábula da praxe, para Rodolfo o saldo final não liquida a dívida predestinada.

No passado, o perigo de que salvara o irmão resultou no desenlace de um Eduardo ligeiramente machucado, carregado às costas do primogénito que de má vontade o resgatara dos malfeitores. Curiosamente, o episódio apresenta nuances inesperadas: o esbelto Eduardo "pesava como chumbo" (OMC, 19), e ao carregá-lo às cavalitas para fora de perigo, Rodrigo vislumbra "nossa sombra no muro, as tiras [da sua camisa rasgada] se abrindo como asas" (OMC, 19). Asas de anjo da guarda ou de vampiro? Quem sabe? Sabemos, porém, que esta narrativa do quotidiano termina com laivos de terror. Em toda a sua desafortunada vida, Rodolfo mantivera uma única esfera de predomínio, um pelouro de atividade em que não era suplantado pelo irmão: o seu relativo sucesso como escritor. Agora, no decurso de uma visita feita pelo carinhoso Eduardo ao seu arisco irmão, o registo da revelação de que até esse último reduto foi capturado evoca o lance final de uma narrativa de terror: "Olhei para sua pasta na cadeira e adivinhei a surpresa. Senti meu coração se fechar como uma concha. A dor era quase física. Olhei para ele.—Você escreveu um romance. É isso? Os originais estão na pasta... É isso? Ele então abriu a pasta" (OMC, 20).

A família transformada em sarabanda de figuras pressupostamente acolhedoras mas efetivamente empedernidas ou até perigosas—aqueles figurantes/figurinos rodopiando numa ciranda (de pedra ou de carne e osso), no romance com esse título—aparenta-se à sua protagonista, Virgínia tão hermética e por fim tão sem solução como a de Rodolfo, com a qual tem semelhanças: uma mãe insondável e um pai indiscernível ("Verde Lagarto") ou desconhecido (*Ciranda de Pedra*, onde quem passara por pai afinal, como se vem a descobrir, efetivamente não o era).

### Amor: O Que É de Natureza Corrosiva

Em Lygia, quase sempre, o amor, e até a amizade, desenrolam-se por vias (de novo cirandas) circunvolutas e perigosas.[17] O que pensar, então, do aterrorizante conto "A Testemunha" (MCE), em que Rolf, amigo inimaginavelmente paciente é assassinado por aquele de quem durante anos (depreende-se) cuidou? Em alguns dos contos, o guião segue as convenções do *slasher movie* tradicional. Em "Venha Ver o Pôr-do-sol" (ABV), o amante rejeitado alicia a antiga namorada a uma armadilha e encarcera-a na catacumba de um cemitério abandonado, onde, pressupõe-se, ela jamais será encontrada. Em "Lua Crescente em Amsterdã," até o título e/ou o protagonista nos engana, a nós e à sua companheira, quando diz que a lua "é crescente, tem o formato de um C" (visto que, como é sabido, no hemisfério norte, a lua é "mentirosa:" o formato de um C indica o quarto decrescente). Neste conto, uma misteriosa conjuntura de circunstâncias entre um par de namorados adquire uma compleição crescentemente (ao contrário da lua) imponderável e, eventualmente, inexplicável: por via de um processo de metamorfose que recusa as leis de qualquer universo pelos protagonistas e por nós decifrável, o humano transforma-se no bestial, o familiar no irresoluvelmente críptico e o amor na morte, tudo isto observado, como tantas vezes em Lygia, pelos olhos semicientes de uma menina em vias de perder a inocência e ser amaldiçoada com gnose.

> Agora vem, vamos dormir naquele banco. Vem, Ana. . . .
> Depositou-a no banco e sentou-se ao lado. . . .
> — E agora? O que acontece quando não se tem mais nada com o amor? . . .
> — Sopra o vento e a gente vira outra coisa.
> — Que coisa?
> — Sei lá. . . . Queria ser um passarinho . . . .
> — Nunca me terias como companheira, nunca. Gosto de mel, acho que quero ser borboleta. É fácil a vida de borboleta?
> — É curta.
> O vento soprou tão forte que a menina loura teve que parar porque o avental lhe tapou a cara. . . . . Aproximou-se do banco vazio. . . . agachou-se para ver o passarinho de penas azuis bicando com disciplinada voracidade a borboleta que procurava se esconder debaixo do banco de pedra. (M, 62-64)[18]

E em "Eu Era Mudo e Só," a esposa inconveniente—inconveniente, embora, algo inesperadamente, por ser demasiado perfeita, carinhosa, atenciosa—é eliminada num daqueles momentos inesperados de transposição do real familiar para o fantástico:

> nesse instante exato eu gostaria que ela estivesse morta. . . . Ergo o olhar até Fernanda. A mãe de minha filha. Minha companheira há onze anos, pronta para ir buscar aspirina se a dor é na cabeça, pronta para chamar o médico se a dor é no apêndice. Sou um monstro. . . .
> 
> Ela então inclinou a cabeça sob o halo redondo do abajur e recomeçou a ler. Que quadro! . . . Guardo o postal no bolso. Fernanda ficou impressa num postal, pronto, posso sair de cabeça descoberta e sem direção: ninguém me perguntou para onde vou nem a que horas devo voltar e se não quero levar um pullover—ah! maravilha, maravilha. (ABV, 179-80)

Até aqui, quer em "Venha Ver o Pôr-do-sol," quer em "Lua Crescente," quer em "Eu Era Mudo," está bem de ver, nada de excessivamente inesperado, visto que em toda a longa tradição da narrativa ocidental, o crime de paixão, com algumas notáveis exceções (Medeia, Clitemnestra) obedece à tradição que dita que o homem ou mata ou salva a donzela, e que esta se deixa ou matar ou resgatar, em ambos casos assegurando que ao sujeito masculino pertence o monopólio do poder e à mulher as limitações de dependência da agência alheia. O que, aliás, só lhes fica bem a ambos, porque manda a regra que o protagonista masculino, para bem ou para mal, é o sujeito da ação (herói ou rufião), enquanto que a heroína, para bem ou para mal, viva ou morta, permanece perpetuamente o objeto. É assim nas fábulas infantis, nos romances de cavalaria medievais, no romance gótico oitocentista, no romance policial contemporâneo e nos filmes de horror, nos quais, quer se trate de princesa sequestrada, castelã sitiada, donzela vampirizada ou heroína ameaçada, ao morrer esta faz o que lhe compete, só ganhando pela transição: "A morte de uma mulher bela é, inquestionavelmente, o tema mais poético do mundo, e os lábios mais adequados para tal tema são, indubitavelmente, os de um amante enlutado" (Poe, 265).

Como entender, então, um mundo virado às avessas como o desta escritora, em que um longo desfilar de jovens machos com tudo a esperar da vida, a perdem inexplicavelmente, de forma mais ou menos misteriosa, mais ou menos sinistra, e quase sempre às mãos daquelas que supostamente os amam?[19]

## O Coração do Companheiro

> *Querida, ao pé do leito derradeiro,*
> *Onde repousas desta longa vida,*
> *Aqui venho e virei pobre querida,*
> *Trazer-te o coração do companheiro.*
> Machado de Assis

No belo poema de amor de Machado a Carolina Augusta, a intenção era clara e a falecida lamentada, mas por que não dar-lhe agora uma voltinha, quer no que diz respeito ao sexo de quem morreu, quer à causa? Não é como se a própria Lygia não tivesse no passado feito perfídias semelhantes aos enredos do seu colega, o bruxo do Cosme Velho.[20] Quase invariavelmente, nesta escritora, onde um protagonista mais ou menos jovem (quase nenhuns chegam a velhos) é introduzido no elenco, convém esperar leitos prematuramente derradeiros. "Herbarium," "Apenas um Saxofone," "A Estrutura da Bolha de Sabão," "A Presença," "A Caçada," "As Pérolas," "O Jardim Selvagem," "A Mão no Ombro." A lista é inquietantemente longa, e, a partir de certo ponto, tenebrosamente previsível. E as circunstâncias abrangem um panorama que se alonga desde instâncias mais ou menos circunspectas (enfermidades e mortes de causa natural), por via de mortes em circunstâncias suspeitas (incluindo o incitamento ao suicídio) e finalmente homicídio, detetado ou não. Mesmo no caso de inofensivas mortes de causa natural, como por exemplo em "As Pérolas," a paisagem emocional de Lygia não renuncia ao luxo de uma certa crueldade, quanto mais não seja a imposição ao futuro finado do espetáculo antecipado do mundo num futuro cruelmente próximo em que ele, mesmo antes de morrer, já foi substituído: "Lavínia, não me abandone já, deixe ao menos eu partir primeiro!" (ABV,187).

As vítimas podem ser pais ou filhos, irmãos ou primos, amantes, esposos ou ilustres desconhecidos. O denominador comum é serem homens, e o fator incomum é serem todos eles meninos nas mãos de bruxas as quais, ou por omissão ou por comissão, participam, ou pelo menos com arrepiante interesse observam, o desenrolar da destruição. Como gatos e ratos? Em *Verão no Aquário*,

> vi um retrato assim do meu pai: um menino débil e louro . . . O olhar ainda limpo do rancor pela bem-amada que havia de traí-lo um dia, pela mãe falhando no momento em que não podia falhar, pelo amigo que não era amigo, por Deus que não apareceria para salvá-lo quando ele próprio se erguesse para ferir o próximo assim como fora ferido também. Os ídolos ainda estão inteiros. O menino então sorri e nem o inimigo mais feroz resistirá a esse sorriso de quem se oferece tão sem defesa. (VA, 26)[21]

## Vela por Mim

Num dos ensaios inclusos no volume *Literatura e Mal*, Georges Bataille propõe que a sexualidade e a reprodução levam à transformação do único no múltiplo, ao sacrifício do Eu para fins da criação de um Outro, e por conseguinte assinalam não a imortalidade, mas antes a morte enquanto perda do indivíduo na sua singularidade (Bataille 13-31). A Deus é possível a quadratura do círculo, ou seja, é concebível ser simultaneamente único e infinito, mas no pelouro humano a transição de um para dois, ou de um para muitos, inerente no facto da maternidade, denota possivelmente a dissolução. Será talvez daí que origina, par a par com a consciência da fragilidade do que é carne da sua carne, o impulso por parte da progenitora de fazer mal ao novo ser que, pelo mero facto de existir, torna aparente a vulnerabilidade daquela enquanto individualidade previamente estanque? No reino da selva (em jardins selvagens), nunca é boa ideia dar parte de fraco. E isso leva-nos em linha reta à questão de mães, ou figuras maternas, e dos seus meninos, na obra de Lygia: "Os homens não se cansam de procurar novas formas de exprimir o ímpeto violento devido ao qual se sentem atraídos para a mulher, mas par a par com este desejo, são impelidos pelo pânico de que através da sua agência possam morrer e desintegrar-se" (Horney, 134).

A teoria psicanalítica pós-Freudiana, incluindo a obra de Melanie Klein (1997), Dorothy Dinnerstein (1987) e Nancy Chodorow (1985), discerne na figura da mãe o terror do ponto iniciático, de uma vida finita e por isso condenada a perecer. Se para o recém-nascido a mãe se afigura toda-poderosa, fonte de tudo o que é tanto benigno como maligno, potencialmente ameaçando a sua existência e apontando para a possibilidade da morte, essa dualidade persistirá no inconsciente do adulto como a ambivalência do desejo de um regresso àquele ventre materno edénico mas, paradoxalmente, aniquilador. A mãe que recorda a dependência absoluta na infância reaviva a memória dessa impotência, dessa iniciática existência rudimentar, inquietantemente próxima do Nada que antecedeu o Ser: estado perigoso, sinónimo do caos, da desordem, da fantasia desregrada, e para o qual a solução, lacanianamente, é a separação edipiana do reino materno, e a trajetória em direção à identificação com o pai, cujo pelouro e cuja lei inauguram a vigência da masculinidade, da linguagem, da lógica e da razão.

Em Lygia, o mundo da fantasia e do fantástico (no sentido de antinatural ou sobrenatural da palavra), ou seja, da desrazão, pode levar, como veremos adiante ("A Presença," "Seminário dos Ratos," "As Formigas"), a cenários de apocalipse (o fim do mundo).[22] Mas a maldade bem entendida, como já ficou dito, começa por casa. Se a intenção é precipitar o fim do mundo, que sítio melhor para começar do que junto daqueles que, segundo os reconhecidos interesses do *commonweal* (bem público) são senhores dele: os jovens (não os velhos), os filhos (não as filhas), os homens (não as mulheres), os fortes (não os fracos), os belos (não os feios).

Em "Apenas um Saxofone," a melancolia de uma existência estéril é exacerbada pelo choque de uma morte escandalosamente sem sentido. Neste conto, o cenário de abertura apresenta-nos Luisiana, uma mulher de certa idade, criatura de nome estrangeiro, "peregrina em terras estranhas" (Atos 7:6), bem-posta na vida mas dela alienada.

Tenho um iate, tenho um casaco de vison prateado, tenho uma coroa de diamantes, tenho um rubi que já esteve incrustado no umbigo de um xá famosíssimo, até há pouco eu sabia o nome desse xá. Tenho um velho que me dá dinheiro, tenho um jovem que me dá gozo e ainda por cima tenho um sábio que me dá aulas sobre doutrinas filosóficas com um interesse tão platônico que logo na segunda aula já se deitou comigo. (ABV, 38-39)

Tudo neste mundo, à primeira vista luxuoso, é afinal falso, desde a sua castelã autodefinida como "puta erudita" (ABV, 35), até à decoração sumptuosa de uma mansão possuída a preço do próprio corpo, até a um decorador tragicamente forçado pelas exigências da profissão a fingir ser o que mais frequentemente os que o são fingem não ser:

Fomos escurecendo juntas, a sala e eu. Uma sala de uma burrice atroz, afetada, pretensiosa. E sobretudo rica, exorbitando de riqueza, abri um saco de ouro para o decorador se esbaldar nele. E se esbaldou mesmo, o veado. Chamava-se Renê e chegava logo cedinho com suas telas, veludos, musselinas, brocados, "trouxe hoje para o sofá um pano que veio do Afeganistão, completamente divino! Di-vino!" Nem o pano era do Afeganistão nem ele era tão veado assim, tudo mistificação, cálculo. Surpreendi-o certa vez sozinho, fumando perto da janela, a expressão fatigada e triste de um ator que já está farto de representar. (ABV, 36)

Nada é o que parece, nem a cronologia narrativa que, tendo-nos apresentado a protagonista, prontamente nos arremessa em *flashback* para um passado em que o monstro que ela virá a ser nos aparece ainda em embrião. Embrião que é, aliás, como veremos, uma das fórmulas mais apetecidas para inspirar terror na obra desta autora: o malefício em gestação mas já imparável, ilimitável na sua futuridade, resultando aqui, num passado/futuro remoto na morte do amantíssimo e vulnerável Xenofonte:

Se você me ama mesmo, eu disse, suba então naquela mesa e grite com todas as forças, vocês são todos uns cornudos, vocês são todos uns cornudos! E depois desça da mesa e saia mas sem correr. Ele me deu o saxofone para segurar enquanto eu fugia rindo, não, não, eu estava brincando, isso não! Já na esquina ouvi seus gritos em pleno bar, "cornudos, todos cornudos!" . . . Outra noite—saíamos de um teatro—não resisti e perguntei-lhe se era capaz de cantar ali no saguão um trecho de ópera, vamos, se você me ama mesmo cante aqui na escada um trecho do *Rigoleto*! Se você me ama mesmo, me leva agora a um restaurante, me compre já aqueles brincos, me compre imediatamente um vestido novo! Ele agora tocava em mais lugares porque eu estava ficando exigente, se você me ama mesmo, mesmo, mesmo... .... Pensei em abandoná-lo mas não tive forças, não tive, preferi que nosso amor apodrecesse....

Enrodilhado na cama, ele tocava em surdina.... Se você me ama mesmo, eu disse, se você me ama mesmo então saia e se mate imediatamente. (ABV, 44-45)

Moços e saxofones, aqui e em outro conto com justamente esse título ("O Moço do Saxofone"), são uma combinação malograda.[23] Mais frequentemente, porém, a tarefa de destruição não é delegada ao próprio ("saia e se mate imediatamente"), mas desempenhada por aquela mais diretamente interessada, contando-se esta quase sempre entre os familiares mais próximos do defunto-a-vir. Em "Herbarium," o amor sem retorno, como é regra, transforma-se em ódio mortífero. Nesse aspeto nada de novo, e antiquíssimo, também, é o ato antinatural mas não incomum em Lygia, do homicídio consanguíneo. Neste conto, uma mocinha ainda quase criança, que ao seu ponto de vista nos recruta por meio da narrativa na primeira pessoa, concebe uma paixão não reciprocada pelo primo em visita de convalescença de uma doença não especificada. Este é jovem, belo, de uma idade que o coloca no pelouro edipiano de irmãos mais velhos ou pais. Como muitíssimos outros objetos de amor em Lygia ("A Estrutura da Bolha de Sabão," "Noturno Amarelo," "Os Objetos," "O Jardim Selvagem," os outros contos já acima mencionados), o ambiente é evocativo de uma fábula para crianças, com todos os elementos de terror, sortilégio e mistério, e toda a simbologia e literalidade tenebrosa da morte ceifeira. De regresso de uma excursão em que recolhera folhas destinadas ao *herbarium* do primo, a jovem heroína presencia a reunião entre aquele e a namorada que o viera buscar de regresso à cidade:

No tufo raso vi uma folha que nunca encontrara antes, única. Solitária. Mas que folha era aquela?

Tinha a forma aguda de uma foice, o verde do dorso com pintas vermelhas irregulares *como pingos de sangue. Uma pequena foice ensanguentada*... Escondi a folha no bolso, peça principal de um jogo confuso. Essa eu não juntaria às outras folhas, essa tinha que ficar comigo, segredo que não podia ser visto....

Através do vidro (poderoso como a lupa) vi os dois.... Ele, de pé e um pouco atrás da cadeira [dela], acariciando-lhe o pescoço....

Estendi-lhe o cesto, mas ao invés de segurar o cesto, segurou meu pulso: eu estava escondendo alguma coisa, não estava? O que estava escondendo, o quê? . . . Enfiei a mão no bolso e apertei a folha, *intacta a umidade da ponta aguda* . . . . Ele continuava esperando, e então? No fundo da sala, a moça também esperava numa névoa de ouro, tinha rompido o sol. Encarei-o pela última vez, *sem remorso, quer mesmo?* Entreguei-lhe a folha. (SR, 47-49, itálico nosso)[24]

O estratagema do uso da primeira pessoa narrativa pode servir, como já se viu, para encurralar o leitor num beco de cumplicidade involuntária, como espetador de um crime impossível de travar. O espetáculo encenado frequentemente inclui uma *femme fatale*, a destruição sem sentido de um belo e prometedor mancebo, e uma jovem que testemunha o "crime" mas não o pode salvar. É este o guião de "A Estrutura da Bolha de Sabão" (OMC) e "O Jardim Selvagem" (M).[25] Duas mulheres misteriosas, versões femininas do Barba Azul tradicional, desposam e depois destroem os seus frágeis companheiros.

### Mortes Anunciadas

Ambos os contos são narrados na primeira pessoa por duas protagonistas cujo papel nunca passa do de espetadoras impotentes perante a agência de duas mortíferas comparsas. Em "A Estrutura da Bolha de Sabão," uma antiga namorada testemunha a aniquilação do seu etéreo amigo, um cientista sonhador cuja vida é consagrada ao estudo do fenómeno epónimo. A esposa deste, "bonita, sem dúvida, mas um tanto grosseira, fora casada com o primo de um amigo, um industrial meio fascista que veio para cá com passaporte falso, até a Interpol já estava avisada, durante a guerra se associou com um tipo que se dizia conde italiano mas não passava de um contrabandista" (OMC, 133), dá credibilidade a estas suspeitas, visto que a atmosfera de "ciúme [que] foi tomando forma e transbordando espesso como um licor azul-verde, do tom da pintura dos seus olhos" (OMC, 132) coincide com a doença súbita do companheiro, a que se segue, para a antiga namorada, a epifania temida. Numa visita ao doente e à esposa, cujo ciúme, aliás, já então se desvanecera sem explicação (a missão uma vez cumprida, o ciúme perde a razão de ser), aquele "duas vezes empalideceu, ficou quase lívido. Comecei a sentir falta de alguma coisa, era do cigarro? Acendi um e ainda a sensação aflitiva de que alguma coisa faltava, mas o que estava errado ali? . . . Então descobri o que estava faltando, ô! Deus. Agora eu sabia que ele ia morrer" (OMC, 135).

## Jardim Selvagem ou Selva *Tout Court*?

> Foi uma infância meio selvagem, livre, e na qual se destacou a figura principal de uma pajem preta, adolescente desbocada e sexual que me fazia confidência e contava histórias, centenas de histórias de lobisomens, almas-penadas, antiquíssimos mortos que se levantam chocalhantes e lá vinham com seu canto fanhoso até nossa porta.[26]

A tal "infância meio selvagem" de Lygia coaduna-se com posteriores escritos em que desfilam sucessivas heroínas vindas não se sabe de onde e, tal qual essa pajem, eventualmente desaparecidas não se sabe para onde, deixando atrás de si rastos concreta ou metaforicamente sangrentos; ou seja, um pouco como aquelas histórias por aquela transmitidas em linhagem feminina-matrilinear à mocinha Lygia que com tanto proveito as herdou.

O "Jardim Selvagem" apresenta-nos outra colegial arrepiante (ecos de "Herbarium"), observadora interessada de um crime indetetável (outro suicídio "induzido" por vontade alheia, como o do frágil Xenofonte), numa cadeia de contágio moral que principia com uma das clássicas protagonistas de Lygia, e se repetirá ao longo da obra da escritora. No conto a que a sua descrição dá nome, Daniela, objecto de fascinação da mocinha Ducha, "é assim como um jardim selvagem." (M, 49)

Daniela: na versão masculina, nome bíblico; na feminina, nome pouco comum, e que por isso dá que pensar. Dá que pensar, mas nem sequer é necessário que nos afastemos muito do original, porque o Daniel bíblico é ele próprio um caráter algo inquietante: supremamente certo dos seus direitos ("Deus é o meu juiz"),[27] forasteiro em terras estranhas onde, não obstante, amansa quer leões quer monarcas hostis, mesmo quando lhes interpreta sonhos agourentos, lhes prevê o apocalipse e os força a enfrentar as duras verdades escritas no muro por mão divina (a única autoridade que ele reconhece, Daniel 5:26-28). Que charme perigoso, o deste Daniel. Que arrogante invencibilidade. Se perante ele até potentados bíblicos sucumbem, quanto mais, perante a sua encarnação feminina, o delicado Ed, frágil homem-criança desde sempre apaparicado por titis solteironas, que na infância "tinha pavor do escuro" (M, 50), e "cujos sonhos eram todos horríveis" (M, 50). Daniela, a noiva misteriosa com quem Ed se casa sem participar (e sem que o possam nem avisar nem impedir), tem todos os sinais de uma compactuante com Satanás: é suspeitosamente imune a sinais de envelhecimento ("lindíssima" embora "meio velha," M, 51); possui fortuna de proveniência incerta ("consta que ela se veste nos melhores costureiros, só usa perfume francês, toca piano," M, 51, tal qual o misterioso gato da fábula—*era uma vez um gato maltês, tocava piano e falava francês*); "anda sempre com uma luva na mão direita, não tira nunca a luva dessa mão, nem dentro de casa . . . já amanhece com ela" (M, 52, sinal porventura de polidactilia, a marca das bruxas); e é dada a rituais estranhos: "montar [cavalo] em pêlo . . . feito índio," M, 55; "quando estiveram na chácara, nesse último fim de semana, ela tomou banho nua debaixo da cascata," M, 51; "até na cascata usa uma luva de borracha," 55).

Daniela tem, ademais, o dom da telequinésia, fazendo mover objetos ("uma noite a mesa do jantar virou inteira," M, 55), e cativa até os leões mais contumazes, incluindo, de início, a tia Pombinha. Todos, de facto, com a exceção do cão de Ed (o seu mais fiel amigo, a quem "só faltava falar," M, 55), animal porventura de instintos impérvios às suas artes de sedução, e que ela mata sem hesitação:

> Encostou o revólver na orelha e pum! Matou assim como se fosse uma brincadeira... não era para ninguém ver, nem seu tio que estava na cidade. Mas eu vi com estes olhos que a terra há-de comer, ela pegou o revólver com aquela mão enluvada e atirou no pobrezinho que morreu ali mesmo, sem um gemido... Perguntei depois, mas por que a senhora fez isso? O bicho é de Deus, não se faz com um bicho de Deus uma coisa dessas! Ela então respondeu que o Kleber estava sofrendo muito, [só porque ficou doente e ela achou que ele estava sofrendo], que a morte para ele era um descanso. (M, 54)

Nestas circunstâncias, o que se segue é apenas o que se esperaria: "tia Daniela telefonou da chácara para avisar que tio Ed estava muito doente" (M, 55), e adiante, "seu tio Ed se matou hoje de manhã! Se matou com um tiro!" (M, 56) A reação de Ducha, mocinha ela própria algo inquietante (alter ego em embrião de Daniela e talvez sua sucessora), confirma as nossas suspeitas ("um tiro no ouvido?" M, 56) e franqueia ainda acesso a outras paisagens se possível mais perturbantes.

Daniela, tal como o seu xará bíblico, herda um reino deste mundo, mas também porventura um do outro, sobrenatural. E como qualquer monarca previdente, lega-o por sua vez a quem lhe siga nas pisadas: neste caso, por via de linhagem matrilinear (ou seja, alheia ao imperativo das genealogias masculinas), a Ducha, sua sobrinha não-consanguínea, aprendiz de feiticeira, e já comprovadamente capaz de administrar à tia, destroçada pela morte de Ed, cinquenta gotas de um calmante, em vez das quinze recomendadas ("carrega[ndo] no açúcar para disfarçar o gosto" M, 55).

Eu chegava da escola quando Conceição veio correndo ao meu encontro: . . .

Dessa vez achei muito bom que eu estivesse na escola quando chegou a notícia. Conceição enxugou duas lágrimas na barra do avental enquanto fritava batatas.

Peguei uma batata que caíra da frigideira e afundei-a no sal. Estava quase crua.

— Mas porque ele fez isso, Conceição?

— Ninguém sabe. . . . Você . . . não acha que foi por causa da doença?

— Acho—concordei, enquanto esperava que caísse outra batata da frigideira. Pensava agora em tia Daniela metida num vestido preto. E de luva também preta, como não podia deixar de ser. (M, 56).

## Tantas Mortes

Em *A Noite Escura e Mais Eu*, o "e," tal como o "y" em outras circunstâncias, é o nó do problema. Em noites escuras, não é de surpreender que "eu" tenha medo; é, porém, verdadeiramente surpreendente que "eu" seja um *partner in crime*, comparsa de não identificadas malfeitorias. O "e," ademais—a noite escura *e* mais eu—é o signo da cumplicidade: eu *e* eles, sejam *eles* quem forem. Durante a noite escura é quando se cometem atos inaceitáveis à luz do pleno dia: o abandono de mortos por enterrar ("Dolly"); a eutanásia (voluntária, é certo, mas que ainda assim a lei condena: "Boa Noite, Maria"); bruxarias inexplicáveis, com tonalidades de lesbianismo e/ou adultério prévio ("O Segredo"); e indiferença ou, quem sabe, regozijo que se aproxima da psicopatologia infantil em relação à morte de pais e irmãos ("A Rosa Verde:" "Eu sou órfã, gritei," NE, 158).[28]

Em "Você Não Acha que Esfriou?," Kori ama Armando que com ela é impotente porque ama Otávio, o qual casou com Kori pela sua fortuna mas a atraiçoa com outra mulher, que dele engravida. Ao som fatídico dos acordes da *Carmen*, abre-se o pano da ribalta, não para esse nascimento, mas para um desenlace tenebroso com tonalidades de uma metafórica morte anunciada, a do doce Armando que cuida do bem-estar de todos, até da esposa do homem que ama, velando pelo conforto dela, tocando a música de que ela gosta, oferendo-lhe carinhosa hospitalidade, tentando até dormir com ela por uma questão de boa educação, e a quem ela agora desfecha o golpe de misericórdia (a vingança da mulher rejeitada) quando lhe revela que Otávio, até então mulherengo descuidado, está agora verdadeiramente apaixonado. Kori, em eco da Luisiana de

"Apenas um Saxofone," destrói o frágil objeto do seu desejo, e ao fazê-lo destrói-se também a si própria: tal qual o oruboros (a serpente com a cauda na boca), ou o escorpião que quando encurralado se pica a si mesmo e morre. Tudo isso, como diriam as nossas avós, "coisas muito feias, credo!" Feias como uma noite de trovões, escura e de trovões, embora até estes tenham uma inegável beleza para quem goste de ter medo. Para o tipo de pessoa que gosta de histórias e filmes de horror. Para quem goste de ler Lygia, seja com a letra "y" ou "i," ou até "e," ou com uma mistura de todas elas, fervendo numa sopa borbulhante: Ligeia, como aquela heroína arrepiante de Edgar Allan Poe, escritor e poeta já citado, necrofilicamente obcecado com donzelas mortas a cujo extermínio os belos defuntos de Lygia oferecem porventura retaliação.

Onde estiveste de noite?

## II—OUTROS MUNDOS: DEUS E O DIABO

> Vi com os meus próprios olhos a Sibila, em Cumas, pendurada num jarro; e quando os moços lhe perguntaram: "o que desejas, Sibila?" ela respondeu: "desejo morrer."
> Petrónio, Satiricon

Numa atmosfera de mistério em que as indicações de bruxaria são claras, o apelo feito aos parâmetros do fantástico provoca duas reações por parte do leitor, ou, mais exatamente, nestes casos, da leitora: incompreensão e participação. O género do fantástico abre a quem o lê mundos de possibilidades alternativas em que se harmonizam os elementos do proibido e do desejado:

> Ao expressar o desejo, a fantasia pode operar de duas maneiras . . .: pode narrar, manifestar ou [representar] o desejo . . . , ou pode expulsá-lo quando ele prova ser um elemento perturbador, uma ameaça à ordem cultural . . . . Em muitos casos, a literatura fantástica cumpre ambas as funções simultaneamente . . . . Desta forma, a literatura fantástica aponta para ou sugere a base sobre a qual repousa a ordem cultural, pois desvenda, de relance, a desordem, a ilegalidade, tudo o que se situa fora da lei, alienado dos sistemas de valores ortodoxos. O fantástico aponta para o não-dito e para o invisível cultural: o que foi silenciado, elidido, apagado e negado . . . Fala da tentativa impossível de realizar o desejo, de tornar visível o invisível e de descobrir a ausência (Jackson, 18, tradução nossa).

Para Jean-Paul Sartre (135-40), a função do fantástico é transformar o mundo, *este* mundo, ao invés de inventar alternativas (de natureza por exemplo mágica, sobrenatural ou extraterrestre), enquanto que para Maurice Lévy quando imaginamos o fantástico substituímos ao nível da imaginação aquilo que perdemos ao nível da fé. Ouçamos ainda Tzvetan Todorov:

> Num mundo que é realmente o nosso mundo, o mundo que conhecemos .... ocorre algo que não pode ser explicado pelas suas leis . . . .. Quem participar nesse evento deve optar por uma de duas explicações possíveis: ou é vítima de uma ilusão dos sentidos, de um produto da imaginação—e essas leis por conseguinte, permanecem estáveis—ou então o evento de fato ocorreu, faz parte integrante da realidade, mas essa realidade, verifica-se agora, é controlada por leis que afinal nos são desconhecidas. . . . O fantástico ocupa a duração dessa incerteza . . . . O fantástico é o nome que damos à hesitação de quem, apenas conhecendo as leis naturais, enfrenta um acontecimento aparentemente sobrenatural. (Todorov, 25)

Para Lygia, as barreiras entre o real e o imaginário não são nem por sombras estanques, ou pelo menos ela pede-nos que suspendamos o nosso ceticismo acerca dessa possibilidade. Às vezes o ceticismo funciona, até bem de mais. Façamos agora um pequeno desvio por paragens que põem à prova a credulidade e a boa vontade de quem ler o que se segue. A conclusão será que quem agora aqui escreve é ou mentirosa ou tonta. Paciência. Correndo embora o risco ou de acusações de falsa ingenuidade ou de estereótipos acerca de portugas típicos, o que se relata abaixo não é mentira. A única circunstância extenuante para a obtusidade aqui confessada é que, num volume intitulado *Invenção e Memória*, lido pela primeira vez de boa-fé como uma compilação de ambos géneros, e em que uma narradora na primeira pessoa (e cujos dados biográficos, ademais incluíam ser ela, tal como a própria Lygia, estudante de Direito em S. Paulo) relata os acontecimentos detalhados em "A Dança com o Anjo," encontrávamo-nos, possivelmente, no pelouro da autobiografia. De boa-fé foi a história do anjo relatada nessas páginas lida e repetida a familiares e amigos. Que se riram muito e aconselharam mais juízo e menos prontidão a cair em lérias. A que se seguiram, por sua vez, afirmações apressadas por parte desta vossa autora, de que claro que os anjos não existem, mas, mas, mas... E depois, após mais investigações, a realização de que afinal a história era mesmo isso... uma história. Uma história da carochinha, um conto, uma fantasia.

Ou será que não? Talvez não? Lygia, será que com a verdade nos engana? Para benefício do que se segue, digamos que sim. *Double bluff*? Digamos que sim e para a frente: em "A Dança com o Anjo," uma jovem estudante de Direito, tendo alcançado dos pais, estes algo contra vontade, autorização para assistir a um suposto "jantar sério, homenagem ao nosso professor" (IM, 23)[29] em certo Primeiro de Agosto, vê-se em perigo de ser apanhada num *pindura*. O *pindura*, como é sabido, ocupa aquele lusco-fusco entre o lúdico e o criminoso, entre o moral e o imoral, no decurso do qual jovens Paulistas, aprendizes da lei (estudantes de Direito), se situam temporariamente (um dia por ano) fora dela, com o objetivo, porém profundamente ortodoxo (pelo menos segundo uma ideologia capitalista), da exploração dos trabalhadores por uma elite (a fuga, sem pagar a conta, de restaurantes onde previamente se banquetearam). Confuso? Para Lygia (digamos que era mesmo Lygia), nesse Primeiro de Agosto, a situação poderia ter-se complicado. A salvação (mas será que é mesmo esse o *mot juste*, no que diz respeito ao resgate de uma futura jurista em risco de ser apanhada em infração da lei?) aparece na pessoa ("pessoa" sendo quase de certeza *não* o *mot juste*) de um angélico moço de cabelos louros e olhos azuis, de origens obscuras mas que dança como se tivesse asas, toca violino (que é, aprendemos adiante, "o instrumento preferido do Anjo Decaído," IM, 28), e possui o dom da profecia:

> Mas o que está acontecendo?—perguntei....
>   — Isto é um *pindura*, minha querida [disse ele], vai acabar muito mal.... Tome um táxi lá em baixo e agora vai!... Ouvi então sua voz já remota mas singularmente próxima, O dinheiro está na bolsa!... Então ouvi as sirenes aflitas dos carros da polícia chegando com estardalhaço. Entrei toda encolhida no táxi... apertando [a minibolsa preta ... no feitio de um missal] que nem precisei abrir porque sabia que a exata quantia da corrida já estava ali. (IM, 27)

Depois dessa noite, o "anjo da guarda" (ou servente de Satanás, dependendo do ponto de vista), desapareceu sem deixar rasto.

Para Freud, a declaração de um tabu assinala, por definição, um ato não, como se pressuporia, repugnante (visto que o que é repugnante não necessita ser interdito para não ser praticado—não é necessário declarar a ingestão de fezes ou de urina tabu, porque com ou sem tabu ela não é cometida) mas, pelo contrário, simultaneamente temível e sedutor.

Os tabus, devemos supor, são proibições de antiguidade primeva que foram, em certa época, externamente impostas a uma geração de homens primitivos; devem ter sido calcadas sobre eles, sem a menor dúvida de forma violenta, pela geração anterior. Essas proibições devem ter estado relacionadas com atividades para as quais havia forte inclinação.[30]

Incluindo, está claro, contacto com personagens sagradas. Como por exemplo anjos? Que depreender, então, na prosa de Lygia, da posição moralmente ambígua de espectadoras intra—e extra-diegéticas (a delas, e por associação a nossa), perante um espetáculo o qual por enquanto contemplamos de fora, embora com o qual a qualquer momento possamos passar a comp(atuar)?

## O Menino da sua Mãe

> *No plaino abandonado,*
> *Que a morna brisa aquece . . .*
> *De balas trespassado,*
> *Duas de lado a lado . . .*
> *Jaz morto e apodrece,*
> *O menino da sua mãe.*
> Fernando Pessoa

Passemos agora a dois contos que, de diferentes formas, tomam o tema do nascimento e da morte de Jesus, e do momento iniciático do Cristianismo como o ponto de partida para o bloqueio de uma variedade de noções de origem no sentido quer metafísico quer temporal do termo (o conceito de criação divina e patriarcal oriunda num Deus/Pai e transmitida a um seu descendente ungido como tal neste mundo e no outro).[31] Na primeira história, "Natal na Barca," a voz narradora na primeira pessoa, tardiamente divulgada como pertencente a uma protagonista do sexo feminino, atravessa num barco misterioso um trecho de água (Aqueronte? Estige? Triângulo do Diabo?)[32] na companhia de uma madona demoníaca que, de bebé nos braços, assusta o narrador com o relato da morte do seu primogénito. Nesta versão revisionista do Divino Verbo, o sagrado Filho morre sem hipótese de ressurreição às mãos de uma madona iconoclasta. Trata-se aqui do fim de um mundo, especificamente o Judio-Cristianismo em que se alicerça a cultura ocidental. Abracadabra, inaugure-se o pelouro do fantástico.

Em "Natal na Barca," a narradora apercebe-se que o bebé nos braços da insólita madona, tal como o primeiro filho antes dele, também está morto.

A consciência desta morte abre as comportas a duas heresias. Primeiro a hipótese de ser o Filho de Deus afinal mortal. E segundo, a possibilidade de ser ele (e a Divindade cuja essência aquele integra dentro da realidade do Verbo feito carne) substituível por um segundo filho. Elaboremos: para Annemarie Schimmel, na cosmogonia judaico-cristã,

> [o número] um tornou-se o símbolo do Um primordial, a divindade sem alternativa, a existência não-polarizada. A unidade real, porém, é inconcebível, porque assim que o Eu pensa em si, produz uma dualidade: o observador e o observado. . . .
>
> Para [Plótino], o Deus Único está para além de todas as formas, porque as formas expressam multiplicidade. . . . E já que Deus é a raiz e a pressuposição de tudo, Ele é também a Unidade absoluta . . ., único no seu ser. (Schimmel, 42-43)

A catástrofe da morte de um segundo filho (ele próprio, por conseguinte, algo herético—visto dever ser impossível vislumbrar a hipótese de dois Messias, em vez daquele supostamente único, inimitável, insubstituível), no decurso de uma mortífera Consoada, não é remediada pela eventual consciencização por parte da narradora, de que o protagonista desta tenebrosa Natividade afinal está vivo: a hipótese da sua mortalidade uma vez articulada, permanece como imaginável (possível) em terrível perpetuidade no contexto de uma cosmogonia em que duvidar é pecar.

"Natal na Barca" "responde a uma pergunta com outra" (ABV, 136), e o resultado, que é também o ponto de abertura da história, nega a barcaça como o local de qualquer possibilidade que não seja a do silêncio absoluto:

> Não quero *nem devo* lembrar aqui por que me encontrava naquela barca. Só sei que em redor tudo era silêncio e treva. *E que me sentia bem naquela solidão.* . . . Já devíamos estar quase no fim da viagem e até aquele instante não me ocorrera dizer-lhe qualquer palavra. Nem combinava mesmo com uma barca tão despojada, tão sem artifícios, a ociosidade de um diálogo. Estávamos sós. E o melhor ainda era não fazer nada, não dizer nada . . . . Ali estávamos os quatro, silenciosos como mortos num antigo barco de mortos deslizando na escuridão. Contudo, estávamos vivos. E era Natal. (ABV, 135-6, itálico nosso)

Se o imperativo Judaico-Cristão proclama que no princípio era o Verbo, estamos aqui perante um silêncio que porém não é a impotência mas antes um *princípio* (em ambos os sentidos do termo) diferente. A barca rudimentar, simulacro daquele antigo estábulo paupérrimo aqui metamorfoseado em presépio horripilantemente profano, não oferece nem doutrina nem certezas. A base em que assenta não é fixa mas flutua; os seus ocupantes são no mínimo inquietantes ("um velho, uma mulher . . . sentada entre nós, apertando nos braços a criança enrolada em panos. Era uma mulher jovem e pálida. O longo manto escuro que lhe cobria a cabeça dava-lhe o aspeto de uma figura antiga," 135); e o destino previsto quase de certeza não é a bem-aventurança eterna. O efeito geral, desestabilizador e mórbido, evoca antes outras associações intertextuais, acarretando a mesma ameaça: uma mãe porventura satânica ou no mínimo perpetuamente de luto (o manto é escuro, não o azul celeste da iconografia mariânica tradicional) por um filho que neste evangelho alternativo está eternamente (hereticamente) morto; e uma Segunda Vinda anunciadora não de salvação mas de desespero a vir:

> Certamente que uma revelação se aproxima;
> Certamente que a Segunda Vinda se aproxima.
> A Segunda Vinda! Apenas profiro essas palavras
> Uma vasta imagem do Spiritus Mundi
> Me perturba a vista . . .
> A escuridão cai de novo; mas agora sei
> Que vinte séculos de sono empedernido
> Se reduziram a pesadelo ao embalar de um berço,
> E que besta bruta, o seu reino enfim presente,
> Se arrasta para Belém para ser dada à luz? (Yeats, 210-11)

Era Natal, (ABV, 135-6), mas o que a figura da Virgem/*Mater Dolorosa* revela é a heresia do vácuo criado pelo abandono divino ("Pai, porque me abandonaste?"), aqui reproduzido num contexto secular ("Meu marido me abandonou" ABV, 137). Este universo desocupado de presença paterna dá lugar a metafísicas (fantasias, feitiçarias) alternativas, de carácter essencialmente feminino. Emasculador? Aqui e adiante, em "Missa do Galo," como se verá, o *Fiat lux* introduz um reino assustador de trevas: uma noite de consoada transmutada em convénio de bruxas, uma Divindade ausente e um filho (ou dois) que em vez de arautas da salvação e vida eterna anunciam a inevitabilidade de perdas repetidas *ad infinitum*: "a nossa jornada ao passado acabou... A lenda inicial do cristianismo está feita, vai findar o mundo antigo!" (Queirós, 1887, 210).

O meu primeiro [filho] morreu o ano passado.
Fiquei sem saber o que dizer. Esbocei um gesto e em seguida, apenas para fazer alguma coisa, levantei a ponta do xale que cobria a cabeça da criança. Deixei cair o xale novamente e voltei-me para o rio. O menino estava morto. Entrelacei as mãos para dominar o tremor que me sacudiu. Estava morto. A mãe continuava a niná-lo, apertando-o contra o peito. Mas ele estava morto. (ABV, 140)

As vítimas deste novo arranjo, como seria de esperar, verificam-se ser o Pai, divino ou temporal, agora irrelevante porque esquecido ou desertor, e o filho morto e abandonado. A aparente resignação da *mater dolorosa* é à primeira vista exemplar ("Bem-aventurados os que choram, porque serão consolados! Bem-aventurados os mansos, porque possuirão a terra!" Mateus 5: 4-5).

Ia contando as sucessivas desgraças com tamanha calma, num tom de quem relata fatos sem ter realmente participado deles. Como se não bastasse a pobreza que espiava pelos remendos da sua roupa, perdera o filhinho, o marido, via pairar uma sombra sobre o segundo filho que ninava nos braços. E ali estava sem a menor revolta, confiante. Apatia? (ABV, 138)

A reação menos serena da narradora ("uma obscura irritação me fez sorrir," ABV, 138) dá lugar adiante ao entendimento de que esta madona tem mais que se lhe diga: "Não, não podiam ser de uma apática aqueles olhos vivíssimos, aquelas mãos enérgicas. Inconsciência?" (ABV, 138). Inconsciência, talvez, ou falta de consciência, ou uma consciência apenas entendível como "a tal fé que removia montanhas..." (ABV, 139): de caráter imponderável, pouco natural, porventura menos ortodoxo do pareceria à primeira vista. Neste cenário de bruxarias em que nem tudo é o que parece, aprendemos que o primogénito morreu porque, como fica bem ao filho de tal mãe, não resistiu à tentação oferecida por Satanás e tentou voar: "Se tu és o Filho de Deus, lança-te de aqui abaixo; porque está escrito: Que aos seus anjos dará ordens a teu respeito, E tomar-te-ão nas mãos" (*Mateus* 4:6); "Subiu no muro, estava brincando *de mágico* quando de repente avisou, vou voar! E atirou-se. A queda não foi grande, o muro não era alto, mas caiu de tal jeito... Tinha pouco mais de quatro anos" (ABV, 137, itálico nosso).

Tentou voar e fracassou, mas até os aprendizes de feiticeiros (feiticeiras) têm direito a repetir o exame, especialmente num mundo agora tão transformado que nem mesmo as montanhas se deixam ficar no seu lugar. Um mundo em que nem Deus nem pais são de fiar, em que as mães tomam as rédeas nas mãos, o freio nos dentes, e nos arremessam, a nós e aos seus próprios filhos, para paragens desconhecidas. O resultado é um mundo de linhagens masculinas abolidas e de conluios femininos em guerra com a demiurgia original, o espetáculo de um Deus desaparecido, de um S. José degradado, de meninos que não passaram quarenta dias no deserto mas quatro anos no mundo, e que não conseguiram resistir à tentação de se jogar de muros (nem sequer pináculos, nem sequer muito altos, apenas que chegasse para desprovar o estatuto divino desses filhos eminentemente mortais).

Por fim, contudo, como aliás faz sentido nos equívocos universos (múltiplos, porque há sempre mais do que um único mundo) de Lygia, talvez permaneça afinal de contas uma possibilidade de ressurreição, de restauração do protótipo original:

Inclinei-me. A criança abrira os olhos—aqueles olhos que eu vira cerrados tão definitivamente. E bocejava, esfregando a mãozinha na face corada. Fiquei olhando sem conseguir falar.

— Então, bom Natal!—disse ela. (ABV, 140)

Bom Natal? Talvez. "Deus disse: 'Faça-se a luz!' E a luz foi feita" (*Génesis*, 1:3)? "No princípio era o *Verbo*, e o Verbo estava com Deus, e o Verbo era Deus (*João* 1:1)? Mas em Lygia, por fim, permanece sempre uma alternativa mais tétrica: "Não quero nem devo lembrar aqui por que me encontrava naquela barca. Só sei que em redor *tudo era silêncio e treva*. E que me sentia bem naquela solidão" (ABV, 135).

## Deus nos Acuda: Literatura como Arma?

Arma, sim. Mas arma de ataque ou de defesa, ou será que é a mesma coisa?

Falhando, não culpar Deus, oh! Por que Ele me abandonou? Nós é que O abandonamos quando ficamos mornos. Quando a vocação para a vida começa a empalidecer e também nós, os delicados, os esvaiados. Aceitar o desafio da arte. Da loucura. Romper com a falsa harmonia, como o falso equilíbrio e assim, depois da morte—ainda intensos—seremos um fantasminha claro de amor. (Telles)[33]

Em "Natal na Barca," as últimas palavras da mãe, antes de desaparecer—"então bom Natal!" (ABV, 140)—são a negação final de reinos quer deste mundo quer do outro, agora suplantados por um vácuo que é também a afirmação de outras possibilidades ainda inarticuláveis.

Se na narrativa na primeira pessoa de "Natal na Barca" a veracidade da narrativa é posta em causa pela narradora diegética ("Não quero nem devo lembrar aqui por que me encontrava naquela barca," ABV, 135), em "Missa do Galo" o processo ganha complexidade já que o conto reescreve, embora preservando título, enredo, protagonistas e até atmosfera, o famoso conto de um progenitor literário: Machado de Assis, o homem mais importante das letras brasileiras do século XIX. Tenha sido ato de homenagem ou profanação (parricídio?)—e não seria esta a única instância disso na obra de Lygia, veja-se por exemplo o guião cinematográfico *Capitu* (exemplo de outro herói machadiano cuja eponímia, ou seja, supremacia, é reivindicada por uma mulher)—a intenção do conto de Lygia permanece ambivalente, não menos na sua escolha de uma epígrafe retirada do conto machadiano e inquietantemente enfatizadora de um espaço de silêncio absoluto no texto precursor: "chegamos a ficar algum tempo—não posso dizer quanto—inteiramente calados" (OMC, 121).

Na "Missa do Galo" de Lygia, o estatuto do narrador é ainda mais equívoco do que em "Natal na Barca." O conto de Lygia, como o de Machado, gira em torno de uma conversa premente de expetativa e tensão, na noite da Consoada, entre um jovem que fica sem nome e Conceição, sua pouco imaculada senhoria. Entre eles, nesta noite supostamente sagrada, paira a possibilidade da sedução do jovem pela mulher mais velha, até então vista como esposa traída e submissa, mas de repente, no decorrer desta reunião noturna, inesperada e perigosamente sedutora. Quer em Machado quer em Lygia a sedução permanece inconsumada, deixando em aberto um espaço de expetativa não realizada. Mas em Lygia, porém, esse espaço que é um vácuo desencadeia outras possibilidades, já discerníveis nos primeiros parágrafos, "sem alterar as superfícies tão inocentes como essa noite diante do que vai acontecer. E do que não vai—precisamente o que não acontece é que me inquieta. E excita" (OMC, 121-22).

Em outro eco de Machado no seu romance mais famoso, *Dom Casmurro* (outra narrativa na primeira pessoa por um narrador pouco de fiar), também Lygia exalta as virtudes ("as omissões. Os silêncios tão mais importantes," OMC, 122) de "livros omissos" que em *Dom Casmurro* tanto aliciaram Machado: silêncios que incentivam a leitura comparticipativa, atenta a uma semântica das entrelinhas como pré-requisito do acesso à verdade textual.

Na versão de Lygia, porém, é o que é ligeiramente alterado, bem como o que não é dito ou o que fica por acontecer que empurra um pouco mais longe as possibilidades deixadas em aberto pelo conto de Machado. Ambos os contos prestam atenção ao detalhe dos quadros que decoram as paredes da sala onde se dá o encontro noturno, mas Lygia introduz o tema já familiar do homem-criança vulnerável, ausente na versão machadiana. Assim, em Machado, "os quadros falavam do principal negócio deste homem. Um representava 'Cleópatra;' não me recordo o assunto do outro, mas eram mulheres. Vulgares ambos; naquele tempo não me pareciam feios" (Assis, 144). Em Lygia, em contrapartida, a encenação salienta a servidão masculina fora do universo da pintura: "Os quadros ingenuamente pretensiosos, não há afetação nos móveis mas os quadros têm aspirações de grandeza nas gravuras de mulheres imponentes (rainhas?) entre pavões e escravos transbordando até o ouro purpurino das molduras" (OMC, 121).

Em Lygia, acentua-se uma atmosfera de confinamento dentro do *panopticon* de uma ótica feminina que na página de abertura permite ao moço o estatuto de "um jovem nítido, próximo" (OMC, 121), mas adiante privá-lo-á de definição e por fim até mesmo de visibilidade num mundo em que a presença masculina se afunda no tal ubíquo "silêncio e treva" (ABV, 135). A confusão de identidade entre a narradora, identificável enquanto observadora externa, e Conceição enquanto protagonista, nunca é totalmente resolvida, fundindo-se ambas figuras numa teia de cumplicidade: "Ela adverte com um sorriso cálido que ele não retribui, nem pode, enredado como está naqueles cabelos, massa sombria tão mal arrepanhada como as saias, ameaçando desabar" (OMC, 122-23). "E do olhar que inesperadamente se concentrou inteiro nele, fechando-o: sentiu-se profundo através desse olhar. . . . Para encará-la de novo já sem resistência: pronto, aqui estou. Mas não disse nada nessa pausa que ela interrompeu, *a iniciativa nunca era dele*" (OMC, 122, itálico nosso).

Ou seja, parecida, em todos os essenciais, esta personagem, com aquela Capitu de Machado, e a outra de Lygia, ambas de cabelos tumultuosos e olhos de ressaca. Criaturas insondáveis e pouco de fiar?

A Conceição de Lygia, "com seu andar de jaula" (OMC, 122), assemelha-se ainda à enigmática Tigrela, outro bicho que tal como é o caso de Capitu, no final da narrativa permanece uma incógnita, possivelmente pecadora, possivelmente vítima.[34] Ou àquela "deusa da gravura" (OMC, 122) cuja potência hierática acompanha uma inegável atração sexual ("magra, mas os seios altos como os da deusa da gravura, os cabelos quase num desalinho de travesseiro" OMC,122). Os seios, está bem de ver, são a caraterística de amantes e aqui de deusas, mas também de mulheres mais velhas, mães que amamentam mas também devoram; que concebem (como indicado pelo próprio nome da protagonista), mas também controlam e porventura destroem. O jovem sem nome acerca do qual a voz narrativa especula "será virgem?" (OMC,127) torna-se o seu "alvo" (OMC, 127), associado à vulnerabilidade do São Sebastião penetrado por flechas de quem ela fala e a quem afirma rezar, deixando o seu jovem interlocutor sem palavras, reduzido a gestos de assentimento, e "seteado de dúvidas como a imagem do santo, não é estranho?" (OMC,127).

Por fim, porém, em Lygia, é o papel destrutivo da mulher (tanto teologicamente, em antagonismo contra o paradigma de uma Criação de origem exclusivamente masculina, como secularmente, através da eliminação de linhagens patrilineares no contexto da família burguesa), que é reiterado neste conto, através de um dos temas habituais nesta escritora, nomeadamente a eliminação do macho. E eliminação ademais, que neste caso específico coloca Meneses, marido de Conceição, na posição de vítima de duas velhas bruxas a ele hostis: nomeadamente a mãe da esposa e a madrinha da amante, unidas no mesmo intuito incendiário em que, para variar, não são as bruxas que são queimadas: "bom para o fogo, esse Meneses" (OMC, 124). Nesta noite de consoada, o mau ensejo das duas velhas destila-se na metamorfose da esposa subjugada em agente das mortes do jovem e do marido: "Mas dormir se o sono é o irmão da morte? . . . um perigo dormir. A gente passa o ferrolho e [a morte] entra pelo vão das telhas feito um sopro, entra em tudo. Mas foi Conceição que entrou . . . num meneio de barco . . . eterna na essência como a noite" (OMC, 124-25).

A Conceição diuturna, sócia de Maria, Virgem luminosa, transforma-se aqui na Virgem heterodoxa de "Natal na Barca," criatura vampírica, habitante das trevas, *memento mori* e origem de um ataque a todos os fundamentos do monopólio masculino sobre o momento de Génese. Ambas são "eterna(s) na essência como a noite," ou seja, previamente "Estrelas da Manhã" ou "Estrelas d'Alva" (*Ezequiel* 28:14), mas agora imponderáveis, luciferinas, excomungadas da luz divina.

Em ambos contos, o momento da Natividade é o ponto de interseção entre dois mundos, a Cristandade e o momento que a antecedeu ou aquele em que desta vez, pela primeira vez em dois mil anos, ela não se renova, e em que jovens indefesos de fato sucumbem: "Vocês sabem que dentro de alguns minutos será o *nunca mais*? Faça com que aconteça alguma coisa!—repito e meu coração está pesado diante desses dois indefesos no tempo, expostos como o Menino Jesus" (OMC, 128). Em "Missa do Galo," o perigo encarna-se na figura da mulher previamente maternal, depois sexualmente apetecida e agora obscuramente sabida e temida. Tal qual a Capitu de Machado e de Lygia:

> Ela apoia as mãos na poltrona e ali fica parada, os olhos muito abertos, respirando fundo. Concentra-se, parece reunir as forças. Quando consegue se aprumar, na sua face descorada mas lisa não há nenhuma marca emocional. Aperta um pouco os olhos. Volta-lhe aquela secreta calma enquanto encara Bentinho. É a Capitu de sempre, lúcida. Insondável. (C, 176)[35]

Tal como no caso de Capitu, porém, também aqui outra possibilidade permanece, inquietante e sem solução, nomeadamente a de um jovem casmurro, manhoso, caluniador:

> Contradições, há momentos em que o sinto dissimulado, um jovem se fazendo tolo diante da mulher desafiante, provocativa. Com olhos que eram castanhos e agora ficaram pretos, mais uma singularidade dessa noite: não é que a simpática senhora ficou subitamente belíssima? Mas não, ele não dissimula, está em êxtase, atordoado com a descoberta, bruxa, bruxa! quer gritar. A hora é de calar. . . . Apago o lampião. (OMC, 127, 129)

*Apago o lampião*. Esta consoada pervertida não é o começo de nada mas é o começo do Nada: o Verbo foi eliminado, a hora é de calar, e *Fiat lux* nunca mais.[36]

Toma um conselho de amigo,
Não te cases, Belzebu;
Que a mulher, com ser humana
É mais fina do que tu. (Machado de Assis, 297)[37]

## III — O FIM DO MUNDO

> *A justiça é o que está estabelecido; e, assim sendo, todas as nossas leis estabelecidas serão necessariamente tidas como justas sem serem examinadas, uma vez que estão estabelecidas. Três graus de latitude subvertem toda a jurisprudência. Um meridiano determina a verdade . . . . As leis fundamentais alteram-se. O que está certo muda com o tempo que passa. Singular justiça que um rio delimita! Verdade aquém dos Pirinéus, errado além.*
> Blaise Pascal

> Morrer.
> Morrer de corpo e de alma.
> Completamente.
> Morrer sem deixar o triste despojo da carne,
> ... Morrer sem deixar um sulco, um risco, uma sombra,
> a lembrança de uma sombra
> em nenhum coração, em nenhum pensamento,
> em nenhuma epiderme.
> Morrer tão completamente
> que um dia ao lerem o teu nome num papel
> perguntem: "Quem foi?..."
> Morrer mais completamente ainda,
> sem deixar sequer esse nome.
> Manuel Bandeira, "A morte absoluta"

Porque mesmo que se deixasse esse nome, já não havia quem o lesse? "A morte absoluta" de Manuel Bandeira evoca, é certo, a morte individual, não coletiva, mas no caso de Lygia podemos contar com versões extremas daquilo que mesmo só por si já nos atemorizava. Para além da morte física, da morte espiritual, da morte moral do indivíduo, mesmo com todas as possibilidades que essa morta acarreta de um contágio moral do bem-estar coletivo (da comunidade, da sociedade), quando mesmo assim nada resulta em uma restauração convincente de parâmetros mínimos de integridade, a única solução em Lygia parece ser a de rasgar o esboço original e regressar à prancheta. Ou, por outras palavras, desencadear o fim do mundo e recomeçar do nada. Essa possibilidade é explorada de forma menos explícita em "As Formigas," e segundo parâmetros mais claramente apocalípticos em "A Presença" e "Seminário dos Ratos."

**Terror, Horror, Pavor**

Em "As Formigas," duas jovens estudantes, futuras representantes do *status quo*, incluindo tudo o que é científica e juridicamente respeitável (uma estuda Medicina, a outra Direito), alojam-se numa pensão cuja senhoria apresenta todas as já conhecidas marcas do heterodoxo, neste caso de uma bruxa (devoradora de meninas), com o seu gato da praxe ("Foi o gato que miou comprido ou foi um grito?" SR, 15): "A dona era uma velha balofa, de peruca mais negra do que a asa da graúna. Vestia um desbotado pijama de seda japonesa e tinha as unhas aduncas recobertas por uma crosta de esmalte vermelho-escuro descascado nas pontas encardidas. Acendeu um charutinho" (SR, 7).

Neste antro pouco de fiar, a reação das jovens é desde logo ilógica e por isso quase de certeza inadequada para fins de autodefesa. Os únicos toques pessoais no quarto que compartilham são um retrato do matemático e linguista Herman Grassmann e, para fins de refúgio emocional (retorno à infância), o urso de pelúcia de uma delas. À medida que as leis inescrutáveis do pelouro do fantástico se afirmam—um exército de formigas faz progresso na montagem de um esqueleto de anão esquecido (ou, mais provavelmente, abandonado) numa caixa pelo prévio ocupante do quarto—duas premissas do *status quo* vigente começam a dar sinais de fraquejar: o domínio do indivíduo sobre os seus próprios mecanismos somáticos (a tensão nervosa reduz a jovem aspirante a médica a um estado de estrabismo agudo); e o domínio reclamado pela espécie humana sobre aqueloutros até então desprezados como aberrações (o anão) ou—no dia-a-dia real, embora não necessariamente nas fábulas infantis, veja-se o exemplo da cigarra e da formiga, como pragas (as formigas). Em ambos os casos (formigas e anões), convém assinalar, trata-se de adversários à primeira vista em desvantagem devido ao seu tamanho.

> E as formigas? . . . Ela apertou os olhos estrábicos, ficava estrábica. . . . Ela estava sentada na beira da minha cama, de pijama e completamente estrábica. Elas voltaram.
> Quem?
> As formigas. Só atacam de noite, antes da madrugada. Estão todas aí de novo. (SR, 12-13)

O instinto que leva as duas jovens, quando verificam que o esqueleto está quase montado, a fugir da pensão, carece de lógica mas faz intuitivamente sentido. A fuga a meio da noite, deixando para trás "a casa, [em que] só a janela vazada nos via, o outro olho era penumbra," encontra eco noutro conto, este um dos mais famosos da autora, em que as dimensões do fantástico e do apocalíptico se mesclam com a da sátira política.

Alusões diretamente políticas (ou seja, para além da política sexual) existem e não são poucas, quer na vida quer na obra de Lygia. Na vida, por exemplo, transposto para a ficção, o acontecimento relembrado no conto epónimo em *Conspiração de Nuvens*, nomeadamente a célebre manifestação de intelectuais que, em 1976, em reação à censura imposta pelo regime militar, elaboraram um documento com mil assinaturas reivindicando a liberdade de expressão. E insistentemente, ao longo das suas narrativas, como pano de fundo de dramas interiores, por exemplo em *As Meninas*, deparamos com a realidade do desapossamento social ("Confissão de Leontina") ou com a sátira plena de ameaças de "Seminário dos Ratos," cujas referências ao período da ditadura já foram amplamente comentadas pela crítica.[38] Este último conto faz a crónica do descalabro de um regime caracterizado por políticos balofos e podres de gota, luxuosamente alojados numa casa de campo remota ("a cúpula se valoriza ficando assim inacessível," SR, 176),[39] e controlando as informações providenciadas à imprensa em regime estritamente vigiado ("é sabido que uma certa distância, um certo mistério excita mais do que o contato diário com os meios de comunicação. Nossa única fonte vai soltando notícias discretas, influindo sem alarde até o encerramento, quando abriremos as baterias!" SR, 176). Em causa está uma conferência (a última de muitas, todas elas até então sem qualquer efeito), convocada pelos poderes internacionais vigentes, para fins de debater o problema dos ratos que estão a tomar conta do planeta.

Mesmo no que se prova ser uma situação *in extremis* ("temos agora cem ratos para cada habitante, . . . nas favelas não são as Marias mas as ratazanas que andam de lata d'água na cabeça," SR, 174; "os ratos do Pólo Norte têm pêlos deste tamanho para aguentar o frio de trinta abaixo de zero, se guarnecem de peliças, os marotos," SR, 175), políticos e diplomatas refastelam-se numa mansão luxuosamente renovada para esse fim, com piscina enchida para a ocasião com água de côco. Pelo país fora a devastação causada pelos ratos já resultou na queda de infraestruturas e em uma população esfaimada, reduzida ao recurso, aliás inteiramente contraproducente, de devorar quem os poderia salvar: "não sobrou nenhum gato na cidade, já faz tempo que a população comeu tudo. Ouvi dizer que dava um ótimo cozido!" (SR, 179). Mas ainda assim, a "cúpula," incluindo o Chefe das Relações Públicas e o Secretário do Bem-Estar Público e Privado (este último dado a reminiscências sobre "quando fiz a Revolução de 32 e, depois, no Golpe de 64," SR, 178), ocupa-se prioritariamente com os detalhes do jantar inaugural: "a mesa decorada só com orquídeas e frutas . . . , a mais fina cor local, encomendei do norte abacaxis belíssimos! . . . lagostas . . . , o Cozinheiro-Chefe . . . nunca viu lagostas tão grandes" e "vinho chileno . . . de . . . safra . . . Pinochet, naturalmente" (SR, 179).

Quando os ratos invadem o casarão e desbandam os ocupantes (ou devoram-nos, visto que embora nada fique claro, essa possibilidade não é excluída, sendo que o Chefe das Relações Públicas, perseguido por uma horda de ratos, se refugia dentro da geladeira, autorreduzindo-se literal e metaforicamente a produto comestível), o que se segue é o fim do mundo: "A casa foi sacudida nos seus alicerces. As luzes se apagaram. Então, deu-se a invasão, espessa como se um saco de pedras borrachosas tivesse sido despejado em cima do telhado e agora saltasse por todos os lados numa treva dura de músculos, guinchos e centenas de olhos luzindo negríssimos" (SR, 184).

Nem perante este cenário de catástrofe, porém, merecem o leitor ou leitora a catarse de um simbólico triunfo (dos oprimidos sobre os opressores, dos pobres sobre os ricos, dos trabalhadores sobre os patrões). Porque afinal de contas, os ratos, que como é sabido, são uma praga, portadora de infeção e de doença, não são um elenco condigno da inauguração de um admirável mundo novo. No caso destes ratos, em particular, o seu comportamento quando de posse das rédeas do poder, assemelha-se em tudo ao dos seres humanos que derrotaram: desde a precaução em controlar os meios de comunicação (os fios de telefone roídos, os carros inutilizados), ao arvorar a aparência do opressor ("de pé na pata traseira . . . me enfrentou feito um homem. Pela alma da minha mãe, doutor, me representou um homem vestido de rato!" SR, 183), e mais inquietantemente, o estabelecimento imediato de estruturas governamentais em tudo semelhantes às dos poderes usurpados:

> Foi andando pela casa completamente oca, nem móveis, nem cortinas, nem tapetes. Só as paredes. E a escuridão. Começou então um murmurejo secreto, rascante, que parecia vir da Sala de Debates e teve a intuição de que estavam todos reunidos ali, de portas fechadas. Não se lembrava sequer de como conseguiu chegar até o campo, não poderia jamais reconstituir a corrida, correu quilômetros. Quando olhou para trás, o casarão estava todo iluminado. (SR, 185)

## Senhores do Mundo

Finalmente, porém, em Lygia, nem sequer os ratos (nem formigas, nem anões: de um modo geral seres pequenos/desprezados/extermináveis mas aqui incontroláveis) são necessários para pôr fim à humanidade. Para isso bastamo-nos nós. Em "A Presença," o ato de auto-extinção da espécie é desencadeado em microcosmo, e o ataque vem de onde menos se espera. Um jovem, belo e sadio, com a vida toda à sua frente, procura alojamento por umas semanas num hotel algo desconcertante, "um hotel só de velhos, quase todos moradores fixos antiquíssimos" (OMC, 165), e cuja reação ao novo hóspede se abeira da hostilidade. O hotel, de onde foram removidos todos os espelhos, fora no tempo da sua inauguração uma estância de férias normal, mas, com o decorrer dos anos "os hóspedes mais velhos foram dominando, à medida que os mais jovens começaram a rarear, não sabia explicar o motivo, o fato é que a transformação embora lenta—fora definitiva. Um museu-mausoléu" (OMC, 166).

Impávido face a uma crescente atmosfera de ameaça o jovem, com toda a insensibilidade da juventude, resiste aos avisos, cada vez mais explícitos do velho porteiro:

> Por mais tolos que esses velhos pudessem parecer, guardavam o segredo de uma sabedoria que se afiava na pedra da morte. Era preciso lembrar que usariam de todos os recursos para que as regras do jogo fossem cumpridas: até onde poderia chegar o ódio por aquele que viera humilhá-los, irônico, provocativo, tumultuando a partida? O jovem se animara com a idéia da piscina. Mas se nessa mesma piscina coalhada de folhas aparecesse uma manhã seu belo corpo boiando, tão desligado quanto as folhas? (OMC, 168-69)

A ameaça torna-se realidade nessa mesma noite quando, depois de uma goiabada com um certo travo amargo e "um chá servido às vinte e uma horas, ele já não se sentia bem" (OMC, 170).

A atmosfera hitchcockiana tem repercussões para além do efeito imediato da narrativa de terror. Um *status quo* em que os maus triunfam já de si não oferece garantias de estabilidade a longo prazo; mas as conotações deste desfecho, mais bem pensadas, adquirem adicionais laivos de apocalipse: um mundo em que o egoísmo reina (de jovens contra velhos e vice-versa) e em que os velhos, em vez de protegerem os novos e velarem pela continuidade das gerações, os exterminam, é um mundo em que o mais básico instinto de perpetuação da espécie desapareceu. E daí ao fim do mundo, ou pelo menos de um mundo em que o ser humano é o rei da criação, é apenas um curto passo, após o qual uma espécie com maior instinto de cooperação (por exemplo a formiga) passará a ocupar a posição de supremacia deixada vaga por uma humanidade fundamentalmente autodestrutiva:

> Essas formigas. Apareceram de repente, já enturmadas. Tão decididas, está vendo? Levantei e dei com as formigas pequenas e ruivas que entravam em

trilha espessa pela fresta debaixo da porta, atravessavam o quarto, subiam pela parede do caixotinho de ossos e desembocavam lá dentro, disciplinadas como um exército em marcha exemplar. (SR, 10)

## IV—O FIM DE MIM

> *Todo o mundo é composto de mudança,*
> *Tomando sempre novas qualidades.*
> Luís de Camões

> *Não há destino exato para a semente no deserto.*
> *Para implacável incerteza desperta.*
> *Para o doer de tigres que desperto.*
> *No tigre dói a não investida,*
> *E assim o tempo cria em mim suas dores.*
> Júlio Almada

Em "O Noivo," Miguel acorda no dia do seu casamento sem qualquer memória de como aí chegou ou do nome da mulher com quem vai casar. Numa atmosfera não propriamente de pesadelo, mas demasiadamente vívida para ser alucinação, veste-se e apronta-se com o encorajamento algo impaciente da empregada, e parte para a igreja rebuscando na memória a lista de todas as mulheres que no passado amara na tentativa de adivinhar quem o espera ao altar. O desenlace deixa o mistério ainda impenetrável: "— Que estranho. Lembrei-me de tantas! Mas justamente nela eu não tinha pensado... Inclinou-se para beijá-la" (MCE, 146).[40]

Quando o mundo perde a razão de ser, ou pura e simplesmente perde a razão (deixa de fazer sentido), o ultimo reduto da antiga ordem estabelecida é o Eu. Encurralado, talvez, sitiado, quem sabe, mas ainda assim inexpugnável. Enquanto eu entendo quem sou, ainda existo. O ruir desse fato, o fim de mim, em certa medida assinala um fim generalizado no contexto daquilo que para mim é entendível. Se as linhas divisórias que distinguem o Eu do Outro se dissolvem, a possibilidade de sentido desaparece, pelo menos de uma perspetiva antropocêntrica, que por definição é a única que nos está disponível (visto que num mundo diferentemente organizado, o *modus antropos* perde tanto significado como relevância e torna-se pior do que a morte, sendo que esta, embora apavorante e abstrata, oferece ainda assim a ilusão de familiaridade. De significado. Ou seja, pelo menos, de algo que não é não-significante. Algo que reconhecemos e entendemos).

Como interpretar, então, o espetáculo da morte do Eu que Lygia concede ou impõe, com alguma frequência, a protagonistas que, em especial quando falam na primeira pessoa, nos arrastam a nós, leitores para abismos vertiginosos. É nesse terreno sem piso que possibilidades obscuras por fim alcançam definição, revelando o espetáculo da morte de quem, até esse momento, era (mas subitamente verifica-se já não ser) o ponto de origem de perceção e de voz. Em "O Encontro," por exemplo, a realidade possível dá lugar ao inexplicável:

> Meus cabelos se eriçaram. Era comigo que ela se parecia! Aquele rosto era o meu.
> "Eu fui você"—balbuciei.—"Num outro tempo eu fui você!"—quis gritar e minha voz saiu espedaçada. Tão simples tudo, por que só agora entendi?...... lembrei-me do que tinha acontecido. E do que ia acontecer.
> "Não!"—gritei, puxando de novo as rédeas. Um raio chicoteou o bosque com a mesma força com que *ela* chicoteou o cavalo. Ele empinou, imenso, negro, os olhos saltados, arrancando-se das *minhas* mãos. Estatelada, vi-o fugir por entre as árvores.
> . . . Por um segundo, por um brevíssimo segundo, consegui vislumbrar ao longe a pluma [vermelha de seu chapéu] debatendo-se ainda. Então gritei, gritei com todas as forças que me restavam. E tapei os ouvidos para não ouvir *o eco de meu grito* misturar-se ao ruído pedregoso de cavalo e cavaleira se despedaçando no abismo. (M, 73-74, itálico nosso)

A fusão do eu confrontado com a sua própria morte e simultaneamente com a consciência de si enquanto testemunha desse espetáculo (sujeito, objeto e observador do mesmo drama) aparece com insistência no imaginário de Lygia, incluindo dois outros contos gémeos de "O Encontro," "A Mão no Ombro" e "A Caçada." Em ambos, o medo do desconhecido dá lugar a algo inquietantemente no limiar do familiar, seguido de um momento de epifania (gnose) cujo preço, porém, é a morte.[41]

Em "A Caçada," um jovem fascinado por uma tapeçaria de origens insondáveis, deixada numa loja de penhores gerida, como já seria de esperar, por uma velha bruxa ("foi um desconhecido que trouxe, precisava muito de dinheiro. . . . Mas já faz anos isso. E o tal moço nunca mais me apareceu"), sente, tal como em "O Encontro," um *déjà vu*, aqui, como alhures em Lygia, ominosamente esverdeado: "Conhecia esse bosque, esse caçador, esse céu— conhecia tudo tão bem, mas tão bem! . . . Quando? Percorrera aquela mesma vereda, aspirara aquele mesmo vapor que baixava denso do céu verde... . . . Teria sido esse caçador? Ou o companheiro lá adiante, o homem sem cara espiando por entre as árvores?" (ABV, 79-80).

O momento de esclarecimento, aqui e em outros contos ("A Mão no Ombro," "A Estrela Branca"), é o momento que antecede a morte.

> Era o caçador? Ou a caça? Não importava, não importava, sabia apenas que tinha que prosseguir correndo sem parar por entre as árvores, caçando ou sendo caçado. Ou sendo caçado?... Comprimiu as palmas das mãos contra a cara esbraseada, enxugou no punho da camisa o suor que lhe escorria pelo pescoço. Vertia sangue o lábio gretado.
>
> Abriu a boca. E lembrou-se. Gritou e mergulhou numa touceira. Ouviu o assobio da seta varando a folhagem, a dor!
>
> — Não...—gemeu, de joelhos. Tentou ainda agarrar-se à tapeçaria. E rolou encolhido, as mãos apertando o coração. (ABV, 83)

E em "A Mão no Ombro,"

> O homem estranhou *aquele céu verde-cinza* com a lua de cera coroada por um fino galho de árvore, as folhas se desenhando nas minúcias sobre o fundo opaco. . . . E o silêncio cristalizado como num quadro, com um homem (ele próprio) fazendo parte do cenário. . . . Está na escada, ele respondeu. Esse caçador singularmente familiar que viria por detrás, na direção do banco de pedra onde ia se sentar, logo ali adiante tinha um banco. Para não me surpreender desprevenido (detestava surpresas) discretamente ele dará algum sinal antes de pousar a mão no meu ombro. Então eu me viro para ver. Estacou. A revelação o fez cambalear, esvaído numa vertigem. . . . se olhasse para trás, se atendesse o chamado. . . . Estendeu a perna e quis contar [à mulher] o sonho do jardim com a morte vindo por detrás: *sonhei que ia morrer*. (SR, 119-23, itálico nosso)

E de novo, aqui, a consciência súbita, no último instante em que qualquer consciência ainda é possível, da realidade do irreal: "Enganar assim a morte saindo pela porta do sono. Preciso dormir, murmurou fechando os olhos. Por entre *a sonolência verde-cinza* viu que retomava o sonho no ponto exato em que fora interrompido. A escada. Os passos. Sentiu o ombro tocado de leve. Voltou-se" (SR, 129, itálico nosso).

Para eles, então, para estes protagonistas a quem é sonegado o direito a um entendimento que não seja o derradeiro, o fim, após uma quebra com a realidade, é brutalmente real. Mas e para nós, leitores, perplexos e abandonados em mundos que também não entendemos, por narrativas que nos recusam o direito básico a uma explicação?

O verde já nos devia ter avisado. Em *Capitu*, Lygia, que já em "Missa do Galo" fora pescar a Machado de Assis dicas acerca de como inquietar o leitor, a ele recorre de novo. Também nesse roteiro cinemático para a obra-prima de incerteza que é *Dom Casmurro*, essa cor figura de novo, em tonalidades tão mutáveis como as possíveis permutações de uma verdade inatingível. Capitu, esposa fiel ou adúltera, traída ou traidora, já até no paraíso lua-de-mel chama a atenção de Bento para uma pequena cobra verde, que ela acha "esperta. E elegante" (C, 21). Segue-se imediatamente um episódio em que ela trinca (sem porém tentar o marido a fazer o mesmo), "uma pequena maçã verdolenga," e gaba-se de uma sabedoria (o entendimento do seu amor de adolescentes) apenas mais tarde adquirido por Bento: "Você demorou para entender, querido. Eu, não." (C, 28) Esses díspares momentos de gnose com os tais ecos esverdeados repetem-se ao longo das instruções de encenação, nas roupas de Capitu, que alternam entre sombrios verdes "cor de musgo" (39) e de "folha caída rolando ao vento" (C, 133), e, incongruamente, no momento terrível da acusação de Bento—"eu disse que Ezequiel não é meu filho" (C, 173)—"um vestido verde-água . . . primaveril" (C, 172). Tão destoante, aliás, da emoção do momento como aquele "romântico negligé num tom rosa-antigo" (C, 91) com um "longo xale branco" que pudicamente "cobre-lhe os braços e os ombros" (C, 99), no episódio em que ela supostamente por um triz é apanhada em flagrante com Escobar.

E está claro que, tratando-se, como é o caso aqui, de Lygia, nem essa impressão de ser o contraintuitivo agora a nova regra (o verde assinalando não esperança mas perdição) oferece garantias, porque em outro contexto não é o verde, mas outra cor bem diferente, que assinala perigo de morte e as chamas do inferno.

Tigrela, como seria de esperar de um tigre, é fulva, da mesma cor que o colar de âmbar que reivindica a Romana. Em outros aspectos que não a cor, porém, em Tigrela as características da espécie atenuam-se e dão lugar a um processo de antropomorfização. Tal como Romana, Tigrela aprecia perfumes e alta-costura, bebe demais e depois fica deprimida, e, tal como o antigo namorado daquela, tem tendência para o ciúme. Embora as caraterísticas sejam ainda de um felino, o animal selvagem dá lugar ao animal de estimação ("um gatarrão que exorbitou, como se intuísse que precisava mesmo se restringir: não mais do que um gato aumentado," M, 94-95), que perde até alguns dos seus traços fundamentais ("Somos vegetarianas, sempre fui vegetariana, você sabe. . . . Tigrela só come legumes," M, 96) embora retendo algumas facetas inquietantes: "desconfio que vê melhor de olhos fechados, como os dragões" (M, 95).

Em "Tigrela," mais claramente do que em "O Encontro" ou "A Caçada," a sugestão de fusão de identidades faz-se logo no parágrafo de abertura, que anuncia também o provável desenlace: "Encontrei Romana por acaso, num café. Estava meio bêbada mas lá no fundo da sua transparente bebedeira senti um depósito espesso subindo rápido quando ficava séria. Então a boca descia, pesada, fugidio o olhar que se transformava *de caçador em caça*" (M, 93).

Tigrela começa por ser a cria de adoção de Romana ("precisou criá-la com mamadeira," M, 93) mas rapidamente se transforma em seu alter-ego:

> Dois terços de tigre e um terço de mulher, foi se humanizando e agora. No começo me imitava tanto, era divertido, comecei também a imitá-la e acabamos nos embrulhando de tal jeito que já não sei se foi com ela que aprendi a me olhar no espelho com esse olho de fenda. Ou se foi comigo que aprendeu a se estirar no chão e deitar a cabeça no braço para ouvir música. (M, 93)

"Às vezes nos medimos e não sei o resultado, ensinei-lhe tanta coisa, aprendi outro tanto, disse Romana esboçando um gesto que não completou" (M. 97).[42]

A sugestão de agressividade mútua (ou será que é amor ardente ao ponto da violência ou ainda ímpeto autodestrutivo?) intensifica-se. A interlocutora repara numa marca roxa no pescoço de Romana e sugere como recomendável a separação do que já então se ia tornando uma relação sufocante, com elementos de amor lésbico ("tinha tanto fervor," M, 99), bestialidade e violência doméstica: "O ciúme. Fica intratável. . . . Aceitara Aninha, que era velha e feia, mas quase agredira a empregada anterior, uma jovem" (M, 95). E o retorno do antigo namorado de Romana, curiosamente, transforma-la até certo ponto, naquilo que ela devia efetivamente ser ("uma fera," M, 98, "entigrada," M, 99): "Quando o sol batia de lado no topo do edifício, a sombra da grade se projetava até o meio do tapete da sala e se Tigrela estivesse dormindo no almofadão, era linda a rede de sombra se abatendo sobre seu pêlo como uma armadilha" (M, 94). E "Romana, não seria mais humano se a mandasse para o zoológico? Deixe que ela volte a ser bicho, acho cruel isso de lhe impor sua jaula, e se for mais feliz na outra? Você a escravizou. E acabou se escravizando, tinha que ser. Não vai lhe dar ao menos a liberdade de escolha?" (M, 99).

À medida que a sugestão de posse (no sentido de endemoninhamento) se acentua ("está ocupando mais lugar embora continue do mesmo tamanho, ultimamente mal cabemos as duas"), aumenta também a atmosfera de isolamento (Tigrela rói os fios do telefone para bloquear o contacto entre Romana e o antigo namorado), de ameaça ("Não usa o fio dental porque não come nada de fibroso, mas se um dia me comer sabe onde encontrar o fio" (M, 97), e de prisão ("Você tem algum compromisso, perguntei, e ela respondeu que não, *não tinha nada pela frente. Nada mesmo*, repetiu, e tive a impressão de que empalideceu," M, 97, itálico nosso).

Tigrela no passado "tenta[ra] o suicídio na bebedeira" (M, 94) e agora, à medida que mulher e tigra se confundem, também a linha divisória entre suicídio e homicídio (mas será que se pode referir a homicídio no caso de um animal?) se esborrata:

> Ao invés de leite, enchi sua tigela de uísque . . . . Uma noite dessas, quando eu voltar para casa o porteiro pode vir correndo me dizer, A senhora sabe? De algum desses terraços... . . . A porta do terraço está aberta, essa porta também ficou aberta outras noites e não aconteceu, mas nunca se sabe, é tão imprevisível, acrescentou com voz sumida. Limpou o sal dos dedos no guardanapo de papel. Já vou indo. Volto tremendo para o apartamento porque nunca sei se o porteiro vem ou não me avisar que de algum terraço se atirou uma jovem nua, com um colar de âmbar enrolado no pescoço. (M, 99)

Suicídio ou crime? Violência ou amor? Certezas, há poucas em Lygia, mas conscientes, embora, disso, deixemos ainda assim a última palavra, ou quase a última, à autora, visto que não temos aliás alternativa:

> A obra de arte é a negação da morte. . . . Não cortaremos os pulsos, ao contrário, costuraremos com linha dupla todas as feridas abertas. E tem muitas feridas porque as pessoas estão bravas demais, até as mulheres, umas santas, lembra? Costurar as feridas é amar os inimigos porque odiar faz mal ao fígado, isso sem falar no perigo da úlcera, lumbago, pé frio. Amar no geral e no particular e quem sabe nos lances desse xadrez—chinês imprevisível, ousar o risco. Sem chorar, aprendi bem cedo os versos exemplares, "não chores que a vida é a luta renhida. Lutar com aquela expressão de criança que vai caçar borboleta, ah como brilham os olhos de curiosidades. Sei que as borboletas andam raras, mas se sairmos de casa certos de que vamos encontrar alguma... o que importa é a intensidade do empenho nessa busca e em outras."[43]

Mas Lygia, querida Lygia, será que é mesmo assim...? As borboletas, como já se viu atrás, "têm a vida curta" (M, 64) e às vezes são devoradas. Ainda há muito para conversar, e o "y" continua difícil de decifrar: "O leitor é o meu cúmplice, isso já foi dito. Recorrendo ao estilo romântico, convido agora o leitor a descansar na mão direita a fronte pensativa e refletir. E julgar. Vamos, leitor, o vosso julgamento será definitivo" (EC, 203).[44]

Definitivo? Permitamo-nos duvidar. Cúmplice? Talvez, mas só até certo ponto, porque até os cúmplices mais vigilantes podem ser ludibriados; aliciados àquela "Escola de Morrer Cedo" em que se matricularam todos aqueles jovens poetas (mas não só eles) prematuramente mortos às mãos de um(a) *deus(a) ex machina* resvaladiça e enigmática, e que no fim (n)os abandona. Abandona-(n)os pendurados ("pindurados") num jarro, em Cumas ou seja onde for, no escuro, e sem anjo da guarda com quem dançar. Querendo morrer? "Apago o lampião."

NOTES

\* Este ensaio foi um dos vencedores do Prémio Itamaraty no Brasil em 2012.

1. *As Horas Nuas*, a partir daqui HN.

2. Nas notas que se seguem serão assinalados trabalhos e publicações de relevância às obras mencionadas mas não necessariamente aos tópicos especificamente debatidos aqui.

3. Carta de Lygia a esta autora, de 12 de Agosto de 1991.

4. Entrevista reproduzida em http://comunidadelft.blogspot.com

5. Sharpe, Peggy a)

6. Para análises do tema do irreal em Lygia Fagundes Telles, consultem-se por exemplo os estudos de: Oliveira, Katia; Pinto, Cristina Ferreira; Silva, Vera Maria Tietzmann a); Chagas, Wilson; Coelho, Nelly Novaes; Coutinho, Edilberto; Lucas, Fábio; Milliet, Sérgio; Monteiro, Adolfo Casais; Rónai, Paulo; Almeida, Maria Antonieta Carbonari de; Bacellar, Maria Angela Silva.

7. Luft, Lya.

8. Zucco, Maria Joana Barni.

9. Veja-se também Magalhães, Carlos Augusto; Cunha, Thereza Cristina L.V. Alves da; Coelho, Nelly Novaes.

10. Veja-se também Castanheira, Cláudia Silva; Pires, Mônica Kalil.

11. *A Disciplina do Amor*, a partir daqui DA.

12. "Venha Ver o Pôr-do-sol" em *Antes do Baile Verde*, a partir daqui ABV.

13. *Ciranda de Pedra*, a partir daqui CP.

14. Sirach, *The Alphabet*. T. Witton Davies (International Standard Bible Encyclopedia).

15. Lei Maria da Penha, Lei N. 11.340/06 de 7 de Agosto de 2006. http://www.espacounicocriativo.com/2011/07/violencia-domestica-contra-homens.html http://www.jusbrasil.com.br/topicos/2785072/violencia-domestica-contra-o-homem http://www.psiqweb.med.br/site/?area=NO/LerNoticia&idNoticia=89

16. 'Verde Lagarto Amarelo' em *Os Melhores Contos de Lygia Fagundes Telles*, a partir daqui OMC.

17. Veja-se Carrozza, Elza.

18. Em *Mistérios*, a partir daqui M.

19. Priore, Mary Del; Bergamaschi; Patrizia Romana de Toledo; Cardoso, Neiva da Silva; Ramos, Isabel Maria Abranches B. Bergamaschi, Patrizia Romana de Toledo; Cardoso, Neiva da Silva; Ramos, Isabel Maria Abranches B.

20. Por exemplo a reescritura por Lygia do conto de Machado "Missa do Galo," ou *Capitu*, o guião para um filme inspirado por *Dom Casmurro*.

21. *Verão no Aquário*, a partir daqui VA.

22. Sobre o tema do Fantástico consultem-se também Ferreira-Pinto, Cristina c) e Moser, Robert H.

23. "O Moço do Saxofone" em ABV.

24. "Herbarium" em *Seminário dos Ratos*, a partir daqui SR.

25. "O Jardim Selvagem," em *Mistérios*, a partir daqui M.

26. Entrevista reproduzida em http://comunidadelft.blogspot.co.uk/2011_06_01_archive.html. Sharpe, Peggy a).

27. Significado bíblico do nome Daniel.

28. *A Noite Escura e Mais Eu*, a partir daqui NE.

29. 'A Dança com um Anjo' em *Invenção e Memória*, a partir daqui IM.

30. Freud, Sigmund. *Totem e Tabu*. Tradução para o português da Lais de Lima, *http://www.palavraescuta.com.br/textos/totem-e-tabu-1913-resenha.*

31. A análise que se segue de "Natal na Barca" e "Missa do Galo" aborda temas previamente explorados de forma menos ampliada, numa publicação em inglês, mas agora revista, aumentada e modificada.

32. Referências na mitologia clássica, ou, no caso deste último a uma região também conhecida como o Triângulo das Bermudas: área geográfica no Oceano Atlântico, entre as ilhas Bermudas, Porto Rico, Fort Lauderdale e as Bahamas, em que famosamente ocorreram números pouco comuns de desaparecimentos de aviões e barcos, e que por essa razão entrou no folclore de acontecimentos sobrenaturais.

33. Entrevista reproduzida em http://comunidadelft.blogspot.co.uk

34. Em *The Brazilian Othello of Machado de Assis*, Helen Caldwell apresenta um argumento persuasivo contra as acusações reunidas por Bentinho contra Capitu.

35. *Capitu*. A partir daqui C.

36. Alguns dos temas sobre "Natal na Barca" e "Missa do Galo," agora largamente revistos, rescritos e aumentados, foram previamente abordados numa versão mais curta em inglês em Lisboa, Maria Manuel, 1999.
37. Machado de Assis b), "O casamento do Diabo"
38. Veja-se, a título de exemplo, J. Paulo Paes.
39. "Seminário dos Ratos" em *Seminário dos Ratos*, a partir daqui SR.
40. "O Noivo," em *Meus Contos Esquecidos*.
41.
42. Silva, Vera Maria Tietzmann; Sharpe, Peggy.
43. Entrevista reproduzida em http://comunidadelft.blogspot.co.uk/2011_06_01_archive.html.
44. "A Escola de Morrer Cedo," em *Durante Aquele Estranho Chá*, EC.

## OBRAS CITADAS (LYGIA FAGUNDES TELLES)

Telles, Lygia Fagundes. *A Disciplina do Amor*. Companhia das Letras, 1980.
———. *A Noite Escura e Mais Eu*. Editora Nova Fronteira, 1995.
———. *Antes do Baile Verde* [1970]. Editora Nova Fronteira, 1986.
———. *As Horas Nuas*. Editorial Presença, 1989.
———. *As Meninas*. Editora Livros do Brasil, 1973.
———. *Capitu* [1969]. Com Paulo Emílio Salles Gomes. Editores Siciliano, 1993.
———. *Ciranda de Pedra* [1954]. Editora Nova Fronteira, 1984.
———. *Conspiração de Nuvens* [2000]. Editora Rocco, 2007.
———. *Durante Aquele Estranho Chá: Perdidos e Achados*. Editora Rocco, 2002.
———. *Invenção e Memória*. Editora Rocco, 2000.
———. *Meus Contos Esquecidos*. Editora Rocco, 2005.
———. *Mistérios*. Editora Nova Fronteira, 1981.
———. *Os Melhores Contos*. Global Editora, 1984.
———. *Seminário dos Ratos* [1977]. Editora Nova Fronteira, 1984.
———. *Verão no Aquário* [1964]. Editora Nova Fronteira, 1984.

## BIBLIOGRAFIA

Almeida, Maria Antonieta Carbonari de. *Aspectos Lexicais dos Contos de Lygia Fagundes Telles*. Universidade Estadual Paulista, 1991.
Assis, Joaquim Maria Machado de. *Dom Casmurro* em *Obra Completa*, vol. 1. Editora José Aguilar, 1962, pp. 805-942.
———. "Missa do Galo" em *Obra Completa*, vol. 2. Editora José Aguilar, 1962, pp. 605-611.
———. "O casamento do Diabo" in *Obra Completa*, vol. 3. Editora José Aguilar, 1962, p. 297.

Ataíde, Vicente de Paula. *A Narrativa de Ficção*. A Editora dos Professores, 1972.

Bataille, Georges (1985). "Emily Brontë" em *Literature and Evil*. Tradução de Alastair Hamilton, Marion Boyars Ltd., pp. 13-31.

Baudrillard, Jean em Mark Poster, organização. *Jean Baudrillard: Selected Writings*, Stanford, 1988, pp. 169-70.

Bergamaschi, Patrizia Romana de Toledo. *Lygia Fagundes Telles: Incursões Artísticas no Universo Feminino*. Universidade de São Paulo, 1993.

Bianchin, Leila Roso. "Espelho, Espelho Meu: Uma Leitura de As Horas Nuas de Lygia Fagundes Telles." *Travessia*. UFSC, 1990, pp. 133-42.

Botelho, Raquel Lima. "O Rito de iniciação nos contos 'As cerejas' de Lygia Fagundes Telles". *Letras*, vol. 3, nº 1, 2004, pp. 61-68.

Caldwell, Helen. *The Brazilian Othello of Machado de Assis*. University of California Press, 1960.

Callado, Antonio et al. *Missa do galo: Variações sobre o mesmo tema*. Summus, 1977.

Cardoso, Neiva da Silva. *O Romance de Lygia Fagundes Telles*. Pontifícia Universidade Católica do Rio Grande do Sul, 1980.

Carrozza, Elsa. *Esse Incrível Jogo do Amor: A configuração do Relacionamento "Homem-Mulher" na Obra de Maria Judite de Carvalho e Lygia Fagundes Telles*. Hucitec, 1992.

Castanheira, Cláudia Silva. *Roteiros do Abismo Interior: A Temática do Desencontro em Lygia Fagundes Telles*. Universidade Federal do Rio de Janeiro, 1996.

Chagas, Wilson. "Presença de Lygia." *O Curso do Mundo*. Instituto Estadual do Livro/Fundo Nacional da Cultura, 1997.

Chodorow, Nancy. *The Reproduction of Mothering: Psychoanalysis and the Sociology of Gender*. University of California Press, 1985.

Coelho, Nelly Novaes. "Antes do Baile Verde." *Revista de Artes e Letras*, vol. 60, 1970, pp. 71-72.

———. "As Horas Nuas: A Falência da Razão Ordenadora." *A literatura Feminina no Brasil Contemporâneo*. Siciliano, 1993, pp. 235-248.

———. "As Meninas, a Crise das Elites e da literatura." *Estado de São Paulo, Suplemento Literário*, vol. 17, 1973.

———. "O Mundo de Ficção de Lygia Fagundes Telles." *Seleta*. José Olympio, 1971.

Costigan, Lúcia Helena. "Literatura e Ditadura: Aspectos da Ficção Brasileira Pós-64 e Alguns dos Escritos de Lyga Fagundes Telles e de Nélida Piñon." *Hispanic Journal*, vol. 13, nº 1, 1992, p. 141-151.

Coutinho, Edilberto. "Três Mulheres e Uma Constante: Lygia Fagundes Telles, Maria Alice Barroso e Clarice Lispector." *Criaturas de Papel*. Civilização Brasileira, 1980.

Cunha, Thereza Cristina L.V. Alves da. *O Desdobramento da Verdade em "As Horas Nuas" de Lygia Fagundes Telles*. Universidade da Carolina do Norte, 1995.

Dinnerstein, Dorothy. *The Rocking of the Cradle and the Ruling of the World*. The Women's Press Ltd., 1987.

Ferreira, Debora. "Pilares Narrativos: A Construção do Eu e da Nação na Prosa de Oito Romancistas Brasileiras (Ercília Nogueira Cobra /Adalzira Bittencourt/ Rachel de Queiroz/Patrícia Galvão/Carolina Maria de Jesus/Nélida Piñon/Lygia Fagundes Telles/Clarice Lispector)." *Luso-Brazilian Review*, vol. 45, nº 1, 2008, pp. 209-210.

Ferreira-Pinto, Cristina a). *Gender, Discourse and Desire in Twentieth-Century Brazilian Women"s Literature*. Purdue University Press, 2004.

——— b). *O Bildungsroman Feminino: Quatro Exemplos Brasileiros*. Perspectiva, 1990.

——— c). "The Fantastic, the Grotesque and the Gothic in Contemporary Brazilian Women"s Novels." *Chasqui: Revista de Literatura Latinoamericana*, vol. 25, nº 2, 1996, pp. 71-80.

Freud, Sigmund. *Totem e Tabu e Outros Trabalhos*. Edição inglesa de James Strachey. Routledge, 1919. Tradução portuguesa: http://www.scribd.com/doc/12707732/ Totem-Tabu, p. 24.

Horney, Karen. "The Dread of Woman." *Feminine Psychology*. W. W. Norton and Company, 1993.

Jackson, Rosemary. *Fantasy: The Literature of Subversion*. Routledge, 1981.

Klein, Melanie. *The Psycho-Analysis Of Children*. Vintage, 1997.

Lacan, Jacques. *Écrits: A Selection*. Routledge, 1985.

Lamas, Berenice Sica. *O Duplo Em Lygia Fagundes Telles: Um Estudo em Psicologia e Literatura*. EDIPUCRS, 2004.

Lévy, Maurice. *Le Roman Gothique Anglais*. Toulouse University, 1968.

Lisboa, Maria Manuel. "Here Be Dragons: She-Devils and Little Boys: The Annihilation of the Male in Lygia Fagundes Telles.". *Other Women's Voices/Other Americas*. Organização de Georgiana Colville. Edwin Mellen Press, 1996, pp. 119-144.

———. "Darkness Visible: Alternative Theology in Lygia Fagundes Telles." *Brazilian Feminisms*, vol. 12. Organização de Solange Ribeiro de Oliveira e Judith Still. The University of Nottingham Monographs in the Humanities, 1999, pp. 133-154.

Lucas, Fábio. "A Ficção Giratória de Lygia Fagundes Telles." *Travessia*. UFSC, 1990, pp. 2-12.

———. "Lygia Fagundes Telles." *Modern Latin-American Fiction*. Organização de William Luis. Vanderbilt University (Detroit) e A. Bruccoli Clark Laymann Book (Londres), 1992.

Luft, Lya. *Três Espelhos do Absurdo: A Condição Humana em "As meninas" de Lygia Fagundes Telles*. Universidade Federal do Rio Grande do Sul, 1979.

Magalhães, Carlos Augusto. *A Fragmentação Romanesco-Existencial em "As Horas Nuas" de Lygia Fagundes Telles*. Universidade de Brasília, 1994.

Mello, Ana Maria Lisboa de e Saraiva, e Juracy I. Assmann. "Variações Sobre um Tema de Machado." *Letras de Hoje*, vol. 24, 1989, pp. 81-101.
Milliet, Sérgio. "Fevereiro 11." *Diário Crítico*. Martins, 1959.
Monteiro, Adolfo Casais. "Um Romance de Lygia Fagundes Telles." *O Romance (Teoria e Crítica)*. José Olympio, 1964.
Moser, Roberto H. *The Carnivalesque Defunto: Death and the Dead in Modern Brazilian Literature*. Center for International Studies Ohio University, 2008.
Oliveira, Katia. *Técnica Narrativa em Lygia Fagundes Telles*. Universidade Federal do Rio Grande do Sul, 1972.
Paes, José Paulo. "Ao Encontro dos Desencontros." *Cadernos de Literatura Brasileira*, vol. 5, 1998, pp. 70-83.
Pires, Mônica Kalil. *As Vozes da Polifonia ou a Arte do Fragmentado*. Universidade Federal do Rio Grande do Sul, 1990.
Poe, Edgar Allan. "The Philosophy of Composition." *The Works of the Late Edgar Allan Poe*. The Edgar Allan Poe Society of Baltimore, vol. 2, 1850, p. 265.
Priore, Mary Del, organização. *História das Mulheres no Brasil*. Contexto, 1997.
Queirós, José Maria Eça de. *A Relíquia* [1887]. Edição Livros do Brazil, s.d.
Quinlan, Susan Canty. "Revisando/Revisualizando Gêneros: A Noite Escura e Mais Eu e Invenção e Memória de Lygia Fagundes Telles." *Revista Iberoamericana*, vol. 71, nº 210, 2005, pp. 275-287.
Régis, Sônia. "A Densidade do Aparente." *Cadernos de Literatura Brasileira*, vol. 5, 1998, pp. 84-97.
Rónai, Paulo. Introdução. "A Arte de Lygia Fagundes Telles." *Histórias Escolhidas de Lygia Fagundes Telles*. Martins, 1964.
Santiago, Silviano. "A Bolha e a Folha: Estrutura e Inventário." *Cadernos de Literatura Brasileira*, vol. 5, 1998, pp. 98-111.
Sartre, Jean-Paul. " 'Aminadab or the Fantastic Considered as a Language." *Situations*, vol. 1, 1947, pp. 135-40.
Schimmel, Anne Marie. *The Mystery of Numbers*. Oxford University Press, 1993.
Sevcenko, Nicolau, organização. *História da Vida Privada no Brasil*. vol. 3. Companhia das Letras, 1998.
Sharpe, Peggy, edição a). *Entre Resistir e Identificar-se: Para Uma Teoria da Prática da Narrativa Brasileira de Autoria Feminina*. Mulheres, 1997.
———— b). "Fragmented Identities and the Progress of Metamorphosis in Works by Lygia Fagundes Telles." *International Women's Writing: New Landscapes of Identity*. Organização de Anne E. Brown e Marjanne E. Gooze. Greenwood Press, 1995.
Silva, Antônio Manuel dos Santos. "Existência e Coisifição nos Contos de Lygia Fagundes Telles." *Revista de Letras*, vol. 26, 1986-87, pp. 1-16.

Silva, Maria Angela. *Chave: Uma Adaptação para o Cinema Baseada em Três Contos de Lygia Fagundes Telles*. Universidade de São Paulo, 1995.

Silva, Vera Maria Tietzmann a). *A Ficção Intertextual de Lygia Fagundes Telles*. Cegraf/UFG, 1992.

―――― b) *A Metamorfose nos Contos de Lygia Fagundes Telles*. Presença Edições, 1985.

Todorov, Tzvetan. *The Fantastic: A Structural Approach to a Literary Genre*. Tradução de Richard Howard. Cornell University Press, 1975.

Yeats, W.B. "The Secod Coming." *Collected Poems*. Picador, 1985.

Žižek, Slavoj. *Welcome to the Desert of the Real*. Verso, 2002.

Zucco, Maria Joana Barni. *As meninas: Sintaxe Narrativa e Tratamento Espaço-Temporal*. Universidade de Santa Catarina, 1978.

MARIA MANUEL LISBOA é Professora Catedrática em Literatura e Cultura Portuguesas na Universidade de Cambridge e é Fellow de St. John's College, Cambridge. Leciona em literturas portuguesa, brasileira e lusófona. É a autora de cinco livros e cerca de sessenta artigos. Um dos seus livros recebeu o Prémio do Grémio Literário em Portugal em 2008 e este ensaio foi um dos vencedores do Prémio Itamaraty no Brasil em 2012. O livro *A Heaven of their Own: Heresy and Heterodoxy in Portuguese Authors from the Eighteenth Century to the Present* está no prelo.

# Reviews

# António Ole.
*Luanda, Los Angeles, Lisboa.* Museu Calouste Gulbenkian, Lisbon (September 17, 2016—January 9, 2017).

António Ole has been recognized as one of the leading figures of contemporary Angolan art, and his exhibition at the Gulbenkian Museum (September to January 2017) confirmed the range and depth of his work. Ole[1] is known for his installations, and for the variety of means that he uses to convey his awareness and visualization of social issues of poverty and displacement, of the hidden pages of Angola's history and of the architecture of the *musseques* on the outskirts of Luanda. He delivers his message with video and photography, with painting and collage, and combines them with objects that he collects in the street. In a documentary that shows the artist at work, we see him with a plastic bag, walking through half-standing buildings, collecting discarded items.[2] He shapes these objects that tell stories of slavery and forced labor, of the colonial war in Angola, independence, and his love for Luanda and the sea. Like other African artists, Ole is dedicated to uncovering what has been hidden in the past and to making it material.

At the entrance to the Modern Collection at the Gulbenkian Museum in Lisbon, an enormous poster in orange and white announced the exhibition. It read, *António Ole: Luanda, Los Angeles, Lisboa.* Ole attended primary school in the 1950s in a village between Figueira de Foz and Coimbra and on his return to Angola as a young artist he did his first photographs in black and white of locals. In 1977, shortly after the coup, he went to Los Angeles to study film at the University of California. He says that with film he felt he had found has path, and that film was a complete art for its immediacy. Yet he has said that he holds no loyalty to any medium, a claim that was apparent in the Gulbenkian exhibition. What linked the extensive number of objects was his ability to bring everything together and to consistently use assemblage to transport the viewer to a place of violence, where individual rights were denied and where escape was impossible.

The links between one work and another were most evident in two powerful pieces that were central to the exhibition: the series, *Hidden Pages Stolen Bodies*

(1996-2001) and *Margins of the Borderland* (*Margem da Zona Limite*) (1995). Together, they anchored the show in their concentration on the theme of displacement and slavery. *Hidden Page Stolen Bodies* consists of eight seven-foot panels based on a photograph of a faceless forced laborer, found by the artist in an archive in Benguela, south of Luanda. In the Lisbon archives he found slave record books with precise indications of the physical characteristics of young slaves: their teeth, the color of their skin, their physical appearance. In each panel there appear found objects from daily life: an empty and rusted tin plate, a cup, yellowing papers with lists of names, all rendered against a background made of natural pigments from the earth. Taken as a whole, the visual assault is a staggering reminder of colonial power and authority over the dehumanized 'stolen body' condemned to live without human rights or recourse to justice. Placed at the entrance of the vast space of the Modern Collection, the series sets the tone for other works that followed.

In *Margem da Zona Limite*, Ole made a boat of scrap metal, split in two halves. In one part he piled old police archives from the colonial period; the other half is filled with bricks. On each half a stuffed crow stands; a video records calm water, and the two broken parts recall a painful past and the future of old objects given new life. In all of Ole's work, what has been rejected from the past is reformed into something that can reconstitute buried and suppressed memory.

The vast space of the Gulbenkian Modern Collection has typically housed a history of the modern art of Portugal. It is a difficult space to use, with its overhead lighting and occasional wall divisions. Ole filled the space handsomely with a sequence that led the viewer from 'stolen lives' to an enclosure dedicated to video, to his murals, including the *Township Wall* (2004), to give a sense of being in a village inhabited by the traces of ghosts. Because of the scale of his work and its architectural qualities, Ole and the curators managed the space to create the way that one might experience that of a lived environment. The *Township Wall* is a re-imagination of parts of the city of Luanda in which Ole cobbled together wooden doors, corrugated iron, windows and glass, to make what appears to be a neighborhood on the edge of town, a *musseque* where one makes do with what's found in order to carve out a life. The effect is a vivid portrayal of the city that Ole loves, its red and pale blue doors, its ladders to nowhere, its textured and cut tin, its battered and abused surfaces. I'm a *caluanda* he has said, a true Luandan, influenced by the ethnologies of Angola, but not beholden to them. The ritual context long admired by ethnologists is no longer the basis for art making, and while

Ole may refer to African objects, the modernity of his work resides in his focus on assembling old objects into themes of war, destruction and Angola's painful past. Ole's work emerges from a social conscience, embodied in everyday reality.

I should mention that adjacent to Ole's exhibition, the Gulbenkian had mounted *Portugal Flagrante/Portugal Exposed*, an examination of Portuguese art since 1900, with supporting documents in art journals from the Gulbenkian library used as explanatory material. Exhibition histories and textual explanations by the curators made this fully researched history a fitting analog to Ole's show, in particular the section that documented the military coup of April 25, 1974 known as the Carnation Revolution, and its effects on Portugal's African colonies. To walk back and forth between these two exhibitions, in which each spoke to the other, was a visual and historical education.

Ole's work has much to say about our own time and place. He explores questions of identity that are relevant to the fragmented and divided time in which we live. He has traveled across Europe where he has exhibited and done research, and has always returned to Luanda. He imagines himself and others with a symbolic freedom that extends to questions of race and belonging, and since his earliest experiments as an artist, he has built fierce and endlessly engaging objects.

Curated by Isabel Carlos and Rita Fabiana. Exhibition Catalogue: *António Ole: Luanda, Los Angeles, Lisboa*. Lisbon: Fundação Calouste Gulbenkian, 2016, with essays by Isabel Carlos, Rita Fabiana, Nadine Siegert, and Teresa Gouveia. The catalogue includes a biography, bibliography and a list of works in the exhibition.

NOTES

1. António Ole is his artistic name, changed from António Oliveira which he thought was too similar to António de Oliveira Salazar. With a few deleted letters, Ole is how he identifies himself.

2. A trailer of the film António Ole, directed by Rui Simões is on Vimeo: https://vimeo.com/71245090. An interview with Ole produced by the Gulbenkian appears in Traveling with António Ole in which the exhibition is discussed on https://www.youtube.com/watch?v=wS67m1G4IVE.

MEMORY HOLLOWAY is Professor of Art History at the University of Massachusetts Dartmouth and Editor of *Portuguese Literary & Cultural Studies*.

## Carlos Cortez Minchillo.
*Erico Verissimo, escritor do mundo: circulação literária, cosmopolitismo e relações interamericanas.*
São Paulo: Editora da Universidade de São Paulo (EDUSP), 2015. 320 p.

What actually is a literary system? The problems and powers involved in dealing with the literary system as a critical phenomenon suggest that what we inevitably struggle with is that which mathematicians call the "chaotic system." If we have more, or, even worse, if we have many, many more variables than equations, how can we figure them out? Examples of the chaotic system are the weather forecast and traffic management in large cities. It is even commonplace to think that when worthy predictions cannot be made, a system appears random, but it is not. Likewise, the retrospective analysis of a subject's performance within one of these kinds of systems may also cause effects of apparent randomness. At least, a sense of mystery about why and how things turned out the way they did is a plausible result.

No matter how taxing the enterprise may seem, many scholars, such as Carlos Cortez Minchillo, embark on cultural studies that reserve room for reflections on the field of culture at large, undeniably a chaotic system, while addressing the links between works and the private lives of authors, or their intellectual growth and the ideologies around them; the zigzagging of aesthetic trends, such as the trajectory of realism-to-vanguard-to-neorealism; the links between private publishers and institutional agencies; or even the tug-of-war between national and international radical transformations, such as wars and political radicalisms.

In this multifaceted study on Brazilian novelist Erico Verissimo (1905-1975), Minchillo, a professor at Dartmouth College, employs a wide variety of approaches to a vast field of variables that have led to Verissimo's development as a writer of very high credentials in Brazil and, at the same time, as an author with little following in the United States or elsewhere outside his native country, despite the fact that a considerable number of his titles have been translated into English and Spanish, despite the point made that he had innumerous friends in the international publishing world, and despite the argument advanced that he held, for several years, a post of substantial intellectual influence in Washington over Pan-American cultural affairs.

In his preface, Minchillo explains that he writes his book at the confluence of intellectual history, the study of critical practices, and literary analysis (21). He has set out to focus on the relationships between Verissimo's international path, particularly within the United States, and the make-up and reception of three of his novels (*Saga*, *O Senhor Embaixador*, and *O prisioneiro*), including the thematic, formalist and ideological changes that resulted from his deep sense of cosmopolitanism and humanism.

Minchillo shows us how, for three long decades (1940s-1960s), strong winds and mighty air masses have mingled and shifted—in and out of the clouds—the traces of Verissimo's moving portrait as author, editor, lecturer, professor, and director of the Cultural Affairs Office of the Pan-American Union. Likewise, there has also been the unfolding narrative of his ups and downs crossing through the high, intercontinental scenario of literature and cultural politics. Verissimo's sui generis case in Latin American literature is indeed one of substantial popular success in Brazil and had caused a significant rise in international recognition and expectations. That is followed, though, by a slide into anonymity among contemporary readers and critics alike, argues Minchillo (21).

What one learns, Minchillo contends, is that "the success or failure of a given work or an author, or else, their greater or lesser insertion into the national or international markets, are not determined exclusively by the lines of the literary text" (21). They derive, actually, from a streak of actions and discourses of multiple natures, whether it is political, economic, market-oriented, diplomatic, or ideological—it is, in a nutshell, "a history written by many hands that echoes many voices" (22).

In order to shed light on Verissimo's circumstances and outcomes, Minchillo investigates the Gaúcho writer's fiction through close reading and ideological analysis, while combining the insight provided by other critics and theoreticians, and by an abundance of archival materials, such as private letters, institutional reports, mass print news media clips and interviews. Apart from the preface, penned by Universidade Federal de Minas Gerais historian Kátia Gerab Baggio, and an introductory essay, *Erico Verissimo: escritor do mundo* has four chapters chronologically and thematically organized. A concluding section offers syntheses and openings for further inquiries.

The first chapter covers Verissimo's young life and early career. The second takes stock of his advances on the concept of universal humanism and explores the identity duality of local tenets vs. cosmopolitan life panaches by highlighting the novel *Saga* (1940). The discussion also dialogues with another three fictional books of his, *Clarissa* (1933), *Música ao longe* (1935), and *Um lugar ao sol* (1936). The third chapter intertwines Verissimo's travel narratives written about his exploits in the United States with a book he wrote on the history of Brazilian literature. In the same chapter Minchillo talks about several issues associated with decisions and consequences of cultural politics between Latin America and the United States over editing and translation projects, and the book market as a whole. The fourth chapter compares and contrasts Verissimo's metamorphosis in terms of how he perceives a cosmopolitan and humanist order in these major works, *México* (1957), *O senhor embaixador* (1965), and *O prisioneiro* (1967).

All things considered, Minchillo's book underscores Verissimo's "relatively eccentric" standing in the Brazilian literary map (22). Minchillo summarizes that assessment: Verissimo was a Gaúcho who was not a "regionalist," a modern writer who distanced himself from the folkloric trend of Brazilian modernism; an experimental writer, at times, without breaking up an easy communication conduit with his readers; a politicized but nonpartisan intellectual; a socialist against communist regimes; a novelist concerned with social reality but never a spokesperson for the working class; and, finally, a writer preoccupied with his nation, but without any concern for literary nationalism, who eventually sought out an international outlet for growth and appreciation (22).

Minchillo's book, which results from his doctoral research at the Universidade de São Paulo, is profound and wide-scoped. Unlike so many academic studies, its language is clear and neutral. Devoid of bias or jargon, it appeals to readers within and beyond high school and college campuses. It undoubtedly constitutes a seminal work on a single author of the utmost importance in the spectrum of Brazilian literature. It offers much more, however. Among other roles, it contributes to the understanding of a particularly complex and intense period of cultural exchanges and ideological manipulations between the United States and Latin America: the heights of the Cold War and the deceptive goals of the Good Neighbor Policy.

Ultimately, Minchillo's book helps us understand considerably better many of the intricacies and hidden factors playing a part in the chaotic systems of literature and cultural politics. At last, here is a teaser for curious reader: while traveling through the pages of Erico Verissimo, *escritor do mundo*, do not rush, but make sure you reach the "Final Remarks" section and learn how, in 1953, Erico Verissimo, Jorge Amado and Pablo Neruda once faced together an elucidating but embarrassing crossroads of art, ideology, and their own symbolic capitals as prominent writers and influential intellectuals.

DÁRIO BORIM is Professor of Portuguese at the University of Massachusetts Dartmouth.